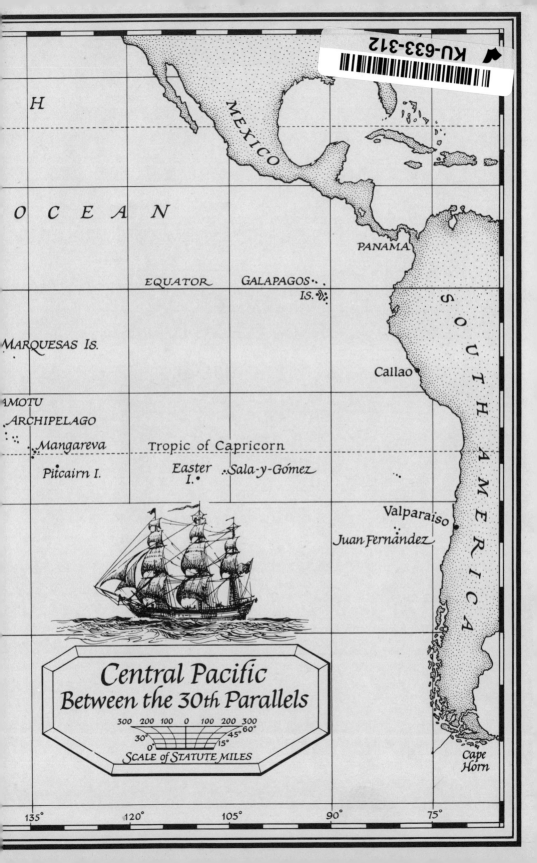

H

MEXICO

OCEAN

PANAMA

EQUATOR   GALAPAGOS
                IS.

MARQUESAS IS.

SOUTH AMERICA

Callao

AMOTU
ARCHIPELAGO

Mangareva   Tropic of Capricorn

Pitcairn I.   Easter   Sala-y-Gómez
                    I.

Valparaiso
Juan Fernández

Cape
Horn

Central Pacific
Between the 30th Parallels

300 200 100   0   100 200 300

30°   45° 60°
        0°   15°
SCALE OF STATUTE MILES

135°   120°   105°   90°   75°

Beyond the Capes

Books by Ernest S. Dodge

NORTHWEST BY SEA

NEW ENGLAND AND THE SOUTH SEAS

British survey ship cruising in the South Seas

Beyond the Capes

Pacific Exploration from Captain Cook to the Challenger
1776–1877

by ERNEST S. DODGE

LONDON
VICTOR GOLLANCZ LTD
1971

All illustrations were reproduced from books, paintings and prints
in the collection of the Peabody Museum of Salem.

Printed in Great Britain by
Lowe & Brydone (Printers) Ltd., London

TO BETSY
MY DEAREST WIFE

Preface

BEYOND the Cape of Good Hope and Cape Horn lies the Pacific Ocean. Before the building of the Suez (little use that is today) and the Panama canals, there was no easy entrance to this vast ocean world. Perforce all ships had to round one of the two great capes or thread the equally troublesome Strait of Magellan. Only slowly did the last South Sea Islands appear, did longitudes become fixed, did coasts become delineated, and did the indigenous Pacific peoples become known.

It has been my joy, as well as my professional obligation over the years, to read the published voyages relating to the Pacific Ocean. For it was through these handsome eighteenth and nineteenth century volumes, written by seamen or naturalists and often accompanied by sumptuous atlases of plates and charts, that the earth's greatest single geographical feature slowly unfolded (and still unfolds) to the eyes of the Western world.

But modern histories of Pacific exploration, and references to it in general works, stop with Captain James Cook's third voyage, as if nothing else had happened in the way of exploration and discovery after that expedition limped its way home following the deaths of Cook and Captain Charles Clerke, his successor. Yet, in fact, for a century after the great navigator's tragic death, the Pacific was the object of many private and government voyages which made important discoveries, charted reef-strewn waters, surveyed unknown coasts, and collected data of primary importance. This book tells the story of those hundred years of Pacific exploration, the story of those intrepid men and stout ships who filled in with detailed strokes the broad canvas left by Cook.

In writing this book I have been keenly aware that geographical names are always a problem in the literature of the South Seas. Some Pacific islands have had as many as five or six European and native names. Even the synonymy is more often misleading than useful. So that, in general, when I have used the frequently obsolete name that appears in a contemporary account, I have identified it with the current nomenclature. On the other hand, I have assumed that readers will understand such well-known synonyms as the Sandwich Islands and Hawaiian Islands, Friendly Islands and Tonga Islands, Navigator Islands and Samoa Islands, Port Jackson and Sydney, and Van Diemen's Land and Tasmania, for example, without further explanation.

While working on this book I have been grateful for the generous and enthusiastic assistance of others. The Trustees and Staff of the Peabody Museum of Salem have been always more than helpful, but I must particularly mention Mrs. Paul Andrews, recent librarian; Markham W. Sexton, photographer, and my meticulous secretary, Mrs. Kenneth Ford, who has worked long over my erratic penmanship and typing. Stephen Phillips's generosity to the Peabody Museum Library has eased my task, and many other friends have given me innumerable hints and suggestions. The work has been improved by the editorial hands of Llewellyn Howland III and Ann Mendez. And I am grateful to Samuel H. Bryant for his clear maps, frontispiece. and jacket painting. Last and most important has been the patience of my long-suffering family, especially my wife who has not only endured many a lonely weekend but made the labor lighter with her unceasing encouragement and good cheer.

Ernest S. Dodge

Salem, Massachusetts

Contents

[xi]

Contents

Illustrations

[xiii]

Maps

Book One

From Magellan to Cook

ONLY yesterday the world was young. There was still half the earth to be explored, still islands to discover, mountains to climb, seas to sail. Not until the second half of the nineteenth century with the opening up of "Darkest Africa" did the last great inhabited geographical area of the globe become known. Even then much of the polar regions, as well as the interiors of New Guinea and Australia, remained to be explored.

The world's greatest single geographical feature is the Pacific Ocean. And yet Núñez de Balboa did not see it until 1513 and Magellan did not cross it until seven years later. By this time Western civilization, even in a rather restricted sense, was several millennia old. Western man, facing the Atlantic, shut in by Asiatic hordes and interminable land miles and mountains to the east and the Sahara to the south, had only the ocean open to him. And this vast highway was substantially closed until ships were developed that could tack and therefore sail by the wind, and until the science of navigation had developed to the point where latitude, at least, could be established. These advances in the arts of naval architecture and navigation were reached in the late fifteenth century, when the three-masted ship in essentially its final form became general and the astrolabe and cross staff joined the compass as indispensable instruments for the navigator. Even so, another two hundred years passed before the development of a reliable chronometer made it possible to figure longitude easily with any degree of accuracy.

Once men and material were equal to the task, exploration by sea proceeded at a rapid rate. However, the Pacific, largest and most distant of the oceans, was the last to be surveyed. Not only was it the last, its survey took the longest: the span from Magellan's voyage to Cook's third expedition was more than two hundred and fifty years. Only when Cook's third voyage was over and the great explorer had met his death at Kealakekua Bay in Hawaii, did the Pacific assume its present form upon the map.

While there were no major features to be added to the Pacific map, there did remain work to be done. Exploration and scientific investigation went on intensely for another century, and in certain aspects still go on today. Following Cook, various governments sent out elaborate, well-equipped naval expeditions. The accomplishments of many of these were published in multivolume reports, which, for the most part until recently, have never been reprinted. Traders seeking products for the China market, whalers in the tenacious pursuit of their prey, and missionaries carrying the gospel to indolent islanders found their share of reefs and atolls, described plant and animal life, and wrote classic descriptions of island cultures. In fact, Pacific exploration after Cook included some of the greatest exploring expeditions ever mounted. This final period of exploration had its triumphs and its tragedies. It was a time of noble men and resolute endeavor.

Generalizations are usually misleading, but it is a convenience to think of Pacific discovery through Cook as being divided into three centuries: the sixteenth, Spanish; the seventeenth, Dutch; and the eighteenth, mostly English. Balboa, looking south from the Panama Isthmus and seeing the Pacific for the first time, named it the South Sea. Magellan, crossing the ocean for the first time in 1520–1521, found the weather so moderate that he named the ocean the Pacific. For centuries the two names were used almost interchangeably, with "Great South Sea" being favored by English writers. Only in the nineteenth century did "Pacific" crowd "South Sea" almost entirely off the maps. Still, the earlier and more romantic name is often heard

The death of Captain Cook at Kealakakua Bay, after Webber
(Atlas to Cook's Voyages)

— usually in a somewhat restricted sense — in association with the islands rather than as synonym for the whole Pacific.*

Magellan's superb feat of seamanship and navigation, and his discovery of Guam on March 6, 1521, marked the beginning of Pacific exploration.† About a week after leaving Guam, Magellan arrived in the Philippines, where he was killed while aiding a friendly chief against his enemies. One of his five ships, the *Victoria*, and eighteen of his men continued the voyage and arrived at Seville on September 8, 1522 — becoming the first to circumnavigate the globe.

The vast breadth of the new ocean came as a surprise to Europe's armchair geographers. They believed that somewhere in its southern part a great continent would be found: the continent was necessary in order to offset the enormous landmasses of the northern hemisphere and to keep the world in balance. This theoretical continent they named *Terra Australis Incognita* (or, the Great Southern Continent) and it played an important part in all Pacific exploration until Cook on his second voyage conclusively disproved its existence.

Following Magellan, several unsuccessful Spanish expeditions sailed west, sent out mostly by Cortez from Mexico. None of these succeeded in sailing back, for all of their attempts to do so were made along their outward course, about 13° north latitude, where they were bucking winds and currents. The first successful return voyage was made in 1565, after Miguel López de Legaspi had sailed from Mexico and established the first Spanish colony in the Philippines. Purely by accident one of his subordinates, Andrés de Urdaneta, found the eastward-flowing winds and currents that swept his ship far to the northward and carried him safely back to Mexico. For the next three hundred years the Manila galleons plied Urdaneta's route between Acapulco, Mexico, and the Philippines, always stopping at

---

* Antonio Pigafetta, gentleman adventurer with Magellan, wrote, "We sailed about four thousand leagues during those three months and twenty days through an open stretch in that Pacific Sea. In truth it is very pacific, for during that time we did not suffer any storm."

† Guam is the principal island of a group early named the Ladrones because of the thievish proclivities of the inhabitants, a name which lasted many years. The Ladrones were renamed the Marianas in 1668 in honor of Queen Maria Anna of Austria, widow of Philip IV.

Guam, discovering nothing, and luring the English raiders Drake, Cavendish, and Anson into the Pacific.

The first Spanish expedition for formal exploration was inspired, as were its successors, both by Inca tales of gold and silver brought from western islands and by the prospect of converting the infidel. The expedition was promoted by Pedro Sarmiento de Gamboa, but command of it was given to Alvaro de Mendaña, nephew of the viceroy of Peru, who sailed from Callao on November 19, 1567, with short provisions and unsuitable ships. Nevertheless, after a voyage of almost two years, Mendaña returned with both vessels and two-thirds of his crew — an excellent record for those days. On this voyage he discovered the Solomon Islands, where he remained exploring and refitting his ships from February 7 until August 17, 1568. Then, sailing north, he discovered barren Wake Island, and turning east, eventually arrived safely at Peru on September 11, 1569, after suffering numerous hardships.

Mendaña was eager to return with colonists to the Solomons, which he regarded as part of *Terra Australis Incognita*. It was over a quarter of a century, however, before he could arrange another expedition. In the meantime, Francis Drake had been in the Pacific (1577–1578). Abandoning any pretense of finding the Great Southern Continent or the western end of the Northwest Passage, Drake refitted his ships on the coast of California and, laden with Spanish booty, returned around the world to England.

On his second voyage, Mendaña left Callao on April 9, 1595, with four ships and with Pedro Fernandes de Queirós as pilot. In July (thinking at first he was back in the Solomons) he made the first discovery of a major group in Polynesia; he named the group Las Marquesas de Mendoza for the Peruvian viceroy. Leaving the beautiful Marquesas, he reached Santa Cruz (another important discovery), again supposing he was at the Solomons. Here he endeavored to establish a colony, but a more unfortunate attempt has seldom been made. Conflict with the natives, mutiny, illness, and starvation came near to eliminating the entire company. Mendaña died, and Queirós, his pilot, gathering the remnants together, brought them to the Philippines, where, after months of recuperation, they returned to the New World, arriving at Acapulco on December 11, 1597.

There was one final voyage in this series of Spanish explorations. Queirós, fired with religious zeal to convert all the heathens of the new lands he had seen, sold the idea to the proper authorities and was dispatched from Callao in late December 1605, with Luis Vaez de Torres in command of his consort. Just as on the previous voyage, when Mendaña had tried to relocate the Solomons and found Santa Cruz, so now Queirós tried to find Santa Cruz and discovered the New Hebrides, which he called Australia del Espíritu Santo. On the way he discovered several of the small islands in the Tuamotus, as well as the Duff Islands, some of the Banks Islands, and, on his return voyage to the north, Makin in the Gilberts. The consort, meanwhile, had become separated from Queirós; its commander, Torres, discovered Malekula in the New Hebrides and then, on the passage to Manila, sailed through the strait later named for him, proving that New Guinea was separated from Australia. (Torres's discovery was, however, forgotten, until the English found his report in some papers obtained in Manila in 1761.)

While the objects of Spanish exploration were gold and the conversion of heathens for the Glory of God, the practical Dutch sent out expeditions to improve their commerce, to find new products and new markets. Dutch independence was achieved in 1581, and in 1609 the Dutch obtained agreement that Spain would not interfere with their trade in the Far East. In 1619 they took over the city of Jakarta on the island of Java and renamed it Batavia. Under the energetic monopoly of a Dutch East India Company their trade increased rapidly and enormously. But successful trading companies never have enough profits and their very success also creates hopeful competitors. Probably by accident the Dutch, who had been following the old Portuguese route to the Indies up the east coast of Africa, discovered that because of prevailing winds and currents it would shorten the voyage to sail due east from the Cape of Good Hope and then north. Thus the western coast of Australia (which the Dutch called New Holland) soon became known — though, since it was an inhospitable land, the Dutch showed little interest in it.

In addition to their explorations along the Australian coast the Dutch made several important voyages into the Pacific. The voyage of Willem Schouten and Isaac Le Maire was an attempt by a group of Dutch merchants, headed by Le Maire, to circumvent the prerogatives of the Dutch East India Company. Under the company's charter, no ships except those of the company could sail to the Indies either around the Cape of Good Hope or through the Strait of Magellan. The assumption was that these were the only ways into the Pacific, since the land below the strait was considered to be a part of the Great Southern Continent and it was known that any northern passages were ice clogged. Le Maire's group called itself the Australian Company and outfitted two ships, which sailed from Hoorn, with Isaac Le Maire's son Jacob in command and Willem Schouten as sailing master.

Leaving in the spring of 1615, the vessels entered the Pacific through the Strait of Le Maire and rounded the southern extremity of South America, which the officers named Cape Horn in honor of their town. In the crossing of the Pacific, Le Maire discovered several islands in the Tuamotus and, on May 19, 1616, the Horn Islands (Fortuna and Alofi). He also discovered in the Bismarck Archipelago several minor islands and the two large islands New Ireland and New Hanover (both of which were thought to be part of New Guinea), as well as a number of small islands in the Admiralty group. After all this, when Le Maire arrived at Batavia his ship (Schouten's had accidentally burned on the coast of Patagonia) was confiscated. The Dutch East India Company authorities refused to believe that he had entered the Pacific by an unknown route. Le Maire and Schouten were shipped home via a naval fleet. On this return trip, Le Maire died.

The greatest Dutch voyage of discovery was sent out from Batavia by the energetic Governor-General of the Dutch East India Company, Anthony Van Diemen. Abel Janszoon Tasman, in command of two ships, left Batavia in late 1642 with orders to sail, if possible, around New Holland. This Tasman did, but except for Van Diemen's

Land (the present Tasmania) he never saw the actual coast. He sailed east from Tasmania and discovered New Zealand, touching first at South Island and then sailing along the western coast of North Island. When belligerent natives prevented his landing, he returned to Batavia, discovering some of the Tonga and Fiji islands on the way. Tasman's voyage proved conclusively that Australia was not a part of an indefinite southern land mass: *Terra Australis Incognita* receded a bit further into the ocean.

The last Dutch expedition was an attempt by the century old Dutch West India Company to break the East India Company's monopoly. Jacob Roggeveen, a retired employee of the rival company, left Texel Island in the Netherlands in command of two ships in August 1721, rounded the Horn, and after an enthusiastic stop at Juan Fernández discovered Easter Island on Easter Day, 1722. Then he sighted the usual batch of islets in the Tuamotus (who did not?), as well as Maupiti and Bora Bora in the Societies, and Manua, Tutuila, and Upolu in the Samoa group. When he arrived at Batavia, Roggeveen met the same fate as Le Maire and Schouten. His ships were seized and the officers and crews shipped back to the Netherlands.

So far, all of the major discoveries in the South Pacific had been considered either promontories of, or island groups off, the coast of the Great Southern Continent. And *Terra Australis Incognita* remained the primary objective of European exploration. Here would be found rich civilizations, markets, gold, people to convert; here would be the land of milk and honey — or at least of apple pie and beans.

Towards the end of the seventeenth and during the early eighteenth centuries, however, English roving buccaneers of less exalted ambitions began sailing the Pacific. One of the most successful of these swashbucklers was Captain Woodes Rogers, who, in a voyage lasting from 1708 to 1711, captured the Manila silver galleon, crossed the Pacific, and returned to England via the Cape of Good Hope.

Rogers's pilot on this expedition was William Dampier, a most remarkable man. A West Country orphan, born in 1651 in Somerset — a region that has produced more of England's great seamen than any other — Dampier went to sea in his early twenties. By the time he shipped with Rogers in 1708 he had sailed around the world three times.

Dampier is important to our story for several reasons. First, on the one voyage during which he was a naval officer rather than a pirate (he was in command of the H.M.S. *Roebuck*), he discovered and sailed through Dampier Strait, which separates New Britain from New Guinea. (Before Dampier, the larger Bismarcks were believed to be part of New Guinea.) Although this was Dampier's principal contribution to geographical discovery, he also had a part in perpetuating the legend of Davis Land. For in the course of his wanderings, he met Captain Edward Davis of the *Batchelor's Delight*, another buccaneer, who told him that in 1687, while bound for Juan Fernández, about five hundred leagues west of Chile in 27° south latitude, he had seen an island with high land behind it. Lionel Wafer, a shipmate of Captain Davis, also reported this discovery. The chances are this was Easter Island and some cloud banks, but captains went off their courses for years seeking "Davis Land," which was thought to be part of *Terra Australis Incognita*. Finally, Dampier was not only a navigator and pilot of superior ability, but an observer endowed with an intelligence and curiosity that made his writings, based on a journal that he began keeping shortly after he first went to sea, best sellers of their day. His books gave early eighteenth-century England the background for the notable series of circumnavigations that began in mid-century with Commodore George Anson's three-year voyage in 1741–1744.*

In 1764, the British Admiralty sent Commodore John ("Foul-Weather Jack") Byron, grandfather of the poet, who had sailed on Anson's voyage, with the *Dolphin* and the *Tamar* on the first of the series of expeditions that established the major geographical features of the Pacific. Byron aroused great public excitement by reviving the legend of the Patagonian giants — monsters first reported by Magellan, but discredited in succeeding decades. The British government

---

* This was considered a successful naval venture — the Spanish prizes were rich — but it was a tragedy in terms of loss of lives and ships. Its contribution to geographical knowledge was nil.

apparently encouraged popular belief in the giants as a smokescreen to other aspects of the voyage. Even the Royal Society swallowed the report of giants hook, line, and sinker. Byron, whose only actual discoveries were Pukapuka (or Danger Island, as he called it), two tiny islands along the northern fringe of the Tuamotus, Atafu in the Tokelau group, and Byron Island in the Gilberts, does not otherwise loom large in the history of Pacific exploration. And yet, in his own time, his voyage was not considered unsuccessful and his experience was useful in planning the voyage of Samuel Wallis.

The Wallis expedition, consisting of the flagship *Dolphin* accompanied by the *Swallow* under Captain Philip Carteret and a storeship, sailed from Plymouth on August 22, 1766. The *Swallow* was a dull sailer and when Wallis cleared Magellan Strait in April 1767 he left Carteret far behind. The two ships thus became, in effect, two separate expeditions. Wallis added to the charts one of the most scintillating jewels of the South Seas by discovering Tahiti, June 18, 1767. Thereafter he found nearby Moorea and several minor islands of the Society group; Uvea in mid-Pacific; and two of the northern Marshall Islands. He arrived back in England on May 20, 1768.

Carteret for his part performed a remarkable navigational feat in working his cranky, slow, misnamed vessel across the Pacific. He discovered Pitcairn Island (which he named for the young man who sighted it). He also discovered the Duke of Gloucester Islands in the Tuamotus, rediscovered Santa Cruz (last seen by Queirós), Buka in the Solomons, the channels separating New Britain from New Ireland and New Ireland from New Hanover, and Tobi (Lord North Island), westernmost of the Carolines. Carteret arrived at Spithead March 20, 1769, ten months after Wallis.

While the *Swallow* was still heading north in the Atlantic a swift sailing ship had overhauled her, broken out French colors, and hailed. This was Louis Antoine de Bougainville in the frigate *Boudeuse*, also completing a circumnavigation. Bougainville passed the slogging *Swallow* quickly, offering any assistance he could give, and arrived at Saint-Malo on March 16, 1769, four days before Carteret reached Spithead.

Bougainville, one of the most charming and attractive of men, had reason to be proud of his accomplishment. Leaving France in November 1766 in a fine new ship, accompanied by the store vessel *Etoile*, he had cleared the Strait of Magellan in January 1768. After passing many of the coral atolls of the Tuamotus, he had, like Wallis, come upon Tahiti. Tahiti, its sweet air wafted off shore, its threadlike waterfalls, its soft green beauty, its amiable people, worked magic on the Frenchman. Bougainville called the island New Cythera. Yet pleasant though it was, he stayed at Tahiti less than two weeks; then he continued his voyage through the New Hebrides and the Solomons and returned to France. After reaching Saint-Malo he went on to Paris, accompanied by a Tahitian named Aotourou, whose story figures also in a later expedition. Bougainville's nautical achievements were slender: he is perhaps most famous for introducing into France the beautiful bougainvillea plant.

This summary now brings us to the three expeditions of Captain Cook.

James Cook was, without doubt, one of the great men of the eighteenth century — a man in all respects perfectly suited by temperament, experience, and intelligence for the work allotted to him. When he sailed on his first voyage on August 26, 1768, over six months before either Carteret or Bougainville had returned to European waters, the main geographical features of the Pacific basin were little known. When his third expedition returned after his death at Kealakekua Bay, Hawaii, there was little of a major nature left to discover.

Cook's explorations fired the imagination of western Europe. The object of his first voyage in the *Endeavour*, when he was accompanied by Joseph Banks, a wealthy supporter of natural science, and Charles Green, a civilian astronomer, was to observe the transit of Venus at Tahiti. Cook then discovered the Leeward Islands of the Society group and Rurutu in the Australs. Next he sailed south to New Zealand (it was the first European contact since Tasman) and circumnavigated both islands to make a remarkable survey of their shores. He followed this with an equally remarkable exploration of a great deal of the eastern coast of Australia inside the Great Barrier Reef and returned via Torres Strait, Batavia, and the Cape of Good Hope to England, arriving July 13, 1771.

A year later to the day — July 13, 1772 — Cook sailed from Plymouth with the *Resolution*, accompanied by the *Adventure*, which was commanded by Captain Tobias Furneaux (who had been Wallis's second lieutenant). This time he was instructed to confirm the existence of the Great Southern Continent and to test the newly developed Harrison chronometers — the first timepieces accurate enough to make possible sure and easy calculation of longitude at sea.

In many ways this was Cook's greatest voyage. Going out around the Cape of Good Hope, he zigzagged up and down between Antarctic ice and the tropics for three years, proving conclusively that *Terra Australis Incognita* existed only in the minds of theoretical geographers. He discovered many small islands in the Tuamotus, Fatu Hiva in the Marquesas, Palmerston, Niue, Norfolk, and several of the New Hebrides; but his most important find was the large island of New Caledonia. Cook arrived back in England the end of July 1775.

Next to the Great Southern Continent, the greatest geographical puzzle remaining to be solved was the existence of the Northwest Passage: an open water route connecting the Atlantic and Pacific via the Arctic. Cook, who had been promoted to post-captain and retired in charge of Greenwich Hospital, was persuaded to accept command for the third time. He sailed with the *Resolution* and *Discovery*, commanded by Captain Charles Clerke, within one day of the anniversary of his second voyage, July 12, 1776. His purpose was to search for the western end of the Northwest Passage. Entering the Pacific again via the Cape of Good Hope, he sailed once more to New Zealand and then explored around the central Pacific, discovering Mangaia and other islands of the Cook group, several small islands of the Tongas, Tubuai in the Australs, and, on December 25, 1777, Christmas Island. His greatest discovery came on January 18, 1778, when he first saw the Hawaiian Islands. From there he went north as soon as the season permitted and established that there was no passage entrance between Vancouver and Bering Strait. Turned back by ice, Cook returned to Hawaii to winter. There he was killed, February 14, 1779, at Kealakekua Bay.

Cook was not only a discoverer, but an explorer and surveyor of the first magnitude. He never missed an opportunity to chart a reef or island, and many of his well-executed charts are still in use. Besides the geographical and hydrographical accomplishments of his expeditions, there were all of the exciting and invaluable observations of people, their cultures, plants, and other resources of the Pacific. Many of the drawings and paintings by Cook's artists were reengraved in innumerable editions of the voyages. His accounts excited popular as well as official interest throughout western Europe.

The voyages of Cook ended an era as far as South Sea exploration is concerned. Thereafter interest in the area turned to politics and national rivalries, trade and commerce and missionary efforts. If, however, major discoveries were no longer possible, exploration of the Pacific in a more refined sense continued for nearly a century. Cook's successes stimulated a series of later expeditions by various nations, and the books on his voyages were emulated by individuals and governments alike. This is the story of these voyages after Captain Cook — naval, commercial, and missionary voyages that contributed to our growing knowledge of the Pacific.

2

Cook's Contemporaries

CAPTAIN James Cook's three expeditions spanned the period from 1768 to 1780. During these years several lesser-known expeditions were dispatched by rival nations. Cook's voyages were so well planned, so competently carried out, so successful, that the considerable accomplishments of the French and Spanish contemporary voyages have faded into the shadow of the story of the great navigator.

The first French expedition after Bougainville was privately organized by a business syndicate and received permission to pursue a voyage for trade from the inactive French East India Company, which held the government commercial monopoly to the South Seas. Jean François Marie de Surville sailed from Brittany in June 1767 — the very month Wallis was in Tahiti — in the 650-ton *St. Jean Baptiste*. He called briefly at Mauritius and continued on to the Coromandel Coast, where his original intention of trading around the East Indies, China Coast, and India was changed when the promoters of the venture heard that the English had discovered a rich island in the South Seas. Since de Surville did not leave India until June 1769, the rumor of Wallis's discovery of Tahiti had apparently reached them and they in turn sent word to de Surville, but it seems to have been mixed up with the old myth of Davis Land off the coast of Peru. Then, too, the legend of *Terra Australis Incognita*, the Great Southern Continent, with its rich cities and civilized people, was still a reality in the minds of many men. Probably the rumor was compounded of all these elements. In any case the object of the expedition was changed from commerce to discovery, with the additional hope that the ship's abundant cargo might be traded for the gold of the opulent natives of the newly found English island. Since they hadn't the faintest idea where the island was, it must have taken a certain amount of credulity on the part of the investors (of whom de Surville himself was one) to give up trade with known ports for a fabulous will-o'-the-wisp.

De Surville was an able officer in his early fifties who had been at sea most of his adult life. His ship had in theory been well provisioned for three years (reality was a different story), and, while he and his officers did not know where they were going, both the personnel and equipment of the expedition were of a quality that led everyone concerned to believe that some successful conclusion would be reached. Never did more sanguine hopes have a more sour finish.

The *St. Jean Baptiste* sailed from the Hooghly on March 3, 1769, and after a couple of brief ports of call to complete cargo arrived at Pondicherry on May 5, whence de Surville took his departure nearly a month later. He worked his leisurely trading way through the Strait of Malacca and up through the South China Sea to the Batan (once known by the more euphonious name of Bashee) Islands, between Formosa and the Philippines, where he turned in a southeasterly direction for the Pacific.

On October 7 a long mountainous coastline came into de Surville's view — the same Solomon Islands' coastline that had been followed by Bougainville the preceding year. Slanting by the reefs off Choiseul, de Surville picked up Malaita off the tip of Santa Isabel. By this time many of his crew were sick and he was looking for fresh water and food. At a harbor that he called Port Praslin the natives were hostile and the water scarce; he departed the place October 21 after an eight-day stay and continued raising new lofty islands along the Solomon Chain — Ulawa and San Cristobal. Still there was no good anchorage to rest his sick and weary crew, so rounding Cape Surville (as the eastern end of San Cristobal is now called), he headed for the New Hebrides, hoping to land at Espíritu Santo. Because he altered course

B

just before reaching there, he missed not only the New Hebrides but the as-yet-undiscovered island of New Caledonia.

Throughout his voyage de Surville's longitude was hopelessly off and he never quite knew where he had been. For instance, he did not know that he had coasted Mendaña's Solomons: when they were astern he wrote that he had "left the land of the Papuans." Now in serious circumstances, he was faced with the necessity of finding hospitable land. Yet the only thing that showed on the charts of his day was the bit of New Zealand discovered by Tasman a hundred years before. Therefore, when he reached the proper latitude he put his ship before the fair westerly wind for New Zealand, which he raised December 12, 1769. Because of bad weather, the vessel did not round North Cape until three days later. (Cook himself was a few miles to the north at this very time and the two navigators missed meeting each other off North Cape by only one day.) Finally, on the seventeenth, the *St. Jean Baptiste* came to anchor in what Cook later named Dauntless Bay.

At first de Surville found the Maoris friendly. Scurvy-ridden sailors began to recover their health. Gifts were exchanged. Supplies were ample. Then the Maoris made off with a yawl that had gone adrift, and de Surville in anger burned houses, destroyed food, and kidnapped the friendly chief Ranginui in revenge — an act of inexcusable barbarity. Having aroused the anger of these proud and warlike people, he could not risk remaining longer. He sailed in the evening of the last day of the year and headed due east across the Pacific.

Because the crew was ill again, de Surville's hope of seeking Davis Land (which he correlated with Wallis's discovery of Tahiti) was abandoned and he decided to make South America as quickly as possible. Poor Ranginui died of scurvy March 24, 1770, and ten of the crew also died. With barely enough men on their feet to work the ship, *St. Jean Baptiste* reached the vicinity of Callao on April 7. Here, in his desperation to get a message ashore concerning his people's condition, de Surville was drowned when his boat capsized on the bar in heavy surf. Two days later the ship was taken to Callao. While the sick were cured, negotiations with the deservedly suspicious Spanish authorities in Callao went on endlessly. In fact the *St. Jean Baptiste* was not allowed to leave South America for three years, finally getting away April 7, 1773. She arrived at Port-Louis, Brittany, in August of that year after a financially disastrous voyage.

The exploratory results of this expedition were not great. But as John Dunmore has pointed out, de Surville "proved that no southern continent existed north of the 40th parallel," and it was his rediscovery of the Solomon Islands, along with Bougainville's and Carteret's sightings, that enabled geographers to conclude that the disputed discovery of Mendaña could again be put on the charts.

The three-year impounding of the *St. Jean Baptiste* was partly to give the Spaniards time to find and take possession of Davis Land, which they believed de Surville had discovered. Consequently, when two Spanish ships sailed from Callao on a secret mission in October 1770, the detained Frenchmen suspected their destination.

The Spaniards had meanwhile become concerned about the English voyages across the Pacific. They felt that the English, as well as de Surville, had probably discovered the Great Southern Continent. The viceroy decided to find Davis Land and take possession of it for His Catholic Majesty Charles III, and thus establish a claim that would be difficult for any other nation to counter. Commodore Don Felipe González had arrived from Cadiz at Callao in the sixty-four-gun ship of the line *San Lorenzo* with troops and military supplies for Lima. The frigate *Santa Rosalia*, in Callao at the same time, was commanded by Don Antonio Domonte, another naval career man. These were the two ships that the viceroy, Don Manuel de Amat y Jumient (who took office in 1761), dispatched to find Davis Land, while he held de Surville's ship and crew.

The expedition sailed on October 10, 1770. By November 14 it had sailed as far westerly as orders required. However, numerous sea birds encouraged González to continue, and all officers agreed at a conference during a calm the next day that these signs of land should be pursued. On the fifteenth, the expedition was rewarded by a sighting of Easter Island; from the sixteenth to the nineteenth, a party sailed around the island in two small boats, taking soundings and making a survey.* At the same time amiable trade was carried on with the natives. On November 20 a party went to the interior of the island, erected three crosses, and fired three volleys of muskets that were answered with twenty-one guns from the ships. Thus did Don Felipe González take possession of the "Island of David," as he called it, for the king of Spain, naming it San Carlos in the king's honor.

Leaving Easter Island on the twenty-first, González explored to the westward for two more days and then turned towards South America. From the island of Chiloé on December 15 González sent a report to the secretary of state for the Indies, saying in part: "I have met with the island commonly called David's although it is badly placed on the French and Dutch charts. I have examined its entire outline with the ship's boats, and explored the interior with an armed party who got as far as its centre; and have prepared a plan after both methods, which I am forwarding to Your Excellency with the log. . . ."

González had done a competent and professional job. He now considered his commission at an end.

When Bougainville returned to France from his circumnavigation in 1769 he brought with him the Tahitian Aotourou. Paris tired of him soon enough. As in the case of Omai, who was brought to London by Captain Tobias Furneaux on Cook's second voyage, lionized, and returned to the Society Islands on Cook's third expedition, the question arose: how to return this displaced South Sea Islander to his home. Aotourou was sent to Mauritius with the rather naive instructions that he should be passed along to Tahiti by any convenient ship. The notion appealed to Nicholas Thomas Marion Du Fresne, a well-heeled resident of Mauritius, who volunteered to do the job at his own expense.† Two ships, the *Castries* commanded by Marion and the

---

* The chart that they drew did not enter the published literature until 1908.
† M. l'Abbe Rochon, the noted astronomer of the Academy of Science, and Philibert Commerçon, the botanist who had sailed around the world with Bougainville, were in Mauritius at this time. Marion thought it essential to have these two scientists on board and he was bitterly disappointed when they were assigned to other duties.

Mascarin under Captain Julien Crozet (upon whose shoulders most of the scientific work would fall), and carrying a contingent of soldiers, sailed from Mauritius on October 18, 1771. At Port Dauphin, Madagascar, where the expedition stopped for supplies, the unfortunate Aotourou died.

The principal object of the expedition was now gone but Marion decided to do a little exploring anyway. He provisioned at the Cape of Good Hope and left there on December 28, 1771 to search for the Great Southern Continent.

On January 13, 1772, he discovered some fog-shrouded islands that he named Terre d'Esperance. As he was about to survey this group, now called the Marion Islands, the *Castries* accidentally rammed the *Mascarin*, taking off her mizzenmast, the poop taffrail, starboard galley, and some of her hen coops. The *Castries* lost her bowsprit and headsails. After three days of repairs *Castries* was still in no shape to explore further to the south, so the expedition continued easterly, roughly along the forty-sixth parallel. Marion discovered another group on January 24 and here Crozet landed and took possession for France by leaving a bottle with a message on a cairn of stones. (The islands were originally called the Iles Froids and are now named after Crozet.) A white pigeon flying over made Crozet feel that the Great Southern Continent could not be far off, but the *Castries* was still in no condition to sail into the more tumultuous waters to the southeast — the direction in which they thought some land existed.*

The two ships arrived at Tasmania (then Van Diemen's Land) on March 3, 1772. There the initially friendly relations between the French and the natives deteriorated when Marion unwittingly annoyed his hosts by lighting a wood pile with an offered brand. He and another officer were wounded in a shower of stones tossed by the

---

* Marion did not know it, but on February 2 he was just a few miles to the north of Kerguelen Island, which was discovered by Yves J. de Kerguelen-Tremarec on the thirteenth of the same month. This was the principal discovery of Kerguelen, who had sailed with two ships, the *Fortune* and the *Gros Ventre*, from Mauritius on January 16, 1772, on his first Antarctic expedition. On his second expedition he left Mauritius on October 18, 1773, and discovered nothing. Kerguelen's voyages were intended for South Sea exploration, but since the first never got beyond Kerguelen Island and the second never got anywhere, neither contributed anything to Pacific exploration and they are not included here. Dunmore gives the best modern résumé of Kerguelen's abortive attempts.

retreating but infuriated Tasmanians. The expedition, which stayed six days at Frederik Hendrik Island without finding fresh water or suitable mast timber for repairs, fared better in New Zealand, where it arrived in mid-April. For when the two ships came to anchor on May 11 in the Bay of Islands, they found not only a well-sheltered harbor but ample water and wood, including a forest of fine straight kaui pines well suited for making new spars for *Castries*. A camp was immediately established for a gang to cut and finish masts and build a road for transporting them to the shore. Another camp for the sick was set up on the small island of Motu-Arohia.

Relations with the Maoris, of whom Crozet distinguished three physically different types, were very friendly and became more and more relaxed as the days went by. Visits between ships and shore were frequent and casual. Marion, who had a particular liking for the Maoris, spent much of his time with them. On one occasion the assembled chiefs surrounded him and stuck four white plumes in his hair to indicate that they were making him a head chief.

All was not as well as it seemed, however, and a clue to what was in the wind came when Crozet's particular Maori friend gave him a handsome present of arms, ornaments, jades, and other valuable local things and would take nothing in return. Even more ominous was the Maori's refusal to eat, and his sorrowful departure. (Indeed Crozet never saw him again.) On June 12 Marion made a landing with sixteen men in the gig to eat oysters and run a seine. When the party did not return at night, no one on shipboard was alarmed for the Maoris' hospitality was well known. There was plenty of everything, the sick were getting well, and the masts for *Castries* were nearing completion.

Early the next morning, the *Castries*'s longboat with eleven men was sent for wood and water. Then at 9 A.M., a man was seen swimming towards the ships. Bleeding from two spear wounds, he was hauled aboard. He reported that he was the sole survivor of the longboat's company and related that when the boat was beached the Maoris appeared their usual friendly selves, and carried the sailors ashore so that they did not get wet feet. He had seen no arms. Nevertheless, as soon as the sailors separated to collect wood, each man was attacked by eight or ten natives, and murdered. He alone had managed to fight off his assailants and flee into the woods, where he watched the massacre and dismemberment of his companions. There was now no doubt in anyone's mind as to the fate of Marion and his party.

The *Mascarin*'s longboat with soldiers was dispatched at once to rescue the shore crew. Crozet, who had gone ashore the day before and was with the mastmaking detachment, saw the soldiers coming and realized that there must be trouble. He ordered the working sailors to arms and, abandoning the masts, joined the soldiers. The combined groups numbered about sixty men. They marched back to the shore closely pressed by Maoris. As the overloaded boat shoved off, the natives attacked, but there were no casualties. Crozet then ordered the soldiers to fire, and several Maoris were killed.

No time was lost in preparing for open hostilities. The sick station on Motu-Arohia was evacuated with the longboat by 11 P.M. The next day, June 14, the natives were driven off that island and their village burned, so that the French had access to the wood and water there. Since the *Castries* was still without a bowsprit and mizzenmast and since the handsome kaui pine could not now be obtained, she had to be jury rigged. In this precarious situation and with only one surviving longboat, it took the French an entire month to load seven hundred barrels of water and seventy cords of firewood into the two ships.

During this time, there was one more fight with the Maoris, a party of whom had sneaked back onto the island — some dressed in clothes of the murdered men. For their part the Frenchmen whammed a cannon ball ashore during the night to let the natives know they were awake. One day a cannon ball cut in two a passing canoe manned by eight or ten men.

The fate of Marion and his men was soon verified. When an armed party was sent to the village towards which Marion had headed, the village chief fled wearing Marion's scarlet and blue cloak; Marion's bloody shirt and the garments of other officers and men were found in houses. Thereupon the enraged Frenchmen burned not only the offending village but another nearby and destroyed two sixty-foot war canoes.

With the leader murdered, the *Castries* crippled, and her best sailors lost, Crozet decided to forego any further search for a Great Southern Continent and to visit only the Tonga Islands before sailing for the Marianas, Philippines, and back to Mauritius. Thus on July 14, 1772, the expedition quit the Bay of Islands (as Cook had called it), renaming it with good reason Treachery Bay. The scurvy-ridden expedition arrived at Guam on September 20 and, after recovering good health, departed November 19 on the last leg of the voyage home.

The geographical contributions of the Marion expedition were slight, but Crozet made good observations on the Maoris, the natural features of the islands, and volcanic activity in the Pacific, and he described various species of animal life, including the only mammal seen — the dog.

The energetic, ambitious, and capable viceroy of Peru, Don Manuel de Amat, decided to follow up the González voyage to Easter Island with another. He feared that the English had established a base somewhere in the islands along the lower Patagonian coast, or perhaps near the Strait of Magellan, as had been recommended by Commodore Anson after his voyage around the world in 1741–1744. The English had not, in fact, done any such thing, but Amat sent cruisers to investigate the situation. He also announced that any and all islands in the Pacific belonged to the Spanish sovereign. To preserve the domain in the name of the Spanish king, he felt it necessary to send naval ships to take formal possession. This González had done for Easter Island. Amat knew of the discovery of Tahiti and he was sure that de Surville had been exploring it and that probably the English were colonizing it. Therefore, following the return of González and Domonte, Amat decided to send an expedition to Tahiti to protect the national interest.

The result was the three voyages of the frigate *Santa María Magdalena*, familiarly known as *Aquila* (the Eagle). These voyages were not intended primarily for discovery, although discoveries were made. And it is a tribute to Spanish secretiveness that, although they were important to the history of their time, the actual conduct of the voyages was barely known, until published by the Hakluyt Society in

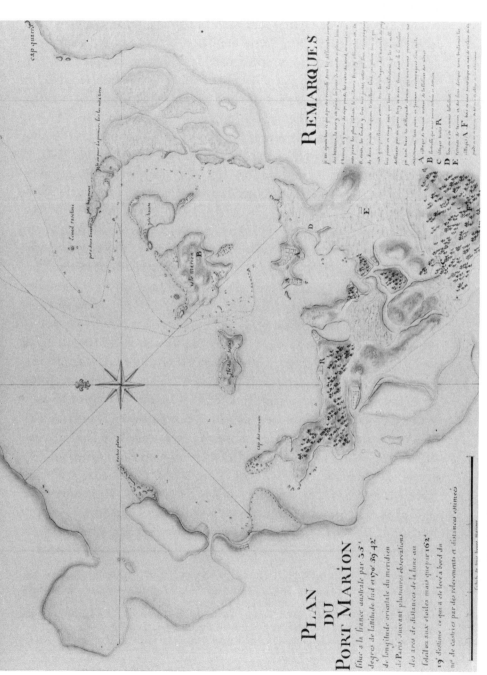

Previously unpublished watercolor chart of the site of Marion du Fresne's death
(In the collection of the Peabody Museum of Salem)

1913. (In the same way, the Spaniards' first visit to Tahiti was known to Cook and others only by rumor.)

The *Aquila* under Don Domingo Boenechea, a naval career officer, sailed from Callao with a fresh southerly breeze on September 26, 1772. When Boenechea opened Amat's instructions and read them to his officers, he found them detailed, businesslike, and sensible, as would be expected of a man of the viceroy's ability and experience. Nearly every contingency was covered. There were recommendations for behavior towards the representatives of other nations and the natives. (For example, four or five Tahitians were to be brought back, if possible, for religious instruction, but not against their will.) The principal purpose of the voyage, however, was to investigate thoroughly the island of Tahiti, to confirm its position as given by the English, to give an account of its resources and natives, and to find out whether or not the British had established a colony there, as was suspected. The secondary purpose was to examine the island of San Carlos (Easter Island) more completely than had been done by González and to obtain permission of the natives to establish a mission there, in order to rescue them from their miserable idolatry and to plant in them the seeds of the Gospel. Boenechea was to be thorough at all times, but as to the sequence of his explorations he could use his own judgment. Boenechea decided to go first to Tahiti and then, if necessary, return to Valparaiso for provisions before going to San Carlos.

On October 28 Boenechea sighted a palm-covered atoll.* A few hours later he approached it in a boat but was unable to land because of the surf. The following day, October 30, he made another discovery in the Tuamotu Archipelago — the island of Haraiki, which he named Isle of San Quintin. Late in the afternoon of November 1 he sighted Anaa, one of the most populous of the Tuamotus.† A party landed on Mehetia, November 6, which he called San Cristóbal.‡ Finally, on November 8, Boenechea sighted Tahiti, although it was not

---

* This island, which he named San Simón y Judas, was a new discovery. It was renamed by Cook the next year (August 11, 1773) Resolution Island. It is today called Tauere (17° 23′ south latitude, 141° 30′ west longitude).

† This island, which he named Todos Santos, had been called Chain Island by Cook April 9, 1769, and was probably identical with the La Sagitaria of Queirós.

‡ Wallis, in H.M.S. *Dolphin*, had discovered this island on June 18, 1767, and named it Osnaburgh.

until November 19, after running hard aground on a reef, that he was able to bring his ship to a safe anchorage.

The *Aquila* stayed for a month at Tahiti, and during that time Boenechea carried out his instructions completely. He sent a boat to circumnavigate the island and even persuaded four Tahitians to accompany him to South America. On December 20 he weighed anchor and, after looking at the island of Moorea, set a course for Valparaiso, where he anchored on March 8, 1773. The damage sustained by *Aquila* when she ran on the reef at Tahiti had necessitated calling off the second part of the voyage to Easter Island.

In 1774 Amat again dispatched the *Aquila* under Boenechea. She was accompanied this time by the storeship *Jupiter* commanded by Don José de Andia y Varela, as before, however, her destination was Tahiti — or, as the Spaniards called it, the island of Amat. Two Tahitians had died and the other two, who had survived their conversion, were to be returned and two missionaries with two other men were to be left with supplies on the island. (A house, cattle, seeds, and farm tools had been sent along for their comfort.)

The expedition sailed from Callao on September 20, 1774 and the two ships met off Tahiti November 14. (The *Jupiter* actually reached the island on November 8.) Here the two surviving Tahitians emotionally greeted their friends and relatives and helped mourn for the two who had died. Trade was brisk and the Tahitians were friendly. Boenechea had no trouble reaching agreement with the chiefs over the site for a house for the missionaries, who moved into their new quarters December 31. On New Year's Day 1775 they celebrated their first mass on shore with a procession and contingent of marines, to the vast entertainment of the natives; and erected a cross with the inscription, "Carolus 3rd Imperat x 1774." (The cross was still standing when Cook arrived in August 1777. Cook actually took the cross aboard ship and had carved on the opposite side, "Georgius Tertius Rex, Annis 1767.1769.1773.1774.1777" and reerected it.) On January 5 Boenechea consummated a treaty with the chiefs acknowledging the sovereignty of the king of Spain.

From January 7 to 20, the two ships cruised to Huahiné and Raiatéa. Then on the eighteenth Boenechea became critically ill. After turning the command over to his first lieutenant, Don Tomás Gayangos, he died at 4:30 on the afternoon of January 26 and was buried with due honor the next day. Two days later the ships got under way for the return, leaving behind two unhappy padres with an interpreter and a seaman. The most important discovery of this expedition came on February 6, when they reached Raivavae and named it Santa Rosa. The *Aquila* was again at anchor in Callao by April 8, 1775, and the *Jupiter* arrived five days thereafter.

The same year the *Aquila* under Don Juan de Lángara sailed again for Tahiti with additional stores for the missionaries. It turned out that, although they had not been harmed in any way, these two faint-hearted characters had been terrified the entire time, and Langara soon saw that it was useless to urge the priests to remain on the island. They were bundled aboard ship and returned in *Aquila* to Callao February 17, 1776. Thus ended any Spanish missionary and colonizing efforts in central Polynesia.

Don Francisco Antonio Maurelle, a Spanish pilot, first made a voyage to the Northwest Coast of North America in 1775. In 1780 and 1781, after bringing a contingent of marines to Manila, he was placed in command of the frigate *La Princessa* by the Governor of the Philippines for a voyage from Manila on a secret expedition. He first proceeded under sealed instructions to the east coast of Luzon where his final orders arrived November 10, 1780, charging him to deliver as quickly as possible dispatches for the Mexican viceroy to either the port of San Blas or Acapulco on the west coast of Mexico.

Leaving Luzon, on November 21 — at exactly the wrong time of year for making a good west-to-east passage along the northern Pacific — he worked his way slowly past various Melanesian islands. ". . . We discovered an island right ahead," he wrote on February 27, 1781, "on which was a lofty mountain, appearing scorched at the summit, but exhibiting a pleasing verdure on its sides covered with trees. We distinguished on it many cocoa-trees, which increased our desire to land, but the faintness of the wind did not allow me to approach nearer than within a league of it, on the western side. From this side several canoes put off with cocoa-nuts and bananas; and a barter presently commenced. The Indians, full of confidence in us, came on board. Their chief expressed the warmest friendship for us. He danced on the deck, and sung songs. Among other presents he gave me a kind of large counterpane, resembling blotting-paper,* composed of two or three leaves placed upon one another, to give the texture more firmness."

This was the Vavau group of the Tonga Islands, one of the most important Spanish discoveries. The enormous size of the people and the grace of the women deeply impressed Maurelle. He replenished supplies and water, drank kava, and watched a Tongan wrestling match. He stayed until March 19 and made the most of his opportunity by giving a good account of the place and people. Eventually he worked his way north to Guam in late May and finally departed there for New Spain June 20, anchoring in San Blas harbor on September 27.

The Spanish expeditions sent out by Amat were impressive for their careful planning, the generally competent way they were carried out, and the kindness and good sense with which the natives were treated. They contrasted strongly with the rather slipshod and haphazard French efforts of the period — besides, Spanish navigation was infinitely better than that of the French.

* Tapa-cloth.

3

The Vanished Frenchman

O N only two occasions in the recorded history of exploration have great government-sponsored expeditions completely vanished. Sir John Franklin's expedition disappeared while searching for the Northwest Passage in 1845. Fifty-three years earlier La Pérouse's vanished after leaving Botany Bay.

The two expeditions had much in common. Each was commanded by a highly regarded officer of proven merit. Each had two ships well supplied and a picked company of officers, men, and scientists. From Melville Bay one vanished into the icy Arctic fastness; the other sailed from Botany Bay into the Pacific unknown. Fortunately, unlike Franklin, La Pérouse was twice able to send home journals and papers — once from Kamchatka and once from Botany Bay — so we have a good account of his achievements up to that point; although, less fortunately, his scientists did not avail themselves of these opportunities. The published result, authorized by the French government, was a handsome two-volume work with a folio of plates and charts — the French answer to the English publication of Cook's third voyage.

Of the five French exploring expeditions sent to the South Seas up to this time, only the first, Bougainville's, had been successfully completed and only the abortive attempts of Kerguelen had official government backing. The success of Cook and of the other British Admiralty expeditions was intensely admired in France. It was felt that France too should send a great scientific expedition to the Pacific, but war intervened in 1778 and the idea did not again occur until peace with England was reestablished in 1783.

The French expedition — the object of which was to increase geographical and scientific knowledge in the Pacific — was ably conceived. Jean François de Galaud de La Pérouse, the man selected to command the venture, was born at Albi in 1741. His entire active life had been spent in the navy, in which he had consistently distinguished himself. He had been severely wounded at the Battle of Belle Isle. As a brilliant career officer he rose rapidly in the ranks during the war with England, aiding American Independence and becoming a captain in 1780. In 1782 he commanded the *Sceptre*, seventy-four guns, and accompanied by two frigates sailed to Hudson Bay to attack the English forts there. Despite ice, shoal water, and gales he successfully accomplished his mission, destroying both Fort Prince of Wales and York Fort of the Hudson's Bay Company and taking their governors prisoner. Thus, like so many other navigators to the South Seas, La Pérouse had had his taste of Arctic ice. Peace came again in 1783 and two years later he was appointed to command the scientific voyage around the world then fitting out at Brest. Competent, humane, and highly regarded, the forty-four-year-old La Pérouse enjoyed the confidence of his peers and the respect of his adversaries.

For the expedition, La Pérouse selected two ships of about 500 tons, each of the type called flutes, one named the *Boussole* and the other the *Astrolabe*. Both vessels were outfitted at the naval yard at Brest, and classed as frigates. La Pérouse chose his old friend of the Hudson Bay expedition, Paul Antoine de Langle, to command *Astrolabe*. Another old companion of that raid, Paul Monneron, went along as shipwright to maintain the two vessels in good condition.

The king's private instructions to La Pérouse were detailed and fill thirty-six pages of the English edition of the printed work. Entering the Pacific around Cape Horn, La Pérouse was to search for the mythical Drake's Land. Then, after visiting Easter Island and searching for the Spanish discoveries of 1773, his two ships were to separate. While La Pérouse sought new islands of the Tuamotu Archipelago, de Langle was to visit Pitcairn and seek some of the islands reported

by Queirós in 1606. After these excursions the vessels were to rendezvous at Tahiti for a month, then visit the other Society Islands,
Tonga, New Caledonia, Santa Cruz, the Solomons, eastern New Guinea, and, if possible, the Gulf of Carpentaria. All the time La Pérouse
himself was to be checking positions, charting coasts, and carrying out
scientific explorations.

But this was just the beginning. He was next instructed to sail to
Sunda Strait and from there explore the western coast of Australia,
and then to proceed along the southern shore to Tasmania and complete the surveys of that island. The expedition's next stop was to be
New Zealand. From there La Pérouse was to sail, via the Marquesas,
to the Northwest Coast, where he was to search for an entrance to a
passage to the Atlantic and truly locate the Aleutians and other islands
between Asia and America. Following this little chore, he was to go to
the port of Petropavlovsk in Kamchatka for provisions, then explore
the Kurile Islands, the coasts of Japan, and the islands as far as Formosa. It would then be time to refit at Canton and Macao or Manila.
Refreshed and ready to be off again, La Pérouse was to survey the
Chinese, Korean, and western Japanese coasts back to the Kuriles and
Kamchatka. On his return he could reconnoiter the Marianas, proceed
to the Ile de France (Mauritius) through the East Indies, and from
there return to Brest in the late summer of 1789 by way of the Cape
of Good Hope. In case the ships were separated, the instructions established nine ports of rendezvous.

Other sections of the instructions detailed political and commercial
objectives to be pursued; the work to be done in astronomy, geography, navigation, physics, and various branches of natural history; conduct towards native peoples; and the precautions to be taken for the
health of the crew. The Academy of Sciences drew up a memoir with
suggestions for studies in geometry, astronomy, mechanics, natural
philosophy, chemistry, anatomy, zoology, mineralogy, botany, geography, and examination of the nature and specific gravity of the air
and waters. Not to be outdone, the Society of Medicine proposed
making what today would be called anthropometric measurements
and observations on all native peoples, as well as ethnological studies
of food, clothing, houses, customs, medicine, diseases, surgery, and

materia medica. Ten experiments in regard to the preservation of water were to be made. The head of the Botanic Garden gave directions for taking useful plants from France to other lands and for collecting, preserving, and bringing back plants that might be grown in Europe.

La Pérouse without doubt realized how impossible these instructions would be to carry out, much less in the time allotted. Fortunately he was given the discretion and latitude to chop the problems down to size.

As with personnel, so with equipment, nothing was spared to insure that this expedition would be a success — a credit to France and worthy of comparison with Cook. But it was to do more than emulate Cook. If possible, in the mass of its results if not in geographical discoveries, it was to exceed his work. Trade goods in great variety were liberally provided. To aid navigation and astronomical research, there were sufficient numbers of all available instruments. There were also apparatus for conducting chemical experiments, ample supplies for the collection and preservation of botanical and natural history specimens, and assorted colors, pencils, and papers for the artists. Finally, a substantial reference library of books on voyages, astronomy, navigation, natural philosophy, and natural history was furnished. Two pinnaces and a twenty-ton boat prefabricated to be set up in the Pacific were carried along for coastal work.

International cooperation was quickly obtained for such an altruistic enterprise. All of the principal maritime nations agreed to aid the expedition in peace and not to interfere with it in war.*

La Pérouse received his instructions on June 26, 1785 and arrived at Brest on July 4. There he found the two frigates nearly ready and supplied. He mustered the crews on the twelfth, although westerly winds held the ships in port until August 1. Because the English had raised the price of wine to an exorbitant level, La Pérouse tarried at Madeira only three days and then went to Teneriffe, where sixty pipes of wine for each vessel were taken on board. He departed Tener-

---

* The engineer Monneron was unsuccessful in obtaining an Eskimo in London to serve as an interpreter on the Northwest Coast, but Sir Joseph Banks sent over two dipping needles that had already been used by Captain Cook.

iffe August 30 with a fair breeze and crossed the line September 29. *Boussole* and *Astrolabe* anchored at St. Catharine's Roads, Brazil, November 6, ninety-six days out. Here ample supplies of all kinds were taken on board. On November 19, La Pérouse headed south.

In the South Atlantic, after searching for the Isle Grande allegedly sighted by Anthony de la Roche in 1675, La Pérouse concluded, correctly, that it did not exist. The Strait of le Maire was entered January 25, and La Pérouse was lucky in having one of the easiest roundings of the Horn on record, from which he concluded that its difficulties were greatly exaggerated. The health of his men was still excellent — not a single one on the sick list. Fresh food has always been important in maintaining health at sea, and as the vessels entered higher latitudes quantities of albatrosses and petrels were killed and served with a rich sauce. (It was said these birds tasted nearly as good as European duck. Only the French could achieve this next-to-impossible culinary feat.) By February 9 *Brussole* and *Astrolabe* were in the South Seas off the western end of the Strait of Magellan, bound for Juan Fernandez.

La Pérouse wasted little time looking for Drake's Land, as he was convinced, again correctly, that it did not exist, but was probably part of Tierra del Fuego or nearby islands. Instead, observing the low stock of his flour and the worminess of his biscuit, he decided to make for Concepción. He anchored off Concepción on February 24, 1786, and found that the Spanish expected him. There was still not a sick man on board — a fact almost unheard of in a ship rounding Cape Horn. The stay at the Chilean port was pleasant and refreshing, with exchanges of entertainment between ships and shore relieving the necessary drudgery of refitting the vessels and getting supplies. The ships sailed March 17, sighted Easter Island on April 8, and dropped anchor in Cook's Bay on April ninth.

During the one day at Easter Island La Pérouse made a landing with about seventy men and dispatched de Langle to examine the interior of the island, to plant seeds, and to distribute sheep, goats, and pigs. Considering the short stay there, La Pérouse's experts made some exceedingly interesting observations. For their part, the hospitable islanders not only offered their women but, rather unnecessarily, demonstrated how they should be used. Although vexed by the wholesale

The statues at Easter Island (Atlas du Voyage de La Pérouse)

larceny committed by these great thieves, La Pérouse behaved with tact and humanity towards them.

On leaving Easter Island La Pérouse decided not to follow his instructions: instead of going to Tahiti, he would sail to the Sandwich Islands and carry out some of his north Pacific orders during the first summer season. La Pérouse did not tarry at Hawaii — he was clear of the islands by June 1 — but again, for so short a stay his observations on the natives are exceedingly good. He also noted that the same school of fish had accompanied his ships all the way from Easter to Hawaii — the individual fish could be identified by harpoon wounds. It was on June 23, 1786, that the expedition sighted Mount Saint Elias on the Northwest Coast. On July 2 it came to a good anchorage at Lituya Bay (which La Pérouse named Port des Français). The expedition settled down to surveying and to seeking a river that might lead into the continental interior.

So far the expedition could not have been more fortunate. The crew was still healthy. The ships were in good condition. But now occurred the first of the three tragic episodes that marked this enterprise as one of the most unfortunate of its kind ever launched. At six in the morning on July 13, less than two weeks after the arrival of the expedition at Lituya Bay, La Pérouse dispatched his two pinnaces and the jolly boat under the command of his first lieutenant, d'Escures, to do some sounding. About ten the jolly boat returned with the dreadful news that both pinnaces had been swamped in the breakers and everyone in them — six officers and fifteen men — drowned. Inevitably, the morale of the expedition was deeply affected.

La Pérouse saw that it was impossible to do any more detailed surveying and still get to Manila by the end of February. He therefore spent August running down the coast, and arrived at Monterey in September to recuperate and take on supplies. He sailed again on September 24. On the passage across the Pacific, Necker Island was discovered on November 3, as well as the nearby hazards to navigation — French Frigates Shoal and La Pérouse Pinnacle. By December 14 the expedition was at Assumption in the Marianas, and on the twenty-eighth at the Bashee Islands. The ships anchored in Macao Roads on

January 3, 1787, then made a twenty-three day run to Cavite and thence to Manila.

La Pérouse departed Manila April 9, and made Formosa twelve days later to begin his Asia coastal survey. He passed through the Ryukyu Islands, was delayed for days by fog in the East China Sea, but cleared the Strait of Korea May 25. After exploring a good deal of the Korean coast the *Boussole* and the *Astrolabe* headed north along the western Japanese seaboard — the first European ships to enter the Sea of Japan. Crossing over to the Tartar coast, La Pérouse followed it through fog; June 23 to 26, 1787 were spent stretching the crew's sea legs on shore; then, continuing north, the expedition entered the strait separating Sakhalin Island from the mainland. La Pérouse made several landings in Tartary, and established effective communications when he discovered that one of the Chinese sailors shipped in Manila could speak the language and would act as interpreter. During this time La Pérouse became convinced that Sakhalin was separated from the mainland by a strait but, although he reached just south of the Amur River, he did not, because of rough seas and shallow water, sail through and prove his point. (The actual passage was not made until 1849.) After an extended stay at a good anchorage named Castries Bay he left the bay, turned south, and passed through what is now called La Pérouse Strait, which separates Sakhalin and Hokkaido islands. Crossing through the Kurile chain, he entered the Bay of St. Peter and St. Paul (Petropavlovsk) by September 6, 1787.

Here Russian hospitality was at its best. After exchanging entertainments and salutes, the Russians gave the French the run of the place. An observatory was set up. The naturalists went on collecting trips. The officers hunted. Kasloff, the cultivated governor, enjoyed having congenial and educated people to talk to. He flatly refused payment for such oxen and other provisions as he could provide. To top it all off, a ball was given in honor of the distinguished visitors, and all the post's women — three Russian and two Kamchatkean — performed their special exhibition dances. "This dance, almost as tiresome to the spectators as to the performers," La Pérouse noted in his journal, "was scarcely finished, when a shout of joy announced the arrival of a courier from Okhotsk." Knowing that the French were anxiously awaiting letters, the governor interrupted the ball for them to read their mail. La Pérouse received news that he had been promoted to the rank of commodore, which set off a renewed chain of celebrating.

In tribute to earlier eminent visitors, brass memorial plaques were subsequently erected on the graves of the French scientist Louis de la Croyère, who had died in Russian service in 1741, and Captain Charles Clerke, who had succeeded to the command of Cook's third expedition and died shortly thereafter. But La Pérouse little knew that his most important order at Kamchatka preserved his name and accomplishments for posterity. Fortunately for history the Russian-speaking de Lesseps was sent overland to Paris with La Pérouse's journal to date and other dispatches, an arduous journey that he successfully completed with his arrival at Versailles on October 17, 1788. After the entertaining and restful stay La Pérouse got his ships under way September 29 and headed once more for the South Seas.

On his voyage south La Pérouse kept his eye peeled for various islands reported by earlier navigators, but he wasted little time over them. As soon as he was in the latitude of Samoa, or the Navigators' Islands (as Bougainville, their discoverer, had named them), he headed west, and he arrived in that group December 6.

He continued his westerly course, sailing slowly through the islands for three days, trading beads and red cloth for hogs and fruit. He also obtained two delicious dogs to eat. (Curiously enough, the Samoans were not interested in hatchets, axes, or iron. They preferred the useless pretty baubles.) On the ninth he anchored off the island of Tutuila, where de Langle was well received when he went ashore with a party in three boats. During the next two or three days trade was brisk and the French procured five hundred hogs, quantities of fowls, pigeons, and fruits. Casks were filled with fresh water and the Frenchmen were charmed by the tame wood pigeons (they bought about two hundred) which ate out of the hand. Tame turtle doves and beautiful parrots were likewise plentiful. It was difficult not to be overwhelmed by the abundance of food, the friendliness of the natives, and the tranquil beauty of the island. The ships, however, were lying in an open roadstead with a heavy swell running. Although the wind was off shore, La Pérouse and de Langle both well knew that they would be on a lee shore in a dangerous situation if the wind changed.

La Pérouse decided to continue his voyage. De Langle requested that he first be allowed to take in more water and to this the commander reluctantly agreed. The result was the second great tragedy of the expedition. De Langle, in command of two longboats and two barges, got his casks ashore at low water. Once they were loaded the sailors waited in the longboats for the tide to come in so they could get back over the coral. A crowd of about 1200 Samoans had gathered; they become increasingly unruly and began throwing stones at the Frenchmen. Soon a barrage hit them with so much force that de Langle, who had discharged his musket, was knocked overboard. The Samoans immediately clubbed him to death. The fighting now became general about the two longboats. In five minutes not a Frenchman was left; those who were not dead had escaped only by swimming to the two barges somewhat farther off shore. Twelve men, including de Langle and one of the naturalists, were killed outright; of the forty-nine who escaped, twenty others were severely wounded. Deprived of thirty-two men, his ships critically shorthanded, La Pérouse christened the place Massacre Island and continued through the Samoan group to trade at other islands.

The printed journal of La Pérouse contains an excellent account of the Samoans he encountered, with useful speculations on their origins and relationship to other South Sea Islanders. "Among these islanders," La Pérouse noted, "there are a few who are below the stature I have mentioned. I measured some who did not exceed five feet four inches; but they are the dwarfs of the country; and though their height seems to come near ours, their strong and brawny arms, wide chests, legs, and thighs, display very different proportions. In fact they are to Europeans what the Danish horses are to those of the different provinces of France.

"The men's bodies are painted or tatooed, so that you would think them dressed, though they are almost naked. They wear nothing but a girdle of sea-weed round their loins, which reaches to their knees, and gives them a resemblance to the river-gods of mythology, that are represented enveloped with reeds. Their hair is very long, and frequently turned up all round the head, so as to heighten the ferociousness of their countenances, which always express astonishment or choler. The least dispute between them is followed by blows from clubs, sticks, or paddles; and often, no doubt, costs the combatants their lives. Almost all of them are covered with scars, which must have been the consequences of these private quarrels. The stature of the women is proportional to that of the men: they are tall, slender, and not ungraceful; but before their spring-time is past, they lose that gentleness of expression, and elegance of form, the mould of which Nature has not yet broken among these barbarians, but which she appears to leave with them only for a moment, and with regret. Among a great number of women, whom I had an opportunity of seeing, I could distinguish but three that deserved to be called pretty: the grossly impudent air of the rest, the indecency of their actions, and the disgusting offer they made of their favours, rendered them worthy of being the wives and mothers of the ferocious beings by whom they were surrounded."

On December 23 La Pérouse quit Samoa and bore away for Tonga — Cook's Friendly Islands. Four days later he was at Vavau, originally discovered by Maurelle. La Pérouse never anchored among these islands and did only small trading with the natives, who seemed uniformly friendly. On New Year's Day, 1788, he bore away for Botany Bay, where ten days later he made landfall. Also at Botany Bay was Captain John Hunter of H.M.S. *Sirius*, who had just ordered the transports of the First Fleet to Australia to sail for Port Jackson fifteen miles away. Hunter took time to send a boat with an officer to assist the French ships into the bay and see them safely anchored before he followed the transports. (In early March, just before La Pérouse was to depart the coast, Captain Hunter sailed to Botany Bay in the *Sirius*'s longboat with a few other officers and spent two days on board the *Boussole*.) At Botany Bay two scientists died, the naturalist-priest Father Receveur and another naturalist who succumbed of wounds suffered in Samoa. La Pérouse dispatched his journal to date, together with various letters and communications; on February 7, he wrote to the Minister of Marine: "I shall proceed to the Friendly Islands, and do everything enjoined in my instructions, relative to the

The massacre of de Langle and his party by the Samoans (Atlas du Voyage de La Pérouse)

southern part of New Caledonia, the island of Santa Cruz of Mendana, the southern coast of the land of the Arsacides of Surville, and the land of Louisiada of Bougainville, and shall endeavour to ascertain whether the latter constitutes a part of New Guinea, or is separated from it. Towards the end of July, 1788, I shall pass between New Guinea and New Holland by another channel than Endeavour's Straits, if any such exist; and during the month of September and part of October I shall visit the gulph of Carpentaria, and all the coast of New Holland as far as Van Diemen's land, but in such a manner, that it may be possible for me to stretch northward time enough to arrive at the Isle of France in the beginning of December, 1788."

The *Boussole* and the *Astrolabe* sailed from Botany Bay on March 11, 1788. When the ships failed to arrive at Ile de France, there was little anxiety for some months. Sailing ship voyages, especially of exploration, were of uncertain duration at best. But by 1790 there was considerable speculation as to the fate of La Pérouse and concern was deep. Later efforts made to find him were unsuccessful, and it slowly became apparent that La Pérouse would never be heard from again.

The tragedy ended all hope that extensive scientific findings would result from this well-equipped and well-planned expedition. Only La Pérouse's foresight in sending back his journals from Kamchatka and Botany Bay saved the endeavor from total loss. Even though the actual geographical discoveries and scientific results described were minor, the journals are one of the classics of Pacific exploration literature.

4

The Northwest Men — Portlock and Dixon

MEN trained under Cook, and those in turn trained under his men, continued sailing the Pacific for many years. The drilling of the master was notable. Anyone who had sailed with Cook almost automatically made observations on fauna, flora, and natives, and diligently charted new coasts — and wrote a book about his voyage.

It was Cook's third voyage, for that matter — or the published account of it — that stimulated the tremendous early interest in the Northwest Coast fur trade, especially trade in sea otter skins. Captain James King, master of *Discovery*, received a total of 800 Spanish dollars (the usual money of the China market) for twenty skins; a few prime skins, clean and well preserved, exceeded this good price and he sold them for 120 each. This exceptional figure was what people remembered and talked about, and while the subsequent trade was lucrative, it is doubtful, in spite of some claims, if the return ever reached that pioneer sale price of Captain King's furs again.

The newly discovered Hawaiian Islands, plentifully endowed with fruit, vegetables, hogs, and good water, were a natural stopping place for Northwest Coast–China voyages. Even when fur-bearing animals, particularly the sea otters, became depleted, the islands remained the ideal place to winter between seasons on the coast, and captains wintering took advantage of the time to refit and clean their ships.

The official account of Cook's third voyage was published in 1784 and the following year Captain James Hanna in the sixty-ton brig *Harmon* made the first commercial voyage to the Northwest Coast.

He got 560 sea otter skins and returned on a second trading venture in 1789, commanding the *Sea Otter*. While the earliest voyages were English, the trade expanded rapidly in the next few years and was soon dominated by Americans. (English traders had to obtain licenses from both the South Sea Company, which held the government monopoly in the North Pacific, and the East India Company, which enjoyed similar privileges east of the Cape of Good Hope. This was almost impossible to do, and the mutually exclusive policies of the two great companies eventually strangled the English trade. In the first years a few trading voyages, however, were made under this restrictive system and other English voyages were made surreptitiously under foreign colors.) The Americans, unshackled by monopolies, found the trade lucrative. The greatest profit was always in the return cargo from China, which the East India Company monopoly prevented the independent British traders from enjoying.

Several of the first English voyages were notable for their published accounts. While most of the information they contained was no longer new, each contributed to the growing literature of the Pacific, and added, however slightly, to our geographic knowledge. Profits from these early English voyages in the trade were not great but as Nathaniel Portlock, one of the earliest participants, wrote: by "enlarging the limits of discovery, [they] made navigation more safe in the North Pacific Ocean [and] . . . familiarized the South Sea islanders to European persons, and manners, and traffic."

In May 1785 a group of London traders headed by Richard Cadman Etches formed an organization for fur trading between the Northwest Coast and China and called themselves the King George's Sound Company (after the name given by Captain Cook to that body of water which is now known as Nootka Sound). This company succeeded in obtaining a license from the South Sea Company, "who," writes Portlock, "without carrying on any traffic themselves, stand in the mercantile way of more adventurous merchants." They were equally successful with the East India Company, which granted them a license and guaranteed to give their ships a freight of tea from Canton.

No time was lost in purchasing and outfitting two vessels, the ship

King George of 320 tons and the somewhat smaller snow *Queen Charlotte* of 200 tons. Among those whose advice was sought and who visited the ships during preparations for the voyage were Sir Joseph Banks and Lord Mulgrave (who had made a notable voyage towards the North Pole). So it is not surprising that two veterans of Cook's last voyage were selected as captains. Nathaniel Portlock, a lieutenant with Cook, was given command of the expedition as well as of the larger vessel; George Dixon, who had been an armorer on Cook's third voyage, was made captain of the *Queen Charlotte*. Both of these men published substantial books on the voyage (although Dixon's, except for the Introduction, was written by his supercargo, William Beresford, as a series of letters signed W. B.). The point of view of the common sailor was supplied in a book by John Nicol, a Scot, who served on the *King George*.

The two ships sailed from Spithead on September 16, 1785, stopping for a few days at the Isle of Guernsey for a stock of liquor. As they neared Madeira an indefinable object was seen floating in the water. The day was warm and the sea calm, so Dixon allowed two sailors to dive overboard and bring it alongside the *Queen Charlotte*. It proved to be a barnacle-covered cask of claret. Nicol, dictating his reminiscences many years later, remembered it as a cask of port wine taken from the sea off Cape Horn — an unlikely performance. Although Nicol hadn't even been on *Queen Charlotte*, he added: "All the crew got a little of it and Captain Portlock gave us brandy in place of the rest."

At the Falklands in January 1786, they met, according to Dixon, Captain Coffin in the American sloop *Speedwell* serving as a tender to Captain Hussey in the ship *United States*, which was at Swan Island in company with the *Canton*, Captain Whippy, for sea elephant oil. Again Nicol's memory of the event was a little different. He writes: "Having watered, we run for the Falkland Islands. When we arrived, we found two American vessels busy whaling; we hoisted our colours, the Anchor and Hope. The Americans took us for Spaniards, and set off in all haste. When we landed we found a great number of geese ready plucked, and a large fire burning; so we set to work and roasted as many as served us all, and enjoyed them much. Next morning the

Americans came near in their boats, and found out their mistake. Captain Portlock thanked them for their treat."

Sailing from the Falklands on January 23, *King George* and *Queen Charlotte* rounded the Horn and headed north across the Pacific. Shark chowder and turtles broke the monotonous diet of salt horse but did not prevent Dixon suffering from scurvy, for which Portlock supplied a cask of mold with salad growing in it, along with kraut, garden seeds, and mineral water. Indeed, whenever scurvy broke out it was kept under control: both captains had learned well the methods of Captain Cook.

On May 12, 1786, in 20° 1' south latitude and 134° 11' west longitude, Portlock expected to find himself in the middle of Los Majos Islands. But three days' searching produced no land and he shaped his course for Hawaii, which was sighted May 24. Two days later *King George* and *Queen Charlotte* dropped anchor in Kealakekua Bay — becoming the first ships to appear there since Cook was killed. By now King Kamehameha (called Maiha Maiha by Portlock) had succeeded Tereeoboo (Kalaniopuu) who had been king during Cook's visit in 1778.* The new king, who seemed to think they had arrived to avenge the death of Captain Cook, did not come on board and the natives who did were disorderly. While the expedition procured hogs, plantains, sweet potatoes, fresh fruits, excellent taro, and salt in abundance, the chiefs actually put a taboo on the watering place: according to Dixon, "by sticking a number of small wands, tipt with a tuft of white hair, round any place they want to keep private. . . ."

Since water was essential, blank shots were fired to clear the canoes away from the ships. Then the ships got under way and cruised around Maui, Lanai, and Molokai for several days, buying more provisions and water in gourds — or, as they called them, calabashes. This unique method of watering was continued at a difficult watering place on the south shore of Oahu, where gourds of water, some con-

---

* Hawaiian names are printed as phonetically transcribed by the explorers except, as in the case of Kamehameha, when the person has become historically important and the name standardized in modern literature. A committee of missionaries in 1826 established the spelling of Hawaiian names as they are today. Previously they were written as heard and it was difficult to distinguish between *k* and *t*, *l* and *r*, and *w* and *v*.

*The river at Honolulu, 1838 (Original sketch by Auguste Borget.
In the collection of the Peabody Museum of Salem)*

*Interior of a Hawaiian house, 1838 (Original sketch by Auguste Borget.
In the collection of the Peabody Museum of Salem)*

taining as much as ten gallons, were purchased for nails and buttons. The principal chief of Oahu, Kahekili, sent Portlock a handsome feather helmet, and he purchased "some cloaks considerably better than that of Captain Clerke's" for an iron plane blade (Captain Clerke, Cook's second-in-command, had given eight or nine daggers to Kamehameha for a feather cloak).

Portlock appears to have been more of an ethnologist than Dixon, or at least he wrote more in this vein. Not only did he collect feather work in Hawaii, but he makes interesting observations on the political changes that had taken place in the eight years since he was there with Cook in 1778. Kalaniopuu and Kamehameha, who had been a lesser chief at that time, was now king of Hawaii and Lanai as well. Kahekili, who had been king of Molokai only, had added Maui and Oahu to his dominions and lived on the latter island. He had also apparently defeated the forces of Hawaii, for the Oahu chiefs now possessed most of the daggers that Cook's expedition had left at Hawaii. Kauai and Niihau were now ruled by a chief named Abenoue (Kaeo). It is obvious that the series of native wars that would culminate in the establishment of the Kamehameha dynasty throughout the entire island group had already begun.

While the captains made their observations and had their problems, the sailors were perfectly happy. As Nicol observes: "Almost every man on board took a native woman for a wife while the vessel remained, the men thinking it an honour, or for their gain, as they got many presents of iron, beads, or buttons. The women came on board at night, and went on shore in the morning. In the evening they would call for their husbands by name. They often brought their friends to see their husbands, who were well pleased, as they were never allowed to go away empty. The fattest woman I ever saw in my life our gunner chose for a wife. We were forced to hoist her on board; her thighs were as thick as my waist; no hammock in the ship would hold her; many jokes were cracked upon the pair."

On June 5 the ships sailed for Kauai and anchored in Waimea Bay (which had been Cook's first landfall in the Hawaiian Islands). Abenoue, the king of Kauai, threw a party for the ships' companies. Girls danced and men fought sham battles, and the natives completely worsted the sailors in a series of wrestling matches. Then came the work of loading additional supplies, including a special trip made to "Yam Bay," Niihau, for yams. The expedition departed Kauai on June 13, 1786 and sailed for the Northwest Coast of America, making Cook Inlet on July 19. Here the Russians were well entrenched, but wood and water plentiful. Portlock gives a good description of the Russians and their settlement.

The summer of 1786 was not a particularly successful trading season, although Portlock explored some of the same coast that La Pérouse had explored the year before, and purchased a few land and sea otters, bear, raccoon, and marmot furs in exchange for plane irons (or "toes" as they were called) and light blue beads — the only kind the Indians would accept. Unfortunately, by September 4 Captain Portlock was feeling so ill that he asked his colleague to come on board his ship. Portlock instructed Dixon to take the leadership of the expedition if he should be too sick to take the deck, and this Dixon actually did for a few days. Then, shortly after midnight September 26, the expedition was hit by stormy and gusty winds. "At three o'clock," according to Portlock, "the wind shifted to the South East, and blew a mere hurricane, which brought on a very heavy sea, and occasioned the ship to labour and strain exceedingly. It certainly was the most dreadful night I ever saw, and to add to the awful scene of a tremendous sea, loud thunder, fierce lightning, and torrents of rain, we had at each mast-head, and at every yard-arm, those meteors called by sailors *compasants*, which gave a light at least equal to the same number of lights hung aloft: besides those on the masts and yards, they were flying about on all parts of the rigging."

Three days later *King George* and *Queen Charlotte* ended the season and departed the coast for the Sandwich Islands, sighting Mauna Kea November 14. Another three days and they were standing off and on the coast of Hawaii, doing an abundant trade with over 1,000 natives in not less than 250 canoes, a trade that kept twenty hands employed killing and salting pork. The difficulties with the natives were magnified by the great crowd: as Portlock writes, they "shewed their usual inclination for thieving; and one man had dexterity enough in his profession to steal a boat-hook out of a boat along-side, though

c

there was a boat-keeper in her, and another crept up the rudder chains, and stole the azimuth compass out of one of the cabin windows, and got clear off with it, notwithstanding a person was set to look after them over the stern." The surplus provisions of Hawaii were cleaned out by Portlock and his men in a couple of days.

On November 30 the expedition anchored once more in King George's Bay, Oahu, where they found all water and provisions tabooed by King Taheeterre. When Portlock sent the king a present and requested that the taboo be removed, the king reciprocated by sending an old priest bearing gifts. A few more formalities were required to get the water line moving, but eventually Taheeterre himself arrived in a large canoe paddled by sixteen husky men. Portlock wrote of him that he "is an exceedingly stout well-made man about fifty years old, and appears to be sensible, well disposed, and much esteemed by his subjects." His visit had the desired effect, and the king gave directions for water and any other provisions to be produced.

The expedition stayed in Oahu for almost a month while multitudes of both sexes played about the ships. During this time the king occasionally paid visits, and the old priest was almost constantly on board the *King George*. Portlock was impressed with the priest's addiction to kava drinking and wrote: "[He] was almost constantly on board, and, according to his usual custom, drank vast quantities of yava [kava], which kept him in a most wretched condition; he seemed quite debilitated, and his body was entirely covered with a kind of leprous scurf [sic]. The old man had generally two attendants on board to chew the yava root for him, and he found them so much employment that their jaws were frequently tired, and he was obliged to hire some of the people along-side to chew for him at a bead for a mouthful."

Portlock's ethnological observations of this period are a rich source of information for scholars. His book is filled with illuminating sidelights, such as a remark made when the king came off through a very high surf that he used a "single canoe, it being much safer in the surf than a double one." Portlock's journal entries do not neglect the day-to-day dangers facing the expedition, either; as, for example, when the old priest warned him that the king and his principal chiefs were planning to attack the ships. This the captain did not think possible since previous relations with the chiefs had been friendly. However, when a god house was built on a hill (a dangerous sign) and covered with red tapa, Portlock had second thoughts. The king was invited on board the *King George* and arrived in a large double canoe attended by chiefs. For his benefit and as a hint of what could happen, Portlock ordered that a hog be shot. The hint worked. Apparently the king's consultation with his gods (Eatoa) was negative and after two days when the natives stayed away a final lively trade developed before the ships weighed anchor for Waimea Bay, Kauai on December 20, 1786.

Christmas Day was distinguished by a visit from Kaiana, a prince of Kauai, who appropriately brought a gift on the occasion. On the *Queen Charlotte* they drank for their holiday libations not the usual grog but rum mixed with coconut milk, "toasting our friends and mistresses in bumpers of this liquor, which, perhaps, pleased more on account of its novelty, than any other circumstance."

Dixon's observation that they found good sugarcane and taro here but no yams and little breadfruit is an indicator of the agricultural specialties of islands within the Hawaiian group. Besides food, "the natives brought bass and grass rope to barter, which we purchased, as it was likely to prove useful for various purposes. The natives, finding we encouraged this traffic, were very busy on shore manufacturing rope, which they did very expeditiously, and brought off whole coils made of green rushes and grass; this we bought for the purpose of rounding the cables, and the bass for running rigging." Trade was brisk in curiosities as well as necessities. On December 30 the king brought Portlock "several elegant feather cloaks," tapa cloth, and mats. Dixon collected more cloaks, feather helmets, mats, fishing hooks and lines, and necklaces. Bright bird skins skewered in strings of ten were popular and live birds even more so.

The remainder of the winter, the crews of the *King George* and the *Queen Charlotte* spent pleasantly at Waimea, feasting on shore, hunting for ducks, watching the warriors' spear-throwing contests, and observing native life. (For example, Portlock noticed a woman simultaneously nursing two puppies, one at each breast.) Weatherwise, however, this was not one of the island's best years. "I think we may with truth affirm," Portlock wrote, "that during the time we were among these islands we had more disagreeable weather and cross winds, than was experienced in the *Resolution* and *Discovery* during their whole voyage, which was upwards of four years."

By the first of March it was time to quit the islands and return to the Northwest Coast. The two ships anchored off Montague Island, Prince William Sound on April 25 and here, near Snug Corner Cove, the expedition discovered it had English company.

For several days the local Indians kept repeating the word "Nootka" and pointing up the sound but the message didn't come through. Finally, though, on May 8, Portlock sent Dixon in a boat guided by Indians up the sound. They found the 200-ton snow *Nootka* commanded by Captain John Meares frozen fast in the ice with the remnants of a crew sick with scurvy. This was the first meeting between the two English captains, who were to carry on for several years afterwards an acrimonious row that probably never was settled to either's satisfaction.

The row, which developed after they had both returned to England, had murky origins. John Meares had sailed from Bengal in March 1786 accompanied by the 100-ton *Sea Otter* under Captain William Tipping, a lieutenant in the navy. Both vessels had been diverted at the beginning of their voyage, the *Sea Otter* to take opium to Malacca and the *Nootka* to take the paymaster general of the king's forces in India to Madras. Therefore, when they arrived on the coast in early August, they found themselves in the midst of Indian canoes busily whaling. A Russian pilot took them into harbor near where Cook had refitted, and Meares's first mate and surgeon distinguished themselves by falling through a hole into an underground Russian house, landing in the midst of a startled family group.

When, from the crews of three Russian galiots at Kodiak, Meares learned that the *King George* and *Queen Charlotte* had been there before him, he decided to winter at Prince William Sound. (Tipping, in *Sea Otter*, left the coast in late fall.) Meares justified his decision on the grounds that his seamen would have deserted in the Sandwich Islands. Dixon, however, was of the opinion that Meares had allowed his men too liberal use of spirits.

This, at any rate, was the situation when Meares, having lost his second and third mates, surgeon, boatswain, carpenter, cooper, sailmaker, and several sailors, visited Portlock. Portlock gave the unfortunate men supplies and lent Meares two sailors to be returned when the ships met in China. Meares had had tolerable luck in his short trading; he mentioned that several other ships from India and China had been on the coast — all of which had inflated the price of skins. Because of this competition Portlock decided that they would get more trade if his two ships separated. Thus, on May 14, 1787, Portlock and Dixon went their separate ways, not to meet again until they were in China.

Both men spent all summer trading up and down the coast. (Dixon did better than Portlock but neither of them made a real killing.) Both men's accounts are filled with interesting ethnological observations and both charted numerous harbors and anchorages. Dixon's discovery of the Queen Charlotte Islands (or at least his proof that they were not part of the mainland) was the most important resulting piece of geographical information. The Indians gave Dixon's men a lesson in catching halibut and in Norfolk Sound he discovered a cave for the disposal of the dead. One old man whom he met remembered seeing Maurelle and his two Spanish ships in 1775.

Dixon also provides a good illustration of how traders may be the means of acculturation between peoples. "One of the Chiefs who came to trade with us," he writes, "happening one day to cast his eyes on a piece of Sandwich Island cloth, which hung up in the shrouds to dry, became very importunate to have it given him. The man to whom the cloth belonged, parted with it very willingly, and the Indian was perfectly overjoyed with his present. After selling what furs he had brought with great dispatch, he immediately left us. . . . Soon after day-light the next morning, our friend appeared alongside, dressed in a coat made of the Sandwich Island cloth given him the day before, and cut exactly in the form of their skin-coats. . . . The Indian was more proud of his new acquired dress than ever London beau was of a birth-day suit, and we were greatly pleased with this proof of these people's ingenuity and dispatch; the coat fitted exceedingly well." *

On St. James Day, July 25, Dixon named the cape for the saint and in early August 1787 he named the Queen Charlotte Islands. While he did not sail around the group, he was the first navigator to realize from the continual evidence of the Indians whom he met from the opposite shore that they must be islands. His trading, which had been reasonably successful, was particularly so off these islands, where he obtained 1,821 sea otters, besides raccoon, martin, and seal skins.

Dixon had another of his fortuitous meetings with a now famous contemporary — this time off King George's Sound (now Nootka Sound), on August 8, when he fell in with Captain James Colnett † in the *Prince of Wales*, accompanied by Captain Charles Duncan in the *Princess Royal*. Both of these vessels had been fitted out by Portlock's and Dixon's owners and had sailed from England in September 1786. They had paused at Staten Island (off the Horn) to set up a factory for getting seal oil before pushing on to the Northwest Coast. When Colnett and Duncan met Dixon, they spoke of meeting two vessels from Bombay, as well as Captain Charles W. Barkley in the ship *Imperial Eagle*, who had sailed from Ostend in November 1786. Colnett had on board John Etches, the brother of the managing owner of the two expeditions. Business on the Northwest Coast was picking up.

Dixon made a good western passage, sighting Hawaii on September 5. Since he was in a hurry to be on his way to China, he set about laying in supplies as expeditiously as possible, buying hogs and fresh vegetables as he was cruising about the eastern islands and filling the water casks once again from gourds at Oahu, where he also obtained wood. He found, however, that the previously friendly natives were cautious and ill at ease, and it emerged that Captain Meares in the *Nootka*, who had beaten Dixon to the islands by about twenty days,

---

* The reverse of this is illustrated by a seal intestine coat in the Peabody Museum of Salem, presented to Captain Thomas Meek by King Kamehameha of the Hawaiian Islands in 1817, who considered it more valuable than a feather cloak. William Beresford, Dixon amanuensis, makes interesting comparisons between the woven cloaks and the fortification of the Northwest Coast Indians and the Maoris of New Zealand, a circumstance first noted by Cook and by many others since.

† Dixon consistently spells it "Colinett."

had quarreled with the people of Kauai, and then sailed off without making any present for the ample provisions with which they had supplied him. By degrees Dixon persuaded the king that he was still friendly. Dixon left Waimea Bay on September 18, plentifully supplied and bound for China.*

By October 22 Dixon was sailing through the southern Marianas, past Tinian and Saipan; on November 8 he picked up an old Chinaman as a pilot, who agreed to take the ship to Macao for $30, after first asking $50. The next day Dixon anchored in Macao Roads to get a chop or license for Canton. Here he found Captain Barkley in the large ship *Imperial Eagle*, which had last been reported by Captain Colnett as being in King George's Sound.

Let us now return to the point on the Northwest Coast where the *King George* and *Queen Charlotte* parted company, and follow Captain Portlock. The ships went their separate ways on May 14, 1787, and on June 7 Portlock had the misfortune to have his whaleboat and yawl run aground on a falling tide that left bare ground for two miles around. In this helpless position the small boats were plundered by about two hundred Indians.

Two days later the *Nootka*, now in deplorable condition, joined the *King George* at Port Etches, and Portlock lent Meares his carpenter to assist in making repairs. Meares departed on the nineteenth, and Portlock left Prince William Sound the end of July.

Portlock's description of the Indians at Prince William Sound supplements Cook's, and is worth quoting. He remarks that in spite of all their love for finery, "They are remarkably filthy in their persons, and not frequently shifting their garments, they are generally very lousy; and in times of scarcity those vermin probably serve them as an article of food; for I have seen them pick and eat to the number of a dozen or more; and they are not very small."

Portlock also recounts an unfortunate experience. "We made use of the alder buds," he writes, "when they were tender as greens, and

* Beresford, in his account of Dixon's voyage, concludes the Hawaiian stay with an excellent descriptive ethnological account of the natives: some of their customs and their material culture, including feather capes and cloaks, tapa, fans, fishing gear, nets, mats, gourds, canoes, and food habits.

when boiled they eat very well. All hands partook of them one day for dinner; but they had a strange effect; not a person on board but what was physicked in a most extraordinary degree. On some it acted as an emetic as well as a purge; it kept us going for about thirty-six hours, when it stopped, leaving us all somewhat lighter than we were. This bout prevented me from sending the boats on a trading expedition two days longer than I intended."

On August 6, at what became known as Portlock's Harbor, Portlock observed that the Indians were entirely different from those in the vicinity of Prince William Sound. Trading with these same Indians three days later, Portlock saw a non-English carpenter's adze marked with the letter B and three fleurs-de-lis. He learned that it had been obtained from two large men-of-war — obviously the La Pérouse expedition.

Portlock also found trade goods that he knew to be from his colleague Dixon and a "Sandwich Island calabash" doubtless from the same source. (This, incidentally, is very good proof of the way ethnological articles were getting mixed up and distributed around the Pacific even at this early date.) Joseph Woodcock, one of the draftsmen and mathematicians of the expedition, who did some of the pictures from which the engravings were made for Portlock's book, was used as a hostage to the Indians occasionally and availed himself of the opportunity to study them.

On August 24 Portlock cleared the coast for the last time and on September 28 sighted Hawaii, where he immediately commenced trading for supplies. At Waimea Bay Portlock received a letter from Abenoue, left for him by Dixon, in which he learned for the first time that Dixon had met Colnett, that Meares in the *Nootka* had sailed from Kauai about a month before, and Dixon, eighteen to twenty days before. The Hawaiians said that the *Nootka* had fired on them, but that Dixon had been friendly.

Portlock completed his supplies and pushed on to China as rapidly as possible, anchoring in Macao Roads on November 21. Here he found two large French ships, a thirty-two-gun frigate and a storeship in Typa. Here, too, were the *Nootka* and *Imperial Eagle*, and a letter from Dixon (who had heard of Portlock's arrival on the twenty-third), announcing his own safe arrival. On November 24 Portlock went upriver and joined Captain Dixon. Portlock and Dixon stayed at Canton until early February 1788, disposing of their skins and loading cargo for the East India Company. At the same time private trading in snakeroot went on between two of the sailors and the Chinese. As Nicol explains it, when they were at Prince William Sound, he "and the quartermaster made an excursion up the river, and discovered a large space covered with snakeroot, which is of great value in China. My comrade, who had been in China, informed me of its value. It is the sweetest smelling plant I ever was near when it is growing. We set to work, and dug up as much as we chose, and dried it, letting no one know, for lessening the value of what we got. It was got safe on board the day before we sailed, and we sold it well at Wampoa." The expedition's skins, consisting of 2,552 sea otter, 434 cub, and 34 fox, were finally sold to the East India Company's supercargo on January 26 for $50,000. Other odds and ends, consisting of 1,080 beaver tails and assorted beaver, raccoon, fox, lynx, and marmot cloaks, were sold by the captains to pay for current expenses. This was far short of what Portlock and Dixon had hoped to realize — Meares and Barkley, for example, had done better — but it was expedient to get back to England. Their cargoes of teas were all on board by January 30. Watering was completed. All was ready for sea. Anchor was weighed at 10 A.M., February 5, and the ships dropped downriver. While *King George* was warping downriver, three sailors stole a boat and were caught buying liquor "sufficient to have kept the ship's company in a state of drunkenness for some days."

Both ships stood down Macao Roads on February 9 and were all clear of the land by next day. On the fourteenth they spoke their old friend of the Northwest Coast, Captain Barkley in the *Imperial Eagle*, now bound to Mauritius. The ships separated on April 1, after an agreement to meet at St. Helena. Portlock arrived there on June 12 and Dixon on the eighteenth. During the wait for his colleague, Portlock met Etienne Marchand, who was on his way home from Bengal, and briefed the French captain on the details of the fur and China trades. Portlock anchored in Margate Roads August 24, and Dixon arrived off Dover September 17, 1788.

Although the voyage did not return enormous profits, the King George's Sound Company nevertheless made a few thousand pounds. The crippling effect of the East India Company on this trade was pointed out by Portlock, who remarked that, if they could have disposed of their sea otter skins themselves any time within a month of their arrival at Canton, they would have brought $80 to $90 each, but by the time they were disposed of through the company supercargoes the price was down to $20 each.

Yet, of course, this was more than a commercial voyage. The charting done on the Northwest Coast was important. Dixon concluded correctly that the Queen Charlotte Islands were not part of the mainland. And the handsome books that resulted from the expedition contain valuable accounts of the Northwest Coast Indians and the Hawaiian Islanders. Throughout, Cook's training of these two men is evident, and Dixon tells us that, in addition to all its duties, the expedition collected natural history and ethnological specimens for the Leverian Museum, John and Isaac Swainson, M. Colonne, the Duchess of Portland's Museum, and that of "Mr. George Humphrey, dealer in natural curiousities, Albion-Street, near Black-Friar's Bridge, London."

5

The Northwest Men—Meares and Colnett

WHEN Dixon arrived at Canton and found Captain John Meares with the *Nootka*, he found also that Meares had brought with him the Sandwich Islands prince, Kaiana (variously spelled by Dixon, "Tyana"; Portlock, "Tyaana"; and Meares, "Tianna"), brother of the king of Kauai.* Both Dixon and Portlock had known the six-foot-two chief in Kauai, and Kaiana was delighted to accompany Dixon along with Mr. Ross, mate of the *Nootka*, on their trips between Macao and Whampoa.

Kaiana gloried in his stature, and on his frequent excursions through the Chinese cities he made himself even taller by wearing his crested feather helmet. Resplendent in this headpiece and a dazzling feather cloak, and carrying a long wooden barbed spear, he terrified the smaller Chinese. He was popular with the gentlemen of the English factory as well as with other foreigners at Canton — all of whom treated him with a respect befitting his rank. But Portlock tells us: "Tyaana often expressed his dislike of the Chinese, particularly that custom of shutting up and excluding the women from the sight of all strangers. And he seemed likewise to have contracted a prejudice, as well against the form, shape, and manner of their persons, as against their practices and customs; and carried it even to hatred and antip-

* This chief was not the first Hawaiian to leave the islands. Mrs. Barkley, wife of the captain of the *Imperial Eagle*, had on their passage to China taken on board an island woman named Wynee as a servant.

athy, insomuch that he was once going to throw the pilot over-board for some trivial matter of offence."

Meares confirmed Portlock's remarks. "The natives of China," Meares wrote, "he considered with a degree of disgust which bordered on extreme aversion; their bald heads, distended nostrils, and unmeaning features, had raised in his mind the strongest sensations of contempt: — Indeed it might be owing to the addition which the natural dignity of his person may be supposed to receive from such a prevailing sentiment, whenever he found himself amongst them, that the Chinese appeared to regard him with awe, and that, wherever he turned, the timid crowd never failed to open to him a ready passage."

This tall, dignified Hercules in his early thirties must indeed have been an awe-inspiring sight to the Chinese. That he was fundamentally kind to them is, however, suggested by an incident that Portlock witnessed. "A Captain Tasker, of the Milford, from Bombay, gave a sumptuous entertainment to a number of English gentlemen," writes Portlock, "and of course Tyaana was among the rest. After dinner, being upon deck, a number of poor Tartars, in small sampans, were about the ship asking alms, as is customary there on such occasions of entertainment and festivity. Tyaana immediately enquired what they wanted, and being told that they were beggars who came to supplicate the refuse of the table, he expressed great concern, saying that he was very sorry to see any persons in want of food, and that it was quite a new scene to him; for that they had no people of that description at Atoui [Kauai]; he seemed to be under great impatience to procure them relief, and became a very importunate soliciter on their behalf."

While he was in Canton Kaiana had painted the portraits from which were made the engravings reproduced in Portlock's and Meares's books. The Woodcock picture is probably the better facial likeness; but it is interesting that both artists reproduced Kaiana's helmet and feather cloak identically. More interesting is Kaiana's own reaction to the Spoilum portrait. According to Meares, "of all the various articles which formed his present wealth, his fancy was the most delighted with a portrait of himself, painted by Spoilum, the celebrated artist of China, and perhaps the only one in his line, throughout that extensive empire. The painter had, indeed, most faithfully repre-

sented the lineaments of his countenance, but found the graceful figure of the chief beyond the powers of his genius. The surprise that
Tianna expressed, as the work proceeded, was various and extreme,
and seemed to follow with continual change every added stroke of the
pencil. When this painting was presented to him, he received it with a
degree of solemnity that struck all who beheld it; and then, in a state
of agitation in which he had never been seen by us, he mentioned the
catastrophe which deprived the world of Captain Cook. He now, for
the first time, informed us that a fierce war had been waged throughout the Islands, on account of a painting, which he called a portrait of
that great man, and which had been left with one of their most potent
chiefs. This picture, he added, was held sacred amongst them, and the
respect they paid to it was considered by them as the only retribution
they could make for their unfortunate destruction of its original."

In January 1788 Meares, with help from British India merchants,
purchased and fitted out two vessels — the *Felice Adventurer* of
230 tons, to be commanded by himself, and the slightly smaller
Iphigenia Nubiana, to be commanded by Captain William Douglas.
No licenses were obtained from the South Sea and East India companies. The ships boldly sailed under Portuguese colors.

One of the lesser reasons for Meares's next voyage was to return the
popular and peripatetic Hawaiian chief to his native land. It had apparently been decided by the merchants and captains in China to return to their homelands all natives that had been brought on ships.
Besides Kaiana of Kauai, the expedition carried Wynee; a stout man
and boy from Maui; and an Indian named Camakela from King
George's Sound, who was so barbarous that not a single civilizing
amenity would rub off on him. The Hawaiians and Indians were divided between the two vessels. The proprietors of the expedition who
had taken on this program obviously did not want to do it again; their
instructions to Meares state: "We particularly direct, that you do not
bring away any of the inhabitants of America, or the Sandwich Islands; as there is no certainty that there will be an opportunity of
returning them to their own country." Each ship also carried six cows
and three bulls, turkeys, goats, rabbits, pigeons, and several lime and

*Kaiana (or Tianna), the Hawaiian chief who visited Canton
(from Meares' Voyage)*

orange trees, few or none of which ever arrived at the Hawaiian Islands.

The two ships sailed from China for the Philippines on January 22, 1788. It was an inauspicious start. The Chinese sailors were seasick and the *Iphigenia*, a dull and heavy sailer, could not keep up and was leaking besides. On February 5 poor Wynee died, and Kaiana, who had cared for her, fell sick with fever. Most of the cattle were dead by the time they reached the Philippines, where Meares stopped at Zamboanga to cut a new foremast for the *Iphigenia*. On February 10 Meares decided to head for the Northwest Coast with the *Felice* only and leave Douglas to follow. Ridding himself of another headache, he transferred Kaiana to the *Iphigenia*, where he would be with his countrymen, and sailed the next day.

The voyage was uneventful until April 9, when Meares made one of his most remarkable discoveries. "About nine o'clock in the morning," he tells us, "a sail was descried from the masthead, and, in about half an hour a large ship was seen from the deck. She appeared to be under an extraordinary croud [*sic*] of sail, and exhibited a very singular figure, for not one of us, even with the assistance of glasses, could make out which way she was standing. The sight of a ship in those seas was such an unusual circumstance, that for some time conjecture was at a loss concerning it. At length, however, it was determined to be a galleon, bound to China from New Spain, and by some casualty driven thus far to the Northward; though the track of those ships to Manilla, is generally between the parallels of 13° and 14° North latitude. In consequence of this opinion, several letters were written to inform our friends in China of our safety, and the progress we had made in the voyage. This extraordinary delusion, for it was no more, continued till we were within two leagues of the object; when, on viewing it with a glass, it was discovered to be a huge rock standing alone amid the waters. . . . As we ranged up with this rock, our surprise was proportionably augmented, and the sailors were more than disposed to believe that some supernatural power had suddenly transformed it into its present shape. It obtained the name of *Lot's Wife* [now known as Sofu Gan], and is one of the most wonderful objects, taken in all its circumstances, which I ever beheld.

[63]

Wynee, the first Hawaiian to go to China (from Meares' Voyage)

"By noon we were abreast of it; when it bore East North East four miles. The latitude was 29° 50′ North, and the longitude 142° 23′ East of Greenwich. The waves broke against its rugged front with a fury proportioned to the immense distance they had to roll before they were interrupted by it. It rose almost perpendicular to the height, according to the tables, of near three hundred and fifty feet."

A month later, May 11, Meares made King George's Sound, where he sighted the *Princess Royal* of London on a fur-trading voyage. On the thirteenth the *Felice* dropped anchor off Nootka Village in Friendly Cove. In twelve days Meares had built a trading house and had laid the keel of a small vessel of forty or fifty tons. Trading was good but there was the usual assortment of unexpected incidents that were common to that wild coast and adventurous trade. For instance, on June 8 a canoe load of Indians offered, along with some sea otter skins, a dried human hand. The hand, Meares and his crew concluded, had once belonged to the unfortunate Mr. Miller of the *Imperial Eagle*, who had been killed in 1787, since they also recognized his seal hanging from an Indian's ear. On June ninth *Felice's* pinnace was stolen, and on the eleventh Meares put to sea, leaving a trading party in residence at the house with instructions on the course of action to be taken when the *Iphigenia* arrived in the fall and if the *Felice* never

The rock called Lot's Wife (Sofu Gar) discovered by Captain Meares
(from Meares' Voyage)

returned. Just before Meares's departure from Nootka, the great chief Callicum returned and offered as presents three of the brass clubs, shaped like New Zealand *patu* (short spatula-like club), which Cook's expedition had left. Each was engraved with the arms of Sir Joseph Banks and the year 1775.

Meares's trading and exploratory cruise lasted until July 26. During that time he coasted from 45° 37′ to 49° 37′ and concluded that Maurelle's chart was useless. He also took possession of Juan de Fuca for Britain and had a fight with the Indians without losing a man. Back at Friendly Cove he found that the fur trading had been good and that the vessel was nearly completed. But trouble broke out on July 28, when a demoted boatswain led a group of eight sailors in an attempted mutiny, aimed at taking the ship to the Sandwich Islands. The mutineers could not get at any arms, and Meares let them choose between two severe punishments: rather than going into irons, the eight men were put on shore, where they became slaves of the Indians. When the *Princess Royal* was sighted once more, on August 6, Meares decided to put to sea on another trading cruise, as the presence of the *Princess Royal* would be added protection to his shore party. The cruise was a short one, and on the twenty-fourth the *Felice* was back at her old anchorage in Friendly Cove, where the mutineers were begging to be taken back.

Three days later the *Iphigenia* arrived. The season was getting on and, after laying in a good cargo of furs, Meares decided to sail with the *Felice* directly for China, leaving the *Iphigenia* and the new schooner, now nearly ready for launching, to clean up odds and ends of trade on the coast before going to the Sandwich Islands for wintering. Before Meares's departure, however, Captain Robert Gray, a man later destined to be famous, arrived with the *Lady Washington* at Nootka Sound. He had separated from his colleague, Captain John Kendrick of the *Columbia*,* off Cape Horn, and Nootka Sound was to be their rendezvous. Gray's disappointment at not finding the *Columbia* was offset by a few congenial days with the English officers. But Meares, always a tricky individual, showed himself a fair-weather

---

* This was the vessel in which Gray would complete the first American circumnavigation and later discover the Columbia River.

friend, if not a downright liar. He offered to take a packet of letters to China and then left them behind with Captain Douglas when he sailed six days later on September 24, 1788. In a mealymouthed letter, he apologized for returning the letters to Gray via Douglas with the excuse that he was not sure where in India he would be going and could not insure delivery. His real reason, according to Robert Haswell, one of Gray's mates, was that some information disadvantageous to him about the fur trade would be sent to China.

Four days before Meares sailed he launched his new schooner *North West America*, the first vessel ever built on the Northwest Coast. She went down the ways like a shot, while Kaiana jumped around on deck, whooping and hollering with jubilant excitement. Because of inexperience in launchings no cable and anchor had been provided to fetch her up; with tremendous way on, the *North West America* surged through the harbor nearly carrying Kaiana out into the Pacific. Boats caught up with her, however, and soon she was safely moored. She stayed on with the *Iphigenia* after the *Felice* had left.

Meares devotes three chapters of his book to the manners and customs of the people of Nootka Sound. His account of their sea otter hunting is an illuminating description of the important part played by the Indian hunters in the trade which for a few years dominated the North Pacific. "The taking of the sea-otter is attended with far greater hazard as well as trouble," he notes. "For this purpose two very small canoes are prepared, in each of which are two expert hunters. The instruments they employ on this occasion are bows and arrows, and a small harpoon. . . . Thus equipped, the hunters proceed among the rocks in search of their prey. Sometimes they surprise him sleeping on his back, on the surface of the water; and, if they can get near the animal without awakening him, which requires infinite precaution, he is easily harpooned and dragged to the boat, when a fierce battle very often ensues between the otter and the hunters, who are frequently wounded by the claws and teeth of the animal. The more common mode, however, of taking him is by pursuit, which is sometimes continued for several hours. . . .

"It has been observed, in the account already given of the otter, that when they are overtaken with their young ones, the parental affection supersedes all sense of danger; and both the male and female defend their offspring with the most furious courage, tearing out the arrows and harpoons fixed in them with their teeth, and oftentimes even attacking the canoes. On these occasions, however, they and their litter never fail of yielding to the power of the hunters."

Meares did stop at the Sandwich Islands, even though he denied that he would do so: *Felice* was making water and he needed provisions. He sighted Hawaii on October 17 and shortly thereafter was buying 400 hogs and boatloads of vegetables. He sent off a present entrusted to him by Kaiana to his uncle Kaeo, the king of Kauai. A few days later Meares cleared his ship of the ever present natives and made sail for Kauai, where he anchored in Waimea Bay, October 23. The principal reason for stopping here was so that he could tell Kaeo that Kaiana would return shortly on the *Iphigenia*. Two days later *Felice* left for China. She anchored in Macao Roads on December 5.

Captain Douglas, the *Iphigenia*, and its returning exiles had been left behind in the Philippines in February, to get a new foremast. Even after the mast was stepped the Spaniards held the vessel for payment of half her iron cargo. Douglas finally got away from the Philippines on February twenty-second. On March 9 in 3° 11′ north latitude and 131° 12′ east longitude he made what he believed to be a new discovery and named it Johnstone's Island. This must have been Tobi, discovered by the ship *Lord North* in 1781. In April he was among the Pelews and on the fourth he sighted two islands, the largest of which he called Moore's in honor of his friend Sir Hugh Moore. By June fifth he was at Cape Trinity and on the seventeenth the *Iphigenia* was running up Cook's River (Cook Inlet), where she anchored in Snug Corner Cove. There Douglas found an inscription reading: "J. Etches, of the Prince of Wales, May 9th, 1788, and John Hutchins." Evidence that Captain James Colnett had been less than a month ahead of him. Douglas left Snug Corner Cove on July 14 and traded successfully down the coast until he joined Meares and the *Felice* in Friendly Cove on August 27. The *Iphigenia* remained here until October 27, when Douglas sailed for Hawaii in company with the *North West America* under Captain Funter — over a month after the departure of *Felice* for China.

By now Kaiana, Douglas's most important passenger, was getting impatient to be home. On December 7 the island of Maui was sighted and Kaiana's brother-in-law, who lived on Maui, came on board to welcome the long-absent chief. The next day friends arrived from Hawaii and on the ninth came more relatives. The king of Maui himself, Kahekili, came in a large double canoe, greeted Kaiana with tears, and gave Captain Douglas "a most beautiful fan, and two long-feathered cloack [*sic*]."

On the crossing to Hawaii, where Kamehameha was king, Kaiana learned from friends and relatives who stayed on board *Iphigenia* that it would be very dangerous for him to return to Kauai. Kaeo, forewarned by Meares, did not want Kaiana to return for political reasons, and was preparing a rough welcome. As a stopgap Kamehameha offered him land on Hawaii, an offer Kaiana accepted. And so Kaiana's treasures, which "consisted of saws of different kinds, gimblets, hatchets, adzes, knives and choppers, cloth of various fabrics, carpets of several colours, a considerable quantity of China-ware, and ten bars of iron," were brought on deck. Kaiana, "after entreating Captain Douglas again and again to bring his family from Atooi to Owhyhee, took a most affectionate leave of him and the whole crew, who had so long been his constant companions and friends; nor were the latter without their emotions of regard, when they saw the chief, whose amiable disposition and superior qualities had won their sincere esteem through the connection of a long and dangerous voyage, about to be separated from them." As Kaiana left the ship, accompanied by a numerous train of his relations in their canoes, Captain Douglas ordered a salute of seven guns, as a mark of esteem to that respected chief, and immediately made sail to the North West.

For four months Douglas moved about the islands collecting provisions. When *Iphigenia* anchored in Waimea Bay, Kauai, the chief Kaeo fled into the mountains, fearing that Kaiana was on board, and Douglas was able to take Kaiana's wife and child from Kauai and reunite the family at Hawaii. By way of reward, Douglas, who was accumulating quite a wardrobe of expensive garments, received yet another feather cloak from King Kamehameha and Kaiana.

Finally, on March 18, 1789, Douglas sailed again for the Northwest Coast and another season's trading. At Nootka Sound a month later, the *Iphigenia* was seized by the Spaniards. Although she was released promptly, the Spaniards confiscated much of her iron and other trade goods, and her season was only moderately successful. By the time she anchored in Macao Roads, October 5, completing her Pacific mission, news of her seizure — combined and augmented by the subsequent seizure of Captain James Colnett in the *Argonaut* — had seriously increased the international importance of the Spanish acts.

Who was Colnett and what was he doing in Nootka Sound? James Colnett was a career officer in the Royal Navy, who had served as a midshipman in the *Resolution* with Captain Cook on his second voyage. His name is preserved at Cape Colnett, New Caledonia, which he was the first man to sight (on September 4, 1774). When Cook returned in 1775, Colnett left the *Resolution* and served on various ships, rising to first lieutenant, until 1786 when he was placed on half pay. Probably to increase his income he obtained the Admiralty's permission to take command of the ship *Prince of Wales*, accompanied by Captain Charles Duncan in the sloop *Princess Royal*, on a trading voyage to the Northwest Coast and China. These two vessels were fitted out by Richard Cadman Etches and his associates — the same investors who had sent Portlock and Dixon in the *King George* and *Queen Charlotte* the year before. On board the *Prince of Wales* was John Etches, younger brother of the governor, representing the company and acting as supercargo. As with Portlock's ship, the company had provided Colnett's vessels with licenses for legitimate trade under both the South Sea and East India companies.

Colnett arrived at Nootka Sound on July 7, 1787, where he found Captain Barkley with the *Imperial Eagle* under the Austrian flag. After a month recovering from his long voyage he met Dixon (as already noted) in the *Queen Charlotte*. Sailing north along the western coast of Vancouver Island, he discovered Klaskish Inlet (Port Brooks) and then traded on along the eastern shore of Queen Char-

The North American, the first vessel built on the northwest coast, in the Strait of Juan de Fuca (from Meares' Voyage)

lotte Islands until September 4. At Calamity Bay, the southern end of Brooks Island, he had serious difficulties with the Indians' stealing from the ships tools, iron — indeed, anything not nailed down. Colnett wintered in Hawaii and returned to the coast in 1788, where the *Princess Royal* spent the season trading around the Queen Charlotte Islands, while Colnett and the *Prince of Wales* cruised Prince William Sound and other Alaskan waters. The two vessels sailed in company from the coast on August 18 for the Hawaiian Islands and thence to China, where they arrived on November 12, 1788.

Apparently Colnett and Meares met in China and decided that it would be mutually beneficial if they joined forces in the trade. Colnett's licenses for his ships from the two great companies would be fair exchange for Meares's greater experience in the fur trade. Since John Etches, one of the partners in the company that owned Colnett's vessels, was present, and since Meares's owners, Daniel Beal and Co., and John Henry Cox, were in Canton anyway, it was an easy matter to organize a joint trading expedition. The new partnership combined the King George's Sound Company and Meares's owners and was called the "Associated Merchants Trading to the North West Coast of America." As soon as an agreement was worked out, John Etches sailed for England on the *Prince of Wales,* giving Colnett authority to act for his company. The new group combined their assets. Meares had left two vessels, the *Iphigenia* and the new schooner *North West America,* on the Northwest Coast. The King George's Sound people had the *Princess Royal* and agreed to outfit another — a snow (*Argonaut,* as Colnett ultimately called her) — to replace the *Prince of Wales.* It is important to note that only the two latter ships would be properly licensed by the two great companies; the other two would continue to collect furs under Portuguese colors and ship them back to China on the licensed vessels.

This was why Esteban José Martínez, the Spanish commander, after capturing all four vessels, let go the two under Portuguese colors but retained those under British colors — the *Argonaut* and *Princess* — and sent their crews to Mexico as prisoners. Colnett was captured July 3, 1789 and released July 9, 1790. The capture of the four vessels created an international incident that nearly brought Britain and Spain into armed conflict. Spain's high-handedness was due to her belief that merely by discovering and taking formal possession of lands and ocean she had done all that was necessary to claim sovereignty. The British and Americans did not share this attitude, and eventually the disagreement was settled in favor of Britain at the Nootka Convention of October 28, 1790. Spain paid Meares damages for his vessels and trade goods. (Meares did not, however, collect for uncaught sea otters, as he tried to.) Colnett's voyage of the *Argonaut* of 1789–1791 is, thus, important largely for its political consequences, rather than for its contribution to exploration or commerce.*

After his release Colnett spent five months — from October 1790 to March 1791 — trading on the Northwest Coast, where he secured some 1,100 sea otter skins. He sailed for Hawaii on March 3, 1791, and arrived at Macao on May 30, only to find that the Chinese (now at war with the Russians) had prohibited the importation of furs at Canton. His trading voyage to Japan was no more successful, although he was the first Englishman to attempt it since the unsuccessful effort of the East India Company's ship *Return* in 1673. Colnett did sell a few skins in northern China. The remainder he sold to the East India Company after his return to England.

Colnett made no real geographical discoveries on this voyage; his ethnological interest was minimal; and his journal, which contains numerous sketches of harbors, landfalls, and elevations from the Northwest Coast to Mexico and from Korea to Japan, was not published until 1940 and thus had no effect on contemporary geographical knowledge. Colnett may, however, have been the first man to show the Indians of Nootka Sound how to use sails; for he writes on December 31, 1790: "In return for this attention the chief having attempted to rig and sail two canoes after the manner of our Boats I caus'd their sails to be properly made and a Rudder for the Chief's Boat." Captain Cook had observed in the same region in April 1778 that "sails are no part of their art of Navigation." Less than two years after Colnett taught them how to set sails, Ingraham wrote at Nootka in July 1792: "We passed a vast number of canoes every one with a

---

* It has been discussed in detail in the Introduction to Frederic W. Howay's two scholarly volumes and in various articles.

sail, which was a new thing to me, as I never saw them make use of any in this part before."

Colnett returned to England in 1792 still a lieutenant on half pay. That same year the Admiralty gave him command of the ship *Rattler* for a voyage to the western coasts of America. The objective was to examine ports suitable for the refreshment and refitting of ships in the extensive British Pacific whale fishery, and otherwise to aid that important industry.

Colnett sailed in his new command on January 7, 1793, carrying a whaling master and a crew of experienced whale men. By February 24 he was at Rio de Janeiro, where he met Governor Phillip on his homeward passage from Botany Bay. Colnett sent home by Phillip a table showing the rate of his timekeepers to Sir Philip Stephens, the Lord of the Admiralty, to whom his book is dedicated. Before rounding Cape Horn he searched in 45° south latitude for the nonexistent Grand Island, which, according to Dalrymple, was supposed to have been discovered by Anthony de La Roche on a passage from the South Seas in 1675. In the course of this fruitless search a storm destroyed his fresh vegetables and livestock and two men were hit by a ball of lightning. Colnett restored them by applying a massage that he had learned from the Tahitians during his voyage with Cook.

Rounding South America, he bypassed Juan Fernández (where he might be troubled by Spaniards) and on May 20 sighted Saint Felix and Saint Ambrose. He attempted to land, "but night was coming on, and it beginning to sniffle and rain," and he decided to return to his ship. He made the Galapagos on June 25, partially surveyed the group, named Chatham and Hood islands, and described the plants, reptiles, birds, and sea life.

Leaving the Galapagos, Colnett stopped by the island of Malpelo, which he found unsuitable for a whalers' rendezvous, and then turned westward for Cocos Island, where he arrived July 25, 1793. This island, which he charted, had a good harbor. As he described it, "It is Otaheite on a small scale, but without the advantage of its climate, or the hospitality of its inhabitants." Colnett completed his survey and left a letter in a bottle tied to a tree and over it an inscribed board, which Vancouver removed some time later when he anchored there. He next skirted the Mexican coast and charted Socorro and other islands of the Revillo Gigedo group. All the while he was also whaling, but not too successfully; he even made a famous dissection of a small sperm whale. On the way back from Socorro to Mexico his men had good fishing and caught many turtles. "Sea snakes were also in great plenty, and many of the crew made a pleasant and nutritious meal of them." Among Colnett's crew was a little boy who was a nephew of Captain Marshall, for whom the Marshall Islands were named.

The only remarkable occurrence on the passage home seems to have been in latitude 24°: "About eight o'clock in the evening an animal rose along-side the ship, and uttered such shrieks and tones of lamentation so like those produced by the female human voice, when expressing the deepest distress, as to occasion no small degree of alarm among those who first heard it. These cries continued for upwards of three hours, and seemed to increase as the ship sailed from it: I conjectured it to be a female seal that had lost its cub, or a cub that had lost its dam; but I never heard any noise whatever that approached so near those sounds which proceed from the organs of utterance in the human species."

By March 17, 1794, the *Rattler* was back at the Galapagos and from there made her return voyage via Saint Felix and Saint Ambrose, the coast of Chile, round the Horn, St. Helena, and home, where she anchored in Cowes Road, Isle of Wight, on November 2.

If Colnett in his Northwest Coast voyages made small contribution in his time, Meares created an enormous stir with the publication of his pretentious but beautifully illustrated volume in 1790. He had made some real discoveries, to be sure, but he also took credit for the achievements of others and his book is an unreliable source. Dixon, especially, took umbrage at many of Meares's remarks, and after the publication of Meares's book there was an acrimonious exchange of pamphlets between the two men.* They had obviously never liked each other since that day when Dixon found Meares frozen in the ice.

* See Howay, 1929, who provides an excellent introduction on this subject and reprints the rare pamphlets.

Meares not only belittles both Portlock and Dixon in his book but uses their charts and others without credit. He places upon his chart a circumnavigation of Vancouver Island by the sloop *Washington* which Captain Kendrick never made. He contradicts himself and lies about the prices of sea otter skins. In short, as Howay says, "Meares was not only lacking in veracity; he was also addicted to the bad, and closely-allied, habits of stating as facts things of which he had no knowledge." Dixon came off much better in the argument. Meares fades into oblivion.

Indeed, in the voyages of Portlock, Dixon, Meares, and Colnett, there is an excellent example of the difference between those who had sailed with Cook — and Meares, who had not. The men trained by Cook were as careful, observant, and meticulous as their instruments and experience allowed in recording their journals. Meares, let us be charitable, was otherwise.

Book Two

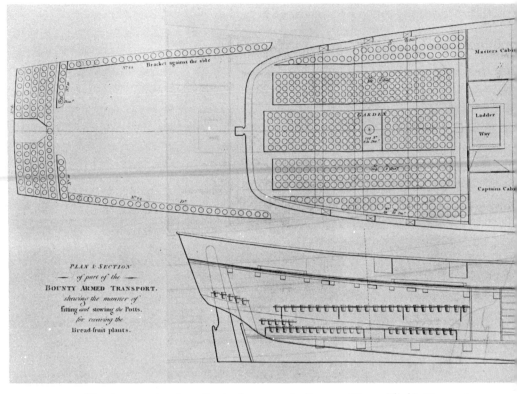

Within the image:
Master's Cabin
Ladder Way
Captains Cabin
GARDEN
Bracket against the side

PLAN & SECTION
of part of the
BOUNTY ARMED TRANSPORT.
shewing the manner of
fitting and stowing the Pots.
for receiving the
Bread-fruit plants.

Plan for stowing breadfruit plants on the Bounty (from Bligh's Voyage)

6

The Breadfruit Tree

THE story of the mutiny on the *Bounty*, Captain William Bligh's extraordinary boat voyage, and the settlement of the mutineers on Pitcairn Island has been written many times. This is not the place to tell it all again. Nevertheless, aside from the adventure and romance, the voyage enriched European knowledge of the Pacific both geographically and ethnologically. Perhaps a brief summary of the voyage should be given here.

The British planters and merchants in the West Indies had requested that the breadfruit tree, a reliable food supply, be introduced to their islands. England, thinking well of the idea, bought a 215-ton ship, the *Bounty*. Sir Joseph Banks developed a plan for stowing and caring for the young breadfruit plants by constructing in the great cabin of *Bounty* a false floor cut full of holes to take the pots. The ship was fitted out at Deptford, and on August 16, 1787, Captain William Bligh was given command of the forty-four officers and men of the Royal Navy who manned her. David Nelson, who had been with Cook in a similar capacity, was retained as botanist and gardener, and William Brown was appointed as his assistant. Bligh was under no illusion that this might be a voyage of exploration. "The object of all the former voyages to the South Seas undertaken by the command of his present majesty," he wrote, "has been the advancement of science, and the increase of knowledge. This voyage may be reckoned the first, the intention of which has been to derive benefit from those distant discoveries."

Because of bad weather, sailing was delayed a month but *Bounty* finally left Spithead on December 23, 1787. Bligh's orders were to proceed to the South Seas around Cape Horn — but if he found this impossible, to go via the Cape of Good Hope. The delay in sailing was critical. For on April 2 and 3 off Tierra del Fuego he encountered the worst storm of his life and finally, on April 21, he gave up fighting the constant westerly gales and headed for Africa. Bligh, in his log, goes to considerable detail to justify his decision. He noted that to continue attempting to round the Horn would unnecessarily lengthen the voyage, that his crew was fatigued, that the ship was beginning to leak, that the seasons in the Pacific would be better if he delayed no longer, and that it was only common sense anyway to run before the wind. On May 22 the *Bounty* came to anchor in Simon's Bay.

Bligh remained at Cape Town for over a month recovering from his grueling experience. He sailed again at four in the afternoon on July 1, 1788.

Late in the month the islands of St. Paul and Amsterdam were passed and on August 19 Tasmania rose over the horizon. Bligh has left some useful observations on the Tasmanians, as did Nelson, the botanist, who collected plants at Adventure Bay. Nelson tells us that on August 28 the date "A.D. 1773" was discovered where it had been carved on a tree by one of Captain Tobias Furneaux's crew on Cook's second expedition, over fifteen years before. Among the inhabitants, who kept their distance, Nelson recognized the same crippled individual whom he had seen when he was with Cook. Bligh describes this party of Tasmanians: "Only a few of them had the Weapon already described, a short small Stick about two or three feet long. The Colour of these people are [sic] naturally black; their skin was scarifyed about the shoulders and breasts, they were middling Stature or rather below it. One of them had his Body discoloured with red oaker, but all the others had laid an additional Coat of black over their Faces & Shoulders, and it was laid on so thick that it totally prevented me at this distance, to say anything exact of their features; but upon the whole, taking things as they first strike one, which often proves a very just Method, they appeared like Negroes. They were certainly Wooly headed as much as ever a Negroe was, and I shall ever continue of that opinion untill I hear of convincing proofs to the contrary."

After leaving Adventure Bay and pushing on eastward around the southern end of New Zealand, Bligh discovered on September 19 a new group of rocky islands, which he placed in 47° 44′ south latitude and 179° 7′ east longitude and named the Bounty Islands after his ship. From here he made a rather fast run to Tahiti, which was sighted at 6 P.M., October 25. The surgeon's examination found all hands free of venereal complaint and *Bounty* came to anchor in Matavai Bay at nine in the morning of the twenty-seventh. During the long — 27,086 miles — run from England to Tahiti, *Bounty* had averaged 108 miles for each twenty-four hours.

No sooner was the ship moored than Tahitians were clambering all over her. They inquired after Captain Cook, for they had heard from a passing ship a few months previously that he was dead. Several local chiefs came on board, as well as those who pretended to be chiefs. Bligh learned that Omai was dead, and received a message from the chief Otoo, now called Tinah, whom he had known in 1777. Certain changes had taken place in the Tahitian way of life since Bligh's previous visit. The natives had already adopted European tools and hatchets and no longer wanted the "toeys" or chisels made in imitation of their former stone tools. Dogs were still plentiful but the indigenous native variety had been replaced by European mutts. The same had happened with hogs, for the native breed had vanished.

Relations with the Tahitians continued to be excellent. Nelson, the gardener, found the two fine shaddock trees he had set out in 1777 and also saw that there was an ample supply of young breadfruit seedlings. Indeed, it emerged that the natives distinguished eight different kinds of breadfruit trees, and by a series of exchanges of gifts and dinners Bligh managed to persuade the Tahitians that he was doing them a favor by carrying off breadfruit plants. Tents were set up on Point Venus to receive the collected plants and by November 6 over a hundred had been potted. Two days later this had increased to 242. By late January *Bounty* had taken on board 774 pots, 39 tubs, and 24 boxes of breadfruit plants, besides a number of other plants thought to be useful.

While Nelson and the crew were busy plant collecting, Bligh, with his keen eye, was making observations on Tahitian culture and noting the many changes that had taken place since he was there with Cook a dozen years previously. There had been a war between the people of Moorea and Tahiti, in which the former had inflicted severe damage. All of the great houses on Tahiti of Cook's day had been destroyed, only two or three of the big canoes were left, and the livestock left by Captain Cook had been slaughtered.

Bligh's ethnological observations are excellent. He remarks, for instance, on the accuracy of Webber's (the Swiss artist on Cook's third expedition) drawings of women's dress, and notes that the natives went surfing on canoe paddles. He also describes harbors and part of the island coast. Of Tahiti and Moorea, in general, Bligh's remarks have an unexpected poignancy. "These two places are certainly the Paradise of the World," he writes, "and if happiness could result from situation and convenience, here it is to be found in the highest perfection. I have seen many parts of the World, but Otaheite is capable of being preferable to them all, and certainly is so considering it in its natural state."

Twenty-three pleasant weeks were spent at Tahiti, but on April 3, 1789, the last of the breadfruit was stowed. The men took sad leave of their girls, and Bligh prepared to sail. The next day presents were made to Tinah and his wife, who took an affectionate leave from the ship, saying, "May the *Eatua* [god] protect you for ever and ever." Tinah took back with him the Webber portrait of Cook that he had left with Bligh when the *Bounty* arrived and that had remained on the ship the entire time she was there. Bligh wrote on the back of the picture his arrival and departure dates and the number of plants he was taking away.

On April 11, Bligh made an important and unexpected discovery. "I had little reason to expect making any New Discovery, as my Track, altho not traversed by any one before, yet was bordering so near on others, that I scarce thought it probable to meet with any land. At daylight however we discovered an Island of a Moderate height with a round Conical Hill towards its northern extreme. The N.W. part made in a perpendicular head, but the S.E. slopes off to a point. As I advanced towards it, a Number of Small Keys were seen from the

Mast head lying to the S.E., and at Noon could Count nine of them. They were all covered with Trees, and the large Island had a most fruitful Appearance. The Shore was bordered with Flat land, with innumerable Cocoa Nutt and other Trees, and the higher Grounds were beautifully interspersed with Lawns. I could not get near the Shore on account of the Wind, nevertheless there appeared broken Water between all the Keys, and I am inclined to think they are all joined by a Reef. I saw no Smoke or any sign of Inhabitants, it is scarcely to be imagined however that so charming a little spot is without them."

Bligh stood off and on all night and the following day received a visit from four Aitutaki men in a canoe, who came on board the *Bounty* and were given beads and food. "Being told that I was the *Earee* or chief of the ship, the principal person came and joined noses with me, and presented to me a large mother of pearl shell, which hung with platted hair round his neck; this he fastened round my neck, with signs of great satisfaction. . . . The name of the large island, they told me, was Wytootackee, and the Earee was called Lomakkayah. They said that there were no hogs, dogs, or goats upon the island, nor had they yams, or tarro; but that plantains, cocoa-nuts, fowls, breadfruit, and avees, were there in great abundance. Notwithstanding they said that no hogs were on the island, it was evident they had seen such animals; for they called them by the same name as is given to them at Otaheite, which made me suspect that they were deceiving me. However, I ordered a young boar and sow to be put into their canoe, with some yams and tarro, as we could afford to part with some of these articles. I also gave to each of them a knife, a small adze, some nails, beads, and a looking-glass."

The island was Aitutaki, the northernmost of the Cook group. Its inhabitants, according to Bligh, "did not differ in appearance from the natives of Hervey's Islands, seen in Captain Cook's last voyage, though much [more] friendly and inoffensive in their manners. They were tattowed across the arms and legs, but not on the loins or posteriors, like the people of Otaheite. From their knowledge of iron, they have doubtless communication with Hervey's Islands, which are not more than eighteen leagues distant from them."

The *Bounty* now set out for Savage Island (Niue), which she passed without landing. Bligh reached the northern Tonga Islands on April twenty-first. At Nomuka (Anamoka or Annamooka) on the twenty-third he met an old man whom he had known when with Cook in 1777. As usual, Bligh's ethnological observations were keen and his descriptions comprehensive.

Five days later, at about five-thirty in the morning, Captain Bligh, sleeping soundly in nightshirt and nightcap, was rudely awakened by Fletcher Christian, master's mate of *Bounty* and a Bligh protégé, and two companions. As he barged into the captain's cabin, Christian said, "Mr. Bligh, you are my prisoner." When Bligh's feet hit the deck he was shouting at Christian, who put a cutlass to his throat and had the captain trussed up. While Bligh endeavored to persuade Christian to change his mind, the launch was put over, provisions and clothing were tossed aboard, and Bligh with eighteen loyal companions went over the side. It was dead calm as the launch, with only eight inches of freeboard, pulled away from *Bounty*, while Fletcher Christian watched motionless from the taffrail. Bligh's journals and commission and some ship's papers, including the logbook, were saved, but all of his surveys and drawings were lost.

Bligh proceeded first to Tofua, where the natives were belligerent and one man was killed. Then he decided to sail for Timor. During that historic voyage Bligh, in spite of cold and wet, kept his reckoning and still made sketches and charts of islands that he sailed by. A group of small islands, now called Bligh Islands, he discovered in the northern New Hebrides. On May 28 he got inside the Great Barrier Reef and landed on an island for the night. Here and at other islands Bligh and his party were refreshed with oysters, clams, sea birds, and wild berries. Timor was sighted on June 12, 1789, and two days later the group landed at Koepang. Poor David Nelson, the botanist, died six days later. Bligh left Koepang August 20 in the *Resource* for Batavia, where he anchored October 1. Here he found a passage home; on the way he encountered one of his great contemporary explorers, Bruni d'Entrecasteaux, at the Cape of Good Hope. Bligh arrived at Plymouth March 14, 1790.

The mutineers took exactly a month to sail the *Bounty* to Tubuai in

Captain William Bligh being sent off in the Bounty's launch by the mutineers
(From an engraving by R. Dodd, 1790. In the collection of the Peabody Museum of Salem)

the Austral Islands. She arrived there on May 28, but as there was no livestock on this island, Christian decided to go to Tahiti for hogs. Much to the Tahitians' surprise, they saw the *Bounty* anchor in Matavai Bay on June 6. Christian shortly returned to Tubuai well supplied with pigs, cattle left by Bligh, and Tahitian women and stowaways. The attempt to establish a colony on Tubuai was a failure because of the hostility of the natives, and by September 22, the *Bounty* was once more in Matavai Bay. Christian knew, for the tentacles of the Royal Navy stretched far, that they could not remain safely at Tahiti, although sixteen of the mutineers elected to stay there. After considering various other islands, Christian decided on Pitcairn Island, which had been discovered by Captain Philip Carteret in 1767. There he sailed with the nine remaining English, six Polynesian men, and ten Tahitian women and a girl. Pitcairn was sighted on January 15, 1790. A landing was made and shortly thereafter came the point of no return, when the *Bounty* was burned for her metal. We shall pick up Pitcairn's story on subsequent voyages.

The first sequel to Bligh's voyage turned out to be nearly as adventurous as the *Bounty*'s journey. The publication of Bligh's account of the mutiny and boat voyage stimulated widespread public sympathy, and the Admiralty hurried to fit out a ship that would bring the mutineers home to justice. The twenty-four-gun frigate *Pandora* was selected, commanded by Captain Edward Edwards and manned by 160 men.

Basil Thompson, in his Introduction to the *Voyage of H.M.S. "Pandora,"* ably sums up Edwards's character. "Edwards belonged to that useful class of public servant that lives upon instructions," Thompson says. "With a roving commission in an ocean studded with undiscovered islands the possibilities of scientific discovery were immense, but he faced them like a blinkered horse that has his eyes fixed on the narrow track before him, and all the pleasant byways of the road shut out. A cold, hard man, devoid of sympathy and imagination, of every interest beyond the straitened limits of his profession. Edwards in the eye of posterity was almost the worst man that could have been chosen."

Actually Edwards did not do too badly in recovering the mutineers who had stayed at Tahiti. Within a day of *Pandora*'s arrival at Matavai Bay, on March 23, 1791, four of the *Bounty* men voluntarily came on board and gave themselves up. Several attempted to flee in the small schooner *Resolution*, which had been built under the direction of James Morrison, the *Bounty*'s boatswain, but they were forced to return from lack of provisions. In short order the schooner and three more mutineers were captured. On April 9 the last six *Bounty* men, who had fled to the hills, were taken. In all, fourteen of the sixteen men who stayed on Tahiti were now prisoners on board *Pandora*. (The other two had previously been killed.) Edwards confined them on deck in a cage known as Pandora's Box, and he fitted out the schooner, which he placed under the command of Mr. Oliver, his master's mate, as a tender for *Pandora*.

The two vessels sailed from Tahiti on May 8 and, after calling briefly at Huahiné, Raiatéa, and Bora Bora in the Leeward group, sailed to Aitutaki in the hope of finding Christian and the *Bounty* there. Palmerston Island was next, and here they found *Bounty*'s driver yard. The search party also "found a double canoe curiously painted, and different in make from those we had seen on the islands we had visited." Like the driver yard it was eaten by sea worms.

At Palmerston, Edwards lost one of his boats and crew. Deciding it was hopeless to search further for the *Bounty*, he sailed for Duke of York Island (Atafu). This island was uninhabited, but he found houses, canoes, paddles, and fishing gear left by the people of Bowditch Island (Fakaofo), who used it as a fishing station. Now in the Union group, he discovered Nukunono on June 12 and saw natives in their sailing canoes. Three days later he stood for Samoa. Manua was sighted on the fourteenth, and the next day a landing was made at Tutuila, where Edwards found clothing and buttons that had belonged to de Langle's massacred boat party. Then, late in the afternoon of June 22, *Pandora* lost sight of the *Resolution* in a heavy squall. The next two days were spent searching for her without success.

For more than a month Edwards cruised through the Tonga and Samoa groups hoping to meet up with the tender, but on August 1 he decided to wait no longer and sailed for England. A week later Edwards made his most important discovery, sighting the island of Rotuma. "We run [sic] down the island, and saw a vast number of houses amongst the trees. It is very hilly, and, from the great height of some of them, may be called mountains. They are cultivated to the top; the reason of which, I presume, is from its being so full of inhabitants. It is about seven miles long; and being a new discovery, we called it Grenville's Island, in honour of Lord Grenville. The name the natives gave it is Rotumah."

On August 11 the ship ran over the shoal now known as Pandora's reef and on the seventeenth sighted Vanikoro in the Santa Cruz group. Unfortunately, no landing was made, for smoke rising from the island could well have been signals from the survivors of the La Pérouse expedition wrecked there three years before. Edwards was now pushing on for home as rapidly as possible.

But *Pandora* was destined never to return. While trying to find a passage through the Great Barrier Reef to enter Torres Strait, she struck, August 28, and sank the next day. Two men were killed when she hit and over thirty of her company and four of the mutineers were drowned. Eighty-nine men and ten of the mutineers survived and were divided among the ship's four boats.

Like Bligh the year before, Edwards now headed for Timor. He reached the Australian mainland September 6. On the seventeenth he arrived at Koepang, and here the governor turned over to Edwards eight men, one woman, and two children — escaped convicts from Port Jackson — who had arrived at Koepang after a remarkable open boat voyage of their own in a six-oared cutter. Edwards embarked his company and prisoners on the Dutch East India Company's ship *Rembang*, on October 6, 1791, for Batavia, where he arrived a month later. On the way, at Samarang, they fell in with the long-lost tender. (After the separation, *Resolution* had waited for five weeks in the Fijis — it was the first vessel to spend time there — and had then gone on through Endeavour Strait headed for Batavia.) The tender was sold and all hands shipped home on three Dutch ships. Edwards and his prisoners arrived at Portsmouth on June 19, 1792, after a voyage nearly as adventurous as Bligh's.

Long before Edwards returned, Bligh had sailed on his second — and successful — breadfruit voyage to Tahiti of 1791 to 1793. Two vessels were fitted out for this expedition: the new 420-ton ship *Providence*, carrying 134 men, and the brig *Assistant*, 110 tons and 27 men. Nathaniel Portlock — like Bligh, a Cook veteran, whose trading voyage to the Northwest Coast in 1785–1788 we have already followed, was given command of *Assistant*. James Wiles and Christopher Smith, two botanists recommended by Sir Joseph Banks, were appointed to care for the breadfruit seedlings and to collect exotic plants for Kew Gardens. George Tobin, third lieutenant in *Providence*, left a remarkable illustrated journal of this voyage. Among Bligh's midshipmen was Matthew Flinders, future surveyor of Australia, and of those with Portlock three had accompanied him on his voyage round the world.

Bligh sailed on August 3, 1791, and by the time he reached Teneriffe for the usual wine, water, and fresh beef, he was so sick that he asked Portlock to move over to *Providence* and take command of the expedition. On November 6 the ships anchored in Table Bay. During the stay there Bligh recovered sufficiently to resume command of *Providence* and of the expedition.* Bligh's ships sailed from Table Bay and exchanged salutes with the fort on December 23, 1791. Two days later Christmas was celebrated with a sea pie for each man.

The island of St. Paul was passed on January 18, but, much to Bligh's disappointment, thick fog prevented a landing. Bligh was not, however, under any of the confusion that plagued many of his contemporaries: he knew the southernmost island was St. Paul.

On February 8, for the third time in his life, Bligh sighted Tasmania. (His young midshipman on *Providence*, Matthew Flinders, was seeing Tasmania for the first time; six years later he would circumnavigate the island with Dr. George Bass.) *Providence* dropped anchor in Adventure Bay. Here wood was gotten where *Bounty* had wooded in 1788 and here water was obtained from the stream where *Resolution* had watered in 1777. It was historic ground.†

* Also while they were there Captain John Hunter, who had been wrecked on Norfolk Island in *Sirius*, arrived in bad shape from Batavia in the chartered Dutch snow *Waaksamheyd*.

† Even while Bligh was here, the French Admiral Bruni d'Entrecasteaux was sailing towards Tasmania to search for the lost La Pérouse. He arrived in April, two months after Bligh's departure.

[89]

During the sojourn in Adventure Bay the botanists Wiles and Smith made extensive collections, and Bligh described the plentiful wildlife (including black swans, great black cockatoos, lizards, the wombat, and a strange animal — the echidna — of which both he and Lieutenant Tobin made sketches). As a memento of his stay at Adventure Bay, Bligh carved on the same tree that bore Cook's date of 1777: "Near this tree Captain William Bligh planted seven fruit trees 1792: Messrs. S. and W., botanists." He also set out oaks, firs, and other useful plants. Bligh left Adventure Bay on February 24, to sail across the Tasman Sea and south of New Zealand.

Arriving in the longitude of Tahiti on the twenty-first of March, Bligh turned north and on April 5 sighted and discovered Lagoon Island (today called Tematangi) — one of the Tuamotus. Three days later he sighted Mehetia near Tahiti and read detailed orders to the crew for establishing good relations with the Tahitians. No one was to speak of the loss of the *Bounty*, or mention that Captain Cook had been killed or that the purpose of the expedition was to obtain breadfruit. Care must be taken to prevent thieving but articles stolen were not to be retrieved by violence. All trade must be carried on through an appointed person and curiosities were not to be kept between decks. No firearms were to be carried on shore without permission and the officer of the watch was not to get into conversation with the natives under any circumstance. Further orders regulated the care of boats, use of awnings, and other shipboard matters.

The ships anchored in Matavai Bay on April 9, 1792. Bligh had no intention of lingering this time. Much had happened since his last visit. He heard for the first time of Fletcher Christian's return to Tahiti with the *Bounty*, of the capture of the mutineers who had stayed on the island by Captain Edwards, and the sailing of *Pandora* on May 9, 1791. He also learned of the visit of Vancouver and Broughton on their voyage of exploration in the ships *Discovery* and *Chatham* (whose course we shall later follow) and their sailing from Matavai Bay only a few months before, on January 24, 1792. The wreck of a ship called the *Matilda*, commanded by Captain Matthew Weatherhead from Port Jackson, in February had caused a native war and Bligh found that the Tahitians had deteriorated economically and physically since his first visit. He began collecting breadfruit plants on April 17. Bligh was always the good observer of life and customs. He was apparently fluent in Tahitian. His descriptions of Tahitian religious services (with their human sacrifices) are among the best.

Bligh set sail from Matavai Bay on July 19, with 2,126 breadfruit plants, 472 other plants, and 36 "curiosity plants" on board. He also carried off two Tahitians (one as a stowaway) and fifteen of the *Matilda's* people. Before leaving, he returned the portrait of Cook (which had again been brought on board when he arrived), noting his time of arrival and departure (which he mistakenly wrote as the sixteenth) on the back. If only this portrait had survived, what a unique record it would have been of famous voyages to Tahiti.

Bligh had given Portlock a letter with instructions for rendezvous should the ships become separated on the way to the West Indies. The first goal was to be the island of Aitutaki, which Bligh had discovered on his first voyage about a fortnight before the infamous mutiny. He wanted to check the latitude and longitude of his previous voyage and explore the island more carefully. (His talent for language is indicated by the fact that he could understand Aitutaki dialect better than the two Tahitians on board.) Bligh made his usual sharp observations, and commented that the Aitutaki tapa is similar to that of Tonga. As to the people: "The men were above the middle size," Bligh observed, "[they] had very good regular features and were fleshy — their heads were covered with strong black hair which was very bushy, and I observed that some had theirs smutted, the remains of it being evident about the eyebrows and under the throat. Their dress was only a marro and the pearl shell pendent from the neck by plaited human hair; their colour is darker than that of an Otaheitan."

Portlock, trading with the natives, also made numerous observations. "I procured from them some small pieces of cloth," he says, "two small mats, four paddles, five spears, and three gorgets. Their cloth is much like that of the Friendly Islands, being stout, and some of it prettily glazed, and printed in a very regular manner, red, black, and white in small squares.

"Their mats were small and coarsely made, and wrought with more taste than the Otaheitans' mat, being made with different coloured rushes, which has a pretty effect. Their paddles are five feet seven inches long and nine inches broad, neatly made, and pains taken to ornament them. One side of the blade nearly at the grasp is cut out like Cornish work, and on the other side just above the point of the paddle is a ridge of about half an inch above the surface of the blade. Besides ornamenting they take pains in staining them with a black dye in variety as their fancy directs. Their spears are about twelve feet and thick in proportion, some of them of the hard toa, very much barbed near the point, others of bamboo pointed with toa wood, and one I got pointed with pieces of the sunray's [stingray] tail, and must be a very dangerous weapon. I also got one weapon about eight feet long, made of toa tree and shaped like an officer's spontoon."

After leaving Aitutaki, July 21, Bligh sighted Savage Island (Niue) on August 1 and continued on towards the Friendly Islands (Tonga). Here, instead of proceeding to his old anchorage at Annamooka, Bligh determined to clear up the confusion of islands that had resulted from the reports of Maurelle in 1781, of Cook, and of himself. In general he found that his observations jibed with those of Maurelle. "The relative positions and latitudes agree very nearly," he explains, "and the longitude is out of the question. [Maurelle] has been exact in which it is unpardonable in a navigator to neglect. I mean his latitude. I shall not, therefore (though he seems to have been a poor unhappy wanderer about this sea, and not unlike many of our modern English navigators about this part of the globe), take away the names he has given to these islands by supplanting them with others which a new discovery would have led me to have done."

Leaving the Vavau group of the Tongas, Bligh proceeded through the Lau group to the Fijis, which he had partially discovered on his launch voyage. Two Fijians from Mothe Island came on board who could understand a few words of the Tonga language and knew of the island of Tongatabu. Bligh noticed that their canoe had the outrigger on the starboard side rather than to port, as did the Polynesian canoes with which he was familiar, and that "one of the men wore a pretty pearl oyster shell at his breast."

As they approached Ngau, Bligh, Tobin, and Flinders all agreed that it was one of the most beautiful islands they had ever seen. "We sailed within a mile of the reef which surrounds the shore. Inside the reef the water is perfectly smooth and shoal and has some fine sandy beaches; there are some openings in the reefs fit for boats. About the reefs we saw many natives striking the fish and tracking the canoes about with poles. On the shore the natives were numerous. As we sailed along they followed us, waving pieces of white cloth. Nothing could exceed the beauty of the country at this time. It was cultivated far up into the mountains in a regular and pretty manner. Fine plantain walks and shades of cocoanut and other trees near were rendered more picturesque by the dwellings that were among them."

Bligh sailed through the middle of the Fijis and left the group, regretting that he did not have a month to spare to survey the whole archipelago. In all he located twenty-two different islands, which he identified by letters and numbers.

Bligh left the Fijis on August 11, and made sail towards the New Hebrides, where he sighted the Banks group on the nineteenth. (It was the same group that he had seen in the launch voyage of 1789. Bligh thought at that time that he was making a new discovery, but in fact these islands had been earlier sighted and named by Queirós and Torres.) Without lingering in the New Hebrides, Bligh now headed for Torres Strait, with Portlock, in the more manageable *Assistant,* as always in the lead. The expedition entered Torres Strait cautiously, by what is even today called Bligh Entrance, and Bligh named several islands and reefs as he slowly threaded his way through this dangerous and difficult stretch of water. Bligh also wrote good descriptions of the natives of Campbell Island off the south coast of New Guinea, and Lieutenant Tobin made further descriptions and sketches of other Torres Straits islands. Yet it was slow going, with boats out sounding constantly, for Bligh was exploring and surveying all the time. When he left the strait via Bligh Channel, he had succeeded in putting his name on the passages at both ends of the straits.

The ships anchored in Koepang Roads on October 2, and Bligh was greeted by old friends, who had helped him so much when he arrived in *Bounty*'s launch. Others of Bligh's former friends were dead, and Bligh himself was now sick with fever, as he listened to the first definite news of Captain Edwards's loss of the *Pandora* and the separation from and reunion with the *Resolution*. Wanjon gave Bligh a journal, since lost, which had been kept by the convicts who had escaped from Port Jackson only to be turned over to Captain Edwards.

The expedition left Koepang on October 10, crossed the Indian Ocean, weathered the Cape of Good Hope without stopping, and anchored at St. Helena on December 17. After a ten-day stay Bligh sailed for the West Indies and anchored at Kingston Bay, St. Vincent on January 23, 1793. There he left 544 of his precious breadfruit seedlings and took on board 465 pots and two tubs of botanic plants for Kew Gardens. He departed St. Vincent on the thirtieth for Port Royal, Jamaica, where he distributed breadfruit plants to various sites around the island. The botanist Wiles was left to care for the plants, and the Tahitian stowaway elected to remain as his assistant.

Because word arrived that France had declared war on England, the ships did not leave Jamaica until June 15 and crossed the Atlantic with a convoy. They anchored by Dungeness on August 2, 1793, and at Deptford a week later.* The mission was successfully accomplished.

The transportation of the breadfruit proved to be of little practical use, as the West Indians did not like breadfruit and much preferred plantain. But if the primary purpose of the expedition was not notable, the contribution to geographical knowledge was considerable. The discovery of Aitutaki was confirmed, new islands in the Tonga and Fiji groups were surveyed, knowledge of the Adventure Bay region of Tasmania was increased, and the best way through the tortuous shoals, reefs, and islands of Torres Strait was discovered and charted.

Between the two visits of Fletcher Christian and the *Bounty* mutineers to Tahiti, during their attempt to establish a colony on Tubuai in the northern summer of 1789, Matavai Bay was visited by another English vessel, the *Mercury*. She was sailing from England, bound by way of the Cape of Good Hope and Tahiti for the Northwest Coast, and she missed meeting the *Bounty*, with her insurgent crew, by days.

---

* On September 2 the Tahitian, Mydiddee, died. He was buried in the New Church Yard, St. Paul's Parish, Deptford.

One can only speculate on what might have happened had they met. The *Mercury* was owned and commanded by an old China hand.

John Henry Cox, the Canton merchant and backer of Meares and Colnett, was in England in 1788. He had the famous naval architect Marmaduke Stalkartt build him a new brig at Deptford for the Northwest Coast trade. The brig, christened *Mercury*, was sharp, hollowsterned, deep, copper-bottomed — a fast sailing vessel not entirely suited to long voyages. Cox, however, was apparently delighted with his new acquisition and decided to see something of the south Pacific on his way to northwest America and China, perhaps adding to the accumulating geographical knowledge of that ocean. Since Cox had to go from England to Canton, he chose to go in command of his own vessel. His shipmate Lieutenant George Mortimer has left us a slim volume on this voyage.

After sailing from the Downs on February 28, 1789, Cox stopped at Teneriffe March 12–25 and on May 9 sighted the Cape of Good Hope. Here the crew caught an albatross with a ten-foot wing spread; the bird made an excellent pie. Early in the evening of May 29 *Mercury* came to anchor at Amsterdam Island, more than halfway between the Cape and Australia. Since the only contemporary description in print of this island was that of the Dutchman Willem de Vlamingh, printed by Dalrymple in 1697, Mortimer devotes several pages to it. He speaks of the multitudes of seals and sea lions hauled out on the rocks or retreating into the long grass or reeds that covered the island, and recalls the landing place in the basin of Amsterdam Island, where they left "a bottle surrounded by a pile of stones, containing a piece of parchment with the ship's name, that of her commander, the date," etc. According to Mortimer, Cox and his party remained on the island until June 9, collecting nearly a thousand sealskins and several casks of good oil before continuing on the voyage.

In early July Cox landed for fresh water on the Australian coast, where he found a native hovel surrounded by roasted scallop, oyster, and clam shells. He arrived two days later, on July 5, at a Tasmanian anchorage he called Oyster Bay. Wood was procured here and, more important, Cox made contact and exchanged gifts with the shy Tasmanians.

Mortimer has left us a valuable account of these unfortunate and little-known people, who became extinct a few decades later: "As the bark [of trees seen] appeared to be newly peeled off, we were in hopes we should soon be gratified with a sight of the natives: and in this we were not disappointed; for the cutter being on shore on the 9th, a smoke was observed on the opposite side of the bay from that where she was stationed. Our third mate immediately went in her towards it; and on landing, saw several of them moving off with pieces of lighted wood in their hands. He approached them alone and unarmed, making every sign of friendship his fancy could suggest; but though they mimicked his actions exactly, and laughed heartily, he could not prevail upon them to stay: he continued advancing, and they retreating, till they passed a marsh, and he was prevented from going any farther.

"The next morning we again saw a smoke, nearly in the same direction as before, and proceeded as fast as possible to the spot. As we approached the shore, we observed several of the natives about the fire, and walking among the trees, some of them carrying very long poles and pieces of lighted wood in their hands. When they perceived we had landed, and were pretty near them, they began to chatter very loud and walk away; upon which we called to them, imitating their noise as well as we could, and had the satisfaction to see them stop at a little distance from us. Several of them having long poles or spears in their hands, we made signs to them to throw them aside, with which they immediately complied; and we in return put away our muskets. They now suffered us to come so near them as to take some biscuit, a penknife, and other trifles from us; but they took great care to avoid being touched. Some of them, indeed, would not accept of any thing unless it was thrown to them; and the whole party kept edging off by degrees. They seemed eager to procure everything they saw; and had a great inclination for our hats. Mr. Cox gave one of them a silk handkerchief; and he threw him in return a fillet of skin that he wore tied round his head. The party which we saw consisted of about fourteen or fifteen men and women; but there were several more concealed among the trees: they were of a dull black, or dusky colour, with woolly heads. Most of them were of the middle size; and, though lean, were square and muscular. We observed several of them to be ta-towed in a very curious manner, the skin being raised so as to form a kind of relief; besides which their bodies appeared to be daubed with a kind of dirty red paint, or earth. They were entirely naked, except one man, who had a necklace of small shells, and some of the women who had a kind of cloak or bag thrown over their shoulders; in which, I suppose, they carry their children, and what few moveables they possess. Upon the whole, they seemed to us to be a timorous, harmless race of people, and afford a fine picture of human nature in its most rude and uncultivated state. We spent some time in endeavoring to inspire these poor people with confidence; but though they appeared to be very merry, laughing and mimicking our actions, and frequently repeating the words Warra Warra, Wai, they kept retiring very fast; and as we imagined they beckoned us to follow them, we attempted it for a little while, but soon lost them among the trees."

A little later, "we found they had kindled a large fire," Mortimer continues, "and near it lay several little baskets made of rushes, in which were most of the articles we had given them, carefully tied up together with a few flints and stones, and a little dried grass; from which circumstance I conclude they produce fire by collision; there were besides, three small buckets for holding of water, made of a tough kind of seaweed, and skewered together at the sides; these seem to be their whole stock of domestic utensils; and their only weapon a rude spear, or lance, which is cut or scraped to a point at one end. Mr. Cox, at the interview we had with the natives, made signs to one of them to throw his spear, which he did, to a considerable distance, and with a good deal of force; but I cannot conceive them to be a danger-ous weapon."

Cox left Tasmania on July 10, 1789, and, except for sighting Tu-buai in the Australs a month later, saw no other land until he came to anchor in Matavai Bay on August 12 (only a few weeks after Chris-tian had sailed for Tubuai with livestock in the *Bounty*). His ship was immediately overrun with a swarm of natives, from whom Cox learned that Omai, returned by Captain Cook, had died. He too found the painting of Captain Cook, owned by the king, Otoo (whom he called Poneow). "On the 15," Mortimer writes, "I accompanied the captain on shore, to see a picture of Captain Cook in oil-colours, left here by that celebrated navigator himself, and in the possession of Poneow, chief of Matavia. On the back of the picture was the following inscription: 'Lieut. Bligh, of his Britannick Majesty's ship *Bounty*, anchored in Matavia Bay the 25th of October 1788; but owing to bad weather, was obliged to sail to Oparre on the 25th of December, where he remained until the 30th of March 1789; was then ready for sea, with one thousand and fifteen bread-fruit plants on board, besides many other fruits, and only waited an opportunity to get to sea; at which time this picture was given up. Sailed the 4th of April 1789.'

"Though we went several times to see this picture, we could never discover where it was kept, as we were always conducted to Poneow's house, who desired us to wait there till it was brought to us. He then dispatched two of his servants for it, who used to bring it wrapped up in a cloth; and after we had viewed it, carried it back again in the same manner."

The *Mercury* had already been visited by Etea, the queen, when on August 16, Otoo, the king, arrived in a double canoe. His Majesty turned out to be a childish fellow. The mate gave Etea a pair of scissors and His Majesty demanded them. The queen refused and Otoo wept like a baby until he was given a similar pair. After Cox presented the king with a tailed coat, he employed a man for several hours to sew additional buttons on the flaps. Meanwhile, the strong-minded queen wielded a knife and fork well, relished a cup of tea, and took a potshot at the ship's buoy, with a musket that Otoo dared not discharge, and hit the target the first time she fired.

While Cox was entertaining the king, Mortimer and the third mate walked to Otoo's house, where the natives, thinking they were exhausted from the hike, gave them the "Kaureumee" treatment which consisted of a system of squeezing and pressing their limbs in the effective Tahitian massage learned by Colnett and other European visitors. The officers were entertained by dancers and then, "as soon as the Heiva [dance] was ended we returned on board, and found the king and queen and a large train there; consisting of several chiefs, the king's feeder, for an Otaheitean monarch is not allowed to feed himself, his Ava-chewers, the Taata-toa or man-killer of Otaheite, who slaughters the victims destined for the human sacrifices, and a variety of other attendants. His Majesty supped with us, and seemed not only to excel most of his subjects in size, for he is a very large man, but in point of appetite also, as he ate a most enormous supper, and drank bumpers of wine to the health of King George as fast as we could fill his glass; expressing a wish to be intoxicated in a slight degree, saying, he was often so on board Captain Bligh's ship, and that it was very pleasant. . . ."

Cox was shown the rather recent grave of the *Bounty*'s surgeon, who had drunk himself to death while Bligh was loading young breadfruit trees. Then, sailing over to Moorea in the brig's cutter to see if the cattle left by Captain Cook were still there, Cox found a bull and two cows in good condition, but useless to the natives, who had never learned to milk. After being entertained at several more native dances (during one of which an Englishman became much smitten by one of the dancing girls, who turned out to be a boy), Cox left Tahiti on September 2. *Mercury* dropped anchor in Kealakekua Bay, Hawaii, on September twenty-third.

Immediately King Kamehameha and Kaiana came on board. They brought a helmet and two beautiful feather cloaks as presents, and Mortimer writes: "His Majesty is one of the most savage-looking men I ever beheld, and very wild and extravagant in his actions and behaviour." After remarking on the similarity of the Tahitian and Hawaiian languages (he commented that Hawaiian is so guttural as to be unintelligible to Tahitians), Mortimer further compared the two peoples. "The great authority of the chiefs," he writes of the Hawaiians, "and their living in towns or villages, so different from the natives of Otaheite, form a distinguishing contrast between the manners and customs of the two nations: their canoes likewise are strikingly different, those of the Sandwich Islands being greatly superior in every respect; but the natives are neither so comely nor so well clad as those of Otaheite." Cox was interested to collect several medals from the Hawaiians left by the Americans on the *Columbia* and *Lady Washington*. "The medals, which are of pewter, and nearly the size of a crownpiece, are very neatly executed. On one side is a representation of the *Columbia* and *Washington*, with the following inscription round the border: 'COLUMBIA and WASHINGTON, commanded by J. KENDRICK.' On the reverse, the inscription round the border is thus continued: 'Fitted at Boston, North America, for the Pacific Ocean'; and in the centre, 'By J. Barrel, S. Brown, G. Bulfinch, J. Darby, Ca. Hatch, J. M. Pintard, 1787.' "

The *Mercury* left the islands on September 25 and arrived a month later at Unalaska. Apparently because of the Russians, little trading was done for skins and on November 6 Cox left the coast for China. The *Mercury* was fast. On December 12 she was anchored at Tinian, which was a harbor neither as good as Commodore Anson nor as bad as Commodore Byron described it on their respective eighteenth century voyages. Mortimer speculates on the famous ruins: "In our different excursions on shore, we met with the remains of several of those curious edifices described by Lord Anson, and supposed to have been erected by the original inhabitants of the Island. These buildings are of a most singular structure, and consist in their present state of two ranges of columns, either of stone or composition, and of a pyramidical form, having large semi-globes placed on their tops, with the surfaces upwards.

"If these structures are really of stone, which I imagine them to be, it is astonishing how a rude and uncivilized people, unacquainted with any of the arts necessary for the purpose, and without proper tools, could have formed and erected them."

The *Mercury* dropped anchor in Macao Roads on December 27 and arrived at Canton on New Year's Day, 1790, "having been only ten months and five days in performing our voyage."

7

Many Little Islands

U NTIL the last two decades of the eighteenth century we knew almost nothing about Micronesia — those vast numbers of tiny islands which stretch across the Pacific from approximately 130° to 178° east and which comprise the Carolines and the Marshalls and the Gilberts. Many of the Carolines, to be sure, had been discovered by the Portuguese in 1527 and annexed by Spain in 1686. But the Marshalls and Gilberts were still undiscovered. Magellan, making the first Pacific crossing, missed them all.

Taongi (or Pokaakku, as it is also called), the northernmost outlying Marshall, was seen by Garcia de Loyasa in 1525. But while the galleons had sailed annually between New Spain and Manila for over three centuries, they followed the westerly trade winds north of Micronesia and even farther north on the eastern passage, missing the Hawaiian Islands as well. Miguel López de Legaspi may have seen four of the northern Marshalls in 1545 and Pedro Fernandes de Queirós probably discovered Makin in 1606. Both Drake and Anson missed them completely. It was not until 1765 that Commodore John Byron, in his record voyage around the world, sighted Nukunau in the Gilberts, which until recently bore his name. Then two years later Captain Samuel Wallis, commanding the *Dolphin* on her second circumnavigation, not only discovered Tahiti but sighted two of the northern Marshalls, Rongerik and Rongelap, identifying them with the Pescadores of old Spanish charts.

The westernmost group of the Carolines, now called the Palau Islands but formerly the Pelews, was apparently vaguely known to the Spanish, and had perhaps been sighted in the late eighteenth century by English ships making the eastern passage to China. It is to one such ship that we owe our first real knowledge of this group and its people.

In June 1783, the Honorable East India Company's 300-ton packet *Antelope*, commanded by Captain Henry Wilson, arrived off Macao. Making a quick turn around, she hurriedly refitted and sailed again on July 21 with sixteen Chinese sailors added to her English complement of thirty-three men. Among the latter were the captain's brother Matthias, a seaman, and his son Henry Wilson, Jr., a midshipman. Fortuitously too, as it turned out, there was Thomas Rose, "a native of Bengal, calling himself a Portuguese," whom Wilson employed as a linguist.

The voyage was uneventful until, in the dead of night on August 10, the lookout's cry of "Breakers!" followed by the grinding tilt of the ship striking a reef, brought all hands on deck. With daylight the boats were loaded, a raft constructed, and men and supplies moved ashore onto Oroolong in the Palaus. Fortunately the *Antelope* was in such a position that she remained available and served as a constant source of nails, lumber, and further supplies and provisions.

On August 12 the first two exploratory native canoes arrived. This was a lucky break for the crew of *Antelope*, for with the natives was a Malay — and it happened that Thomas Rose was fluent in the Malay language. In addition, the Malay, who claimed to be a shipwrecked sailor, spoke a little Dutch. An immediate rapport was established between the crew of the *Antelope* and the natives, which lasted throughout Wilson's stay in the Palaus. And Wilson solidified good relations with the local king, Abba Thulle, by lending men with firearms for his skirmishes with rival chiefs on neighboring islands. Meanwhile the keel of a schooner was laid, and the craft, built from local timber and the wreck of the *Antelope*, progressed rapidly. On November 9, 1783, the schooner was launched. She was christened *Oroolong*, after the island.

The friendships that had been made during the three months were hard to break and one of the sailors, Madan Blanchard, remained be-

"King" Abba Thulle of the Pelew Islands
(from Wilson, Account of the Pelew Islands)

hind at his own request, amply provided with clothing and tools from the wreck and good advice from Captain Wilson. At the urgent request of Abba Thulle his second son, Prince Lee Boo, was taken along to visit England. Before *Oroolong* left the island the English hoisted a pennant on a tall tree and to another nailed a copper plate with the following inscription:

The Honorable
English East India Company's Ship
the ANTELOPE
HENRY WILSON, Commander
Was lost upon the reef north of this island
In the night between the 9th and 10th of
August;
Who here built a vessel,
And sailed from hence
The 12th day of November 1783.

On November 12, provisioned with coconuts, native sweetmeats, and supplies from the *Antelope*, the *Oroolong* sailed for China. She arrived at Macao on the thirtieth. Prince Lee Boo, the Palau tourist, was a curiosity to the Chinese, who referred to him as the "new man." But Captain Wilson did not linger for them to get better acquainted with their exotic visitor. Releasing his men to take berths wherever they could be found, he and his charge sailed for home in the ship *Morse*.

Prince Lee Boo was the first of his race to visit England, and he became as popular on the dinner circuits as Omai the Tahitian had been a decade before. Then, sadly, the bright young Micronesian died of smallpox. He was buried at Rotherhithe churchyard, where the East India Company erected a tomb with the following inscription:

To the Memory
of Prince LEE BOO,
A native of the PELEW, or PALOS islands;
and Son to ABBA THULLE, Rupack or King
of the Island COOROORAA;
who departed this Life on the 27th of December 1784,
aged 20 Years;
This Stone is inscribed,

Captain Henry Wilson's camp in the Pelew Islands (from Wilson, Account of the Pelew Islands)

by the Honourable United EAST INDIA COMPANY,
as a Testimony of Esteem for the humane and kind Treatment
afforded by HIS FATHER to the Crew of their Ship
the ANTELOPE, Captain WILSON,
which was wrecked off that Island
in the Night of the 9th of August 1783.

Stop, Reader, stop: — let NATURE claim a Tear —
A Prince of *Mine*, LEE BOO, lies bury'd here.

The book on the wreck of the *Antelope* and Prince Lee Boo, written by George Keate and handsomely published in London in 1788, is one of the great adventure tales of the sea. This classic also contains the most extensive account of any Micronesian people up to that time. Thus, the misadventure of Captain Wilson and his shipmates considerably increased the knowledge of a little-known group of islands, even though, as Keate writes, "the *Antelope* was not a ship particularly sent out to explore undiscovered regions, or prepared to investigate the manners of mankind." The story of Prince Lee Boo was published for young readers in innumerable editions for years,* and a Northwest Coast fur-trading vessel was named for him.

The decision of the British government to establish a convict colony in New South Wales resulted in the sending out in 1787 of the so-called "First Fleet": eleven vessels carrying 776 convicts, under Governor Arthur Phillip. During the ships' return, several of the officers were to make important discoveries. Among them was Captain John Hunter of H.M.S. *Sirius*, who has already come into our story in connection with La Pérouse and will later with d'Entrecasteaux. Others who contributed to Pacific exploration were Lieutenant Henry Lidgbird Ball, commanding the armed tender *Supply;* Lieutenant John Shortland, agent for the transports; Captain Sever commanding the transport *Lady Penrhyn* and Captain William (or John) Marshall and Captain Thomas Gilbert, commanding the transports *Scarborough* and *Charlotte*, respectively. The remaining transports, the

---

* *The History of Prince Lee Boo a Native of the Pelew Islands brought to England by Capt.ⁿ Wilson* (London, n.d.; Philadelphia, 1802).

Alexander, Friendship, and *Prince of Wales,* and three storeships completed the convoy.

The fleet arrived at Botany Bay in January 1788, and later removed to Port Jackson. On February 14, Governor Phillip sent Lieutenant Ball in the *Supply* to take a small group of people for settlement on Norfolk, the rich uninhabited island discovered by Captain Cook. On his passage out Ball came upon two hitherto unknown bits of land — which he named in honor of Lord Howe — about 380 miles off the Australian coast. "And on his return he stopt and surveyed it [Lord Howe]; at that time he caught a quantity of fine green turtles, of which there were great numbers. . . . They found no fresh water on the island," Ball noted, "but it abounds with cabbage-palms, mangrove and manchineal trees, even up to the summits of the mountains. No vegetables were to be seen. On the shore there are plenty of ganets, and a land-fowl, of a dusky brown colour, with a bill about four inches long, and feet like those of a chicken; these proved remarkably fat, and were very good food. . . ."

On May 5, 1788, before Shortland departed Australia, Captain Sever in the *Lady Penrhyn* had left Port Jackson on the return passage via China, and, for some reason not wholly clear, sailed east as far as Tahiti. On May 31 Sever discovered, and the next day named, Curtis and Macauley islands in the Kermadec group. These islands yielded nothing green, however, to alleviate the scurvy that was distressing his crew. Nor, because of east winds, was Sever able to get relief for his men until July 10, when he anchored in Matavai Bay. (Sever's steward had been at Tahiti before when he was a sailor with Cook in the *Resolution.* He recognized Otoo, who, as was his habit, produced the Webber portrait of the great navigator for Sever. To the plentiful supplies of hogs and chickens, fruits and vegetables, the Tahitians eagerly brought cats [introduced by Cook] and dogs for trade. Lieutenant Watts, the writer of the Sever account, observes that many natives had perished in recent years from venereal disease.) *Lady Penrhyn* left Tahiti July 23. On August 8, according to Watts, "they saw a low flat island, bearing from east to north-east seven or eight miles distant; it appeared to be well clothed with trees, but the weather at that time being squally allowed them a very imperfect view. Captain

Sever named it Penrhyn's Island." This island, a new discovery, is now known by its native name of Tongareva. No more new landfalls were made by Sever, who brought the *Lady Penrhyn* into Tinian on September 19 and to Macao exactly a month later.

Six months after the fleet arrived in Botany Bay, Governor Phillip ordered his agent of transports, Lieutenant Shortland, to return to England by way of Batavia with official dispatches. Shortland sailed from Port Jackson in the *Alexander* on July 14, accompanied by the *Friendship*, *Prince of Wales*, and the storeship *Borrowdale*. Shortly after sailing, the two other vessels separated from *Alexander* and *Friendship* and were seen no more during the voyage.

Shortland discovered Middleton Reef and sailed north until he sighted New Georgia in the Solomons. He then ran along the south coast of this island making observations. He named the small Treasury Islands and, sailing through what became known as Shortland's Straits, gave the name New Georgia to the two islands on either side and the Treasury group as well.* With the ships' crews suffering severely from scurvy, Shortland fell in with the Palau Islands on September 10. This was the end of Shortland's explorations. When, on September 27, he sighted Mindanao, so many men had died of scurvy that he was forced to abandon and sink the *Friendship* to man the *Alexander*. He arrived at Batavia in a helpless state on November 18. He was assisted by the Dutch, and arrived back in England on May 29, 1789.

The most important discoveries resulting from the return voyages of Governor Phillip's transports were made by Captains Gilbert and Marshall. Very little is known about these two men, and even Marshall's Christian name is uncertain. Captain William (as he is usually called, though on the track chart in Governor Phillip's *Voyage* he is called John) Marshall in the *Scarborough* and Captain Thomas Gilbert in the *Charlotte*, having discharged their convicts, sailed on May 6, 1788, from Port Jackson for Canton to take on cargoes of teas for the East India Company. Gilbert beat Marshall to Lord Howe Island,

---

* Only the largest of the islands still bears the Treasury name. A chart of the coast was made by Shortland's son, who is called Thomas; George on the chart and John George in the text of Governor Phillip's book.

Man of Duke of York Island (from Hunter, Journal)

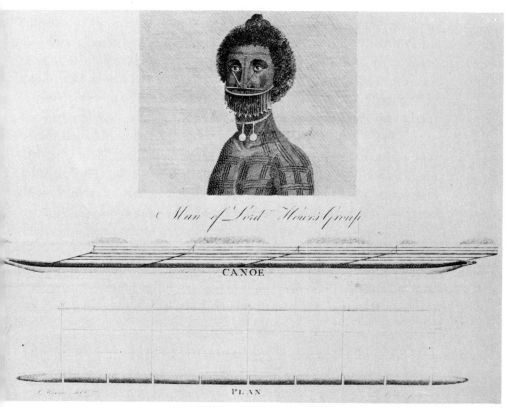

Man and canoe of Lord Howe Island (from Hunter, Journal)

where he collected the fresh supplies with which the island abounded. Ball in the *Supply* and Sever in the *Lady Penrhyn* were there at the same time for the same purpose. Marshall arrived on the seventeenth and the next day the two ships sailed in company for China. Sighting Norfolk Island and discovering Matthew Rock south of the New Hebrides (named for the owner of the *Charlotte*), they made a wide swing to the east, probably with the thought of avoiding the big Melanesian Islands. (They apparently were planning to pick up the easterly trades when they reached the right latitude.) The *Scarborough* and *Charlotte* may have been the first two vessels to sail directly from Australia to China.

The two ships proceeded north and on June 18 sighted the three atolls of Abemama, Aranuku, and Kuria. These were named by Captain Marshall Hopper's, Henderville's, and Woodle's islands. Gilbert "saw many canoes or proas on the beach, and could observe that a considerable number were making towards the ship." He adds that the three islands extend about fifteen or sixteen miles and "seem to be narrow, and all of them have fine white sandy beaches."

Captain Gilbert writes of the first European look at the inhabitants of these islands in the group that now bears his name. "I counted thirty proas," he says, "making towards the ship; and could plainly see many more of the natives launching in a great hurry off the beach. At four the headmost proa, that seemed to conduct the whole, tacked in a very expeditious manner, by shifting its latteen sail (by which means the head became the stern), and went off at a great rate. She had got within half a mile of the *Scarborough*, when Captain Marshall fired a shot at her, to my great regret and vexation, as I thought it commencing hostilities with them too soon, even if they had been hostilely inclined; and would effectually prevent our having any intercourse with them. In order to dispel their apprehensions, and invite a nearer approach, I displayed a white flag; on which two of the proas, one much larger than the other, bore down; but the rest kept aloof."

On the twentieth more islands showed up, and Gilbert sighted an atoll with several islands around it that could be either Abaiang, Tarawa, or Marakei.* He named the atoll Marlar's Islands, and the larg-

* Morison inclines to the belief that it was Tarawa.

A canoe and natives of the Mulgrave Islands (from Philip, Voyage to Botany Bay)

est of the cluster he called Matthews Island. The next day Gilbert mentions three islands in a chain, which he calls Marshall's, Gilbert's, and Knox's, although it is not clear whether these are part of the cluster he mentions previously.*

After leaving the Gilberts, the ships encountered no islands for five days and then entered the easterly, or Radak, chain of the Marshall group. Gilbert, on June 26, discovered Arno Atoll (which he thought to be two islands and named Daniel's and Pedder's) and Majuro, which he called Arrowsmith's. Meanwhile, on June 25, Captain Marshall found Milli and named it Lord Mulgrave's Range. On June 28 Gilbert named Aur the Ibbetson's Islands, and later in the day came upon Maloelap, calling it Calvert's. The next day he discovered Erikub and Wotje and named them Chatham's Islands. The last island he saw was probably Utirik (called Button Island on the charts). This may be one of the Spanish Pescadores reported by Wallis on his circumnavigation.

The *Charlotte* and *Scarborough*, now clear of the islands, picked up the trades, and laid a course for China. Since both crews were sic'· with scurvy they stopped briefly at Tinian for fresh food; there they were forced to cut their cables due to rough weather. They anchored in Macao Road on September 9, took a pilot to Whampoa on the twelfth, and were loaded with cargoes of teas and china ware for England.†

Many ships and men participated in the discovery of the other Marshall, Gilbert, and Ellice islands. Those of the Ralik chain — Namorik, Ailinglapalap, and Namu — were found by a Captain Bond in the British ship *Royal Admiral* in 1792. Captain John Fearn in the snow *Hunter* in 1798 charted Eniwetok and discovered Nauru, which he named Pleasant Island. More or less simultaneously Captain Charles Bishop, an Englishman in the Northwest Coast fur and China

---

* They could be all part of Tarawa or, as Morison suggests, perhaps Makin, Little Makin, and Butaritari (appearing as a separate island from the rest of Makin). It is almost impossible to say.

† Because of the publications of both captains' accounts of this voyage and their discoveries, the names Gilbert and Marshall became fixed on English charts; and after Krusenstern used the names in his great atlas of 1827 (*Atlas de L'Ocean Pacifique*), they became firmly established internationally.

trade, ignorant of the discoveries of Marshall and Gilbert, sailed through the southern Gilberts in the brig *Nautilus* and named them the Kingsmill Islands. This alternative name for the group was used for many years and is still occasionally found on charts. Bishop's *Nautilus* explored Tabiteuea, Nonouti, and Abemama atolls, which Captain Bishop named Bishop's and Drummond's (both parts of Tabiteuea), Sydenham's, and Roger Simpson's, respectively, and they were so published on Alexander Dalrymple's chart of 1822. The only name of Bishop's that has survived is Nautilus Shoal. In the Marshalls, Bishop charted Maloelap, Erikub, and Jemo and bestowed names to islands already discovered by Gilbert and Marshall.

Islands in the Micronesian groups continued to be discovered and charted well into the nineteenth century. Kwajalein was found by Captain Mertho in the British ship *Ocean* in 1804. An American, Captain Crocker, discovered Kusaie in the Carolines and named it Strong's Island. Captain Arent Schuyler de Peyster, an American in command of the British brigantine *Rebecca*, sailed through the Ellice Islands in 1819, discovering Funafuti and Nukufetau and naming the entire group for an English friend who was a member of Parliament.

But, while there were islands left to discover after Gilbert and Marshall, it is these otherwise obscure captains whose names ornament two of the most far-flung archipelagoes in the Pacific. By the end of the eighteenth century the main groups were known and the names established. Credit goes to the officers of Governor Phillip's "First Fleet" for a not inconsiderable number of new discoveries.

8

Furs for France and the Search for a Hero

Two French expeditions — one led by a merchant, one by an admiral — entered the Pacific from opposite sides in 1791. Their goals were very different, but each made significant contributions to our knowledge of the Pacific. Marchand, the trader, hoped to bring French competition to the fur trade on the Northwest Coast, where the English and Americans were prospering. D'Entrecasteaux, the admiral, was sent on an errand of mercy, long delayed by a sluggish government, to search for the lost La Pérouse, now vanished for over three years.

Captain Etienne Marchand, a thirty-three-year-old West Indian–born merchant captain, first got the notion of a fur-trading voyage in 1788 (the year La Pérouse disappeared), when he met Captain Nathaniel Portlock, completing his circumnavigation, at St. Helena. Marchand was returning to France after a voyage to Bengal. The Frenchman eagerly absorbed every detail of information concerning the Northwest Coast fur trade from his English acquaintance. He was impressed by the profits to be made from a cargo of furs, if the China market was advantageous, and by the further profits to be gained on the silks and tea taken from China to Europe.

Arriving in Marseilles, Marchand passed his new information along to the house of J. and D. Baux. The merchants of this eminent company thought well of the idea and immediately made plans for outfitting a ship for such a voyage. All was ready by June 1790, but Marchand's departure was delayed until late in the year by "The Nootka Incident" — the dispute between Spain and England concerning property in Nootka Sound — and by the threat of war in Europe and America.

A new 300-ton ship, the *Solide*, had been built especially for Marchand's expedition. She was copper fastened and sheathed, stocked with appropriate merchandise for trade, supplied with everything for the comfort and health of the crew. Marchand selected two other captains, Pierre Masse and Prosper Chanal, as his seconds-in-command. His brother Louis was one of his three lieutenants. There were, besides, two surgeons, three volunteers, and a crew of thirty-nine. With the signing of a treaty at the Nootka Sound Convention, it became certain that there was to be no war between England and Spain, and the Baux merchants dispatched the *Solide* from Marseilles on December 14, 1790.

Marchand had intended to make the long run from the Cape Verdes to the Northwest Coast without putting in to any port, but lack of water forced him to change his plans. Choosing the Marquesas Islands as the most convenient port for watering, he shaped his course towards them on April 19 and sighted the first island on June 12. He sailed past Fatu Hiva and Hiva Oa and anchored two days later at Resolution Bay (which he called La Madre de Dios Bay) on the west coast of Tahuata, where Cook had been seventeen years before. Here a typical South Sea reception awaited *Solide*.

Chanal sounded ahead of the ship, and was met by canoes and swarming Marquesans. Obviously in authority were two or three chiefs in a large double canoe, propelled by some twenty chanting paddlers, who announced their approach with the low tones of a conch. "They soon shewed that they knew what want had brought the strangers into their bay," Chanal writes. "They pointed, on one side, to the rivulet which empties itself into the north cove, and on the other, to the spring which issues from the rock situated between the two coves: some of them even brought fresh water in calabashes. Several women and young girls, grouped on the shore, embellished the scene; and the men who surrounded the boat informed our sailors, by signs which were by no means equivocal, that the ladies were at their service; while the belles themselves, by expressive looks and attractive gestures, that language of all countries, confirmed with eagerness the offer which the men made of their persons."

Chanal distributed glass beads and traded nails for coconuts, breadfruit, and fish, while five hundred Marquesans in the flotilla of canoes pushed past him to meet the *Solide*. Toys and looking glasses were distributed in exchange for fresh fruit and laughing girls. According to Chanal, the crowd "soon increased to such a degree, that it was no longer possible to work the ship: they were solicited to return to their canoes; to this they consented with a good grace. . . ."

Familiarity bred the inevitable increase in thefts. A shot fired above the canoes, meant to discourage the light-fingered, only angered them, and for a short time the Marquesans became antagonistic. But soon the lively trade was flourishing again. Besides fruit and vegetables, the mariners procured "various little articles and implements, together with arms, cloths, and ornaments in use among the natives." The girls were "loaded with nails, small looking-glasses, little knives, coloured glass-beads, ribbands, bits of cloth, and other productions of our arts, which they had bartered for the only commercial article that they had at their disposal."

Marchand, accompanied by Chanal and eight men, landed and explored along the shore. Multitudes of curious men and women tagged along; one bold old man gravely rubbed noses with the Frenchmen, and an ancient chief, as an expression of friendship, solemnly presented four hogs, each delivered with a suitable speech for which the orators were rewarded with trinkets. Good fresh water filled the casks, and sails and rigging were repaired. Fruit and vegetables (including the excellent Marquesan watercress) were taken aboard. Only hogs were hard to come by. Well supplied and with crew refreshed, the *Solide* sailed from Resolution Bay after one week's stay.

Chanal's and Claude Roblet's account of Tahuata, which they called Santa Christina, with their excellent descriptions of the Marquesans and their customs, is among the important early records of these islands. The flamboyance of the tattooing, the diversity and beauty of personal ornaments, the singularity of the stilt walking, the weight of the stone adzes (some were twenty-five pounds) were all recorded, as were descriptions of household arts, fishing methods, and canoe construction.

While the *Solide* was in Resolution Bay, Roblet remarked "that, among the canoes of different islands which came to traffic with the ship, and each of which returned, every evening, to its respective island, one or two always directed their course towards a point of the horizon where hitherto navigators knew no land."

After leaving the bay *Solide* followed the course of the two canoes and soon sighted the island of Ua Pu, which was not laid down on any chart. Ua Pu was appropriately renamed by the ship's officers Marchand Island. Ranging along the island's shore, *Solide* reconnoitered for an anchorage and eventually landed. Marchand took possession of the island for France by the unique method of giving a sealed bottle, documenting his claim, to each of three people — an old man, a warrior, and a young girl.

Marchand continued on his way, discovering Nuku Hiva on the twenty-second of June and naming it, for his employers, Ile Baux. He made no attempt at exploration here, as it was imperative that he reach the Northwest Coast in time for the fur season. Before again sailing empty ocean, however, Marchand passed the three islets now called Moto Iti, which, because he saw only two of them, he named Les Deux Frères. He also observed the islands of Eïao and Hatutu, honoring them with the names of his two captains, Masse and Chanal. Marchand named the northern Marquesas the Iles de la Revolution and concluded correctly that these islands should be recognized as part of the Marquesas group.

From June 25 land was not seen again until *Solide* raised the South American coast on August 7. Subsequently Marchand anchored in what he thought to be Dixon's Norfolk Sound (but which was probably another sound on the west of Baranof Island) and immediately began trading for furs. The Baranof Indians, he discovered, were dressed partly in European clothes and one young man wore two Massachusetts copper coins as ear pendants.

Two weeks of bartering later, Marchand owned several hundred assorted skins, few of them prime; he left Norfolk Sound on August 21 and sailed south along the west coast of the Queen Charlotte Is-

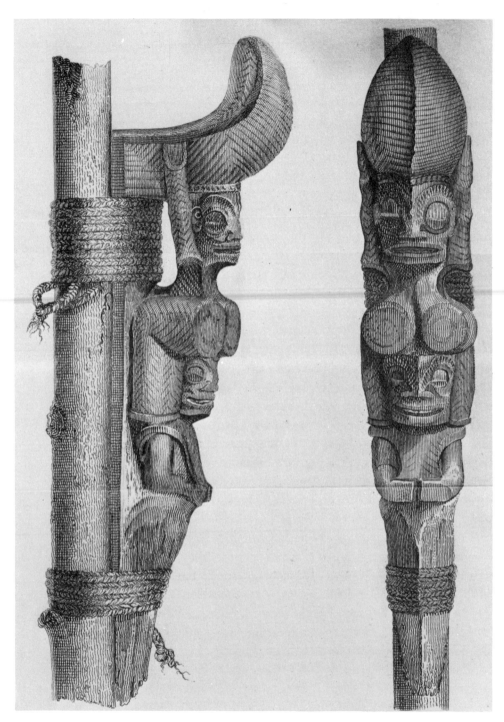

Carved footrest of a stilt, Marquesas Islands
(from Marchand, Voyage)

lands. Trading was desultory, and by early September Marchand decided that he had been anticipated everywhere. Rather than follow others and get few furs, he concluded that it would be better to arrive in China with his small cargo ahead of other ships while the market was high. He sighted Hawaii on October 4 and hurriedly provisioned *Solide*. In three days he was shaping his course for China.

When Marchand reached Macao in late November, he found that the sale of furs, especially sea otters, was now forbidden — apparently because of a new commercial treaty concluded between the emperor of China and the Russian empress. There was no point in going to Whampoa, either, where he would be obliged to pay a heavy duty. He did not even consider resorting to smuggling, his only other alternative. Instead, Marchand elected to proceed to Ile de France (Mauritius) as soon as possible. He sailed from Macao on December 6 and reached Ile de France on January 30. After loading a cargo of coffee at Réunion, *Solide* proceeded home around the Cape of Good Hope. Marchand anchored at Toulon on August 14, 1792, at 5:30 in the afternoon, having completed the first circumnavigation by a Frenchman since Bougainville. Less than a year later, on May 15, 1793, Marchand died at Réunion.

Ironically enough, it was during *Solide*'s nine days in Macao that Marchand learned of the prior American discovery of the northern group of the Marquesas. Marchand's source was Roblet, *Solide*'s surgeon, who had been asked to attend the discoverer, Captain Joseph Ingraham, as he lay ill in Macao. How disappointed Marchand must have been when he heard of Ingraham, whose discovery had anticipated his by so little time. But he could console himself with the reflection that his charts and observations were the more effective, for Ingraham had merely sailed through the islands bestowing names.

Marchand's expedition was a commercial failure, but he was fortunate in his amanuensis, for C. P. Claret Fleurieu's book on the voyage is a valuable contribution to the history of Pacific exploration, not only because of the account of the voyage itself but because his long introduction contains details of other expeditions not found elsewhere. The book also contains valuable appendices of Marquesan words; extracts from the journal of Captain Josiah Roberts of the ship

Jefferson from Boston, who sailed for the Northwest Coast on November 29, 1791, and stayed at Resolution Bay for four months (Fleurieu does not consider him very reliable); and extracts from Lieutenant Richard Hergest's journal of the *Daedalus*, which arrived at Resolution Bay on May 22, 1792. Hergest, who was bringing supplies to Vancouver, thought that he had discovered a new group and gave all of the islands names that were published by Aaron Arrowsmith in his *Planisphere*. (As these were English, Fleurieu thought they were the names bestowed by Ingraham.) Thus, to everyone's confusion, for many years the Revolution, Washington, or northern Marquesas islands each had four sets of names, including the native ones by which they are now known.

Nothing had been heard from La Pérouse's well-equipped expedition after it had sailed from Botany Bay, March 11, 1788. La Pérouse's tentative plans had been to visit Tonga, New Caledonia, Santa Cruz, the Solomons, the Louisiades, the northern coast of Australia, and Tasmania; he hoped to arrive at Ile de France in December 1788. When he did not arrive, there was no immediate concern. The schedules of voyages of exploration were uncertain at best. As the months lengthened into years, however, it was realized, even in that day of slow communication, that some disaster must have befallen the expedition that was to have been the answer of France to Cook's voyages. Even in the midst of the Revolution concern for the vanished men was great.

Eventually the sluggish government was prodded into action by the Parisian Society of Natural History, which appealed to the National Assembly on January 22, 1791, to dispatch a search party. The National Assembly issued a decree on February 9 that the king be petitioned to order all his representatives in foreign countries to request of all governments that their navigators in the South Seas search for any sign of the frigates *Boussole* and *Astrolabe* or their ships' companies. The National Assembly would recompense any services given to the lost mariners. It was further decreed: "that the King be petitioned to give orders for the fitting out of one or more ships, having on board men of science, naturalists, and draughtsmen, and to charge the commanders of the expedition with the two-fold mission of searching for M. de la Pérouse, agreeable to the documents, instructions, and orders which shall be delivered to them, and of making inquiries relative to the sciences and to commerce, taking every measure to render this expedition useful and advantageous to navigation, geography, commerce, and the arts and sciences, independently of their search for M. de la Pérouse, and even after having found him, or obtained intelligence concerning him."

The expedition, promptly organized, consisted of the former store-ships *Recherche* and *Espérance*, together with 219 men under the command of Admiral Antoine Raymond Joseph Bruni d'Entrecasteaux. The admiral was an experienced and able navigator, who had formerly been a naval commander in India and a governor of Ile de France. (Indeed, d'Entrecasteaux had actually sent assistance to La Pérouse when he was in Manila.) Huon de Kermadec, who had sailed with d'Entrecasteaux before, was captain of *Espérance*. All the officers were experienced and able and some later became distinguished: Edouard de Rossel, who wrote an account of the voyage; Jean Baptiste Willaumez, who became an admiral and wrote a famous marine dictionary; Charles François Beautemps-Beaupré, the young hydrographer, who did excellent charting in the Pacific and in a long life compiled a new French *Pilot* of the Atlantic; the naturalist Jacques Julien de La Billardière, who made great contributions to the knowledge of the flora, fauna, and people of the Pacific. These were, however, troubled times politically, and such troubles would eventually lead to the disintegration of the expedition.

The *Recherche* and *Espérance* sailed from Brest on September 28, 1791, and anchored in Table Bay at the Cape of Good Hope on January 17, 1792. Here they received a letter from Saint-Felix, the naval commander at Ile de France. The letter erroneously stated that two French merchant captains had learned from Captain John Hunter that, while he was returning from Botany Bay on a Dutch vessel after his shipwreck off Norfolk Island, he had seen Admiralty Islanders dressed up in French naval uniforms; a rumor that was already circu-

E*

lating at Cape Town.* Ironically, Captain Hunter himself was at the Cape when d'Entrecasteaux's expedition arrived, but he left a scant two hours after they cast anchor and he and the admiral did not meet. Hunter later said that there was no foundation for the statement. Captain William Bligh, on his second breadfruit expedition, left the cape about three weeks before d'Entrecasteaux arrived and had promised to investigate the Admiralty rumor if he had the opportunity.

D'Entrecasteaux spent exactly a month at the cape. When the expedition departed, it was his thought to sail north of Australia and New Guinea and reach the Admiralties as soon as possible. However, he was frustrated by the monsoon with its contrary winds and by the clumsy sailing qualities of his ships, and was forced to sail south of the continent and around Tasmania.

Only two incidents interrupted the voyage to Tasmania. First, a drunken sailor jumped overboard and was rescued. Then Amsterdam Island (which d'Entrecasteaux called St. Paul — the two names moved back and forth between the northern and southern of these twin islands) was sighted and was discovered to be devastated by a forest fire so hot that the ships had to stay to windward of it. When towards the end of April the ships anchored in Tempest Bay, Tasmania (which they called Port D'Entrecasteaux), the Frenchmen were amazed to see swans as black as those of Europe were white. They were also impressed by the tall blue gums towering above the forest.

This was a great opportunity for La Billardière, who energetically made collections and observations of all aspects of Tasmania's natural history. Nothing — forests, plants, birds, animals, native habitations — escaped his quick eye. Although the Tasmanians, a shy people, were at first seen only at a distance, La Billardière found their campsites and collected their utensils and left European articles in exchange.

Later there were mutually surprising encounters between the watchers and the watched. "One of the officers of the *Recherche*," La

---

* This piece of misinformation may have thrown d'Entrecasteaux off his search, for he ultimately visited the Admiralties twice when he might otherwise have spent more time in the area of Santa Cruz with greater chance of success.

Captain John Hunter (from Hunter, Journal)

Billardière writes, "following a beaten path made by the savages through the woods, met six of them walking slowly towards the south, who were all stark-naked, and armed with javelins sixteen or eighteen feet in length. Their surprise at so unexpected a rencounter [*sic*] was visible in their countenances; but their number inspiring them with courage, they approached at the invitations of the European, and bound round their heads a handkerchief and neckcloth which he offered them. They, however, appeared terrified at the sight of his hanger, which he shewed them how to use; nor were their fears quieted till he made them a present of it. He endeavoured in vain to persuade them to come to the place where our ships lay at anchor: the savages walked away, following the same path in a direction opposite to that which led to the shore.

"Some of our men having landed on the other side of the strait, came to a large fire, round which eight savages, each of whom had a kangarou wrapped round his shoulders, sat warming themselves under the shelter of four fences against the wind. They immediately ran away as soon as they saw our people.

"An old woman who had the care of their provisions, which she did not choose to leave behind her, was soon overtaken by some of the sailors. She accepted with an air of satisfaction, an handkerchief that was given her, but was so terrified at the sight of a hanger, which they presented to her, that she leapt down a precipice more than forty feet in height, and ran away amongst the rocks, where they soon lost sight of her.

"I do not know whether those who related this adventure in a different manner, wished to make themselves merry at the expence of the rest, when they asserted that the age of this woman was no security for her against the attempts of some of the sailors: however, she was still young enough to make her escape, leaving behind her two baskets, in which were found a lobster, some muscles [*sic*], and a few roots of a fern, which I recognised to belong to a new species of *pteris*, of which I had before collected a considerable quantity."

Meanwhile the naval officers surveyed the coasts, including d'Entrecasteaux Channel, which separated Bruni Island from Tasmania. On May 16, 1792, d'Entrecasteaux had his frigates (as they were

rather grandly called) towed towards the entrance of the newly
found passage, which he was determined to sail through if possible. It
was possible, and he found that the passage communicated with Tasman's Storm Bay. On May 28 he emerged from the channel and
shaped his course for the southwest coast of New Caledonia, to continue the search for La Pérouse.

Off the southern point of New Caledonia lies the Isle of Pines, discovered and named by Captain Cook. The mastlike line of trees that
distinguishes the island was sighted by the French party on the morning of June 16, and New Caledonia itself came over the horizon in the
late afternoon. The next thirteen days were devoted to examining
the long southwest coast of New Caledonia, as Cook had examined the
northeast. The admiral than moved on to the Solomons, where he
completed the exploration of the western shores of Bougainville and
Buka, as his countryman Bougainville had done of the eastern coasts
of those islands. At one point nine natives came off to the *Recherche*
in a canoe. "We received a very fine bow and some arrows," writes La
Billardière, "in exchange for a few handkerchiefs, which we let down
to them by a rope. As they did not observe that we possessed this kind
of weapon, they endeavoured to make us sensible of its value, by
showing us its use."

A war canoe with sixteen paddlers visited the *Espérance* at Buka.
According to La Billardière, "those warriors showed no hostile disposition; they seemed very fond of the wine and brandy which was
given to them, but did not eat bacon, without a degree of repug-
nance."

Leaving the Solomons, the ships proceeded to Carteret Harbor,
New Ireland where they anchored on July 17. Here "the continual
rains," La Billardière tells us, "have rendered some species of spiders
very industrious. They construct excellent places of shelter, in the
middle of their webs, consisting of a snug fabric, in the shape of a
cornet of paper, four-fifths of an inch in height, and one-fifth of an
inch broad in the base, with its top elevated and a little inclined towards the south-east, in order that the prevailing winds may have the
less force on this little habitation. The rain glides off this kind of cone,
without being able to enter it, or to press it down, being stretched on

all sides by threads fastened to the neighbouring branches. The spider, being perfectly sheltered in this habitation, never leaves it, but to seize the insects which fall into her toils."

The admiral had intended to remain at Carteret Harbor for over a fortnight, but the excessive rains (if not the spiders) forced an early departure. The ships sailed through St. George's Channel, past the island of New Hanover, and on towards the Admiralty Islands.

Had d'Entrecasteaux actually met Hunter at Cape Town, he would not of course have been detoured by this red herring; nor would his hopes have been raised at the Admiralties by "a large tree standing above the breakers [which] was taken by some for the wreck of a ship; but the branches and roots which were distinctly seen left no doubt that it was a tree, which had been detached from the coast." Captain Huon de Kermadec was of the opinion that an island to the east of the one coasted should be visited. "In fact," La Billardière continues, "according to one of the depositions which had been sent to the Commander of the expedition, it was on the most easterly island that the savages had been seen cloathed in the uniform of the French marine." The Admiralty Islands were well and diligently searched, and trade was conducted with countless Melanesian inhabitants. Not a one wore a French uniform.

Discouraged, the party continued west past the tiny Hermit and Ninigo islands, where Manus Island was discovered on August 4. They sighted the Schouten Islands on the twelfth and then, after coasting the Vogelkop Peninsula of New Guinea, continued on to the famous spice island of Amboina, where they arrived on September 6, 1792. The Dutch reluctantly allowed them to anchor among the eighteen Dutch ships in the harbor.

Refreshed, repaired, and rested, they left Amboina on October 15; passing north of Timor, they sailed southwest, then easterly, until they sighted the southwest corner of Australia. It was a trying passage. In the intense heat the stench of the livestock rose from between decks. Torment was increased by thousands of cockroaches swarming throughout the ships, consuming biscuits, linen, paper, and even the ink out of the inkwells. At last, however, d'Entrecasteaux reached Australia and proceeded along the southern shore.

The first anchorage he found was a bay behind some islands, and here the names of the ships were perpetuated by Esperance Bay and the Recherche Archipelago. Here, too, landings were made and herds of seals, new plants, and exotic birds discovered. The vessels next completely encircled Australia and New Guinea; they dropped anchor at Recherche Bay, Tasmania, on January 21, 1793.

In mid-February the ships moved from Recherche Bay to D'Entrecasteaux Channel, where both were briefly grounded. Then the ships proceeded through the strait for the second time and anchored in Adventure Bay, on February 24. A Tasmanian indicated that another ship had recently been at Adventure Bay; according to La Billardière, "probably he spoke of Bligh, who had anchored there in the beginning of 1792, as we learned some days after from several inscriptions, which we found carved on the trunks of trees." Later La Billardière says that the inscriptions "acquainted us, that Captain Bligh had anchored in this bay in the month of February 1792; when he was on his voyage to the Society Islands for bread-fruit trees, which he was to carry to the English colonies in the West Indies lying between the tropics." Six of the seven fruit trees planted by Bligh were still living.

On the morning of March 1, a year after Bligh's visit, d'Entrecasteaux left Tasmania for the last time. He now proceeded more easterly than when he departed Tasmania the first time, and headed for New Zealand. The ships left New Zealand without incident and sailed north through the Kermadec Islands (named for d'Entrecasteaux's second-in-command), discovering two new bits of land that were named L'Esperance Rock and Raoul Island.

They reached the Tonga group at Eua on March 24. In a short time the ships were surrounded by canoes laden with fruit, hogs, and poultry. "All these canoes had eatables on board," La Billardière records with relish, "one excepted, in which we observed none, and which, therefore, we imagined, had nothing to offer us. But we were mistaken: it was navigated by two men, whose countenances expressed much gaiety, while they pointed out to us two women, who were paddling with them; and the signs they made left us no room to doubt, that they were making us very gallant proposals."

D'Entrecasteaux moved to Tongatabu, where a chief and his party obtained a dozen hogs for them in less than an hour in return for a hatchet for each. The French "were much amused to see them [Tongans] holding their little pigs under their arms, and every now and then pulling them by the ears to make them squeal, that we might know they had them to sell." Shortly they were visited by Feenou, a warrior chief bearing on his chest the scars of spear wounds from fighting Fijians. His features were close to European, his hair powdered with lime. "Feenou made a present to the General [Admiral] of the largest hog that we had yet seen since we had been at anchor," says La Billardière. "He gave him likewise two very fine clubs, made of *casuarina* wood, inlaid with plates of bone, some cut round, others in stars, and others in the shape of birds, of which, however, they were but poor resemblances. This chief appeared well satisfied when the General [Admiral] gave him a hatchet, a large piece of red stuff, and a few nails. To testify his gratitude, he took each of these articles in his left hand, and touched the left side of his forehead with it."

The members of the expedition settled down to enjoy the good life. Tents were pitched on shore for an observatory, kava was drunk, gifts were exchanged, the ships were surrounded by canoes trading eatables. "Besides, these canoes carried on another sort of trade, still more rigorously prohibited by the orders of General [Admiral] d'Entrecasteaux: but the sentries not being very strict in this point, many young girls easily evaded their notice, and were creeping in at the port-holes every moment." Chiefs were presented with suits of blue and scarlet and were entertained by being shown the engraved plates of Cook's *Voyages*. (King Toobou, the supreme chief of Tongatabu, Vavau, and Anamouka [Nomuka], was welcomed on board *Recherche* to deliver a criminal whom he wanted to execute on the spot, a request that was not granted. Both he and Feenou were given scarlet suits.) *

According to La Billardière, the Tongans were fascinated by Euro-

---

* In exchange they received finely carved and polished war clubs. La Billardière tells how they were made. "The natives had already sold us a great number of clubs of various forms, and fashioned with skill, and we saw several who were employed in cutting out others with shark's teeth fixed at the extremity of a piece of wood. We were astonished to see them cut with a chisel like this the wood of the *casuarina*, notwithstanding its extreme hardness. Others already handled the iron tools they had obtained from us with considerable dexterity. All these workmen had a little bag of matting, containing pumice-stones, with which they polished their work."

pean shaving techniques: "These islanders shave with the edge of a shell, and the operation takes up a great deal of time. They were struck with astonishment, when they saw how quickly our barber took off the beards of several of our crew, and every one was desirous of experiencing his skill. Among the rest, he had the honour of shaving his majesty himself." La Billardière indicates that the curiosity was reciprocal. "Traversing the interior of the island," he writes, "we saw a barber employed in shaving one of the chiefs, after their fashion. The chief sat with his back leaning against his hut. The barber's razor consisted of the two shells of the *solen radiatus* (violet-coloured, or radiated razor-sheath), one of which he held firmly against the skin with the left hand, while with the right he applied the edge of the other to the hair, as near the root as he could and by repeated scraping, brought it away, scarcely more than a hair at a time. We were astonished at so much patience, and left him, as might be supposed, long before he had finished his operation."

When corpulent Queen Tine, consort of King Toobou, was given a musical entertainment, she returned the compliment by having a girl sing a song whose length was exceeded only by its monotony. The king, however, later gave a fine reception for the explorers; gifts were exchanged, music was played, and kava was drunk until "the King very soon fell asleep, and snored aloud, with his legs crossed, and his head bowed down almost to his knees."

On Cook's last visit to Tonga, he, Omai, and Captain Clerke had each been presented with rare and valuable tropic feather headdresses. Now Feenou brought d'Entrecasteaux "as a present a diadem, made with the beautiful red feathers of the tropic-bird, with some other very small feathers of a brilliant red colour."

According to a Fijian chief who arrived at Tongatabu shortly after the frigates anchored, it would take three days to sail back to Fiji with a fair wind. This is a long voyage for canoes, but Tongans and Fijians had been visiting, trading, and warring back and forth apparently always. The Fijians' reputation for cannibalism did not detract from their artistic skills, it was agreed that "the arts are much farther advanced at Feejee than at the Friendly Islands; the inhabitants of which never failed to inform us that the finest articles they sold us came from

Feejee, being careful to give us to understand that they were very decidedly superior to those which they fabricated themselves."

Greatly refreshed by the stay at Tongatabu, the ships departed on April 10, 1793. Six days later they sighted Tana in the New Hebrides, discovered tiny Beautemps-Beaupré Island in the northern Loyalties, and then saw the mountains of New Caledonia loom up on the eighteenth. The next day they were visited by eleven New Caledonians in a double canoe and later by four canoes under sail.

They spent over three weeks at New Caledonia and made numerous expeditions ashore. La Billardière collected natural history specimens, took astronomical observations, and examined native houses. He found clear proof of cannibalism, and noted that the inhabitants were so hungry that they often ate a greenish earth (steatite). A cooperative cannibal demonstrated with a special implement having a circular greenstone blade how a slain enemy was dismembered and prepared for cooking.

One day a large double canoe built like those of New Caledonia arrived under two sails. There were seven men and a woman on board, but they were not local people, for they spoke Polynesian. They said that their island was called "Aouvea" and lay a day's sail to the east. (This would be Uvéa, the northernmost of the Loyalty group.) The French noticed that a varnished plank from a European ship was built into the canoe, but surprisingly d'Entrecasteaux did not follow up this possible clue to La Pérouse. It may be that he was concerned over the illness of Captain Huon de Kermadec, who died of a fever May 6 or 7 and who, as he requested the Admiral, was buried on a small island in the dead of night with no monument, in order to conceal his corpse from the natives. Command of the *Espérance* was now given to Alexandre d'Auribeau, who moved to that ship from *Recherche*. Since La Pérouse was supposed to have explored the western coast of New Caledonia, d'Entrecasteaux made two visits there and to the eastern coast as well, but neither revealed any intelligence of that ill-fated expedition's whereabouts. *Espérance* and *Recherche* departed the island May 10.

Ten days later, off Santa Cruz, the ships were met by men with bows and arrows in outrigger canoes. One sailor, hit in the forehead by an arrow, later died of the wound. On May 22 seventy-four canoes approached the vessels. La Billardière says: "I remarked in their possession a necklace of glass beads, some green and others red, which appeared to me to be of English manufacture, and which they agreed to exchange." At about this time a new uncharted island was seen southeast of Santa Cruz and named Ile de la Recherche. Unfortunately it was not visited — for this was Vanikoro, where, as Peter Dillon discovered in 1826, the wrecked ships of La Pérouse actually lay. How close d'Entrecasteaux came to the principal goal of his expedition and the possibility of finding at least two survivors, whom Dillon learned had remained there for several years, of La Pérouse's ships who may still have been living there! But the Santa Cruz Islands were explored no more and the ships sailed west for the Solomons. The rescue expedition had missed its chance.

D'Entrecasteaux now coasted San Cristobal, and the Solomon Islanders attacked the *Espérance* with bows and arrows at the same place where the admiral's countryman de Surville had been attacked years before. By the first of June the ships began ranging the southern coast of Guadalcanal. A week later they left the Solomons and they arrived in the Louisiades on the twelfth. Northwest of the Louisiades another island group was named for d'Entrecasteaux, and beyond that a further cluster was called the Trobriand Islands for Denis de Trobriand, senior lieutenant of the *Espérance*. (The group names have survived but the French names for the individual islands have not.)

The expedition did not linger much longer in Melanesia. New Britain was sighted on June 30; the ships sailed along the northern coast and arrived at the Admiralties once more on July 11. Scurvy was now emaciating the crew, and on the twenty-first disaster struck when d'Entrecasteaux, who had been ill for two days, died. Command now fell on Alexandre d'Auribeau and the survivors hurried on round New Guinea and on August 16 were at the island of Waigeo off New Guinea's western end. Here they stayed for twelve days, feasting on the giant turtles with which the waters abounded. Recovered from the scurvy, they went to Buru, where the Dutch resident was most hospitable, and they met several people who had known Louis de Bougainville when he had anchored there.

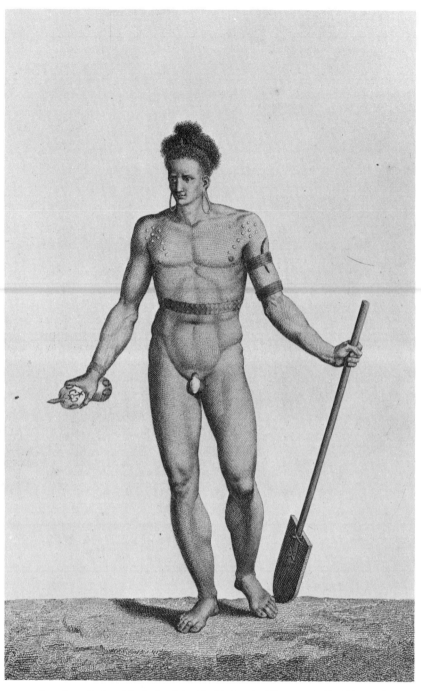

A native of the Admiralty Islands (Atlas du Voyage de La Pérouse)

Tragedy struck again in the East Indies, when the crew was stricken with dysentery. Many died. At Buton they could not land until the nature of the expedition was explained to the sultan's satisfaction. By the end of November they were at Surabaya, where they were made captives, as the Dutch were now at war with France. To further complicate matters, England and France were also at war, the French king was dead, and the Revolutionists were in command.

D'Auribeau and most of the officers were Royalists, but a few, including the naturalist La Billardière and the draftsman Piron, sided with the Revolutionists. On February 19, 1794, d'Auribeau had La Billardière arrested by the Dutch and took his collections. He failed in an attempt to get the naturalist's journal. The disrupted ranks were thinning out. D'Auribeau died at Samarang on August 22, 1794, and Rossel took command of the expedition. So many debts were incurred, however, to supply the needs of the expedition in Java, that Rossel was forced to turn the *Recherche* and *Espérance* over to the Dutch in payment. The expedition, as such, was over and the men began finding their way home as best they could. Several left Batavia in January 1795 in a Dutch convoy. Rossel and Trobriand were on the *Hooghly*. Others, including M. de Giradrin, purser of *Espérance*, were in the *Dordrecht*. (De Giradrin, who died on board, turned out to be a woman, who had obtained her position on the expedition through the kindness of the sister of Captain Huon de Kermadec.) At the Cape of Good Hope Rossel left the *Hooghly* to return home in a Dutch warship. She, however, was captured by the English, and Rossel accepted his captors' employment in the Hydrographical Department at Whitehall, where he wrote the history of the expedition. La Billardière and Piron sailed from Batavia for Ile de France March 29, 1795, arriving there in mid-May and leaving in late November. They landed in France March 12, 1796, and La Billardière went to Paris. Meanwhile his collections had been sent to England; they were only returned to him through the influence of Sir Joseph Banks.

D'Entrecasteaux's expedition did not achieve its primary purpose of finding La Pérouse. But it was one of the more important expeditions to the Pacific. D'Entrecasteaux's name and the names of his officers and ships stud the western Pacific Islands. Gulfs, straits, peninsulas, reefs, and rocks bear witness to his diligence. Beautemps-Beaupré's charts remained the standard references for the northern Louisiades for a century, and the books of Rossel and La Billardière perpetuate and record the admiral's achievements. When one considers that, in addition to the geographical accomplishments, La Billardière's natural history and ethnological observations are classic records, the expedition, in spite of its disintegration, was an unqualified scientific success.

9

Vancouver's Survey

THE same year — 1789 — that the Spanish seizure of English traders on the Northwest Coast was creating the "Nootka Incident,"
plans were being made in London to solidify the English position in
that part of the world. A convict colony had already been established
the year before at Port Jackson (Sydney) in Australia. Now one of
the principal backers of the fur trade, Richard Cadman Etches, proposed that a similar colony be established on the Northwest Coast. He
further suggested that the coast be surveyed from Nootka Sound to
Cook Inlet. Thus, a foothold would be established between the Spanish and Russian settlements; thus, the intricate and hazardous waters
would be charted for traders' benefit; and thus, just possibly, one of
the myriad unexplored channels might prove to be the western entrance to a navigable Northwest Passage, that phoenix of the Age of
Exploration.

The convict settlement came to naught. But by the end of 1789
plans were well advanced for completing the survey of the Northwest
Coast begun by Captain Cook. A new ship of 340 tons was purchased
by the Admiralty. She was especially fitted out for survey work,
named *Discovery*, commissioned as a sloop of war, and the brig
Chatham selected as her consort. Captain Henry Roberts, who had
been a lieutenant on both Cook's second and third expeditions, was
selected as commander of the expedition, while George Vancouver,
who had been a shipmate of Roberts on the same two Cook voyages,
was chosen as his first lieutenant. Shortly after *Discovery* was com-

missioned, Vancouver reported for duty at Deptford. He spent the next three months getting supplies on board. By April 1790 the ship was ready for sea, but news of the "Nootka Incident" at first postponed and then forced abandonment of plans for the expedition. A general impressment was ordered, a fleet mobilized, support requested of Dutch and Prussian allies, and in a remarkably short time Britain was on a war footing. During the mobilization Vancouver was assigned to the *Courageux*, operating with the Channel fleet.

War between England and Spain was averted, doubtless because of this quick show of power. (As Vancouver remarked, "the uncommon celerity, and unparalleled despatch which attended the equipment of one of the noblest fleets that Great Britain ever saw, had probably its due influence upon the court of Madrid.") And with peace now assured, the Admiralty lost no time in deciding to send another expedition to the Northwest Coast for the dual purpose of receiving restitution of territories from the Spaniards and of completing the survey between 50° north latitude and Cook's River (now called Inlet) as originally planned. The importance of the whale fisheries and the fur trade with China made it all the more imperative to act expeditiously. The *Discovery*, which had been prepared for such a voyage a few months before, was available and suitable. The brig *Chatham*, 135 tons, built at Dover, was chosen as her tender. Thus, the same vessels selected for the Roberts expedition were again chosen, but George Vancouver was now appointed commander.

The expedition was manned by one hundred men in the *Discovery* and forty-five in the *Chatham*, which was commanded by William Robert Broughton. Among the officers were Peter Puget, second lieutenant in *Discovery*, whose name was later given to Puget Sound, and Archibald Menzies, surgeon and botanist, who had been to the Pacific before on a fur voyage. Both vessels were armed and well supplied, equipped, and victualed.

Besides receiving back the territories from the Spaniards and examining the coast between 30° and 60° north, Vancouver's orders were to look for a passage through the continent, to ascertain if there were settlements on the coast by other European nations, to pay particular attention to the Strait of Juan de Fuca, to survey Hawaii while wintering there, and, above all, to avoid any controversy with the Spaniards. If time permitted, he could examine the west coast of South America south of Chiloé Island and return via Cape Horn. In all this he was left great discretion.

Vancouver joined the *Discovery* at Deptford on December 16, 1790, but the *Chatham* was not ready until January 6, 1791. Some doubt was expressed regarding the seaworthiness of the *Discovery* after her upper works had been altered to provide more comfortable accommodations. The doubt, however, was unfounded and, after completing their ordnance stores at Deptford dockyard, both ships proceeded downriver to Portsmouth on January 26. Here orders were received to take on board a young Hawaiian named Towraro (or Towereroo, as he is afterwards called throughout Vancouver's book) and return him to the Hawaiian Islands. He had been brought to England in July 1789 and, unlike the famous and gregarious Tahitian, Omai, had lived in obscurity during his entire stay in England.

As they proceeded to the Downs and thence to Spithead, the ship's head was damaged and a man lost overboard. Then Vancouver paid a last visit to London, and the *Discovery* went on to Falmouth, where she arrived March 12. The *Chatham* followed and the two ships sailed on All Fool's Day. As he had no specific instructions in the matter, Vancouver decided to proceed to the Pacific via the Cape of Good Hope; the expedition arrived at Simon's Bay near Cape Town on July 10 and remained until August 17. Fresh provisions and livestock were taken on and arrangements made for a rendezvous in case the ships became separated. *Discovery* and *Chatham* made a rough passage to Australia, passing between the islands of Amsterdam and St. Paul. The voyage was further aggravated by dysentery contracted at the cape.

Fetching Australia, Vancouver surveyed one hundred ten leagues of the coast and gave the name King George Sound to the only secure haven in that distance. Subsequently, he sighted Van Diemen's Land, but he did not stop there, instead shaping a course for Dusky Sound, New Zealand, where the vessels anchored on November 2, 1791. This was Vancouver's fifth visit to New Zealand and here a heavy gale endangered the ships; after it moderated, Vancouver, as always, began surveying. (One arm of the bay not completely examined by Captain

Cook had been called by him "No Body Knows What." After exploring it Vancouver renamed the water "Some Body Knows What.") Much refreshed by twenty days of rest, plentiful fish, and spruce beer the expedition left Dusky on the twenty-second. That same night the two ships were separated in a severe storm.

Passing south of New Zealand in moderating weather, Vancouver, in *Discovery*, discovered and named the rocky islets called the Snares. He then headed for Tahiti, discovering the island of Rapa (which he called Oparo) on the passage. Vancouver wrote a good description of the natives — whose canoes surrounded the ship — and Towraro, the Hawaiian passenger, attempted unsuccessfully — for he had forgotten much of his own language — to hold a conversation with them. On the thirtieth of December, Vancouver anchored in Matavai Bay, and found to his joy the *Chatham* already there.

Chatham's story was the more dramatic. After running before the gale that separated the ships, *Chatham* had lost her jolly boat. (Her crew had also sighted the Snares — naming them Knight's Islands — a few hours after Vancouver had seen them, but they had not seen the *Discovery*.) *Chatham*'s skipper, Broughton, had then decided to make for the rendezvous in Tahiti at once. Taking a course somewhat to the eastward of Vancouver, Broughton discovered a new island. As he approached the shore natives gathered on the rocks with their canoes beached nearby. Making a landing and taking possession, he named it Chatham in honor of the great earl. Then, "after drinking His Majesty's health, I nailed a piece of lead to a tree near the beach, on which was inscribed, His Britannick Majesty's Brig *Chatham*, Lieutenant William Robert Broughton commander, the 29th November, 1791. And in a bottle secreted near the tree, was deposited an inscription in Latin to the same effect." The formalities concluded, Broughton took a close look at the canoes and fishing gear, faithfully recording his observations for eventual publication. "They seemed a cheerful race," he wrote, "our conversation frequently exciting violent bursts of laughter amongst them. On our first landing their surprise and exclamations can hardly be imagined; they pointed to the sun, and then to us, as if to ask, whether we had come from thence."

Accompanied by a group of natives, the party walked along the bay but dared not go too far from their boats. Finally the Morioris (as the inhabitants of Chatham are now called), who were armed with short stone clubs and spears five to ten feet long, became hostile. In the ensuing skirmish one of them was shot and killed. Broughton's final reflection as he left Chatham on November 29 was to "lament . . . the hostility of its inhabitants that rendered the melancholy fate that attended one of them unavoidable, and prevented our researches extending further than the beach, and the immediate entrance of the adjoining wood."

Sailing north, Broughton sighted Raivavae (mistaking it for Tubuai), then arrived at Point Venus on December 26 and anchored in Matavai Bay, where the *Discovery* joined him four days later. Vancouver had passed about twenty leagues north of Chatham Island, just as Cook had done in 1777. (In 1773 Cook had sailed about the same distance south of it.)

There was much to do. New boats had to be built for the *Chatham* to replace her storm losses. Before getting down to work, however, New Year's Day, 1792, was celebrated in an appropriately English manner. "Sunday morning ushered in the new year," Vancouver recounts. "The surf had in some measure subsided, though it still broke with great violence on the shore; which induced me to make new-year's day a holiday. Everyone had as much fresh pork, and plum-pudding as he could make use of; and lest in the voluptuous gratifications of Otaheite, we might forget our friends in old England, all hands were served a double allowance of grog to drink the healths of their sweethearts and friends at home. It is somewhat singular that the gunner of the *Discovery* was the only married man of the whole party." The next day an encampment was set up on shore in charge of Lieutenant Puget.

Vancouver's visit to Tahiti on this occasion lasted only a little over three weeks and came between the visits of Captain Edwards in the *Pandora* and Bligh's second breadfruit voyage. As with all mariners at this time the famous portrait of Cook was brought on board: "Amongst the several chiefs who visited us, was Poeno, Chief of Matavai, who brought with him a portrait of Captain Cook, drawn by Mr. Webber, in the year 1777. This picture is always deposited in the house of the chief of Matavai, and is become the public register. On the back of it was written, that the Pandora had quitted this island the 8th of may 1791." Most of the friends that Vancouver had made among the Tahitians when he was there with Cook were now dead. Otoo was now called Pomare and his son had taken the former name.

The Tahitian chiefs were wined and dined. King Pomare at dinner and afterwards drank an entire bottle of brandy, which threw him into violent convulsions. After four strong men gave him the native massage treatment he fell into a sound sleep and awoke sober. Within a few days he acquired a great respect for "Ava Britarne," as he called rum or brandy, and confined his drinking to a few glasses of wine. Pomare returned English hospitality with presents of large hogs, fowls, vegetables, and tapa cloth. Three men each brought one of the rare Tahitian mourning costumes — the most lavish gift the island afforded and a valuable addition to the ethnographical collections that would accumulate during the voyage. In describing the mourning customs, Vancouver recorded that it was the duty of the chief mourner to keep the inquisitive away from a chief's body "and to maintain as far as possible a profound silence over a certain space in which he parades, having a kind of mace, armed with shark's teeth, borne before him by a man almost naked, whose duty is to assail any one with this formidable weapon, who may have the temerity to venture within reach."

Vancouver's contribution to the history of Tahiti concerns the changes that had taken place in native life since he had been there on Cook's last voyage in 1777. "So important are the various European implements, and other commodities, now become to the happiness and comfort of these islanders," he writes, "that I cannot avoid reflecting with Captain Cook on the very deplorable condition to which these good people on a certainty must be reduced, should their communication with Europeans be ever at an end. The knowledge they have now acquired of the superiority and the supply with which they have been furnished of more useful implements, have rendered these, and other European commodities, not only essentially necessary to their common comforts, but have made them regardless of their former tools and manufactures, which are now growing fast out of use, and, I

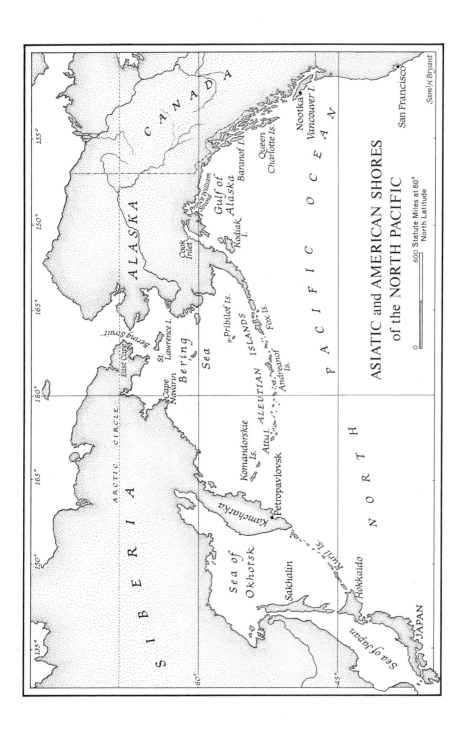

ASIATIC and AMERICAN SHORES
of the NORTH PACIFIC

600 Statute Miles at 60°
North Latitude

Sam'l.H.Bryant

CANADA

ALASKA

SIBERIA

JAPAN

Hokkaido

Sakhalin

Sea of
Okhotsk

Kamchatka

Petropavlovsk

Komandorskie
Is.

Attu I.

ALEUTIAN ISLANDS

Andreanof
Is.

Fox Is.

Pribilof Is.

Bering
Sea

Cape
Navarin

St.
Lawrence I.

East Cape

Bering Strait

ARCTIC CIRCLE

Kurli Is.

Sea of Japan

N O R T H

P A C I F I C   O C E A N

Gulf of
Alaska

Cook
Inlet

Kodiak
I.

Prince William
Sound

Baranof I.

Queen
Charlotte Is.

Nootka

Vancouver I.

San Francisco

135°   150°   165°   180°   165°   150°   135°

60°

45°

may add, equally out of remembrance. Of this we had convincing proof. . . ."

The expedition left Tahiti and set a course to the northward on January 24, 1792. By this time, according to plans made in England, Vancouver should have been leaving the Hawaiian Islands for the American coast. A month had been spent examining the southwestern Australian coast, but the delay was due more to adverse winds and the indifferent sailing qualities of the vessels than to procrastination on the commander's part. Vancouver sighted Hawaii on March 1, and the ships bore to the westward of South Point for Kealakekua Bay.

The first Hawaiian on board *Discovery* was the peripatetic Kaiana whom Meares had brought back from China in 1788. Kaiana, now a prominent chief on Hawaii, inquired after Meares and mentioned Captain Colnett's visit.* Kaiana knew of every ship that had visited the islands, including several American brigs, but much to Vancouver's despair his own expected storeship was not among them.

Kaiana was not the only traveling Hawaiian. As the *Discovery* coasted the island in a light breeze she passed a canoe and was hailed in English by a young man named Tarehooa (perhaps better known as Jack), who had sailed with Captain Ingraham in 1791 with a cargo of furs to China and thence to Boston in New England. Jack had returned to the islands in a brig some months before, and Vancouver promptly engaged him as an interpreter to sail to the Northwest Coast.

The season was getting late, and the vessels had to push on to America. They made a brief stop at Oahu, then at Kauai, for water. Here, Vancouver heard of the capture of the *Fair American* and the massacre of young Metcalf and his crew.† A Kauai chief produced certifi-

---

* After some urging by Vancouver, Towraro decided to stay with Kaiana, although his home was on Molokai. Nevertheless, Towraro did not trust the many possessions which he had brought from England to Kaiana, but left them on the *Discovery* to be brought back to him when Vancouver returned to the islands for the winter.

† In 1789, Captain Simon Metcalf of New York was lying off Maui in the brig *Eleanora* when, in revenge for native thieving, he fired a broadside into a fleet of 300 canoes, killing over a hundred men, women and children and wounding many more. Two weeks later the schooner *Fair American*, commanded by Metcalf's son, arrived at the same place. She was attacked by the Hawaiians and the entire crew killed, except for the mate Isaac Davis. Davis and John Young, boatswain of the *Eleanora* who had been left on shore, both became advisers to Kamehameha I.

cates of commendation from the commanders of four trading vessels who had been there within a year. The first was James Colnett of the *Argonaut*, April 1791. He was followed by Joseph Ingraham in the *Hope*, Thomas Barnet of the *Gustavus*, and John Kendrick of the *Lady Washington*, whose certificate was dated October 27, 1791. Two beachcombers showed up at Kauai — one named Coleman, who had deserted from Kendrick's vessel, and the other an Englishman named Rowbottom. The islands were changing rapidly, becoming the crossroads of the Pacific and a hangout for deserters.

Vancouver took his departure from the Hawaiian Islands on March 18, 1792. A month later he was coasting New Albion, as Drake had named California, and on April 30 had anchored inside the Strait of Juan de Fuca. Then began negotiations with Quadra and the first of three long hard summers surveying the intricate coastline from California to Cook Inlet. It was a stupendous assignment. Only the general charts of Cook and a few details by fur traders were available when Vancouver began his task. Whatever surveying had been done by the Spanish was their own carefully guarded secret. Much was accomplished that first summer of 1792, however. Puget Sound was found and named. Cooperation was given to two Spanish surveying vessels, and from them Vancouver learned that Don Juan Francisco de la Bodega y Quadra was awaiting him at Nootka to carry out the terms of the Anglo-Spanish treaty. In early August the *Discovery* ran on the rocks but was successfully floated again.

There was a dramatic meeting with Captain Robert Gray in the *Columbia* of Boston, from whom Vancouver learned just how untrustworthy Meares's book was, and also, to his chagrin, that he had missed discovering the Columbia River. On the foggy morning of August 28 the *Discovery* arrived at Nootka, where the *Chatham* was already at anchor. To Vancouver's delight, the storeship *Daedalus* was awaiting him there, too.

The *Daedalus*, commanded by Lieutenant Richard Hergest, had not had a happy voyage. She had entered the Pacific and anchored in Resolution Bay, Marquesas Islands, on March 22, 1792. Here she had parted her cable and been driven out of the bay by a gale, at which point it was discovered that she was on fire. (The powder was put overside in a boat and the fire extinguished with much effort.) *Daedalus* had further difficulty while getting water from the Marquesans. After proceeding to the Hawaiian Islands, both Lieutenant Hergest and Mr. Gooch, the astronomer, were killed by the Hawaiians on Oahu. Another severe loss to the expedition was the spoilage of large quantities of the stores in *Daedalus* due to improper stowage.

Meanwhile Vancouver's negotiations with Quadra over the treaty dragged on in a friendly but unsatisfactory way. Vancouver finally sent his first lieutenant, Zachariah Mudge, to England on the trader *Fenis and St. Joseph* with copies of charts, journal extracts, and a request for further instructions. Mudge was succeeded by Puget; other officers were promoted accordingly. Before the *Discovery*, *Chatham*, and *Daedalus* left Nootka on October 12 and 13, 1792, two Hawaiian girls, who had been kidnapped and brought to the coast on the fur trader *Jenny* (although Captain Baker of that vessel claimed they were stowaways), requested Vancouver to take them back to their home on Niihau, which he consented to do. With this addition of pulchritude, sail was set for San Francisco, where the vessels arrived in mid-November. Here negotiations with the Spaniards proceeded no better. William Broughton was now sent to England with dispatches from Vancouver, and Peter Puget took over the command of the *Chatham*. The two ships sailed on January 14, 1793, for their second wintering in the Hawaiian Islands.

Before shaping a direct course for the islands, however, Vancouver decided to search for Los Majos Islands, which were shown on some Spanish charts. Certain scholars have thought that they may have indicated Spanish discovery of the Hawaiian Islands and were thus deliberately misplaced. Since Los Majos do not exist, Vancouver concluded "that the Spanish sea officers have no faith in the existence of these islands; the only authority which they are acquainted with for their insertion in the Spanish charts, is their having been so found in a chart of the pacific ocean, constructed many years ago by an old pilot who had frequently passed between South America and the Philippines. . . ." As the Los Majos Islands had been laid down completely off the old pilot's courses, however, even Spanish captains believed that he had placed them on the chart from hearsay.

Vancouver's ship Discovery on the rocks in Queen Charlotte Sound (from Vancouver, Voyage)

Hawaii was sighted by Vancouver on February 12 and his survey began immediately. The two ships separated. Puget in the *Chatham* began his survey from East Point and followed the eastern shore south around South Point, then went on to Kealakekua Bay. Vancouver in the *Discovery* began his work at East Point, surveyed the north coast and around to the bay. The two vessels met at Kealakekua Bay on February 18.

Before arriving at Kealakekua Bay, Vancouver found it necessary to land a bull and cow, both somewhat the worse for wear from the voyage, but the first of their kind ever brought to the islands. Kamehameha, obviously the most powerful chief on the island, arrived with a retinue of relatives and retainers. Presentations were made to him and he assisted in distributing gifts to all of his people. Vancouver, thinking the king was rather niggardly at times, added to the presents and incidentally to his own popularity. "This distribution being finished," Vancouver wrote, "and the whole party made very happy, the king, in addition to what he had before received, was presented with a scarlet cloak, that reached from his neck to the ground, adorned with tinsel lace, trimmed with various coloured gartering tape, with blue ribbons to tie it down the front. The looking glasses being placed opposite to each other displayed at once the whole of his royal person; this filled him with rapture, and so delighted him that the cabin could scarcely contain him."

At Kealakekua Bay, Kamehameha returned the compliments. As Vancouver describes it, "[Even] before the ship was well secured, eleven large canoes put off from the shore with great order, and formed two equal sides of an obtuse triangle. The largest canoe being in the angular point, was rowed by eighteen paddles on each side; in this was his Owhyhean majesty, dressed in a printed linen gown, that Captain Cook had given to *Terreoboo;* and the most elegant feathered cloak I had yet seen, composed principally of beautiful bright yellow feathers, and reaching from his shoulders to the ground on which it trailed. On his head he wore a very handsome helmet, and made altogether a very magnificent appearance. His canoe was advanced a little forward in the procession, to the actions of which the other ten strictly attended, keeping the most exact and regular time with their

Kamehameha I, King of Hawaii (*Kotzebue*, Voyage of Discovery, *Vol. I*)

paddles, and inclining to the right or left agreeably to the directions of the king, who conducted the whole business with a degree of adroitness and uniformity, that manifested a knowledge of such movements and manoeuvre far beyond what could reasonably have been expected. In this manner he paraded round the vessels, with a slow and solemn motion. This not only added a great dignity to the procession, but gave time to the crowd of canoes alongside to get out of the way. He now ordered the ten canoes to draw up in a line under our stern, whilst, with the utmost exertions of his paddlers, he rowed up along the starboard side of the ship; and though the canoe was going at a very great rate, she was in an instant stopped, with that part of the canoe where his majesty was standing immediately opposite the gangway." Following this impressive arrival, "he then presented me with four very handsome feathered helmets, and ordered the ten large canoes that were under the stern to come on the starboard side. Each of these contained nine very large hogs, whilst a fleet of smaller canoes, containing a profusion of vegetables, were ordered by him to deliver their cargoes on the opposite side. This supply was more than we could possibly dispose of; some of the latter he was prevailed upon to reserve, but although our decks, as well as those of the *Chatham*, were already encumbered with their good things, he would not suffer one hog to be returned to the shore."

Five more cows and some sheep were landed at Kealakekua Bay, and the shore party was stationed in exactly the same spot where Cook had had a similar establishment in 1779. Kamehameha gave assurances that the tents and observatory which Vancouver wanted to set up on shore would be safe, and Vancouver adopted the regulations suggested by the Hawaiian king for governing all dealings between the Hawaiians and English. He added further precautions, however, for the safety of his men, ever mindful of Hawaiians' responsibility for Cook's death.

Vancouver became greatly interested in the politics of the islands. He met and talked extensively with both John Young and Isaac Davis, the survivors of the *Eleanora* and *Fair American* episodes, who were now Kamehameha's advisors. These two men, whom Kaiana had once prevented from sailing with Colnett, briefed him on the character of the various Hawaiian chiefs. Although other chiefs were maneuvering politically it was obvious even now that Kamehameha was the dominant personality on Hawaii, as he would become on the entire group, excepting Kauai.

Vancouver also paid proper respects to his late commander when, accompanied by some of his officers and Kamehameha, he visited "first of all the fatal spot, where Captain Cook so unexpectedly, and so unfortunately for the world, yielded up his valuable life. This melancholy, and ever to be deplored event, the natives are at much pains exactly to represent, to produce reasons for its taking place, and to show that it fulfilled the prophecies of the priests, who had foretold this sad catastrophe."

With the refitting of the vessels completed, observations taken, and chronometers regulated, Vancouver made preparations to leave Hawaii. There was feasting, and Vancouver provided fireworks. Kamehameha had some of his best warriors stage a sham battle to show their skill and dexterity. Just how dextrous they were, Vancouver vividly recounts.

"In their left hand," he writes, "they held their spear, with which in a contemptuous manner they parried some of those of their opponents, whilst with their right they caught others in the act of flying immediately at them, and instantly returned them with great dexterity. In this exercise no one seemed to excel his Owhyhean majesty, who entered the lists for a short time, and defended himself with the greatest dexterity, much to our surprise and admiration; in one instance particularly, against six spears that were hurled at him nearly at the same instant; three he caught as they were flying, with one hand, two he broke by parrying them with his spear in the other, and the sixth, by a trifling inclination of his body, passed harmless."

On March 5, 1793, the king made Vancouver a final present — "the superb cloak that he had worn on his formal visit at [Vancouver's] arrival. This cloak was very neatly made of yellow feathers; after he had displayed its beauty, and had shewn me the two holes made in different parts of it by the enemy's spears the first day he wore it, in his last battle for the sovereignty of this island, he very carefully folded it up, and desired, that on my arrival in England, I would present it in his name to His Majesty, King George. . . ."

Three days later the ships sailed over to Maui and anchored off Lahaina. Here, while Mr. Whidbey began surveying the island, Vancouver concerned himself with native politics. On the sixteenth he sent Puget with *Chatham* off to Nootka. After leaving Maui on the eighteenth, he dropped anchor off Waikiki two days later with the purpose of finding those who killed Lieutenant Hergest and Mr. Gooch. In this he was successful; the three murderers were identified, apprehended, and shot. All during this pursuit of justice Mr. Whidbey was surveying the south coast of Oahu. On native advice, however, Vancouver made no attempt to get into Honolulu Harbor. Instead he sailed over to Kauai on the twenty-sixth.

Vancouver's principal reason for going to Kauai was to return the two Hawaiian girls. From Kauai they could easily get to Niihau if they so desired. Vancouver delivered them to Kauai on the twenty-ninth and the next day took his departure from the Hawaiian Islands.

By May he was at Trinidad Bay, where he found a cross erected by the Spaniard Maurelle. He proceeded to his rendezvous with the *Chatham* at Nootka, arriving there on the twentieth to find that Puget, who had reached Nootka on April 15, had left two days ago in accordance with orders. Vancouver now sailed northward and joined *Chatham* in Fitz Hugh Sound on May 26. For the remainder of the season both ships were engaged with the meticulous survey of the coast, their progress tedious but consistent. By October 5 they were back in Nootka, leaving there on the eighth to sail south. Between San Francisco and Monterey they fell in with the *Daedalus*, now commanded by Lieutenant James Hanson, bringing much needed stores and provisions. The ships sailed leisurely south to San Diego. In December they left the California coast for the third wintering visit to the Hawaiian Islands.

The three vessels, sailing in company, arrived once more within sight of Hawaii on January 9, 1794. Even before they anchored in Kealakekua Bay, which they did on the eleventh, Kamehameha was aboard. Also in the bay was Captain John Kendrick in the American brig *Lady Washington*. More cattle, brought from California, were landed to reinforce those left the previous year and to guarantee their successful establishment in the islands. Vancouver's real goal on this visit, however, which he knew would be the last of the expedition, was to complete the survey of the Hawaiian Islands. In order to accomplish this he still needed to examine the north sides of Maui, Oahu, and Kauai and he decided to allow time to do so.

Before beginning this work, he had one further duty to perform. King Kamehameha had expressed a desire to cede Hawaii to the king of Great Britain. Therefore, on February 25, 1794, the king, queen, and principal chiefs "all assembled on board the *Discovery*, for the purpose of formally ceding and surrendering the island of Owhyhee to me for His Britannic Majesty, his heirs and successors; there were present on this occasion besides myself, Mr. Puget, and all the officers of the *Discovery*." All of the chiefs made speeches. Puget with some officers immediately went on shore and "there displayed the British colours, and took possession of the island in His Majesty's name, in conformity to the inclinations and desire of *Tamaahmaah* and his subjects."

Of the ceding Vancouver mused: "whether this addition to the empire will ever be of any importance to Great Britain, or whether the surrender of the island will ever be attended with any additional happiness to its people, time alone must determine. It was however a matter of great satisfaction to me, that this concession had not only been voluntary, but general; that it had not been suggested by a party, nor been the wish of a few, but the desire of every inhabitant with whom we had any conversation on the subject; most of these having attended the external ceremonies, without shewing any other signs than those of perfect approbation; and the whole business having been conducted by the King and his advisers with great steadiness, and in the most serious manner, left me no doubt of the sincerity of their intentions to abide strictly by their engagement."

Having added this Pacific paradise to the realm, Vancouver quit Kealakekua Bay and spent the first half of March completing his survey of the islands. During this process he met Kendrick and the *Lady Washington* twice more, and found the two women whom he had

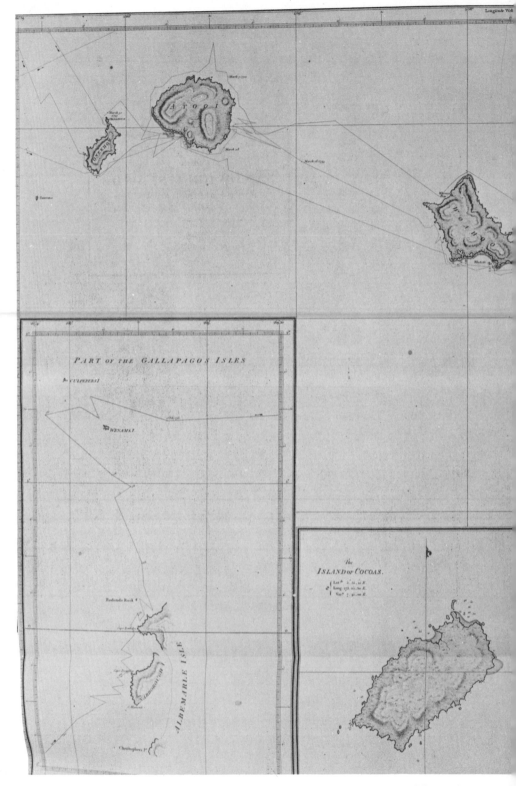

Vancouver's chart of the Hawaiian Islands (from Vancouver, Voyage)

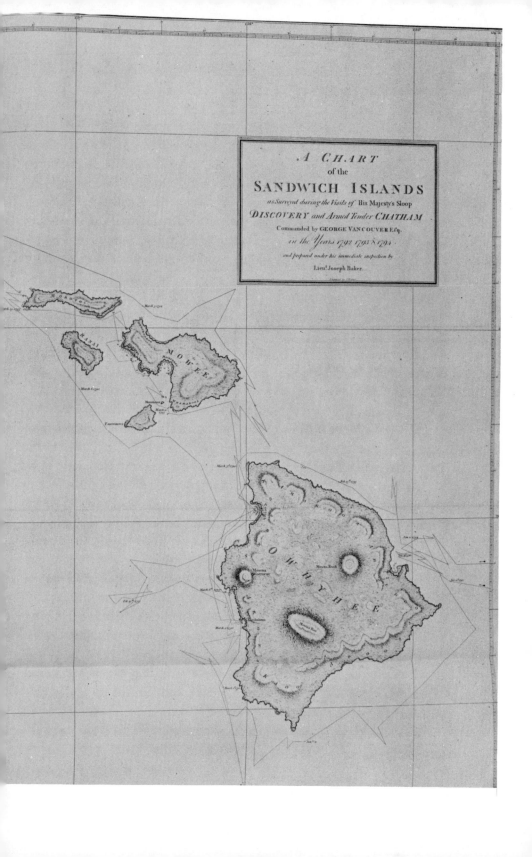

A CHART
of the
SANDWICH ISLANDS
as Surveyed during the Visits of His Majesty's Sloop
DISCOVERY and Armed Tender CHATHAM
Commanded by GEORGE VANCOUVER Esq.
in the Years 1792 1793 & 1794
and prepared under his immediate inspection by
Lieut. Joseph Baker.

returned to Kauai comfortably settled at Waimea. Within two days of completing the survey he left the islands for the last time, bound for Cook River (shortly renamed Cook Inlet), Alaska, to finish the far more difficult Northwest Coast survey.

The expedition was assisted in getting clear of drift ice on April 30 by ten Russians, whose language Vancouver could not understand, and about a score of Indians who fortuitously arrived in a large open boat. The survey was pushed rapidly along from the inlet to King William's Sound. More Russians visited the English and the two ships separated for surveying purposes. By late June the survey was completed to Port Mulgrave (Yakutat) and the two ships met again at Cross Sound.

With the tedious survey completed, the expedition arrived at Nootka Sound on September 2, 1794. Here they found several Spanish, English, and American vessels, including the ubiquitous John Kendrick again in *Lady Washington*. Señor Quadra, the governor, had died and had been succeeded by Brigadier General Don José Manuel Alava. Neither Alava nor Vancouver, however, had the proper documents for concluding the treaty. While he awaited dispatches (which never came), Vancouver put his ships in the best possible condition for the voyage home. He also sent off a letter to the Admiralty, via a Spanish ship, stating that he had completed the survey of northwest America. By October 16, with the ships ready and the summer season drawing to a close, Vancouver sailed from Nootka bound for Monterey. He was followed by Señor Alava in the Spanish *Princessa*. It was hoped that dispatches with instructions for completing the treaty would be awaiting them.

Arriving on November 6 at Monterey, where Puget in *Chatham* had beaten him by four days, Vancouver heard of Broughton's safe arrival at Madrid. Five days later Governor Alava received his instructions from the viceroy of New Spain respecting the cession of Nootka to Great Britain, but nothing arrived for Vancouver. Vancouver was finally let off the hook for concluding the treaty when Alava informed him that everything had been settled amicably between their two governments at home. Therefore, as Vancouver says, "one of the great objects of our voyage, the survey of the coast of

North West America, being now accomplished . . . I did not long hesitate, but determined on making the best of my way towards England, by the way of Cape Horn. . . ." Deserters from the *Chatham* and *Daedalus* who had been detained by the Spanish authorities were collected, and the expedition sailed from Monterey for England on December 2, 1794.

After rounding Cape Horn, the two vessels parted company; they were united again at St. Helena, where they arrived in good health on July 3. Here they found that they had gained a day and that it was Sunday, July 5 rather than Monday, July 6. Puget with the *Chatham* was dispatched on July 11 for the coast of Brazil. There he was to go in convoy to England if possible.

As England was at war again, Vancouver had the good luck to capture a Dutch East Indiaman coming into St. Helena, on which he put a prize crew. They sailed from St. Helena in mid-July and by August 21 had caught up with a convoy of twenty-four sail escorted by H.M.S. *Sceptre* bound home.

Vancouver's voyage immortalized his name on the Northwest Coast, and rightly so. His prime objective — the great survey — was brilliantly completed. His expedition, however, contributed equally to our knowledge of Pacific islands: Vancouver's observations on the politics and ethnography of those islands are outstanding. Also, George Vancouver did not live to see his monumental book published. He died in May 1798 and was buried in Petersham Churchyard, Surrey. His nearly completed work was finished by his brother John.

10

Surveyor, Missionary, Trader

THE late years of the eighteenth century and the beginning years of the nineteenth saw three important English voyages in the Pacific. Their purposes were diverse indeed, but each increased western knowledge of the lands and people of the Pacific basin.

Early in his negotiations with the Spanish, Vancouver had sent two of his highest-ranking officers home with official dispatches. Both messengers, William Robert Broughton and Zachariah Mudge, had delivered their letters to London successfully. However, Vancouver himself was not to return until three years after Broughton had brought the details of the frustrating impasse at Nootka. Broughton was then sent on to Madrid to assist with the interminable negotiations that led to a final settlement of the episode. During this three-year interval, Vancouver completed the survey of the Northwest American coast from California to the Alaskan Peninsula. But the eastern coasts of Asia were only a little less known than the American coast when the Vancouver survey began. Although Vancouver himself had not had time to carry out his instructions to chart the South American coast from Chiloé Island south to Cape Horn, the Admiralty decided to continue the survey to its conclusion.

For this effort what better choice could have been made than a sound and proven ship? The *Providence*, a 420-ton, copper-bottomed, 16-gun sloop of war (the same vessel commanded by Captain Bligh on his second and successful breadfruit voyage) was selected for the arduous task. Nor could the Admiralty do better than to appoint

William R. Broughton commander, with Zachariah Mudge as his first lieutenant. This was done on October 3, 1793, and the *Providence* was commissioned the same day with a complement of 115 men.

Broughton sailed in *Providence* with a West Indian convoy on February 15, 1795, and after the usual stop at the Canary Islands anchored at Rio de Janeiro, where he remained until May 24. Here he found Captain John Hunter, now going out to New South Wales as governor, in H.M.S. *Reliance* with a convoy. (Matthew Flinders, who was an officer on *Reliance*, must have had a pang of nostalgia when he saw his old ship the *Providence* sailing into Rio Harbor.) Broughton, going by the Cape of Good Hope, took Hunter's orders for Port Jackson, where he arrived on August 27, anchoring at Sydney Cove. On September 8 the governor arrived from Rio and caught up with him.

After caulking, refitting, getting fresh food, and rating the chronometers, Broughton laid a course for Tahiti. He observed, however, that "during our stay we entered several good seamen from merchant ships and the colony to complete our complement: our ship's company was in perfect health. We abstained from following the example of other ships that have touched at this colony, by not taking away any of the convicts: a practice very general in merchant ships, which has tended to corrupt the morals of the South Sea islanders." An uneventful passage carried Broughton to Matavai Bay. It was here that *Providence*, warping into a safe anchorage, hooked onto and retrieved the *Bounty*'s old anchor, which had lain six years since the mutineers cut their cable to sail with their Tahitian companions to Pitcairn.

Broughton tarried less than a fortnight at Matavai Bay. He put out to sea on December 11, and on New Year's Day, 1796, was off the Hawaiian Islands. At Kealakekua Bay, now the most familiar port of call in the Pacific north of the equator, he was saluted by the American brig *Lady Washington* with seven guns. (He returned five.) Here, too, he heard that Vancouver, with the *Discovery* and *Chatham*, had sailed for England the previous summer. Broughton learned that Kamehameha was away on Oahu with his chiefs and 16,000 men, having subjugated all of the islands but Kauai. John Young, however, was on hand and took care of all of Broughton's needs. The cattle that

Vancouver had left had bred and were thriving, and goats, Broughton observed, "multiply prodigiously." After moving to Maui, where he found the people in wretched condition, Broughton anchored at Waikiki Bay on February 7. Almost immediately he was visited by Kamehameha and his chiefs, resplendent in feather cloaks and helmets. A brief call at Kauai for hogs (where a young chief presented a small feather cloak) and at Niihau for yams (which could not be obtained because of a great swell preventing the boats from landing) ended the visit.

Broughton sailed for Nootka Sound, where he anchored at Friendly Cove on February 27, 1796, with all his people in good health (excepting those unfortunates who had contracted venereal disease in the Hawaiian Islands). Maquinna, the chief of the village, brought letters that Vancouver had left for Broughton the previous year. These letters informed Broughton that the Northwest Coast survey had been completed and that, to find out where to start in next, he should sail to Monterey and consult the Spaniards. So, after careening his ship to repair a troublesome leak, Broughton sailed south and spent a June fortnight at Monterey. When he learned that Vancouver had sailed southwards a year and a half before, Broughton presumed that Vancouver would have had time to complete the survey of the southern portion of the west coast of South America. His instructions left it up to him what work was to be carried out "in such a manner as might be deemed most eligible for the improvement of geography and navigation." Broughton therefore ordered his officers to write down their opinions as to what should be undertaken, and they all agreed with his own idea: to survey the northeast Asian coast from Sakhalin Island 52° north to the Nanking River at 30° north, including the Kuriles and Japan — now the least-known area of the north Pacific.

Broughton spent the summer crossing the Pacific, and his one brief stop — again in the Hawaiian Islands — ended in terror and bloodshed. Two marines were killed and in reprisal every house, canoe, and plantation was burned for a mile around the spot where the tragedy happened.

After weathering a violent storm, the *Providence* arrived on September 12 off Hokkaido, which Broughton called Jeso. This was the name given the northernmost of the Japanese islands by the Dutch a century before, referring to the hirsute inhabitants now known as Ainu. When Broughton anchored in Volcano Bay at the southern end of the island, a delegation of the short, stocky, bearded Ainu came on board. He was also visited by another people, whom he took correctly to be Japanese. They presented him with a Russian chart and one of their own, told him that foreigners were not welcome, and urged him to depart.

Broughton described the Ainu houses, boats, and customs in detail. His commentary on the people was no less circumspect. "The men in general were of a short stature," Broughton wrote, "their legs inclining to bend outwards, and their arms rather short in proportion to their bodies. Their beards were thick and large, covering the greatest part of the face, and inclining to curl. The hair of the head was very bushy, which they cut short before on the forehead, and below the ears: behind it was cut strait [*sic*]. Their bodies were almost universally covered with long black hair; and even in some young children we observed the same appearance. The women have their hair cut short round their heads, but much longer than the men: the backs of their hands and forhead [*sic*] were tatooed, as well as round the mouth. . . .

"The features of the woman were pleasing," Broughton adds, "though much disfigured by the mode of cutting their hair. Their behaviour was modest, reserved, and becoming their sex. The children went entirely naked. The men saluted us in the most humble manner, sitting down cross-legged, stroaking [*sic*] their beards after stretching forth their hands, and bowing nearly to the ground."

Broughton now made a running survey northeast along the coast of Hokkaido and the Kurile Islands, where he visited an abandoned Russian trading post and saw a few crosses marking graves. Foul weather forced him offshore and during a gale his arm was broken in a fall. He fled south and did not approach the land again until off the southwest point of Honshu, the main island of Japan, where he took up surveying again along the outer easterly side of the chain of the Ryukyu (or Loochoo) Islands, between Japan and Formosa, before entering Macao.

For some unknown reason — perhaps in the interests of economy — the *Providence* had been sent out on her lonely mission without a consort. Ever since Cook's *Endeavour* was nearly lost on the Australian coast, it had been customary to send two ships on government exploring expeditions. Doubtless the dreadful weather encountered around the Kuriles and off Japan persuaded Broughton that he should find another vessel to accompany him on his return to those stormy seas. He found a suitable little schooner of eighty-seven tons in nearby Lark's Bay and purchased her for £1500. It was lucky that he did. Already this remarkable vessel had a history of long voyaging. We have met her before. She was the schooner *Resolution*, built by James Morrison in Tahiti for the *Bounty* mutineers. She was taken by Captain Edwards of the *Pandora* when he rounded up the mutineers left on Tahiti; he commissioned her as his tender under Mr. Oliver, his master's mate, and we have already followed her voyage across the Pacific to the East Indies, where she was sold.

With a consort and his ship repaired, Broughton waited at Macao most of April for a fair wind. The favoring breeze came finally on the twenty-eighth; Broughton coasted Formosa and intended to sail northward, surveying on the opposite side of the chain of islands between Formosa and Japan to complete the work begun on his voyage south.

He did not get far. On the evening of May 17, 1797, as the *Providence* was bowling along at four and one-half knots, she "struck upon a reef of coral rocks. Having felt the shock, which was not violent," Broughton relates, "I instantly went upon deck, and by the way met Mr. Vashon coming to acquaint me with the disaster. The officers and men were upon deck in a moment, and the sails directly braced aback. It appeared to me the helm was a-weather, and the ship's head about E.N.E., sails all full. Had the helm been put a-lee on seeing the danger, I think we should have escaped it.

"The proper signals were made to the schooner, and the master sent to anchor her as near as possible, with her head to the eastward; and we hauled up the mainsail, shivering the other sails, to let her go round without acquiring head way: before she paid off to the southward, she again struck fore and aft, and remained fixed at last with her head due

South. Breakers were then upon each bow, and we had from five to fifteen fathoms in the starboard chains, and only 2½ fathoms at times both a-head and a-stern. Having choked [*sic*] the rudder, the topmasts were struck; and we began hoisting the boats out, the lower yards having been kept up for that purpose. At this time the ship did not strike violently, and had only made 19 inches water. Unfortunately, the wind freshened from the N.N.W., and the sea began to break with great force, which soon knocked the rudder off: we secured it with hawsers."

The boats were gotten over, in the hope that it might be possible to heave off with the help of the schooner. But with the increasing wind, the water rising in the hold, and the violent pounding of the ship, it soon became obvious that the *Providence* was lost. By 11:00 P.M. all of the crew had been transferred safely to the now badly overcrowded schooner.

Little was saved from the wreck. On June 5 Broughton had his schooner anchored at Whampoa and a week later he discharged four petty officers, twenty-four seamen, and fifteen marines into H.M. sloop of war *Swift*, commanded by Captain Thomas Haywood, who had been a loyal midshipman with Bligh in the *Bounty* and had also been with Captain Edwards in the *Pandora* pursuing the mutineers. Sadly, none of these men ever saw England, for the *Swift* was lost with all hands on the voyage home. (Thirty other men went home in various East India Company ships and Broughton retained thirty-five to complete the schooner's complement.)

Undaunted, Broughton decided to continue his survey with the schooner alone. "We now sailed a second time [on June 26]," he writes, "in the prosecution of our voyage, not with the most flattering hopes of succeeding, from the season being so far advanced, and the vessel inadequate in many respects to the purpose. But still there was some prospect of acquiring geographical knowledge of the Tartarean and Corean coasts; and I was unwilling, even under the existing circumstances, not to use every endeavour to the utmost of my power, that could tend to the improvement of science by the exploration of unknown parts. The officers and men were equally disposed with myself to do their respective duties, and we departed in good health."

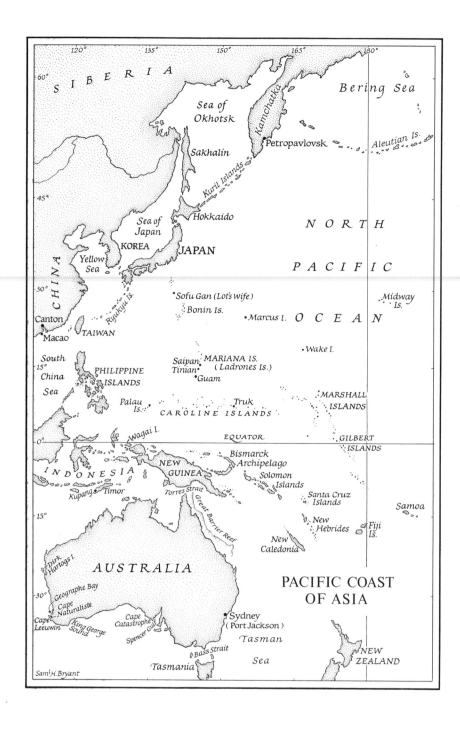

PACIFIC COAST
OF ASIA

Energetically pursuing his work with makeshift equipment, Broughton made observations along the Ryukyu chain, the southern and eastern shores of Japan, and the strait between Hokkaido and Honshu. (Here the Japanese once more politely asked him to leave. Helpfully they gave him "a very compleat map of the Japanese islands, with strong injunctions not to acknowledge from whom I procured it." Probably they hoped to persuade him that there was no necessity for him to repeat work which they considered already done.) Broughton subsequently pushed up along the western coast of Hokkaido and penetrated as far as possible, until stopped by shoal water, between Sakhalin Island (which he thought to be a peninsula) and the mainland. He then turned south, surveying the mainland down to and along the eastern coast of Korea.

Broughton left his arduous work and returned to Macao Roads on November 27, 1797, after a profitable season. When he arrived back in England in February 1799, after a four-year absence, there was little primary work left to do in the northern Pacific.

Solid middle-class England had been rather shocked by the published tales of returning explorers (and doubtless, too, by the gossip emanating from the waterfront) about life in the South Seas — especially Tahiti — and the morals of the Polynesians. To bring these and other unfortunate heathen to their senses, the London Missionary Society was formed in 1795.

The next year the London Missionary Society raised some money, bought the ship *Duff*, and assembled volunteers to sail for the South Seas in order "that a mission be undertaken to Otaheite, the Friendly Islands, the Marquesas, the Sandwich, and the Pelew Islands, in a ship belonging to the Society, to be commanded by Captain Wilson, as far as may be practicable and expedient."

Captain James Wilson, the youngest of a large seafaring family, was about thirty-five years old and of a religious turn of mind. On reading of the missionary society's proposed enterprise, he had immediately volunteered his services, which were accepted, and he thus became captain of the *Duff*. He chose as his first mate his nephew William Wilson, who was largely responsible for the published account of the voyage and entirely so for the charts in the book. The crew was especially selected for their piety and abstemious life. Among the thirty-nine souls originally included in the mission party were four ordained ministers and three children, one an infant. The remainder were craftsmen of various kinds and wives. The *Duff* sailed down the Thames from Blackwall on August 10, 1796, with the missionary flag, showing three silver doves with olive branches in their bills on a purple field, flying brightly at the mizzen topgallant masthead. By the sixteenth *Duff* was at Spithead, where a butcher and his wife, unable to conquer their seasickness, disembarked and one of the children died.

Delays, mostly caused by the weather, prevented the actual departure from England's shores until October 24, when the *Duff* sailed in a southbound convoy. She made her fresh food stop at the Cape Verdes and then ran for Rio de Janeiro, where she was moored on November 13. Wilson considered doubling the Horn but wisely decided, as Bligh had before him, to run before the wind by the Cape of Good Hope, pass south of Australia and New Zealand, and then turn north to Tahiti. During the voyage the members of the missionary party decided who would stay at Tahiti and who would go to the Friendly Islands (Tonga) and the Marquesas. Somewhere along the line the Hawaiian and Palau islands got left out.

Tahiti was sighted on March 4, 1797, and the next day in Matavai Bay the *Duff* was surrounded by seventy-four double and outrigger canoes. As usual Webber's portrait of Captain Cook was produced, "upon the back of which were written the names of his Majesty's ships and their commanders who had visited Matavai since that great navigator's time." After leaving the missionaries, complete with supplies, at Tahiti, it was decided to make the trip to Tonga before putting two other missionaries, John Harris and William Crook, ashore at the Marquesas. Two Tahitians taken on board for the voyage to the other islands proved very useful when Wilson stopped at Palmerston Island for fresh coconuts: they were expert tree climbers.

Duff arrived at Tongatabu on April 5. On April 12 Wilson began landing the Tonga missionaries and their gear. Three days later he headed for the Marquesas. Sailing a southerly course well below the

Missionary's house at Tahiti (from Wilson, Missionary Voyage 1796–98)

Society Islands, the *Duff* approached the southern extremity of the Tuamotu Archipelago and on May 23 discovered the island of Timoe, which Wilson, from the shape of its lagoon, named Crescent Island. Wilson made the most important discovery of the voyage the following day, when mountainous Mangareva showed above the horizon. "At three P.M.," he wrote, "a gale sprung up at E.S.E. and it again became hazy with rain. We directed our course W.N.W. towards an island with two high hills that lie contiguous to each other, and are so lofty as to be discovered when distant fourteen or fifteen leagues. These for distinction's sake, were named Duff's mountains.

"When within three leagues, we saw a reef ahead, and the sea breaking very high upon it: this obliged us to alter our course to N.N.W. which we expected would lead us clear of every danger which lay on the east side of the island; but in this we were mistaken; for after running thus about an hour we had a better view, and it appeared that Duff's mountains were part of an island about three leagues in length, with several of considerable height and extent to the south and southeast of it; the whole forming a group five or six leagues long, lying in a direction nearly N.E. by N. and S.W. by S.; and a reef which lies off about three miles from the main island, and probably encircles the whole as a defensive barrier, extended as far each way as we could see with the eye. Upon this reef were several dry spots, upon which clusters of trees grew, and appeared like so many small low islands without the higher ones. . . . The natives on the north end of the island had observed our approach, and they, to alarm their countrymen, as soon as it was dark made a large fire, which at times presented a very curious phenomenon, appearing like six or seven detached lights, then presently joining shewed as if the side of a mountain was wholly in a blaze. This light, which they kept burning till near daybreak, proved a real benefit to us as a guide; for the night was very dark, with variable winds and squalls, and heavy rain. . . . The main island, and those scattered about it, are, as being noticed, all high, and the reef keeping the sea quite still about them, they present a view romantic, wild, and barren: the valleys, however, appeared covered with trees, but of what kind we could not perceive, though some said they could distinguish cocoa-nut trees; and it is certainly likely they should have the fruits and roots common to the other islands, and must have abundance of fish." Wilson named his new discovery Gambier Islands "in compliment to the worthy admiral of that name, who, in his department, countenanced our equipment."

Now having sufficient easting, Captain Wilson set a course to the northward for the Marquesas. He arrived at Resolution Bay, Tahuata on June 5. The next day, Wilson goes on, "our first visitors from the shore came early; they were seven beautiful young women, swimming quite naked, except a few green leaves tied round their middle: they kept playing round the ship for three hours, calling Waheine! until several of the native men had got on board; one of whom being the chief of the island, requested that his sister might be taken on board, which was complied with: she was of a fair complexion, inclining to a healthy yellow, with a tint of red in her cheek, was rather stout, but possessing such symmetry of features, as did all her companions, that as models for the statuary and painter their equals can seldom be found."

The enthusiastic and conscientious twenty-one-year-old clergyman William Crook was landed with his bed and clothes on the seventh, but the Reverend Mr. John Harris, eighteen years his senior, "seemed entirely to have lost his firmness and ardour." A week later, however, he had screwed up his courage sufficiently to be landed with all his things. In the course of trade and entertainment with the natives, the captain presented a Marquesan with an unusually large conch shell. Wilson little realized what a hit he was making. "The conch-shells they use when they go a-visiting from one valley to another, and as they gain the summit of the hills, they blow them with all their might, and take great delight and pride in listening to the long reverberating echoes."

John Harris did not last long ashore. At daybreak on the twenty-fourth he was found on the beach, where he had been most of the night with his chest. The majority of his possessions were stolen. There was a reason for this debacle. The chief had wanted to take Crook and Harris on an excursion to another valley. Crook readily agreed to this outing, but Harris declined the invitation and "the chief seeing this, and desirous of obliging him, not considering any favour

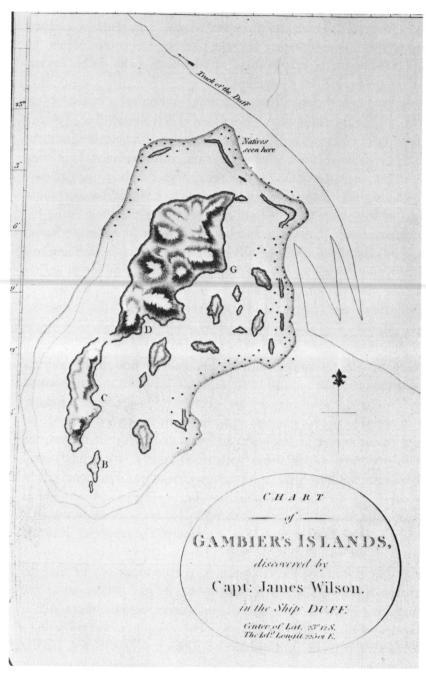

Gambier Islands (Mangareva), discovered by Captain James Wilson
(from Wilson, Missionary Voyage 1796–98)

too great, left him his wife, to be treated as if she were his own, till the chief came back again. Mr. Harris told him that he did not want the woman; however, she looked up to him as her husband, and finding herself treated with total neglect, became doubtful of his sex; and acquainted some of the other females with her suspicion, who accordingly came in the night, when he slept, and satisfied themselves concerning that point, but not in such a peaceable way but that they awoke him. Discovering so many strangers, he was greatly terrified; and, perceiving what they had been doing, was determined to leave a place where the people were so abandoned and given up to wickedness; a cause which should have excited a contrary resolution."

On June 27, 1797, after Harris was snugly aboard and after Crook was sent some soap he had forgotten, Wilson weighed anchor and ran over to the northern Marquesas to check on the related positions of Trevenen's (Huapu) and Sir Henry Martin's (Nuku Hiva) islands to Santa Christina (Tahuata). Two days later he took his departure from Sir Henry Martin's and bent a course for the Society Islands. By July 3 he was back in Matavai Bay.

The remaining iron and steel and other trade goods were now divided between the Tahitian and Tongan missionary groups. Harris decided to throw in his lot with the Tahitian contingent. Wilson gave a dinner party on the ship for the missionaries' wives, and made a tour of the island. On August 4, carrying packets of letters for home, the *Duff* left the missionaries at Tahiti for the last time and sailed off through the Leeward Islands of the Society group for Tongatabu, where she arrived exactly two weeks later. All but one of the Tonga missionaries were found well. Wilson remained here until September 7 and then laid his course for China.

As *Duff* passed Rotuma on September 16, several canoes came alongside and one man, bolder than his companions, allowed himself to be hauled on board by a rope. Even though this was Sunday, which prevented the personnel of the missionary ship from trading, the man was rewarded for his courage and leaped for joy upon being presented with an axe and a few fishhooks.

From Rotuma the *Duff* sailed in a northwesterly direction for eight days. On the morning of the twenty-fifth, the officers saw, much to their surprise, land from the masthead bearing northwest by north. Captain Wilson immediately steered for it. "The weather being gloomy, with drizzling rain, we had no observation for the latitude," Wilson notes. "About five o'clock in the evening, as we drew near to the land, we found that it consisted of ten or eleven separate islands, two or three of which were of considerable size, and saw a canoe coming towards us, in which were two men: they approached within hail, but would come no nearer; they stood up and brandished their paddles, and using many wild gestures, hooped and hallooed in a harsh tone, not seemingly as a menace or defiance, but the effect of surprise and a mixture of other passions at so wonderful a sight, having, in all probability, never beheld a ship before."

This newly discovered group of some eleven islands Wilson named for his ship the Duff group, and the largest of the cluster he called Disappointment Island. It was Wilson's last discovery. *Duff* sailed to the Palaus and then to China, arriving on November 21, 1797, at Macao, where Broughton found her when he arrived six days later. In January, loaded with a cargo of tea for the East India Company, the *Duff* sailed for home. She anchored in the Thames on July 11, 1798.*

In the year 1799 two young men, John Buyers and John Turnbull, made a voyage to China as first and second officers in the ship *Barwell*. Like many others who arrived at Canton in those late years of the eighteenth century, Buyers and Turnbull were impressed by the lucrative fur trade of the Americans from the Northwest Coast. Upon their return to England they persuaded several merchants to invest with them on a trading voyage. A new ship, the *Margaret*, built wholly of stout English oak, was purchased and armed with ten carriage guns, two swivels, and plenty of small arms. Buyers was given command of the new vessel and Turnbull became her supercargo. Both men were part owners. The necessary license to trade in eastern waters was obtained from the East India Company, and they sailed from England with high hopes on the evening of July 2, 1800.

* The published account of the voyage, aside from its recording of the important new geographical discoveries, contains a wealth of ethnographical and historical information, both in the journal text and in an ample appendix about the islands visited.

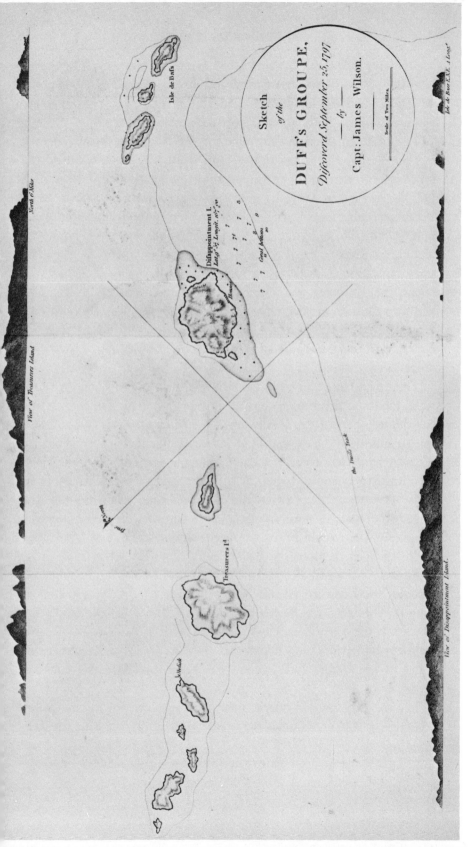

Duff Group discovered by Captain James Wilson (from Wilson, Missionary Voyage 1796–98)

Margaret raised the Cape of Good Hope November 7. One month later she passed south of Australia and through Bass Strait — a course which had become standard procedure for vessels making the eastern passage to China. She arrived at Port Jackson in January.

Turnbull remained in Australia and on Norfolk Island, where he had gone on a whaler, for over a year, while Buyers took the *Margaret* to the Northwest Coast. Buyers's northwest speculation was a failure; he returned to Australia and then went to Bass Strait for sealskins. Because supplies were scarce in Port Jackson, Buyers picked up Turnbull at Norfolk and they left there on August 9, 1802, bound for Tahiti. At Matavai Bay, on September 24, they found H.M.S. *Porpoise* collecting hogs for Port Jackson. According to Turnbull's account, the *Margaret* was visited by the missionaries left by the *Duff* and by a Captain House, whose brig, the *Norfolk*, was wrecked here, as well as by "a Mr. Lewin, a landscape painter sent hither from Botany Bay, for the purpose of taking view, and making drawings of objects in this island."

There were also the usual visits by Tahitian royalty and girls. The royal family at this time had a drinking problem. As Turnbull writes, "all the members of this family were indeed extremely eager to obtain spirits; and, with the exception of Pomarre, all equally outrageous and brutal when intoxicated." Indeed, things were changing in Tahiti. About thirty Europeans were living there, and the missionaries, in the midst of a destructive native war that had been going on for some time, had converted their dwelling into a sort of fortress by mounting the guns of the wrecked *Norfolk* on the second story.

Buyers spent a month at Tahiti collecting hogs, then took on six Tahitians who wanted to go to the Hawaiian Islands, and cruised out through the Leeward Islands of the Society group. At Huahiné he found a former crew member who had deserted on the ship's first passage to the Northwest Coast in 1801. At Raiatéa *Margaret*'s cables were cut by natives who hoped that the ship would strike so that she could be plundered. Everywhere the Tahitians urged the sailors to desert.

The six Tahitians on board, who had been terrified by the sailors' crossing-the-line ceremonies, were calm enough by the time the *Mar-*

garet reached Oahu on December 17, 1802. At Kauai on December 26, Turnbull observed of their compatriots that "the voyage of vancouvre [*sic*] has made a most eminent and permant [*sic*] change in the situation of these islanders."

At Kealakekua Bay, Young, Kamehameha's advisor for fourteen years, came on board. The king's accomplishments since Vancouver's day had been considerable. The great surveyor had laid the keel of His Majesty's first vessel, and now the king owned twenty vessels ranging in size from twenty-five to seventy tons. As Turnbull describes it, "his palace is built after the European style, of brick, and glazed windows, and defended by a battery of ten guns. He has European and American artificers about him of almost every description. Indeed his own subjects, from their intercourse with Europeans, have acquired a great knowledge of several of the mechanical arts, and have thus enabled him to increase his navy, a very favourite object with him. I have no doubt that in a very few years he will erect amongst these islands a power very far from despicable." Many Hawaiians had become inveterate travelers since Kaiana's visit to China. They made frequent voyages to the Northwest Coast and visited New England and the Orient. A number had settled in Tahiti.

On January 21, 1803, the *Margaret* left Hawaii for a third visit to Tahiti. Because of contrary winds she passed well to the leeward of the Society Islands, sighted Mangaia, and then worked her way east and north until she was off Makemo and Taenga in the middle of the Tuamotus. She then sailed to Mehetia (or Osnaburg) Island, about a degree east of Tahiti, and anchored again in Matavai Bay a few days later. Knowing that *Margaret* had arrived from the Sandwich Islands, the Tahitians swarmed her in search of Hawaiian tapa, which they preferred to their own.

Margaret's primary purpose here was to get hogs — the Tahitian pork trade was flourishing. Since it was imperative that she get to China to pick up an East India Company cargo for England, Turnbull disembarked at Tahiti to slaughter hogs and salt pork, while Buyers in the ship supposedly went westward for more hogs. Buyers was to be gone three weeks. When two months went by and the *Margaret* failed to return, Turnbull became worried. Shortly thereafter some Tahitians discovered her wreck about three leagues north of Tahiti. The captain had decided to go to windward to trade for pearls. The vessel was wrecked on a reef in the western Tuamotus, and the Tahitians on board the *Margaret* stole the only boat. The captain and crew landed and built another, but were unable to get it over the reef. They then built a punt of planks from the ship and in this miserable craft eighteen men got safely back to Tahiti in five days.

Once in Tahiti, the crew dispersed. Only Turnbull, Buyers, the mate, and the cook kept together. They had lived there three months when, on August 27, 1803, a ship appeared. And simultaneously came the sudden death of the best-known man on the island. Pomare (the Otoo of Captain Cook) "had got his hogs in the canoe, and was halfway to the ship, when he was seized suddenly with a fit, and falling with his hands on the side of the canoe, expired." When the ship sailed, on September 2, 1803, Turnbull and his three companions obtained passage in her to Port Jackson. They stopped in the Tonga group on the way, where they "purchased some clubs, paddles, and spears; but paid at least three times the price that they would have cost us at any of the other islands." By the end of 1803 the shipwrecked mariners were again anchored in Sydney Cove, Port Jackson.

Ill, but apparently not discouraged by their long, unprofitable adventure, Turnbull and Buyers boarded the *Calcutta* on March 16, 1804, for their passage home. After a tempestuous passage south of New Zealand they rounded Cape Horn on April 27, stopped at Rio for repairs, and left there June first. "At length, after an absence of four years, and twenty-one days, the long-lost shores of Albion made their appearance."

To be sure, this voyage was not notable for its geographical discoveries, but Turnbull's book is important for its ethnographical information and illuminates the growing and ever more involved history of the Pacific.

Book Three

11

Terra Australis

ALTHOUGH with Broughton's survey completed most of the continental and large island coasts of the north Pacific had been charted, the great continental landmass of the southern hemisphere, Australia, remained still largely unexplored. Its coral-strewn coasts were dangerous, and with the founding of Port Jackson, Australian shipping was increasing.

We have seen that most of the vessels entering the Pacific via South Africa crossed the southern Indian Ocean, sighted the southwestern corner of Australia, and then stopped for refreshment near the southern tip of Tasmania. Inevitably this part of Tasmania (then called Van Diemen's Land) had been partially explored by Marion Du Fresne, by Furneaux on Cook's second expedition, by Cook himself on his third voyage, by Bligh, and by d'Entrecasteaux. D'Entrecasteaux had also surveyed a small section of the southern coast of Australia near Esperance, and Vancouver had charted from King George Sound to Termination Island in 1791. Earlier, the Dutch and William Dampier had made known the western coastline, and Cook had outlined the entire eastern seaboard.

The northern coast of Australia, however, especially from Cape York around the Gulf of Carpentaria to Cape Arnhem and beyond, was still virtually unknown. It was not even sure whether Australia was one land or two: some suspected that an ocean channel from the Gulf of Carpentaria to the Great Australian Bight divided the land. Tasmania, on the other hand, was still reckoned an extension of the

G

mainland, although Furneaux, while separated from Cook on his second voyage, had sailed north to see if it was connected with New South Wales. (Although his diversion proved nothing, the Furneaux Islands perpetuate his name.)

The great surveyor of the Australian coast was Matthew Flinders, who was about four years old when Captain Cook landed at Botany Bay in 1770. Flinders was born in Lincolnshire, the county that produced Sir Joseph Banks, Sir John Franklin, and other eminent names in the annals of exploration. His naval service began when he was fifteen, and he was a midshipman with Captain William Bligh on Bligh's second breadfruit voyage in H.M.S. *Providence*. It was on this long voyage with Bligh that Flinders learned hydrography — a subject that fascinated him, although he realized that mastery of it was not the quickest way to rise up the ladder of command.

After a tour of duty in H.M.S. *Bellerophon*, during which he saw naval action in Admiral Howe's "Glorious First of June" in 1794, Flinders was appointed master's mate of H.M.S. *Reliance*. *Reliance* was taking Captain John Hunter to succeed Arthur Phillips as governor of New South Wales. She sailed February 15, 1795.

While he was in *Reliance* Flinders became very friendly with one of his fellow officers, the surgeon George Bass, another young Lincolnshire man with an interest in exploration. Arriving at Port Jackson in September 1795, the two young men found that very little charting beyond the Port Jackson anchorages had been carried out on the eastern coast of Australia since Cook's general survey. Overcoming some opposition, Flinders and Bass, in between their regular duties, managed to explore along the shore in the tiny *Tom Thumb* — only eight feet long, and manned by themselves and a boy.

Late in 1797 the governor provided Bass with a whaleboat, in which, with a crew of six volunteers, he made an important eleven-week voyage. He examined the coast for some six hundred miles. Finding that from Cape Howe the coast trended west, not south to Van Diemen's Land as Furneaux had supposed, Bass proved to his own satisfaction that Tasmania was separated from Australia by the strait that now bears his name. During this voyage he also found seams

A view of Botany Bay, New South Wales (from Philip, Voyage to Botany Bay)

of coal. While Bass was inspecting the mainland coast, Flinders was sailing as a passenger in the schooner *Francis*, making a second voyage to the Furneaux Islands for the purpose of rescuing the crew and salvaging as much as possible from the wreck of a vessel called the *Sydney Cove*. This gave him the opportunity to explore for five days by boat around that group.

In order to confirm the existence of Bass Strait, Governor Hunter in September 1798 gave Flinders the twenty-five-ton schooner *Norfolk*. Accompanied by Bass and eight volunteers, Flinders made a successful voyage of a little over twelve weeks, during which he explored sections of the hitherto unseen north coast of Tasmania, found the Hunters Islands off Cape Grim, and, on the south, investigated the Derwent River where Hobart now stands. Bass sailed for England at the end of this voyage, but its success gave Flinders (who was now highly thought of by Hunter) the opportunity to make one more excursion, in 1799, to the north of Port Jackson as far as Sandy Cape and to chart Hervey Bay. H.M.S. *Reliance* cleared Sydney Heads on March 3, 1800. She arrived at Portsmouth August 26. Thus concluded the preliminary voyages of Flinders and Bass, which set the stage for the next act.

When Flinders, now a lieutenant, arrived in England, he had completed a manuscript on the explorations that he and Bass had conducted during the previous four years: "Observations on the Coasts of Van Diemen's Land, on Bass's Strait and its Islands and on Part of the Coasts of New South Wales, Intended to Accompany the Charts of the Late Discoveries in Those Countries." Its publication in London the following year enhanced Flinders's reputation. He wisely dedicated his book to Sir Joseph Banks, who had taken a particular interest in everything connected with New South Wales ever since he had been there with Cook in the *Endeavour* thirty years before. Flinders had developed a plan for a survey of the entire Australian coast and he needed a patron. Banks approved of his work and of him. With this powerful backing, the plan was laid before the Admiralty, which gave it quick approval. The king directed that the voyage should be undertaken. Flinders was given command.

Flinders chose for the voyage a North Country ship, the same kind that had carried Cook so successfully around the world. She had been in naval service for some time, but being newly repaired and coppered was considered the best available. Her name was changed from *Xenephon* to *Investigator*. Flinders took command of her at Sheerness on January 25, 1801. Since this was to be a voyage of exploration Flinders obtained permission of the Navy Board to lay in higher quality and larger supplies of stores than would normally be allotted to a vessel classed as a sloop. Aged officers and crew members, unless they wished to volunteer for the voyage, were discharged; in their stead, Flinders chose eleven men from a list of nearly 250 young volunteers. Isaac Coffin, that distinguished Nantucketer who later became an admiral in the Royal Navy and a baronet, was at this time the resident naval commissioner at Sheerness; he gave Flinders every facility in preparing his ship for the voyage. Mr. Whidbey, who did so much of the surveying on Vancouver's expedition, offered invaluable advice and assistance in selecting proper stores.

Flinders, with the whole southern summer for work before him, was anxious to get away and arrive upon the Australian coast. Guns, astronomical and surveying instruments, copies of every chart relating to the area, and a library of reference books and voyages to the South Seas were taken on board. Cooperation even came from the directors of the staid old East India Company, who, because the voyage was to be within the limits of their charter, voted a sum of £600 for the tables of the scientists and officers and a similar sum to be given them at the conclusion of the voyage.

On July 17 Flinders received his final instructions, some advice from Alexander Dalrymple, and a passport from the French government declaring his scientific expedition neutral to the war. The following day he sailed from Spithead with eighty-eight people on board, ten of whom were supernumeraries.* Samuel W. Flinders, the captain's younger brother, was one of the *Investigator*'s lieutenants, and John Franklin, later governor of Tasmania and commander of the

---

* One passenger that Flinders had hoped to take on the expedition was missing. In April he had married Ann Chappell, his Lincolnshire sweetheart, in the expectation that she would be allowed to accompany him to Port Jackson. Alas, the Lords of the Admiralty took a dim view of this happy arrangement and Mrs. Flinders, already on board, disembarked as soon as her husband received his sailing orders.

ill-fated Arctic expedition seeking the Northwest Passage, was one of the midshipmen.

Flinders, through William Bligh, was a true disciple of Cook. He kept a clean and aired ship, saw that the crew exercised regularly, and made the men use antiscorbutics liberally. With a healthy crew Flinders had no need of a long stop at the Cape of Good Hope. He was soon running his easting down to Australia along the thirty-seventh parallel: a wise choice, for he had a fair-weather run and averaged about 150 miles per day all the way to Cape Leeuwin. Although he was repeating work done by Vancouver and d'Entrecasteaux, he made a running survey from Cape Leeuwin to King George Sound, where he arrived on December 8. "It was then dark," Flinders wrote, "but the night being fine, I did not hesitate to work up by the guidance of captain Vaucouver's [sic] chart; and . . . anchored at eleven o'clock, in 8 fathoms, sandy bottom." Here he paused to put his ship in good order for the close examination of Australia's southern coast, taking advantage of this delay to make a completely new survey of the sound, while the naturalists began their studies and the artists sketched and painted. Flinders generously states that there was little difference between his survey of King George Sound and Vancouver's, except for the soundings, which could well have changed in the decade between 1791 and 1801.

Leaving King George Sound on January 5, 1802, Flinders began the long plotting of the southern coast. As he reached the eastern side of the Great Australian Bight he entered virgin territory, for both d'Entrecasteaux and Vancouver had veered off for Adventure Bay in Van Diemen's Land, while Nuyts, the seventeenth-century Dutchman who had sailed off these shores, had not gone beyond this point. Flinders spotted the head of the Great Bight and identified Nuyts Archipelago as the islands laid down by the Dutchman in 1627.

So far this had been a fast survey. Everything had gone well. Flinders had not left England until after mid-July, and by the third week of February an enormous amount had been done. On February twenty-first, however, there occurred the first of several tragic events that Flinders was destined to suffer before he saw England again.

The *Investigator* had arrived off the western headland of Spencer Gulf. John Thistle, the master, William Taylor, a midshipman, and six able seamen had gone in the cutter to search the shore for water. They were seen returning under sail at dusk, when suddenly they disappeared. Two hours passed and still no cutter came. A light was shown, and Lieutenant Robert Fowler, taking a lantern, went in a boat to search for the lost cutter. No sign of the boat or men could be found, but at the place where the cutter was last seen, Fowler met with a tide running so strong that he was nearly capsized. This was undoubtedly what had happened to Thistle and his companions. The next day the stove cutter was found bottom up and towed back to the ship. No sign of the men emerged from the shark-filled waters; only an oar and a few bits of wreckage were ever found. This disaster was, of course, a severe blow to the expedition. In Thistle, Flinders had lost not only a shipmate and friend, but an able master and competent surveyor.* Taylor was one of his most promising midshipmen, and the six sailors were all young and able volunteers.

Flinders named the western headland Cape Catastrophe, and began charting the coast as it turned north. There seemed to be the possibility that they were in a channel separating New Holland from New South Wales, but on March 9 Flinders realized that he was in a gulf; the water shoaled out and the shores contracted. Penetrating nearly to the head of the gulf, Flinders moved quickly down the other side. Both the gulf and the point marking its eastern entrance were named Spencer, in honor of the Earl who was First Lord of the Admiralty at the time the voyage was being planned.

Kangaroo Island and the Gulf of St. Vincent (named for John Jervis, Earl of St. Vincent, another Admiralty lord), on which the city of Adelaide now stands, were discovered next. The peninsula separating the two great gulfs was named York for Charles Philip Yorke, who followed Spencer and St. Vincent as First Lord of the Admiralty. The water separating Kangaroo Island from the York Penin-

* Curiously enough, while *Investigator* was lying at Spithead, a fortune teller had told John Thistle that he would be lost on the voyage — a tale with which the master had often regaled his messmates.

sula became Investigator Strait, and its eastern end from the mainland Cape Jervis was named Backstairs Passage. Indeed, Flinders bestowed names liberally on all geographical features. Most of the names are still in use today.

As *Investigator* pushed eastward on April 8, 1802, the lookout reported a white rock ahead. Soon, however, it proved to be a heavy-looking ship. She flew the French ensign and, as she passed to leeward of the *Investigator*, Flinders veered his ship to keep his broadside towards her, not trusting the flag of truce flying from both vessels. The stranger turned out to be the *Géographie*, one of the two ships of the French exploring expedition sent to Terra Australis under Captain Nicholas Baudin.

Flinders went on board the French ship and the two captains showed each other their passports. Baudin had been examining the southern and eastern coasts of Van Diemen's Land; in Bass Strait during a heavy gale he became separated from his consort, the *Naturaliste*. Baudin had also lost a boat and its crew somewhere on the Tasmanian coast. He was far less interested in hearing about what Flinders was doing on the coast than he was in telling about his own work, so the English captain let him talk. But when Baudin criticized the English chart of Bass Strait, published in 1800, Flinders pointed out a note on the chart explaining that it was done from an open boat offshore without any good means of fixing either latitude or longitude. The two explorers parted amicably, and Flinders promised to watch out for the *Naturaliste* and inform her captain to rendezvous with Baudin at Port Jackson. The French at this meeting admitted all of Flinders's discoveries around the Great Bight and the two gulfs and used their names. Later on, when the two groups met again at Port Jackson, Louis de Freycinet (Baudin's second-in-command) remarked to Flinders in the presence of Governor King, "Captain, if we had not been kept so long picking up shells and catching butterflies at Van Diemen's Land, you would not have discovered the South Coast before us." The meeting place with Baudin was named Encounter Bay.

Now the eastward examination of the coast was resumed, and Flin-

ders approached a section of the shore line that had previously been
visited by Captain James Grant in H.M. brig *Lady Nelson,* the vessel
which Flinders was to take as his consort later when he reached Port
Jackson. By April 21 the *Investigator* had entered Bass Strait, where
Flinders was anxious to establish the location of a large island in the
strait's western mouth, reported by Port Jackson whalers. (Actually,
although Flinders was at this time ignorant of it, the northern end of
the island had already been seen by Captain John Black of the brig
Harbinger in January 1801, and named King's Island.) Flinders found
the island and explored it, then ran back to the mainland and continued along the seacoast. On Sunday, May 9, the *Investigator* anchored in Sydney Cove. There were still details to fill in, but basically
Flinders had successfully completed the first part of his assignment.
The south coast of Australia was now laid down.

As soon as his ship was secure Flinders went ashore to pay his respects to Governor Philip Gidley King, who had succeeded John
Hunter. He also carried orders to the governor that the brig *Lady
Nelson* should be turned over for his use and that the *Investigator*
should not be employed on any other service than surveying. The
Lady Nelson was in port and so, too, was Baudin's consort *Naturaliste,* commanded by Emmanuel Hamelin, to whom Flinders gave Baudin's message that the *Géographie* would be returning there. He also
found out that *Géographie*'s lost boat and crew had been picked up in
Bass Strait by the brig *Harrington,* and all were now safely on board
*Naturaliste.**

Governor King was gracious and generous with assistance to Flinders in preparing *Investigator* for continuing the work. During July,
alterations were made in the *Investigator* to provide for a greenhouse
for plants to be taken to Kew. The *Lady Nelson,* especially suitable
for shoal water and river work, was taken over as a tender under Lieutenant John Murray. Seamen and convicts were shipped to replace the
eight men lost in Spencer Gulf and two others who were sick (one

---

* On June 20, Baudin in *Géographie* arrived with his men in pathetic condition. His
crew of 170 had been reduced by scurvy to only twelve capable of duty. Here was
where the tradition of Cook's training paid off. Flinders had arrived with his crew
in perfect health.

from being bitten by a seal on Kangaroo Island). Now all was ready to continue the survey northward. The *Investigator* and her consort *Lady Nelson* sailed in company from Port Jackson on July 22.

On the passage north to Cape York it was Flinders's intention to survey sections of the coast that Cook had passed in the night and that he himself had not surveyed on his voyage to the north of Port Jackson in the *Norfolk* in 1799. Flinders, always a daring surveyor, kept in soundings, charting harbors as he went. Murray, in the more conservative tradition of the sea, kept well offshore, only barely in sight of land. As he moved north, Flinders found that Cook, who had no chronometer, was considerably in error in his longitudes: the error soon increased to about half a degree by Cape York, the northern tip of the westerly trending coast.

Meanwhile, a constant but unsuccessful watch was kept for the still undiscovered remains of La Pérouse's ships. Meanwhile, too, everyone was working — the botanists collecting, William Westall, the artist, making sketches and profiles, sailors getting wood and water. The constant shipboard duties were multiplied by working in intricate shallow waters, especially for the *Lady Nelson*, which, due to the loss of two of her three movable keels, was so leewardly that she became a drag on the expedition. Indeed, when she also lost some of her anchors and Flinders was unable to spare replacements from the *Investigator*, he decided to send her back to Port Jackson. Flinders took most of her stores and provisions, and dispatched the *Lady Nelson*, along with an account of his work to date and a request to Governor King that the brig be repaired and equipped to rejoin the expedition the following year.

Two days following the departure of the *Lady Nelson*, and after much vexing trial and error, Flinders found his way, by what is now called Flinders Passage, through the Great Barrier Reef into open ocean. He sought to reach Torres Strait before the northwest monsoon set in. Keeping well off while making his northing, he discovered and named the coral banks called the Eastern Fields, and then entered Torres Strait by the passage used by Captain Edwards in the *Pandora* in 1791. He pushed through the strait quickly, proving that the pas-

A canoe of the Murray Islands (Flinders, Voyage to Terra Australis, Vol. II)

sage could be made in three days and thus cut the sailing time from Sydney to Batavia by nearly six weeks.

Flinders got around Cape York before the beginning of the north-west monsoon, and by early November had begun his examination of the east coast of the Gulf of Carpentaria. He named Duyfhen Point (which had been seen by the Dutch yacht *Duyfhen* in 1606 — the first vessel to discover any part of Carpentaria). He discovered and laid down the Wellesley Islands, where he found evidence of a European shipwreck. The seven-foot teak carling of a ship's quarterdeck had washed up on Bentinck Island where there were the stumps of at least twenty trees that had been felled with an axe, together with the broken remains of a jar. The identity of the vessel has never been determined.

Flinders wrote of the Wellesley Islanders: "Whether these people reside constantly upon the islands or come over at certain seasons from the main, was uncertain; canoes, they seemed to have none, but to make their voyages upon rafts similar to those seen at Horse-shoe Island, and of which some were found on the shore in other places. I had been taught by the Dutch accounts to expect that the inhabitants of Carpentaria were ferocious, and armed with bows and arrows as well as spears. I found them to be timid; and so desirous to avoid intercourse with strangers, that it was by surprise alone that our sole interview, that at Horse-shoe Island, was brought about; and certainly there was then nothing ferocious in their conduct. Of bows and arrows not the least indication was perceived, either at these islands or at Coen River; and the spears were too heavy and clumsily made, to be dangerous as offensive weapons: in the defensive, they might have some importance."

It was in these waters that Flinders received one of his bitterest disappointments. His intention had been to complete the coastal survey of the continent all the way around to Point Leeuwin. However, on November 23 carpenters engaged in some caulking reported finding rotten planks, timbers, and treenails throughout in the ship. Flinders became alarmed and ordered the master and oldest carpenter to make a complete survey of the *Investigator*. Two days' examination showed that she was in such a dreadfully rotten state that it would be impossible to complete the survey in her. Flinders quit the Wellesley Islands on December 1, 1802, although he continued surveying to Cape Vanderlin, which he found to be an island, contrary to the old Dutch chart in his possession.*

The *Investigator* continued her voyage northward, past Cape Maria (which was shown on Flinders's Dutch charts as mainland, but proved to be an island), Bickerton's Island, and Cape Barros (both of which were named by Flinders). Then came Groote Eylandt, where, to add to Flinders's woes, the crew of the *Investigator* had a fracas with the natives. (Although none of the crew were killed one man was wounded by several spears and another, Thomas Morgan a marine, died of sunstroke after losing his hat. The next day *Investigator* inflicted several casualties on the natives and took a thirteen-and-a-half-foot bark canoe.) After Cape Arnhem was passed on the morning of February 11, 1803, and Cape Wilberforce and Melville Bay had received their names, the examination of the Gulf of Carpentaria and the exploration of its bays and islands was successfully completed.

At the Wessel Islands the condition of the ship forced Flinders to quit the coast. "The accomplishment of the survey," Flinders wrote as he set a course for Timor, "was, in fact, an object so near to my heart, that could I have foreseen the train of ills that were to follow the decay of the *Investigator* and prevent the survey being resumed, — and had my existence depended upon the expression of a wish, I do not know that it would have received utterance. . . ."

Now Flinders's real object was to reach Port Jackson before his ship disintegrated. Speed was also imperative, because of the condition of his crew. There was no scurvy, but several had died and nearly a score were in their hammocks with fever and dysentery. After passing through Bass Strait, the worn-out ship and men arrived at Port Jackson on June 9, 1803, completing the first circumnavigation of Australia.

Flinders immediately reported his arrival to Governor King and made arrangements to have his sick men transferred to the hospital. (For four of the sick crew it was too late — they died in a few days.)

---

* The group of islands of which Vanderlin is the largest was named for Sir Edward Pellew.

View of Coupang, Timor, showing the Géogra

He found that Lieutenant Murray in the *Lady Nelson* had arrived safely, after a tedious passage from the Great Barrier Reef. He also found out that Baudin, with the *Géographie* and *Naturaliste*, had not sailed to the South Coast until some months after *Investigator* had left Port Jackson. Waiting for Flinders was James Inman from the Royal Naval College, Portsmouth, an astronomer sent out by the Board of Longitude to replace Mr. Crosley, who had left at the Cape of Good Hope. The astronomical instruments were immediately put under Inman's charge.

Governor King, at Flinders's request, appointed a committee of officers to survey the condition of the *Investigator*. The result showed that she was in even worse shape than had been suspected — an unbelievable state of rottenness and incapable of any further service. The governor, therefore, decided to offer the much smaller *Porpoise*, with the *Lady Nelson* as a consort, for the survey's completion. Further investigation showed that the *Porpoise* could not be put in condition

the Naturaliste (*from* Atlas *to Baudin's voyage*)

for the work for many months, so Flinders decided to take passage home in the *Porpoise*, lay his charts and journals before the Admiralty, and request another ship to complete the survey of Australia.

The *Porpoise*, in company with the ships *Cato* and *Bridgewater*, an East Indiaman under command of Captain E. H. Palmer, sailed from Port Jackson on August 10, 1803. A week later the *Porpoise* and *Cato* piled up on Wreck Reef in the night. Incredibly, the *Bridgewater* sailed off without making the slightest attempt to rescue the marooned crews, or even to supply them with provisions. The ninety-four men were therefore forced to salvage provisions and water from the wreckage. For nearly two months all but fourteen of the men lived on the exposed sandbank. The inhumanity of Captain Palmer received a certain just reward when the *Bridgewater* was later lost with all hands after leaving Bombay for Europe.

On August 26 Flinders, with the captain of the *Cato* and twelve men, set sail in the largest surviving cutter, named the *Hope*, for Port

Jackson. They arrived thirteen days later. Governor King immediately ordered the ship *Rolla* and the schooners *Cumberland* and *Francis* to the rescue of the stranded men (although they did not sail for another thirteen days). The *Rolla* was bound for Canton and so Flinders was given one of the schooners, the little twenty-nine-ton *Cumberland*, to return to England in after he picked up his charts and journals at the reef. Six weeks to the day after Flinders left the reef, he was back with the three rescue vessels. Men and stores were taken on board the *Cumberland* for the voyage to England. The remaining men either returned to Port Jackson in the *Francis* and a new little vessel built at the sand bank, or, like Flinders's brother, sailed in the *Rolla* for home via Canton.

Flinders successfully passed through Torres Strait and arrived on December 15 at Mauritius, where to his apprehension and dismay he found that war had broken out between France and England. In Port Louis he found out that the *Géographie* had sailed for France the day before his arrival and that Captain Baudin had died at Mauritius shortly after he arrived there. The French, on a technicality, refused to honor Flinders's passport, saying it was for the *Investigator*, not the *Cumberland*. He was not allowed to leave until June of 1810, a detention of over six years. He never returned to complete his magnificent survey. Back in England, in precarious health, he devoted his time to writing his great two-volume work, which was published in June 1814. Matthew Flinders's brilliant career came to an end when he died on July 19, 1814, aged forty years.

The unjustifiable treatment of Flinders by the French in Mauritius is in marked contrast to the British aid and assistance given to his contemporary, Nicholas Baudin, at Port Jackson during his exploration of some of the same coasts.* Baudin's expedition, sent out by Napoleon with the backing of the country's learned societies and the government, was to explore the coasts of Australia and part of New Guinea

---

* In fact, there has been speculation that Flinders's captivity may have been to give François Péron and Louis de Freycinet time to get their books published before those of the English expedition, but there is little evidence for this assumption. Péron, the naturalist who wrote the first volume on Baudin's expedition, placed new French names on many geographical features.

and make scientific collections for the Museum of Natural History in Paris. Its dual purposes were reflected in the names of its two ships — the *Géographie*, a corvette of thirty guns, and the *Naturaliste*, a heavier, poorer sailing, but more seaworthy storeship. Captain Baudin was well chosen to command the expedition and the *Géographie*, for he had led a scientific expedition along the Gulf coast of Mexico. Captain Emmanuel Hamelin was given command of *Naturaliste*. Among the personnel were the zoologist François Péron, who later wrote up the scientific achievements of the voyage, and Louis de Freycinet, who published the geographical and nautical accomplishments.

Manned by some 180 sailors, as well as botanists, artists, mineralogists, and natural historians, and armed with several casks of medals for distribution to impress the natives of the savage islands, the expedition sailed from Le Havre on October 19, 1800. On May 27, 1801, they raised Cape Leeuwin at the southwestern corner of Australia and headed north along the western coast, large sections of which were surveyed with certainty for the first time.*

More than once, the two vessels were separated by a storm. Nevertheless Baudin succeeded in surveying the coast as far as Cape Leveque to the north; and, on another approach (after refreshing at Timor) in surveying a great deal of the Tasmanian coast. Baudin did some important work ranging the hitherto unexplored coast from Cape Banks to Encounter Bay, where, as we have already seen, he met Flinders on April 8, 1802, working eastwards. Following this extraordinary meeting of the two explorers, Baudin continued westward, naming St. Vincent Gulf "St. Josephine" and Spencer Gulf "Gulf Bonaparte." (Actually, both had already been discovered and named by Flinders, and Baudin knew this from the chart the Englishman had given him. Larceny of this kind was, alas, not uncommon then. Nor is it now.) Near the head of the Great Australian Bight Baudin put to sea and, sailing out around Tasmania, made Port Jackson, his crew sick with scurvy, on June 22. There the *Naturaliste* awaited him and there Bau-

---

* The ships' names were perpetuated at Cape Naturaliste and Geographe Bay. At Dirk Hartogs Island off Shark Bay the expedition found a pewter plate, partially disintegrated, spiked to a tree with an inscription saying that Dirk Hatigs [*sic*], master of the ship *Endraght* of Amsterdam, arrived there on October 25, 1616, followed by the ship *Naban* two days later and by five other Dutch ships on February 1, 1697.

din remained during the winter, recuperating with his men and reorganizing his expedition, while the *Naturaliste* proceeded home via Mauritius. At this time Baudin purchased a thirty-ton schooner named *Casuarina* for inshore work; he gave command of her to de Freycinet. Leaving Port Jackson with his reorganized expedition after six months there, Baudin passed through Bass Strait for the second time, touched at King Island, charted the south coast of Kangaroo Island, and spent eleven days exploring around King George Sound and along the coast in detail back to Cape Leeuwin. He then once more worked his way up the western coast, clearing up numerous details. He continued along the northwestern coast as far as Bathurst and Melville islands. From here Baudin sailed for Mauritius, where he arrived August 7, 1803. He died there on September 16.

The results of this expedition were notable. In contrast to Flinders's treatment, Baudin was given every assistance at Port Jackson. Not only that, but when the *Naturaliste* was captured upon her arrival in the channel in June 1803, she was sent in to Portsmouth: after it was ascertained that she was an exploration vessel, her crew were given every refreshment and she was sent on to France with her botanical, zoological, and mineralogical collections, curiosities (ethnological collections), drawings, views, and charts intact. (They consisted of between 1200 and 1300 packages in all.) When the *Géographie* returned to France in 1804, she brought further collections and data.*

Even though the French, due to information obtained from Flinders in Mauritius, were able to publish the first complete chart of Australia in 1807, their grandiloquent names for Spencer and St. Vincent gulfs and Terre Napoléon for Australia's southern coast could not survive the publication of Flinders's great atlas. Although work on the precise charting of Australia continued for many years, the main features of the continent's outline assumed modern form after the publication of Flinders's work and the volumes on the Baudin voyage.

---

* The natural history collections were added to the museum in Paris, and the ethnological collections became part of the foundation of the Musée de l'homme. In 1807 François Péron published the first volume of his natural history work on the voyage. (The second volume did not follow until 1816.) Louis de Freycinet edited the volume on navigation, cartography, and geography, which appeared in 1815.

12

The First Russian Circumnavigation

Flinders completed his circumnavigation of Australia on June 9, 1803. A scant two months later, on August 7, an expedition sailed from Kronshtadt that was destined to bring to the South Seas a hitherto unseen flag.

Until the nineteenth century, Russian exploration and discovery in the Pacific had been confined to the extreme north: the shores of Bering Sea, the Aleutian Islands, and the Alaskan coast to a little south of Sitka. Vitus Bering and Alexei Cherikov in 1728 and 1741, G. A. Sarychev and Joseph Billings (an Englishman in Russian service from 1785 to 1794) had added immensely to the knowledge of this fogbound, tempestuous region. To supply the posts of the fur traders, the early representatives of the Russian-American Company had to haul supplies overland across Siberia. In the course of this work they made important natural history and ethnographic observations, discovered islands, and drew maps of the area. But no Russian ship had ever brought supplies from Europe by sea or sailed across the broad Pacific.

In the reign of Czar Alexander I, 1801–1825, who had a deep interest in the Russian-American Company, it was decided to carry supplies and equipment to the fur posts of Alaska by ships sailing from the Baltic around Cape Horn or the Cape of Good Hope. There were few men in the Russian Navy capable of commanding a ship on such a voyage, and of those few the majority were Englishmen. But there was a close naval connection between the two countries. It had been

Russian policy to send a limited number of promising young officers for training in the British Royal Navy. From this program emerged one man perfectly suited to command such a voyage.

Captain A. J. von Krusenstern, an Estonian, was born in November 1770. He cut his naval teeth fighting in the Royal Navy in the 1790's. Krusenstern sailed in the frigate *Thetis* off North America, toured the seaboard towns of the United States, met President Washington, and visited the West Indies, returning to England in 1796 in the frigate *Cleopatra*. During this time he was involved in several engagements with the French.

Among Krusenstern's preoccupations was the possibility of opening Russian trade in the Far East; he was determined to go to China if possible, although the English officers discouraged the idea. Finally, with two of his fellow officers (one of whom was Urey Lisiansky, later to be his second-in-command), he managed to reach the Cape of Good Hope in the ship of the line *Raisonable*, where he was given permission by his superior commanders to continue to the East Indies in the frigate *Oiseau*. The leaky condition of the *Oiseau* discouraged the other two officers from sailing in her, but Krusenstern stayed on and she luckily reached Calcutta. Krusenstern cruised in the Bay of Bengal and fell seriously ill in Malacca, but nothing deterred him from his goal of reaching Canton. He eventually arrived there in a small merchant vessel and he was immediately impressed with the profits being made by fur-laden ships from the Northwest Coast. He returned to England in an East Indiaman in 1799 and hastened to Russia, where he presented plans to the government for a circumnavigation.

This voyage was intended to prove that it would be far more efficient to supply the fur-trading posts of Alaska by sea than by the tedious overland route across Siberia. After unloading supplies in Alaska, the theory went, the ships would take a cargo of furs to Canton, where they would load oriental goods; they would then return to Russia via the Cape of Good Hope. By this means, necessary heavy goods — anchors and cables, for example — could be freighted by sea. And the relatively quick run from Alaska to Canton meant less loss of and damage to furs than they sustained over the caravan route.

Experienced naval men in Russia did not think that a voyage of this

Admiral von Krusenstern, the first Russian circumnavigator
(*from Ross,* Memoir)

magnitude was possible unless the ships were manned by English sailors. Krusenstern was convinced that it could be accomplished by Russian sailors. The times were unsettled. There were exasperating delays. But after several years the plans were brought before the czar, who was now a member of the Russian-American Company and who, with great enthusiasm, decided to put them into effect at once. Captain Urey Lisiansky, who had trained in the British Navy and journeyed to the Cape with Krusenstern, was sent to England to purchase suitable ships for the voyage. There, in February 1803, he bought and equipped two vessels — *Nadeshda* (Hope) of 450 tons and *Neva* of 370 tons — and brought them to Kronstadt.

Ironically, Krusenstern, who had so strongly urged the dispatch of an expedition of this kind, was now (as a recently married man of some wealth) not anxious to command it. He remained, however, the only Russian officer of sufficient rank with experience in Far Eastern waters. Reluctantly he consented. As his second-in-command and captain of the *Neva*, he chose Captain Lisiansky.

Meanwhile the expedition had taken on greater dimensions. Not only were a year's supplies to be carried to the fur posts, but the voyage was to be one of discovery. Furthermore, the Russian government decided that this would be an appropriate occasion to attempt to open diplomatic relations with Japan by sending an ambassador. There was some reason to be optimistic about this, too. Ten years earlier, in the reign of Catharine II, an embassy to Japan had been well received, and written permission had been sent back at that time for a Russian ship to trade annually at Nagasaki — the same arrangement enjoyed by the Dutch. No opportunity had been convenient to accept the invitation, but this appeared to be a suitable time to take up the option. To defray any loss to the Russian-American Company, Alexander I assumed all expenses of *Nadeshda*. Since the Japanese proposal allowed only one ship to enter Nagasaki Harbor, the two vessels were to separate at the Hawaiian Islands. Lisiansky would proceed directly to the Northwest Coast with the *Neva*, while Krusenstern took the ambassador, M. de Resanoff, and his suite to Japan.

Nadeshda and *Neva* arrived at Kronstadt on June 5, 1803. In early July the czar came to see the ships that would take the Russian flag around the world for the first time. Krusenstern had assembled an excellent assortment of astronomical, hydrographical, and other useful instruments, together with the latest charts and a selected library. Dr. I. Horner, a Swiss, had been employed as astronomer, and two noted naturalists, Councillor W. Tilesius and G. H. von Langsdorff, had been engaged, although they were not yet on board. Among the officers were two who would lead great Russian expeditions in the future — Baron Bellingshausen, fifth lieutenant of *Nadeshda,* and Otto von Kotzebue, cadet. Pilots, physicians, and a surgeon completed the officer complement. In all, including the ambassador and his retinue, there were eighty-five people in *Nadeshda* and fifty-four in *Neva.* It was a well-organized and well-prepared expedition on the successful English model.

Krusenstern sailed from Kronshtadt on August 7, 1803, and arrived ten days later at Copenhagen, where the astronomer and the two naturalists joined the *Nadeshda.* Despite delays caused by re-storing the ships' cargoes, the expedition left in the middle of September. Her next stop was Falmouth, to lay in Irish salt meat, while the astronomer went to London for additional instruments. She sailed from Falmouth October 5.

Nadeshda's crossing of the equator was celebrated by an eleven-gun salute and toasts to the czar; for the first time Russian sailors heard tropical breezes keening through the rigging. After Krusenstern spent several days searching unsuccessfully for the island of Ascension, he anchored at the island of St. Catharine, Brazil, on December 21. Here *Neva* lay for five weeks while her rotten masts were replaced. During this time the ambassador and his suite enjoyed the hospitality of Don José de Carrado, the governor, on shore.

The two ships sailed from St. Catharine on February 4, 1804, after agreeing to rendezvous at Nuku Hiva in the Marquesas should they become separated beyond Cape Horn. They also agreed to spend one day at Easter Island. The Horn was rounded on March 3: perhaps because of their experience rounding Arctic promontories, the Russians did not consider it especially difficult. On the twenty-fourth the two ships became separated in drizzly, foggy weather. Lisiansky set the *Neva's* course for Easter Island, which he sighted on April 16. Because of the squally weather he was unable to land. He did, however, make a survey of the island coast and obtain a few fruits and vegetables from the islanders who swam to one of his boats in Cook's Bay. At the end of five days *Neva* steered for the Marquesas.

Krusenstern also planned to make Easter but was prevented by adverse winds and had to bear away for Nuku Hiva — a circumstance that greatly disappointed the expedition's scientists. He sighted Nuku Hiva on May 5. Coming into Port Anna Maria Harbor (Taiohae), the ship was approached by a canoe flying a white flag. The captain's surmise that this indicated a European on board proved correct: Edward Roberts, an Englishman who had lived nine years in the Marquesas and married a chief's daughter, came to offer his services as an interpreter. His services were invaluable, as events turned out. No sooner was the ship anchored than she was surrounded by Marquesans trading coconuts, bananas, and breadfruit for axes, hatchets, and hoop iron. While the shy, elaborately tatooed chief came on board to receive gifts, about a hundred girls swam around the vessel. (They were eventually allowed to board the ship and spend the night with the sailors.) A second European also turned up. He was a Frenchman, called Jean Baptiste Cabri in Langsdorff's account (Krusenstern calls him Joseph Cabritt), who, it soon became obvious, was the interpreter Roberts's mortal enemy. They had been trying, unsuccessfully, to get each other killed for some time.

Meanwhile, Lisiansky in *Neva* raised the first of the Marquesas, Fatu Hiva, on May 7, and made numerous observations of several islands before rejoining his commander in Anna Maria Bay at Nuku Hiva on May 11. After the *Neva*'s arrival Krusenstern, Lisiansky, and the scientists made an excursion ashore to visit the house of the chief and to call on Roberts and his family.

Substantial amounts of ethnological information were collected at Nuku Hiva and published by Krusenstern, Lisiansky, and Langsdorff in their handsome books. The unusual richness of the information was due to the two Europeans, Roberts and Cabri, who acted as interpreters and informants. Langsdorff remarks that the reason there are occasional differences in information between his book and Krusenstern's is that he collected most of his data from Cabri, whereas Krusenstern relied principally upon Roberts. He further says that he relied more on Cabri for his knowledge of native life, but trusted Roberts more for doing business. Lisiansky, like his commander, received most of his information from Roberts. Each of the three writers dwells upon most aspects of Marquesan life, although they vary in detail and emphasis.

We learn from Lisiansky that the polyandrous life of the Marquesan women did not go unnoticed. "In rich families," Lisiansky wrote, "every woman has two husbands; of whom one may be called the assistant husband. This last, when the other is at home, is nothing more than the head servant of the house; but, in case of absence, exercises all the rights of matrimony, and is also obliged to attend his lady wherever she goes. It happens sometimes, that the subordinate partner is chosen after marriage; but in general two men present themselves to the same woman, who, if she approves their addresses, appoints one for the real husband, and the other as his auxiliary: the auxiliary is generally poor, but handsome and well-made."

The clothing of the Marquesans was minimal, but in its place their entire bodies were embellished with elaborate tattooing. "Among all the known nations of the earth," Langsdorff writes, "none have carried the art of tattooing to so high a degree of perfection as the inhabitants of Washington's Islands. The regular designs with which the bodies of the men of Nukahiwa are punctured from head to foot supplies in some sort the absence of clothing; for, under so warm a heaven, clothing would be insupportable to them. Many people here seek as much to obtain distinction by the symmetry and regularity with which they are tattooed, as among us by the elegant manner in which they are dressed; and although no real elevation of rank is designated by the greater superiority of these decorations, yet as only persons of rank can afford to be at the expence attendant upon any refinement in the ornaments, it does become in fact a badge of distinction."

Marquesans also decorated themselves with the greatest variety of head, ear, and breast ornaments used in Polynesia. Black cock feather headdresses, pearl and tortoise shell crowns, whale tooth and human bone ear ornaments, and finger rings mounted with long tropic bird

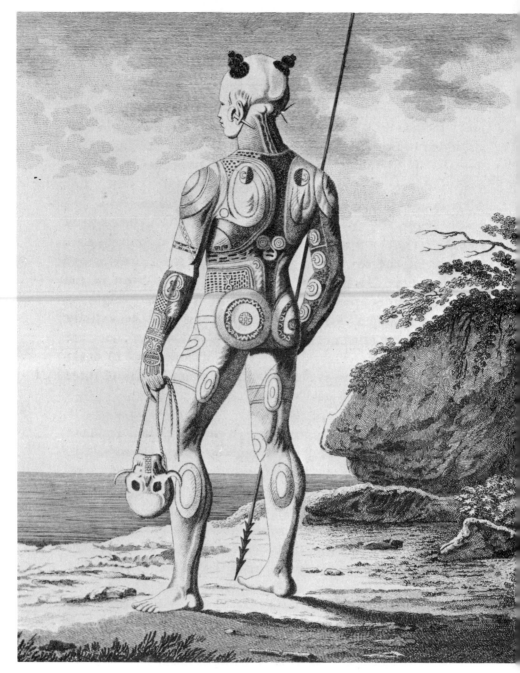

A tattooed Marquesan from Nuku Hiva
(*from Langsdorff*, Voyages and Travels in Various Parts of the World)

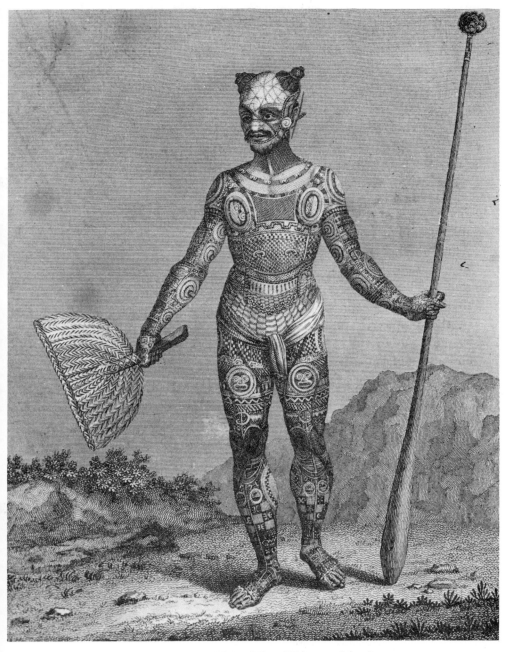

A young man of Nuku Hiva, Marquesas Islands
(*from Langsdorff*, Voyages and Travels in Various Parts of the World)

feathers often accented their already striking appearance. They also showed ingenuity in their hairdressing. As Lisiansky reported, "the men wear their hair in different forms. Some cut it quite close, and shave a little space upwards from behind; others shave half the head lengthwise, leaving the hair long on the other half; and others again shave off all the hair, except a tuft on each side, which is twisted into the shape of horns. Some daub themselves over with yellow paint only, and others with cocoa-nut oil and yellow paint mixed. They all wear ear-rings and necklaces."

Nuku Hiva had been discovered by Ingraham only thirteen years before, in 1791, but in those few years trade for iron with European vessels had nearly eliminated the use of stone tools. "Their tools are extremely simple," Krusenstern writes, "and consist of a pointed stone to bore holes with, and an axe made of a flat black stone. This latter they never use but in the total absence of all European tools; for the smallest piece of iron that they received from us, they instantly fastened to a handle, after sharpening the edge of it."

The Marquesans had a reputation as bloodthirsty warriors. According to Langsdorff, "when they are going publicly to battle, they appear with their hands and feet ornamented with feathers, and a sort of veil on their heads made of cocoa-nut threads woven together, which a stranger would rather suppose to be intended as an article of finery than worn as a part of the accoutrements of war. The most distinguished heroes have then the skull of the enemy formerly slain bound to the hip or the foot." Like all South Sea Islanders, however, they viewed this intertribal or village warfare as more in the nature of a sport or game. One man killed was usually sufficient for an engagement and for a return raid.

But though the casualties were light, the treatment of the unfortunate victim was savage. Langsdorff continues: "The conqueror, or hero, who kills an enemy, has the head as his portion; he cuts it off immediately, parts the skull asunder at the sutures, and swallows the blood and brains upon the spot. The skull is afterwards cleaned from the flesh, ornamented with hog's bristles, and the under jaw fastened to it ingeniously with threads from the cocoa-nut. It then serves at future opportunities as a token of valour, being for that purpose fastened to the cloth which is worn round the waist. During our stay we had several opportunities of examining these skulls."

Religious necessity sometimes caused wars to erupt. It was Lisiansky who spoke of "the most barbarous honours . . . paid here to priests, on their decease. Roberts assured me, that, on the death of a priest, three men must be sacrificed; two of whom are hung up in the burying-ground, while the third is cut to pieces, and eaten by visitors; all but the head, which is placed upon one of the idols. When the flesh of the first two are wasted away, the bones that remain are burnt. The custom of the country requires, that the men destined for sacrifice should belong to some neighbouring nation, and accordingly they are generally stolen."

Fortunately, as in all Polynesia, there was a lighter side of life. "In days of plenty," Langsdorff writes, "these gay people have a variety of amusements of different kinds. At the time of year when the bread-fruit is ripe, so that there is great abundance of it, the chiefs and principal people of the valley make popular festivals: for this purpose they collect swine, cocoa-nuts, bananas, and many kinds of roots, so as to feast the people for some time. The principal of these assemblies are the dancing festivals. . . . The music at these festivals consists of a wild sort of cry, and the beating of several drums, some of them very large. They have the form of an upright cylinder or cask, and are four feet, or four feet and a half high, with a diameter of a foot and a half or two feet; over the top is stretched the skin of a shark: the workmanship is extremely neat."

The popularity of the peculiar Marquesan sport of stilt running is another aspect of island life well documented. It is attested to by the number of beautifully carved Marquesan stilt footrests in museum collections, and described in Langsdorff's eyewitness account. "Next to dancing," Langsdorff says, "one of the favourite amusements among these people is running on stilts, and perhaps no nation upon earth can do this with so much dexterity as the inhabitants of Washington's Islands. At their great public festivals they run in this way for wagers, in which each tries to cross the other, and throw him down; if this be accomplished, the person thrown becomes the laughing-stock of the whole company. We were the more astonished at the dexterity shewn by them as they run on the dancing-place, which, being paved with smooth stones, must greatly increase the difficulty: children are thoroughly habituated to this exercise, even by the time they are eight or ten years old."

Many other aspects of the life and culture of the people of Nuku Hiva are meticulously recorded by the expedition scientists and officers. After the publication of the works on this expedition, the European world had a far more complete picture of the people of the Marquesas Islands than had previously been possible.

On May 17, 1804, Krusenstern, his water and provisions replenished, attempted to leave Nuku Hiva but was blown back into the harbor. The next day the two ships left so precipitously that Cabri was unable to get ashore and was carried from his adopted home and family.*

Off South Point, Hawaii, according to plan, *Nadeshda* and *Neva* separated. Because provisions were scarce and high priced, Krusenstern wasted no time; after three days' cruising along the shore, he put to sea again and steered for Kamchatka, where he arrived at Petropavlovsk Harbor on July 13. Here, too, Krusenstern was anxious to spend as little time as possible, in order to arrive at Nagasaki before the northeast monsoon set in. Nevertheless, he had much to do. After the long voyage it was necessary to repair or replace all sails and rigging, and the entire cargo for Kamchatka (except about 120 tons of iron) was unloaded. Several members of the ambassadorial suite left the expedition, as did Cabri ("the wild Frenchman," as Krusenstern calls him), and set off overland for St. Petersburg. New men were added to the embassy group, along with an honor guard of eight soldiers. Constant fog and drizzle made the stay unpleasant, but everything was finally ready for *Nadeshda* to sail on September 6.

Krusenstern now took the opportunity to look for various islands that had appeared on Spanish and French charts. (He proved to his

---

* This extraordinary individual had a colorful later career. As a tattooed man par excellence, Cabri appeared on the stage in Moscow and St. Petersburg, where he also performed Marquesan dances. Because he had become an expert swimmer in the islands, he was appointed swimming instructor to the marine corps cadets in Kronshtadt, where he settled down. With the passage of time his tales lost nothing in the telling and he came to be regarded as a second Baron Munchausen.

satisfaction that they did not exist.) The passage to Nagasaki was a stormy one, culminating in a typhoon that almost brought an end to the voyage a week before *Nadeshda* arrived at the entrance to Nagasaki Harbor on October 8. She waited in the outer harbor and not until December 22 was *Nadeshda* towed to the inner harbor.

At Nagasaki the Russians spent over six frustrating, even humiliating, months. Week after week interminable negotiations with minor officials on minor matters went on. The Russians were allowed to land only on one tiny bit of rocky shore, which was surrounded by a bamboo fence and watchtowers. Only the ambassador's personal bodyguards were allowed, under protest, to keep their muskets; all other guns and powder were removed from the ship. It was a month before the ambassador and his suite were allowed to move to the large, wellguarded house assigned to them. Except for one meeting with the captains of the two Dutch ships on their annual visit, no contact was allowed between the representatives of the two European nations. About the only good part of *Nadeshda*'s reception was that all of Krusenstern's requests for provisions and material to repair his ship and boats were met promptly and without cost.

Eventually, in early April 1805, the ambassador was granted two interviews with a representative of the Japanese emperor, who promptly refused the letter and presents from the czar, and gave the ambassador a letter saying that never again should a Russian ship come to Japan. The *Nadeshda* was provided with two months' supplies gratis and every assistance was given to hasten her sailing, which took place on April 17. The embassy was a total failure.

As Krusenstern did not want to get back to Kamchatka until the end of July, he took advantage of the time to chart and make observations along the northwest coasts of Honshu and Hokkaido, as well as Sakhalin and some of the Kurile Islands. He even made a landing on the north coast of Hokkaido, much to the consternation of the local Japanese official. Then, after exploring Aniwa Bay at the southern end of Sakhalin and up the east coast as far as Patience Bay, Krusentern returned to Petropavlovsk, where he received the surprising news that Bonaparte had been made emperor of France. At this point Langsdorff left the expedition to visit the Aleutian Islands and Alaska. (He eventually returned to St. Petersburg overland across Siberia.) The ambassador and his suite also left the ship and returned to the capital by the same route.

A case of smallpox on board and contrary winds delayed, until July 5, 1805, Krusenstern's voyage to complete his survey of Sakhalin. When at last the remaining eastern coast of the island was charted, Krusenstern, like Broughton before him, concluded that Sakhalin was a peninsula rather than an island. He returned to Kamchatka and anchored in Petropavlovsk Harbor on August 30. It was now time to prepare the ship for her voyage back to Russia.

During the weeks of refitting the officer of the ship decided to renew the monument to Captain Clerke, who was buried here under a large tree. La Pérouse had replaced the original plaque; now Krusenstern renewed it again. John Webber's original painted escutcheon of Clerke's arms was found in the portico of a house. According to Krusenstern, the inscription that La Pérouse had expressed on a copper plate read:

> At the root of this tree lies the body of
> Captain Charles Clarke
> Who succeeded to the command of His Britannic
> Majesty's ships, the *Resolution* and
> *Discovery*, on the Death of Captain James Cook, who
> was unfortunately killed by the natives
> at an island in the South Sea,
> on the 14th of February in the Year 1779,
> And died at sea of a lingering consumption the
> 22nd August in the same year, aged 38.

In erecting a new monument the grave of Louis de la Croyère, the astronomer who died on Bering's expedition in 1741, was also found beside the grave of Clerke; a tablet to Clerke was placed on the opposite side of the monument. Finally it was recorded on the monument in Russian: "In the first voyage round the world, undertaken by the Russians under command of Captain Krusenstern, the officers of the ship *Nadeshda* erected this monument to the memory of the English Captain Clerke on the 15th September, 1805." The whole monument was surrounded by a ditch and a fence with a locked gate, the key to which was left with the governor.

On October 9, 1805, Krusenstern left Kamchatka for the last time, bound for Macao on his voyage home. On the passage to China Krusenstern endeavored without success to find various mythical islands that had appeared on the earlier charts. There was little time to spare, however, as he was late for his rendezvous with the *Neva* at Macao, and the passage was stormy. Rounding the southern tip of Formosa through Bashi Channel and safely passing a Chinese pirate fleet, he cast anchor in Macao Road in the evening of November 20, 1805. The *Neva* showed up a fortnight later with a rich cargo of furs.

Following the separation of the two ships off South Point, Lisiansky in *Neva* had cruised along Hawaii until he had an opportunity of anchoring in Kealakekua Bay on June 11, 1804. Kamehameha was fighting his war on Oahu, and Young was in command, although not immediately present. A hundred young women swam about the ship offering their favors, but to their astonishment Lisiansky would not allow any of them on board — not from prudishness, but because his crew was free of venereal disease and he did not want it introduced into the ship.

After two days' trading Lisiansky made an excursion ashore, and afterwards called at the chief's house and "the royal temple, which is a small hut, fenced round with paling. Before the entrance stands a statue of a middling size, and further on to the left six large idols are seen. We were not permitted to enter this holy place, in which, we were told, his majesty takes his meals during the taboo days. Near to this was another enclosed spot, containing different idols." Of the great heiau, Lisiansky wrote: "This temple is merely a piece of ground, enclosed chiefly with wooden rails, but here and there with stones, and of the form of an oblong square, the extent of which is about fifty yards by thirty. On the side towards the mountains is a group of fifteen idols, which were wrapped in cloth from the waist downwards; and before them a platform, made of poles is erected, called the place of sacrifice, on which we saw a roasted pig, and some

H

plantains and cocoa-nuts. On the side to the right of the group of
fifteen, are two other statues; further on, on the same side, is an altar
with three more; and on the opposite side another group of three, one
of which is in a state of great decay." Lisiansky was not especially
impressed with this dwelling place of the gods. "These temples," he
writes, "were by no means calculated to excite in the mind of a stranger religious veneration. They are suffered to remain in so neglected
and filthy condition, that, were it not for the statues they might be
taken rather for hog-sties than places of worship."

Another two days and John Young arrived with a present of hogs
and apologies for not showing up sooner, but he had only just heard
of the Russians' coming: the local chief had kept the information and
trade to himself. Now well supplied, Lisiansky sailed on the sixteenth,
and three days later lay anchored in Waimea Bay, Kauai. Four canoes
paddled up. One was manned by five men who "had nothing to sell
but a few spears, and a fan of exquisite beauty, made of the feathers
of the tropic birds, which I obtained for a small knife."

The king of Kauai, anxious to hear of the whereabouts of Kamehameha and his warriors, paid Lisiansky a royal visit. "The King was
waited on in the vessel by one of his subjects, who carried a small
wooden bason [*sic*], a feather fan, and a towel," Lisiansky writes.
"The bason was set round with human teeth, which, I was told afterwards, had belonged to his majesty's deceased friends. It was intended
for the king to spit in; but he did not appear to make much use of it,
for he was continually spitting about the deck without ceremony."

Lisiansky left an interesting account of the islands as they were
when he saw them. He departed for the Northwest Coast on June 20,
1804. He reached Kodiak Island on the tenth of July, and here he was
given a message that the Russian port at Sitka had been taken by the
Indians: he was to proceed there with assistance. He did so, skirmish-
ing with the Indians and burning the fort, which they abandoned. He
returned in November to Kodiak, where he wintered. Leaving Kodiak again on June 14, 1805, he sailed down the coast to Sitka, where
the famous Aleksandr Baranov, superintendent of the Russian-
American Company, came on board. Lisiansky spent the entire sum-

mer on the coast, acquiring furs, surveying, and studying Indian customs. He sailed for Canton in September 1805.

One night in mid-October was nearly disastrous for the *Neva*. Earlier on that day the Russians had seen greater numbers of fish and birds than they had ever observed before — but no land. About ten in the evening *Neva* struck a coral reef. Once guns and other heavy articles were thrown overboard, she floated free, but hardly was she clear when a sudden squall drove her on an even more dangerous bank. By further lightening and great labor, *Neva* was again floated by nightfall of the next day. When Lisiansky landed and examined his newly discovered island, he found it lacked water and was inhabited only by seals, birds, and turtles. The ship's company unanimously agreed to honor their commander by naming the island for him.

As he pushed westward Lisiansky, like Krusenstern, weathered a damaging typhoon, during which part of the cargo of furs was lost from water in the hold. On the evening of December 3, 1805, the *Neva* arrived at Macao, where Krusenstern and Lisiansky were reunited after a separation of nearly eighteen months.

The Chinese were in some confusion as to whether the Russian ships were men-of-war or merchant vessels, and, therefore, whether or not they would be allowed to go to Whampoa. At last, however, both vessels were towed upriver. The furs were disposed of to the hong merchant Lucqua, and teas, chinaware, and nankeens taken on for a return cargo. Further misunderstandings arose with Chinese officials before the ships were allowed to depart. Fortunately Mr. Drummond, the head of the English East India Company factory at Canton, had great influence with the Chinese and cleared up all difficulties for the Russians. Passports were at last issued, and on February 9, 1806, both ships weighed anchor and dropped downriver. They sailed out past Macao on the twelfth.

After keeping company down through the South China Sea and through Sunda Strait, the two ships became separated during the foggy night of April 15. In the south Atlantic on April 26 they sighted each other briefly, but they made their independent ways home where they arrived on August 19, 1806.

This is an important but often neglected expedition in the history of Pacific exploration: it was successful in all its goals except for negotiating a commercial treaty with Japan. Incidentally, because of the British training of both Krusenstern and Lisiansky, who conducted their work on the English model, there was no suffering from scurvy. Krusenstern's surveys in the northwest Pacific, particularly his work on the coasts of Japan, Sakhalin, and the Kuriles, added materially to geographical knowledge of the area. He determined the longitude of Nagasaki for the first time. He made innumerable temperature and salinity tests of ocean waters, accumulated quantities of hydrographical and meteorological data, and observed the direction and velocity of ocean currents. Lisiansky, while separated from his commander, did some creditable charting along the Northwest Coast and discovered Lisiansky Island. The ethnological observations in the works of Krusenstern, Langsdorff, and Lisiansky on the Marquesas and Sandwich islands and on the northern Pacific coasts of Asia and North America are classic. Krusenstern's great atlas is one of the monuments of Pacific cartography.

It is a pleasure to record that Krusenstern, who was in his thirties when he made his circumnavigation, lived a full and distinguished life. He was a man of great kindness and many friendships, and was deeply mourned when he died — on August 24, 1846 in his seventy-fifth year.

13

Americans in Trade and War

YANKEE fur traders to the Northwest Coast in the last fifteen years of the eighteenth century contributed materially to discoveries in that region and to our knowledge of coastal Indian tribes and of the Sandwich Islanders.

The most important Pacific discovery by a Northwest man was made by Joseph Ingraham in the brigantine *Hope* of Boston when he came upon the northern Marquesas. On April 14, 1791, he had touched at Dominica (Hiva Oa) in the Marquesas. Leaving Dominica, he steered north-northwest. On the nineteenth he sighted two islands at 4 P.M. and two more an hour later. Ingraham was unable to find these on any chart, so he assumed that they were a new discovery and named them Washington (Huahuna), Adams (Huapu), Franklin (Motuiti), and Federal (Nuku Hiva). At 6 P.M. the following day he discovered a fifth island, which he called Franklin, and on April twenty-first he found the final two islands of the group, Hancock (Hatutu) and Knox (Eïao).

Ingraham described what happened as the *Hope* drew abreast of Washington: "A canoe in which were three men came towards us; when they were within about 300 yards of us, they laid still a while as it were to view us; frequently calling out *hootah*, which is, *land*, or, *on shore*, in the language of the Sandwich Islands, and I judged theirs was the same. After many gestures and signs of friendship, we prevailed on them to come near enough to receive a few *cents* and nails. They talked to us a great deal but to little purpose, as all we understood was an invitation to go ashore; but as I saw no place proper to anchor in, I bore away more to the W. and they paddled in shore again, giving us a song, as at the Marquesas. . . . The canoe was curved at each extremity, both being alike and resembling the stern of those at the Marquesas."

Ingraham, the first white man to see these craft, further wrote that "the bottom of their canoes is dug out of a single log, and the sides are sewed on with line made of coco nut fibres. At the head and stern they have a small piece of board fixed perpendicularly, which repels the water and prevents it entering the canoe as she goes ahead. The stern is considerably higher than the head, being a curve terminating in a point. The prow is flat and horizontal, so that the water continually washes over it. The single canoes have outriggers, the double ones are lashed together. Their sails are made of mats in a triangular form; but neither canoes nor sails possess that neatness which marks the superior genius of the Sandwich Islanders."

Ingraham had with him a Hawaiian, Opye, who had visited New York and Boston. He attempted to talk with the Marquesans, but, as Ingraham writes, "I was much surprised to find that Opye could not understand the natives of the Marquesas; but still more to find he could converse but very indifferently with the people of his own country. Nay, on our first arrival, I could apparently talk better with them than Opye; for he, by blending the American language with his own, formed a kind of jargon unintelligible to every one but himself; but it soon wore off, and his mother tongue became natural."

Ingraham's was a major discovery and for many years the seven new islands of the northern Marquesas were known as the Washington and Ingraham group.

Further knowledge of the Pacific and its people resulted from the American search for sandalwood and bêche-de-mer, from sealing, from whaling — and from war.* But as the geography of the region became better known, it was the official exploration voyages and sur-

---

* The recent monumental publication *American Activities in the Central Pacific 1790–1870* (Gregg Press, 1966–1967, 7 vols.) is filled with reports of chance discoveries of rocks, reefs, and shoals.

veys sent out by various governments, rather than the mercantile voyages, that cleared up the fine points. Two reasons for the decreasing importance of commercial voyages in this respect were the unreliability of their longitudes and the inaccessibility of the reports of their discoveries. Even stories appearing in the newspapers were apt to have limited currency; more often, a new-found reef was buried in the privately owned and unpublished logbook of the ship that had found it. Accounts of the observations of government expeditions, on the other hand, were usually published — often sumptuously, with folios of magnificent plates, charts, and views.

A few American traders, however, were writers whose books were published. Some even became best sellers. One sometimes suspects, that the stories, being told by sailors, did not lose in the telling. But there is enough straightforward reporting by these men to give their works considerable value. Four such accounts are discussed here. The first two overlap with Krusenstern's Russian expedition.

Amasa Delano was one of the most adventurous of the many seamen whom the town of Duxbury, Massachusetts produced in the late eighteenth century. He was born on February 21, 1763. During the Revolution he served in the army and first went to sea at age fourteen as a privateersman, and then made several voyages to the West Indies and Europe.

On March 28, 1790, Delano sailed from Hancock's Wharf, Boston, for China as second officer of the new ship *Massachusetts*, which, at 800 tons and armed with thirty-six guns, was the largest merchant vessel to sail from Boston up to that time. *Massachusetts* was owned by Samuel Shaw and commanded by Captain Job Prince. With uniformed crew and midshipmen, she was intended to be the Yankee answer to the English East Indiaman. Unfortunately she had no chronometer on board, and not a single officer knew how to take lunar observations. Unfortunately, too, her skipper found it impossible to exchange the *Massachusetts*'s miscellaneous cargo at Batavia for goods salable in China, as he had originally planned. Prince therefore headed for Macao, where, after weathering a typhoon, he arrived September 30. The voyage was a flop and the *Massachusetts* was sold to the

Danes at Canton. Her officers and sailors were forced to find their own passage home or other employment.

For several months Amasa Delano and his younger brother Samuel worked for the Danes repairing a ship damaged in the typhoon. Samuel then shipped for a voyage to the Northwest Coast and Amasa found an opportunity to go on his one real voyage of exploration. The East India Company was fitting out two Bombay Marine snows — the *Panther*, of 200 tons, and the smaller *Endeavour* — for an expedition of discovery and survey: as Delano writes, "to the eastward, to the Pelew Islands, New Guinea, New Holland, the Spice Islands, and others. . . ." The captain was to be John McClure. Delano was taken on as an officer in the *Panther*. The two snows sailed from the island of Taipa on April 27, 1791, bound for the Palaus, where they arrived on June 9.

In the Palaus, where Captain Henry Wilson had been wrecked eight years before, Abba Thulle (his title, actually) was still king. Delano made a hit by building for him a model of Wilson's ship *Antelope*. The Duxbury boy had apparently been on board this vessel once when she was in Boston and named the *Franklin* and, therefore, knew what she looked like.

In this first meeting with Micronesians, Delano was astonished by their fair-play rules of warfare. "Although I was a Christian," he wrote, "and was in the habit of supposing the Christians superior to these pagans in the principles of virtue and benevolence, yet I could not refrain from remonstrating against this conduct on the part of the king. I told him, that Christian nations considered it as within the acknowledged system of lawful and honourable warfare, to use stratagems against enemies, and to fall upon them whenever it was possible, and take them by surprise. He replied, that war was horrid enough when pursued in the most open and magnanimous manner; and that although he thought very highly of the English, still their principles in this respect did not obtain his approbation, and he believed his own mode of warfare more politic as well as more just. He said, that if he were to destroy his enemies when they were asleep, others would have a good reason to retaliate the same base conduct upon his subjects, and thus multiply evils, where regular and open warfare might be the

means of a speedy peace without barbarity. Should he subdue his re-
bellious subjects by stratagem and surprise, they would hate both him
and his measures, and would never be faithful and happy, although
they might fear his power, and unwillingly obey his laws. . . . Christians might learn of Abba Thulle a fair comment upon the best principles of their own religion." Delano made extensive descriptions of the
islanders and their customs, amplifying those of Captain Wilson.*

The *Panther* departed the Palaus on June 27, 1791, and by July 19
was among the islands off New Guinea's western tip. On September
24 she sailed to Amboina, which was one of the two islands (the other
was Banda) where the Dutch allowed nutmeg and clove trees to
grow. Mid-October found the expedition back at the western end of
New Guinea, searching for the strait that was thought to divide the
island. McCluer Gulf, as it is now called, was the obvious place for
such a possibility and Captain McClure surveyed the great bay until
November 3, when he found that it narrowed to a river flowing from
the eastward.

The charting was accomplished amid attentions from curious and
not always friendly Melanesians. "We always kept two wall-pieces
mounted on the tafferel [*sic*]," Delano recounted, "which the commodore had ordered to be cleaned and loaded, after the canoes came in
sight. They had however been poorly cleaned, and one only was
loaded, which was slightly lashed by the breech. While I was unlash-
ing it, with as little motion as possible, so as not to excite suspicion, I
received an arrow in my breast, which was shot with such force, that
although it hit directly upon the bone, it stuck fast. I immediately
drew it out with my hand, and looked for vengeance upon these
false savages from the grape shot and balls with which I knew the wall-
piece was loaded. The natives were only twenty yards distant; but in
attempting to fire among them, the powder flashed in the pan without
effect, and to my great disappointment and vexation, I had only
shown my disposition to hostility, and had killed nobody. A cloud of
arrows now flew at every part of our vessel, at the men in the tops, at

---

* It will be recalled that one of Wilson's men, Madan Blanchard, chose to remain
in the Palau Islands when his companions sailed for Canton in their homemade
craft. He became a powerful and influential man, but his arrogant and unpleasant
behavior, Delano tells us, finally resulted in his death.

H*

those going up, and at all who were upon deck, where it became dangerous to stand. The sails and rigging were bristled with the weapons of the natives. Our people immediately mustered from below, and with the muskets in the tops and on deck, opened a brisk fire upon the canoes, while the *Endeavour* luffed from under our bow, and brought her broadside to bear directly against them. This they could not stand, and very quick dropped astern. They were apparently thrown into a panic after the discharge of our guns, as they all collected together, instead of separating their canoes, and retreating, as they would have done, had they not been unprepared for the effect of our fire arms. Before we began the fight on our part, we saw the negroes shoot several arrows into Nicholson, and hew him down with a large instrument like a butcher's cleaver." *

Following this harrowing experience and satisfied that no strait existed, McClure crossed over to the north Australian coast and was, by late January 1792, at Koepang, Timor. Here he remained until March 24, when he sailed to Benkoelen, a pepper port and the principal English settlement on the Sumatra coast. At Benkoelen the vessels were refitted with new masts and rigging. But the unhealthy climate cost the expedition twenty men, and the *Endeavour* was so overrun with pestiferous wildlife that exceptional measures were necessary. "We sunk the *Endeavour* at this place," Delano writes, "for the purpose of destroying the vermin and insects, with which she was overrun. They consisted of centipedes, scorpions, innumerable black ants, some rats, millions of cockroaches, and some small snakes. The usual mode, in which they get into a ship, is by the wood which is brought on board. Wherever white ants in particular are found, it is a rule never to take in wood. There are two kinds of ants much dreaded by masters of vessels; the black, whose bite is extremely painful, and the white, which will eat the timbers of the ship so as to ruin it in a few months. In half a year, they have succeeded in making the beams fall out of their places, not being able to bear their own weight.

"In sinking the *Endeavour* we scuttled her between wind and water, where she was empty at low tide, and might be easily raised

---

* Dr. Nicholson had been the ship's surgeon. He expired almost instantly.

again by stopping the scuttle. The expedient freed her from the swarms of immigrants, with which she was colonized."

With the vessels seaworthy once more, Delano departed Benkoelen on August 17, arrived at Batavia a month later, and reached the Palaus again on January 20, 1793, after an adventurous passage through the Sulu Sea. Abba Thulle had died since Delano's previous visit and the island government was in disorder. Nevertheless, the two vessels remained a couple of months before they returned to Macao. Then Delano (richer by some £130) set sail for home.

Amasa Delano did not enter Pacific waters again until 1800, having taken his departure from Boston Light on November 10, 1799, in command of the ship *Perseverance* on a sealing voyage. He spent some time along the Chilean coast and at Más Afuera and Juan Fernández. He left descriptions of San Ambrosio and San Félix islands, as well as of Easter Island. (His brother Samuel in the tender *Pilgrim* visited Sala-y-Gomez and named it Pilgrim Island, thinking it to be a new discovery.) Delano made several visits to the Galápagos Islands and was fascinated by the giant tortoises and iguanas so plentiful there. He attempted to introduce three hundred Galápagos tortoises to Más Afuera, but half of the creatures died from overeating after starvation and the remainder were soon killed for food by the sealers. At last, with a cargo of sealskins, he sailed from Galápagos on November 9, 1801. He arrived at Boston, via Canton, Mauritius, and the Cape of Good Hope, on November 1, 1802.

Amasa Delano's third and last long voyage was another sealing venture in the *Perseverance*, with the schooner *Pilgrim*, under brother Samuel, as tender. They sailed from Boston on September 25, 1803, and spent most of the year 1804 sealing around Tasmania, especially in Bass Strait (where *Perseverance* and *Pilgrim* had running fights with Sydney sealers). On October 24 the two vessels departed Tasmania for South America. Late in the same year they were on the Peruvian coast. Then the Galápagos and Sandwich islands. Then Macao. *Perseverance*'s cargo was completed in time for her departure from Macao late in January 1807. The two ships returned safely to Boston on July 26, 1807 after an absence of almost four years.

Like Delano, Captain Edmund Fanning first went to sea at the age of fourteen, coming from cabin boy up through the grades of seaman to second and first mate. In his early years he made many coasting voyages. His introduction to sealing was as first mate of the brig *Betsey*, on a voyage from Stonington to the Falkland Islands in 1792. Five years later he was off on another sealing voyage in the *Betsey* (altered to a ship in the Cape Verde Islands), to the Falklands and around the Horn. *Betsey* reached the great seal island of Más Afuera on January 19, 1798. At Más Afuera the second mate, despite the high surf and a warning by Fanning not to land, found himself unable to resist, when he saw between three and four thousand fur seals sprawled over the rocks, and smashed up his boat. However, with seals in such numbers, *Betsey*'s remaining boats had no difficulty mounting a swift, cruel hunt that produced a full cargo of dried skins by April 2.

Fanning left the island three days later, China bound. He headed first for the Marquesas to get the food and water needed for the long passage. The natives were shy — frightened by the sight of guns — but Fanning established a certain confidence and traded hoop iron, knives, and nails for coconuts, breadfruit, fish, poi, and fish lines. (Curiously enough, looking glasses, toys, and bright buttons were not easy to trade.) After a couple of days the *Betsey* moved over to Tahuata and attempted, unsuccessfully, against a head wind to get into Resolution Bay. When canoes circled the ship, Fanning noted that "the double war canoes had each on its bows, by way of ornament, four human skulls, and as we were examining these, the chiefs offered to part with them in barter; but not being the sort of refreshment for which we were seeking, their proposal in this case was refused." The canoes were dispersed by a rain squall.

About mid-afternoon on the twenty-second, two men in a small canoe were seen hastening towards the ship. As they came alongside, Fanning was astonished to be hailed: "Sir, I am an Englishman, and now call upon [you], as I have come to you, to preserve my life." Fanning took the refugee on board. Only the year before, the Reverend William Pascoe Crook had been landed on Tahuata by Captain James Wilson of the London Missionary ship *Duff*. Now, dressed in a

Sealers at a South Pacific island (from Fanning, Voyage Round the World)

loincloth and tanned nearly as dark as a Marquesan, the same Reverend William Pascoe Crook was fleeing for his life.

Crook's missionary labors had been interrupted by an armed Italian deserter, who made his life miserable. But for the protection of a friendly chief, the clergyman would probably have been killed. Crook revealed that the Italian, with his friends, was plotting to capture the *Betsey* if she came into Resolution Bay. Crook was full of information. He gave Fanning his first awareness of the existence of the northern Marquesas — or Washington Islands — recently discovered by Captain Ingraham. Crook also enlightened Fanning on local customs: "It had been observed," Fanning wrote, "that at the time when the natives were very numerous around the ship, then laying off Resolution Bay, some of them would take fish, from four to six inches in length, just as they were caught, and eat them, beginning by first biting off the head, so on by a mouthful at a time, until the whole was eaten, or they had finished. On mentioning this to Mr. Crook, at the same time asking whether it was not customary for them to cook their fish, he replied, if the fish was large, and their provisions were plenty, they did cook, but owing to their wars, and the attendant famine, their sufferings for provisions, which were now very scarce, had been great; concluding this to be the case with those we had seen; adding, that himself had been driven to so great distress at times for food, as to do the same thing . . . he said it was a fact also, that the natives, when pushed by famine, would make use of all the art they possessed, to get one of their enemies into their hands, for the purposes of food, it being altogether out of his power to put a stop to so inhuman and horrid a custom."

Supplies were not coming in fast enough, so Fanning decided to try the new Washington group. Moving over to Ua Pu on May 23, he got himself in a desperate situation in a bay with no soundings. There was no wind, it was too deep to anchor, and a heavy swell moved the ship ever closer to the head of the bay. Canoes filled with hostile natives had to be frightened off by the firing of a musket. Finally the ship's boats were lowered. It took several hours of backbreaking work to tow the ship out of the bay to safety.

Fanning had better luck at Nuku Hiva. Here Crook was invaluable as an interpreter, water was in abundance, and friendly islanders aided in filling the casks. Arranging to have certain chiefs remain on the ship as hostages, Fanning and Crook went ashore to visit the young king of the island. They took with them a large, bright, homemade medal, suitably inscribed and fitted with a crimson ribbon, to present to the king. At the beach they were escorted by two chieftains, preceded by the regent, to the royal residence. The regent, Fanning later wrote, "wore on this ceremonious occasion, a most beautiful head-dress, made principally from the plumes of the tropic bird, intermixed with the feathers of other birds, the whole making a very splendid article; he had on also a breastplate of the mother-of-pearl shell. Thus arrayed, he took the lead which station he kept during the march. A row of eight chiefs, bearing long, black, and yellow rods, or canes, made of hard wood, having on one end bunches of human hair, marched on each side of us, while close behind us, came six chiefs in double files, and after all these, a vast multitude of the natives came slowly on in double Indian file, paying, however, no very great respect to their dressings."

The royal residence, eighty feet long by twenty wide, was surrounded by a grove of breadfruit trees with coconut palms beyond. Lush grass grew between the building and the ocean. The floor was paved with smooth stones covered with mats, and four rows of stone seats extended the length of the front. On the tier of seats the handsome young king, who was about fourteen years old, sat with the queen mother, a corpulent Polynesian woman, attended by about two hundred ladies. As Fanning describes them, "the ladies, were all arrayed in snow white cloth garments, with turbans of head-dresses of the same stuff, each one also had made all due diligence first to besmear her personage with a mixture of the oil of the cocoa and the perfume of sandal wood: but here, the disagreeable odor of the oil destroyed the fragrance of the sandal wood, and had it not been for the presence in which we found ourselves . . . I do not know how our olfactories could have prevented us from breaking off, and having no further communication with so anti-fragrant a company." In these exotic surroundings the captain from Connecticut presented the homemade medal to the king — a gesture so successful that, what with heat and the excited crowd, he records: "it presents a situation that I have no very great wish ever to be caught in again." Nevertheless, results were immediate. After Fanning returned to the ship, trade was brisker than ever.

The craftsmanship of the Marquesans fascinated the captain: "In the workmanship of their war-clubs, spears, clubs, and paddles, their canoes, as well as their mother-of-pearl fish hooks, and gear, which are all surprisingly neat, and extremely curious, considering they were not made with steel or iron tools, but by their rough implements of stone, shell, or bone, they have shown themselves to be first rate natural mechanics. We purchased many fathoms of their fishing lines and ropes, made from the bark of a tree, both of which were very neat articles; the last we found answered as running rigging very well indeed."

Fanning's stay at Nuku Hiva was, in every respect, a great success. As he himself put it, "the time spent at these most beautiful islands, cannot in any wise be said to have been foolishly squandered." Indeed, although Fanning had offered to take Crook with him to New York if he wished, the people of Nuku Hiva were so friendly that the missionary decided to remain with them when the *Betsey* sailed on May 29, 1798.

Setting a course generally northwesterly, Fanning was somewhat to the south of the track usually followed in a Pacific crossing to China. On June 11 at three o'clock in the morning the lookout at the masthead cried out, "Land ho!" and the officer of the deck replied, "Where away." "Direct ahead, and close aboard," came the answer. With this time-honored exchange, a new island was discovered. The ship, with studdingsails set, was running before the wind. In this perilous situation with breakers close aboard, the light sails were got in, the helm was put down, the yards braced up, and the ship brought on the wind. After an anxious hour the ship got to the northward of the reef, the wind dropped, but a swell carried her past the atoll now called Fanning Island. It was a narrow escape.

Finding a passage into the lagoon on the western side of the island, Fanning hove to outside the lagoon and went ashore. Sharks swarmed in the passage, biting the oars and rudder of the boat as they rowed through. Fish (they proved to be delicious) filled the lagoon. On shore, under a grove of palms, the coconuts lay three feet deep. After a stroll into the interior, Fanning and his boat returned to the ship late in the afternoon, laden with fresh fish and coconuts for all hands.* Fanning left a good description of the pass and anchorage at the island. "There is sufficient depth of water through the passage," he wrote, "for any merchant ship to pass in, and on the inner or bay side is smooth and convenient anchoring, which, together with the abundance of wood and water, the tropical fruits, best of fresh fish, and excellent turtle, here to be obtained, make this a very desirable place, for the refitting of a ship, and refreshing a crew. The soil, generally speaking, as it appeared throughout the interior, was rich and luxuriant."

The next day, June 12, Captain Fanning made a second discovery. "A little before noon," his account runs, "the seaman at the masthead again called out, 'Land ho!' adding, that the same was half a point off the lee-bow. At meridian, this newly discovered island bore west by north four leagues distance. This was of a much greater elevation then Fanning's Island, and was, moreover, covered with plants or grass, presenting to our eyes a beautiful, green, and flourishing appearance. With the unanimous approbation of every individual on board, both officers and seamen, and with feelings of pride for our country, we named this, Washington Island, after President Washington, the father of his country."

Fanning's third discovery came, after he had a premonition involving sleepwalking, during the night of June 14. The *Betsey*, plowing along under full sail, narrowly escaped being wrecked in the mast-

---

* Fanning Island, lying in 159° 20′ west by 3° 50′ north, is uninhabited. Fanning's narrative, however, includes the following incident. Captain Donald MacKay, in a vessel sent out by Captain Fanning a few years after the island's discovery, "being at anchor some weeks at Fanning's Island, while procuring a cargo of beach la mer, turtle shell, &c. for the China market, reported on his return home, that during this stay he frequently walked into the interior, and in one of these walks had come across some heaps of stones, which, to all appearance, from their order and regularity, were thus placed by the hands of men, although from the coat or crust of weather moss with which they were covered, it must have been at some very remote date. Being prompted by curiosity, and a desire for further information upon this subject, he caused one of these piles to be removed, and found it to contain, a foot or two under the surface of the ground, a stone case, filled with ashes, fragments of human bones, stone, shell, and bone tools, various ornaments, spear and arrow heads of bone and stone, &c."

high breakers of Kingman Reef. This was enough of unknown islands for Fanning. He hauled to the northward to get in the known track of the Spanish Manila ships and steered for Tinian. He also claimed, in his book published thirty-five years later, that he discovered Palmyra Island thirty miles southeast of Kingman Reef, but it has been pointed out that this could probably not be possible. It is generally considered that Palmyra was discovered by Captain Sawle on November 7, 1802.*

When Fanning arrived at Tinian on July 14, 1798, he found a wrecked East India Company ship, whose survivors had been living on shore for thirteen months. Fanning took the European members of the crew to Macao, leaving the Lascars to stand by the wreck. The captain's widow and her little girl, accompanied by a maid, created a landing problem for Fanning in China, as European women were not welcome there. The problem was eventually solved, however, and Fanning departed Canton the end of October, doubled the Cape of Good Hope and arrived at New York on April 26, 1799. He netted $52,300 on the voyage.

This was the most important of Fanning's voyages as far as exploration is concerned. His two published books, however, contain numerous valuable observations and descriptions of incidents and island life drawn from his subsequent voyages and from those which he and his partners sent out. In fact, Fanning's most notable contribution to Pacific exploring was his effort to get a United States exploring expedition under way. In 1829 and 1830 he teamed up with Jeremiah N. Reynolds to send Benjamin Pendleton in the brig *Seraph* and Nathaniel B. Palmer in the brig *Annawan* on a combined sealing and exploring expedition to the Antarctic. On February 5, 1821, when the fog lifted, Palmer found himself bracketed by the ships of the Russian exploring expedition under Captain Thaddeus Bellingshausen at Yankee Harbor, Yaroslov Island. Pendleton and Palmer made some important discoveries (which are, however, a part of the study of the Antarctic, rather than the Pacific). In addition, Fanning was indefatigable in his efforts to get a government exploring expedition sent to

---

* Andrew Sharp, *The Discovery of the Pacific Islands* (Oxford, 1960), pp. 182 and 185.

the Pacific, and his efforts ultimately contributed to sending out the Wilkes Expedition.

In 1812 Captain David Porter took the United States frigate *Essex* around the Horn and into the Pacific, where he raided British shipping, especially whalers. Although war and not exploration was the purpose of the voyage, Porter established a base at Port Anna Maria, Nuku Hiva, in October 1813, and during his stay of over a year in these islands, Porter made good use of his time. His relations with the Marquesans was troubled and his treatment of them at times harsh. But his book is one of the primary sources for ethnological information on the Marquesas Islanders, who, incidentally, are among the best documented of any Pacific islanders for the early nineteenth century.

Among Porter's observations is his unique description of the use of the toggle harpoon. The Marquesans were the only Pacific islanders to use this implement, so typical of the far north, although found archaeologically in New Zealand. The Marquesan harpoon, made of human or whale bone, is rare in collections, and of all the early voyagers only Porter records the usual way in which it was employed.

Porter's ethnological observations came to an end when the *Essex* was captured by the British frigate *Phoebe* and sloop of war *Cherub* in a bloody engagement fought in Valparaiso Harbor on March 28, 1814.

Captain Benjamin Morrell, Jr., who was born July 5, 1795, was cast in the same mold as Amasa Delano and Edmund Fanning of a generation earlier. Like them he was a sealer, and like Fanning he was a native of Stonington, Connecticut, where his father was a noted shipbuilder. The Falklands, Cape Horn, Chile, and Más Afuera were his usual stamping grounds. Unfortunately, Morrell's account of his voyages is so filled with exaggeration and mistakes that it is usually ignored. He mixes the experiences of others with his own to such an extent that it is often impossible to tell whose they actually were. And yet, through it all there is a solid base of voyages which he himself made. His book has value — if it is used with caution.

On his first deep-water voyage, in 1812, Morrell was taken prisoner and spent about eight months in a hulk at St. John's, Newfoundland. On his return he declined his father's offer of an education; shipping on a privateer, he was captured a second time and ended up in Dartmoor prison, where he remained until early May of 1815. After his return he made several voyages before the mast and then worked his way up to being a captain.

He made a sealing voyage to the Falklands, the Antarctic, and South America that lasted from June 30, 1822, to May 18, 1824. The Pacific part of this voyage was confined to the western coast of South America and its adjacent islands. One of his observations in 1823 is a description of the sailing balsa rafts on the coast of Peru, made famous by Thor Heyerdahl's *Kon-Tiki* voyage. "The Indians from the continent visit these islands every year," he reported, "for the purpose of sealing and fishing, and gathering eggs, which they sell on the main. They come hither on a kind of raft, well known on this coast by the term *catamaran*. This craft is composed of a number of large logs of a light and buoyant nature, lashed together with cordage made of a certain species of grass. They are generally from twenty to twenty-five feet in length, and sometimes even fifty feet. In the middle there is raised a kind of box, three or four feet in height, for the better security of the mast, which is stepped in the centre bottom log. They have likewise a short bowsprit rigged out forward, to which the tack of the sail is fastened. The latter is nearly square, and bent to a yard, by which it is hoisted to the mast, the halliards being bent on to the yard about one-third of the distance from the forward end; the other end, abaft the mast, being always the longest and the most elevated. The tack of the sail is then hauled down to the extremity of the bowsprit; and the after-leach, or sheet, is hauled aft, in the same manner as a ship's mainsheet. These catamarans are steered with large wide-loomed oars, which are shipped on the after end of the logs, about two feet high. They will beat to windward like a pilot boat, and I have seen them fifty miles from land. This is the only way the Indians transport their produce to market at the different towns along the coast."

Two months after his return in 1824, he sailed again from New York in the schooner *Tartar*. This time, after sealing on the usual grounds, he went to the Sandwich Islands. (It is typical of his exaggeration and unreliability that he remarked that Mauna Kea is perpetually covered with snow.) Without lingering very long he worked his way out through the small barren islands of the Hawaiian chain, hoping to find seals. On July 6, 1825, he landed on Lisiansky Island. Morrell sensibly cautions his readers on the dangers of running through those low, coral-strewn seas. "In crossing between these two latitudes," he says, "a vessel should never run in thick weather; and even in the clearest of weather, they should always have one or two men at the mast-head, day and night. These reefs, which are all formed of coral, may be seen from the mast-head, by their light reflecting on the top of the water, day or night, double the distance that they can be seen from the deck, and in time sufficient to avoid them, if there be a breeze of wind.

"As another reason for keeping a look-out from the mast-head, I would observe, that in running free, or before the wind, a vessel is running on the back of the breakers, the foam of which cannot be seen from the deck until the vessel is close on board of it. But from the mast-head a man can see the foam over the breakers at a sufficient distance to give time enough to tack ship, or haul off. . . ."

Two days after he left Lisiansky Island, Morrell "landed on Pearl and Hermes Island; or, more properly, a group of sand-pits and coral reefs, so called on account of two British whale-ships having been lost here on the same night, one of which was named the Pearl, and the other the Hermes. They both went ashore at nearly the same time, and met their fate about ten miles from each other. These dangerous reefs lie so low, and so near the surface of the water, that the wreck of the Pearl was seen by the man at our mast-head before he discerned the land, which cannot be seen more than six or seven miles from a ship's top." Morrell continues with a description of the harbor, beaches, wildlife, and adjacent water depths of that lonely reef.

Morrell did not cross the Pacific on this voyage, but returned to New York, where he arrived on May 8, 1826, by way of the Galápagos and the Falklands. Then, after making a voyage to Africa and back in the new schooner *Antarctic* in 1828 and 1829, he sailed again in the *Antarctic* on September 2, 1829, accompanied by his wife Abby

Jane. After stopping by Tristan da Cunha, he passed south of the Cape of Good Hope, crossed the Indian Ocean, and, searching for seals, visited Auckland Island (of which he leaves a quite detailed description) south of New Zealand. Still looking for fur seals he visited the Snares, which had been discovered by Vancouver.

At Molyneux's (Waikawa) Harbor the Morrells made the acquaintance of the New Zealand Maori and collected material from them. "Both sexes are clothed alike," Morrell observes, in a somewhat boastful passage, "having a garment made of the silky hemp, which is a natural production of the country. These robes are five feet long, and four broad, and this is their principal manufacture, which is performed by knotting and running the warp on the ground, and working in the filling by hand. Their war mats are made in the same manner, and are sometimes highly ornamented. I brought home a number of them, two of which I presented to the proprietor of Peale's Museum in Broadway, New York, together with a New-Zealand axe made of jasper, and a number of their bows, arrows, spears, war-clubs, paddles, &c. &c. I made a similar donation to Scudder's American Museum, where they have been much admired; and also to the Museum in the city of Albany."

Moving north, the *Antarctic* arrived at the Bay of Islands on January 20, 1830, and left five days later. Captain Morrell had failed to get a cargo of furs; he now decided to go to Manila and attempt to obtain a freight for Europe or America. On this passage Morrell became a self-styled geographical discoverer of the first rank. In rather rapid succession, he claims for himself the discovery in the Carolines of Losap (actually discovered by Louis Isidor Duperrey), which he named Westervelt's Islands; of what is apparently Nama, which he called Bergh's Group; and of Namonuito (according to Duperrey, known as early as 1824), which he named Livingston's Island. When Morrell failed to discover a freight in Manila, he decided to go to the Fijis for bêche-de-mer. This put him on another island-discovering spree, and he reported Skiddy's Shoal on May 8, and then Skiddy's Group (actually Namoluk, discovered by Fedor P. Lütke in 1828), both named by him for Captain William Skiddy of New York.

Also in the Carolines, he landed on Mortlock. For once he did not claim discovery. Rather, he spoke kindly of the natives, who "were all unarmed, and appeared to be very friendly. They are straight, active, muscular, and well-made, with an average height of about five feet nine inches. Most of them wear a tapper round their loins, which reaches about half-way to the knees, and is made from the bark of tree. The married women wear the same modest covering, highly ornamented in front with feathers and shells; but the unmarried women expose all their charms, being, 'When unadorned, adorned the most.' They sport in the surf, as if the water was their natural element."

Next Morrell dropped down to the Solomons, among some islands where unfriendly Melanesians prevented him from getting a cargo of bêche-de-mer, with which the waters abounded. In one attack he lost fourteen of the twenty-one men in his shore party. Fleeing these Massacre Islands,* as he bitterly named them, he returned to Manila on June 26, to ship replacements for his decimated crew. By September 14, he was back at his old anchorage in the Massacre Islands and now he bombarded the village whose inhabitants had killed his crew members. Shortly afterwards, a single painted wretch was seen paddling hurriedly towards the *Antarctic*. It turned out to be Leonard Shaw, the one lucky member of the crew who could run faster than the Solomon Islanders and had been in hiding for three months. Following the chastisement of the natives, Morrell once again started collecting bêche-de-mer, but once again the hostility of the islanders forced him to leave.

On November 3 Morrell sailed west to Buka, New Britain, and New Guinea. He claims to have then discovered a new group of islands abounding in all good things, but since he gives no location it must be considered fictitious. He returned to Manila and there took a freight for Cadiz, Spain. He arrived in New York on August 27, 1831, after a voyage of two years and six days, bringing with him two Melanesians named Sunday and Monday. Morrell's second wife, who ac-

---

* Morrell's Massacre Islands are now called Tauu on the modern charts. They lie about one hundred and twenty miles northeast of Bougainville and consist of about twenty islands on a circular reef. They were first seen by LeMaire, who named them Marcken for an island in the Zuyder Zee. Subsequently they were called Cocos by Captain Wilkinson in 1790 and then Mortlock after that captain who saw them in 1795.

companied him on this voyage of the *Antarctic* published an account of it that complemented Morrell's own.

For all his voyaging, Morrell still wanted so badly to be an explorer that in 1837 he volunteered his services for Dumont d'Urville's second expedition. His services were not accepted. Finally Morrell applied for a job to the leading English owner of whalers, Charles Enderby. Morrell's career was epitomized by Enderby's response: "he had heard so much of him that he did not think fit to enter into any engagement with him." *

* H. R. Mill, *The Siege of the South Pole* (New York, 1905), p. 111.

14

The Later Russian Voyages

CAPTAIN Cook's expeditions had trained a generation of commanders for British exploring and surveying voyages. Krusenstern's circumnavigation developed a similar, albeit lesser, tradition among officers in Russia. A dozen years later Krusenstern was advising His Highness Count Romanzov, Grand Chancellor of the Russian Empire, regarding preparation and plans for an expedition to search for a passage across North America through Bering Strait beyond Cook's farthest penetration. The original plan had called for another Russian expedition, to be commanded by an American, paid for by Count Romanzov, and sent from east to west — historically the traditional direction in which to search for the Northwest Passage. The latter expedition was never dispatched, however. Instead, the decision was to wait until the return of the Pacific expedition before sending out the other; by that time the English were embarking Sir John Ross's first expedition for the same purpose.

Krusenstern had his doubts concerning the discovery of a Northwest Passage, but he considered that the sciences and navigation would reap four important benefits from the search. The first was a matter of national pride — it would be a satisfaction to have made another attempt.* Second, Krusenstern believed that by employing a smaller vessel it would be possible to examine the northern American

* Since the return of Krusenstern's expedition, the only Russian discovery in the Pacific had been that of the uninhabited island found by Captain Mikhail Lazarev, in command of the Russian-American Company ship *Suvorov*, who named it for his ship.

coast in shallow water more closely than Cook had been able to do. Third, he planned to send a party overland to the north, in order to ascertain the extent of the territory. Last (and, as it turned out, the only part of the plan that was fully consummated), he felt that crossing the South Sea twice in two directions "would certainly not a little contribute to enlarge our knowledge of this great ocean, as well as of the inhabitants of the very numerous islands scattered over it; and a rich harvest of natural history was to be expected, as the Count had appointed, besides the ship's surgeon, an able naturalist to accompany the expedition."

Krusenstern's enthusiasm, experience, and knowledge undoubtedly aroused the absorbing interest of the energetic count. The veteran admiral recommended that the expedition be commanded by Lieutenant Otto von Kotzebue, son of the celebrated writer, who had served as a cadet in *Nadeshda* in the voyage of 1803–1806. With the commander selected, Krusenstern and Kotzebue went to Abo in Finland, then part of Sweden, in 1814, to arrange for the construction of a fir-planked vessel of 180 tons. (While small, this was considerably larger than the craft of eighty tons originally planned: quite sensibly, it was decided that the latter would be too tiny to carry sufficient men for defense against South Sea Islanders.) After contracting for the building of the ship they returned home and then, Krusenstern went to London, where he purchased a selection of instruments for astronomical and physical observation, together with charts, maps, surgical instruments, and clothing. Sir John Barrow, secretary of the Admiralty, arranged to have given to the Russians an unsinkable lifeboat recommended by the Admiralty.

On January 22, 1815, Kotzebue left his home town of Revel in Estonia and journeyed overland via St. Petersburg to Abo, walking most of the way. The *Rurick*, as Romanzov had named the new vessel, was launched on May 11 and by the twenty-sixth Kotzebue had her in Revel. In June he took her to Kronshtadt, where the party was joined by the scientific supernumeraries (two naturalists, Adelbert von Chamisso of Berlin and a Dane, Martin von Wormskiold, who volunteered his services, came on board at Copenhagen but left the expedition at Kamchatka). Louis Choris, another volunteer and a fortuitous one, was the artist of the expedition. Ivan Escholtz, the ship's surgeon and an entomologist, made up the fourth member of the scientific party.

As plans developed, Kotzbue decided to abandon any attempt at land exploration in America. However, the South Sea aspect of the voyage was more strongly stressed, even though, as Krusenstern wrote in his introduction to Kotzebue's work: "important discoveries cannot now be made; here and there an island, or group of islands, which is unexpectedly met with, is all that the most fortunate discoverer can now hope for; yet still a new voyage to the South Sea appears to me to be important; there are still so many deficiences to fill up, so many errors to correct. Such a voyage must be considered as the concluding expedition to the South Sea, for the revision of all preceding discoveries."

As an example of the sort of work that the expedition might accomplish, Krusenstern noted that while the Caroline, Solomon, and Louisiade islands were all generally known, they were imperfectly explored. The rigorous scientific basis for the expedition was summed up by Dr. Horner, scientific advisor to the expedition, with the admonition "to measure every thing measurable." He emphasized the importance of accuracy in determining latitude and longitude, the surveying of coasts, the sketching of land profiles, maintaining magnetic records of the dipping needle, and observations on tides, currents, and waves.

The *Rurick* sailed from Kronshtadt on July 30, 1815, and arrived on August 9 at Copenhagen, where the two naturalists, Chamisso and Wormskiold, joined the expedition. Eight days later *Rurick* began a tedious passage to Plymouth, where she dropped anchor on September 1. Here Kotzebue sought the advice, willingly given, of Mr. Whidbey, Vancouver's experienced surveyor, who was then building the Plymouth breakwater. Kotzebue also corrected his chronometers and picked up the thirty-foot unsinkable lifeboat that Sir John Barrow had had especially constructed for the Russians. It was an innovation that turned out to be so big and heavy that it was abandoned in Kamchatka. Finally, on October 4, Kotzebue left Plymouth for the Pacific, by way of Cape Horn.

As *Rurick* neared the tempestuous cape, Kotzebue escaped drowning by a miracle. "I was lying on a hen-coop," he wrote afterwards, "the storm raging round me, without suspecting any danger, when this wave suddenly seized me and my couch, and swept us together overboard. I must have been inevitably lost, had not some ropes, which were fastened to the ship, fallen down with me, and caught me as it were in a net. I was stunned, and did not recover my senses till the cable threatened to break, and just gave me time to swing myself on the deck. The coop, with forty fowls, on which I had been lying, together with my pillow, swam in the sea past the ship: I thanked God for my safe deliverance, and patiently bore the loss of the roast fowls, upon which we had all reckoned, for those that were in both the other coops also perished by the violence of the waves."

The *Rurick* arrived at Concepción Bay, Chile, in mid-February 1816, and sailed for Kamchatka the following month. On March 28 she reached Easter Island, where shy natives traded fruit and vegetables for hoop iron. When the Russians attempted a landing, however, they were pelted with stones, and it took a few musket shots before they gained the beach. Nor was the visit ashore a friendly one. "Scarcely had the savages perceived [that we had landed]," Kotzebue writes, "when they surrounded us with still more importunity. They had painted their faces red, white, and black, which gave them a terrific appearance, danced with the most ridiculous motions, and contortions of the body, making such a terrible noise, that we were obliged to halloo in each other's ears to understand what we said." When Kotzebue felt a stone strike his hat, he once more resorted to gunfire to force the Easter Islanders to retreat. Even then, the islanders' hostility prevented further exploring, and a hail of stones attended the premature Russian departure.

The voyage continued towards Kamchatka through the Tuamotus, and Penrhyn was sighted on April 30. The *Rurick* next sailed on to the Radak chain of the Marshalls, and past Utirik and Taka atolls, which Kotzebue, believing he had made a new discovery, named Kutusov and Suvarov.* (Actually they were the Button Islands of Gilbert and Marshall.)

---

* An entirely different island from the Suvorov discovered by Lazarev in 1814, which is still on the charts.

Interior of a house in the Radack chain, Marshall Islands (Kotzebue, Voyage of Discovery, Vol. II)

Kotzebue pushed on to Kamchatka, in order to make his summer voyage into the Arctic. In mid-July, he passed through Bering Strait and conducted a notable exploration of Kotzebue Sound, Alaska. He then sailed down the Alaskan and Northwest Coast to California and entered the Golden Gate on October 2, 1816, anchoring in San Francisco Bay, where the *Rurick* remained for the rest of the month. The Spaniards gave a warm welcome to the Russians and provided for them as well as was possible from their meager supplies.

About November first, Kotzebue departed for the Sandwich Islands. He sighted Hawaii three weeks later, and on the twenty-fourth he reached Kealakekua Bay. Here Kotzebue landed at the invitation of King Kamehameha, who met him at the shore and escorted the Russian commander to his "straw palace." * Kotzebue was disturbed to hear from the Hawaiian monarch of the activities of Georg Anton Schaffer, the conniving German who worked for Aleksandr Baranov and who was endeavoring to establish Russian sovereignty over Kauai in order to ingratiate himself with Alexander I. Kotzebue assured Kamehameha that the Czar was unaware of Schaffer's intrigues.†

Kamehameha presented the Russian explorer with a brilliant feather cape and entertained him in the most lavish Hawaiian manner possible. Furthermore, it was directed by Kamehameha that the astonished Russian sailors should be treated in the same manner. "After we had dined," Kotzebue wrote, "and left the house, the king was very anxious that my rowers should be well entertained; he gave orders to this effect, to one of the chiefs, and the table was immediately laid out again. They were obliged to sit down, and were served with the same attention as had been shown us. The sailors were certainly never in their lives treated with so much ceremony; for each of them had, like us, a Kanaka standing behind him, with a tuft of feathers to drive away the flies." Following this repast, Kotzebue accompanied the king to a morai: "While the king is gone into the morai [temple] nobody is

---

* Choris's famous portrait of the king corresponds exactly to his commander's description: "Tamaahmaah's dress, which consisted of a white shirt, blue pantaloons, and a red waistcoat, and a coloured neckcloth, surprised me very much for I had formed very different notions of the royal attire."

† For a full account of this episode see Richard A. Pierce, *Russia's Hawaiian Adventure, 1815–1817* (Berkeley and Los Angeles, 1965).

allowed to enter; and during that time we admired the colossal idols, cut in wood and representing the most hideous caricatures."

Royal orders were given for Kotzebue to receive forty-three hogs, as well as fowls, geese, fruit, and all the wood he wanted at Oahu, whither the *Rurick* sailed on November 25, On her arrival she was towed into Honolulu Harbor by eight double canoes, propelled by sixteen to twenty paddlers each. Honolulu was now the busiest place in the islands, and Kotzebue met all of the Hawaiian, American, and European dignitaries who resided there. He also had his cold northern blood warmed by the sight of a Hawaiian hula. Kotzebue's description of the hula deserves to be quoted in full.

"We took our seat," he writes, "and the dance immediately commenced. The musicians were four men, who beat with small sticks on a hollow gourd, which produced a noise, that might serve for time to the song. Three dancers by profession, who go from one island to another, and show themselves for money, now stepped forward, entirely naked, except bracelets of hogs' tusks, and half armour for the feet, made of dog's teeth. They placed themselves opposite to us, close to each other; and expressed the words to the accompanying song, by the skilful movements of the whole body. . . . The spectators were enraptured, and at every pause, entered the circle to make presents to the dancers; and, in the end, in their enthusiasm, gave even their silk handkerchiefs. After the men had sufficiently distinguished themselves, the scene changed, and a number of young girls arranged themselves in three rows. Their heads and shoulders were tastefully ornamented with wreaths of flowers; the neck adorned with pearls, and various fantastic things; besides this, they had only the lower part of their body covered with a coloured tapa. This group had a very pleasing effect, as they accompanied the monotonous music with graceful movements. The last rows conformed to the first, and always imitated the movements of the foremost dancers. The whole bore the impression of pure nature, and delighted me more than a skilfully executed European ballet."

Following a walking excursion from Honolulu nearly to Pearl Harbor, Kotzebue reboarded his ship and left Oahu, on December 14, 1816, bound for the Marshalls. After searching without success for

Cornwallis Island,* Kotzebue sighted a low coral atoll on January 1, 1817, and named it New Year's Day Island — a name now shortened to New Year Island. (New Year Island, or Miadi, is in the Radak chain of the Marshalls.) Seven canoes with hulls built of very small boards, each manned by a crew of five or six tall, well-shaped, tattooed men with bright brown eyes and aquiline noses, approached the ship that New Year's Day, and since the sea was calm, Kotzebue sent two armed boats ashore under First Lieutenant Gleb Simonovich Schischmarev, accompanied by Choris, the artist. A brisk barter in coconuts, fruit, and native manufactures brought an ever increasing and unruly crowd of about two hundred Marshallese, who prevented a proper landing.

Sailing westerly, Kotzebue raised a chain of small coral islands — the substantial atoll of Wotje — which he named Romanzov (Rumiantsov) Islands. Although he had to spend a risky night moored to the reef while the trade wind kept his ship off, he eventually found an entrance on the southeast (it is still called Rurick Pass) and got his ship into the great lagoon. This lagoon he called Christmas Harbor, for here the crew of the *Rurick* celebrated the holiday in the old style on January 6, 1817.

The islet itself he named Goat Island, after a billy goat released there that terrified the inhabitants. The thirteen Goat Islanders, the only inhabitants, were friendly and the "men were painted with different squares of a dark blue colour." From another islet, meanwhile, a thirty-foot sailing canoe arrived at the ship with twenty-five men tattooed differently from the Goat Island inhabitants.

After a reconnaissance of the lagoon by boat, the *Rurick* was moved over to Otdia Island. During the nearly three weeks' stay at Otdia, Kotzebue and his men made a good survey of Wotje, which was calculated to consist of sixty-five islets around the reef. Kotzebue subsequently began a leisurely cruise south through the Radak chain. In succession he named Erikub Atoll Tschitschagov Island for the Russian Minister of Marine, Maloelap Atoll for the Russian General Saltikov, and Aur Atoll after the Russian Minister of Naval Affairs,

---

* Now called Johnston Island for Charles James Johnston, who discovered it in 1807 while in command of the ship *Cornwallis*.

Captain Kotzebue's reception in the Marshall Islands (Kotzebue, A New Voyage Round the World, Vol. I)

Traversé. All are now known by their Marshallese and not their Russian names. At Aur he found two Caroline Islanders who had been blown from Ulle, fifteen hundred miles to the west, about three years before. One of the Carolinians, named Kadu, announced his determination to stay with the *Rurick:* a piece of good fortune that enabled Kotzebue to learn of other islands, including the Ralik chain. In fact, it was from these two islanders that he learned for the first time of the names Radak and Ralik for the windward and leeward chains of the Marshalls.

Kotzebue left the islands in late March and headed for Unalaska, surviving on April 13 a storm of hurricane force, with hail, snow, rain, and gigantic waves, during which *Rurick*'s bowsprit was broken and she suffered much other damage. Once *Rurick* was repaired, she spent the summer exploring along the Alaskan coast and St. Lawrence Island. But with the coming of fall she turned south again and on September 26 sighted lofty Mauna Kea.

Although this was to be a brief visit, the Hawaiian king granted Kotzebue the same amount of provisions as before, and even sent a chief along to Oahu on the *Rurick* to see that his orders were carried out. Already Honolulu Harbor was becoming a crossroads of the Pacific. Eight ships were there — six American, one Hawaiian, and a Russian-American Company vessel on the beach.

The *Rurick* sailed from Oahu on October 14, bound home, and doubled the Cape of Good Hope on March 29, 1818. At Table Bay, Kotzebue met and exchanged visits with Captain Louis de Freycinet in the corvette *Uranie*, on a French expedition to the Pacific. After various stops on a generally uneventful voyage, Kotzebue arrived at Revel on July 23, and on August 8 anchored in the Neva opposite Count Romanzov's palace.

It must have been a source of great satisfaction to Kotzebue to realize that his expedition had contributed more to the knowledge of the Pacific than any other expedition since Cook's. To Kotzebue's own accomplishments must be added the work of the talented Chamisso and Choris, both of whom published extensively on the voyage.*

* Some years ago Choris's original watercolors turned up in a London shop and they are now in the collections of California and Honolulu institutions.

Training on the Krusenstern circumnavigation also produced the commander of another Russian expedition, one that was to make significant additions to our knowledge of the Antarctic regions as well as of the central Pacific. This expedition was not, however, well known to English historians until 1945, when the Hakluyt Society published a translation of the original Russian account.

The story properly begins in March 1819, when Czar Alexander I announced that twin naval expeditions, each consisting of two vessels, would be dispatched to explore the polar regions. This tremendous effort in exploration had actually been promoted by the Minister of Naval Affairs, the Marquis de Traversé.

The northern expedition, or Second Squadron as it was called, consisting of the corvette *Otkryitie* (Discovery) and the *Blagonamyerenny* (Well-Intentioned) under Commander Vasilev, was to make yet another search for the Northwest Passage (that had eluded Kotzebue.) The southern expedition, or First Squadron, the one that concerns us here, was to make a survey of the higher latitudes of the Antarctic seas. For this the sloop *Vostok* (East) and the transport *Mirnyi* (Peaceful) were selected.

Command of the First Squadron was originally offered to a Captain Ratmanov, a veteran of Krusenstern's voyage. However, he was in poor health, and the choice fell upon another of Krusenstern's old shipmates, Thaddeus Bellingshausen, an excellent seaman then commanding the frigate *Flora* in the Black Sea. This taciturn Estonian hastened to St. Petersburg to learn that he had been selected to command the expedition "to carry out a voyage of discovery in the higher southern latitudes, and to circumnavigate the ice-belt of the southern Polar circle."

At St. Petersburg Bellingshausen found his ships. The 129-foot sloop of war *Vostok* was an almost new vessel, built of softwood that had been reinforced and copper-sheathed for the voyage. She was selected because her build and dimensions were identical with those of the sloop *Kamchatka*, in which Captain V. M. Golovnin made a successful but uneventful circumnavigation in 1817–1819, Bellingshausen at once saw that the *Vostok* was badly oversparred for the tumultuous seas she was to sail, and ordered her rig considerably reduced. *Mirnyi* (the converted merchantman *Ladoga*), although nearly the same size as *Vostok*, was of much greater depth and was a clumsy, slow-sailing workhorse. She could never have kept up with the *Vostok* had not Bellingshausen kept his flagship under reduced sail for most of the voyage. *Mirnyi* was commanded by Lieutenant Mikhail Lazarev, an affable and competent officer who had served for four years in the English Navy. Professor Ivan Simanov of Kazan University was appointed the astronomer, and Paul Mikhailov of the Imperial Academy of Fine Arts the artist, of the expedition. (Two Germans, who were employed as naturalists, unfortunately failed to meet their rendezvous at Copenhagen. Hence the elaborate reports on natural history and native races that had been anticipated never materialized.)

In all, 117 men sailed on *Vostok* and 72 on *Mirnyi*. Both naval and civilian personnel were liberally rewarded for their dangerous undertaking and the ships were well equipped and supplied. Silver and bronze medals, with Czar Alexander I on the obverse and the names of the sloops with the date 1819 on the reverse, were specially struck at the St. Petersburg Mint for presentation to important personages and for distribution at newly discovered islands. A large and varied supply of trade goods was stowed aboard to barter for fresh provisions and to cultivate native goodwill. Bellingshausen was given general instructions for ports of call but he was also given wide latitude to use his own discretion and make his own decisions, always bearing in mind that the principal object of the expedition was "exploration in the closest possible vicinity to the South Pole." The orders were sensible and humane.

From inception to readiness of the expedition, Bellingshausen worked with great dispatch. On July 4, 1819, he sailed from Kronshtadt (in company with the Second Squadron) with the cheers of enthusiastic spectators ringing in his ears.*

Vostok and *Mirnyi* spent seven days at Copenhagen, laying in additional supplies and equipment and attempting to find volunteer naturalists to replace the dilatory Germans. On June 28 the Russians an-

---

* The dates in this narrative are Old Style and have been retained. The Russians did not adopt the Gregorian Calendar until 1923. Twelve days must be added for the corresponding English date.

chored in Portsmouth Roadstead, where to their delight they met their compatriots in the sloop *Kamchatka*, under Captain V. M. Golovnin, returning from the voyage of 1817–1819 around the world.* From Portsmouth, where the *Vostok* and *Mirnyi* lay, Bellingshausen and Lazarev went to London for the books, charts, and nautical and other instruments required for the voyage. In London, Sir Joseph Banks endeavored to find a naturalist for them, but without luck. The captains returned to their ships on August 10, although their instruments did not show up until ten days later. They did not sail from Portsmouth until August 26, 1819.

The real work of the expedition began three months later at South Georgia, where Bellingshausen surveyed the part of the coast that had not been charted by Cook forty-four years before; in effect, he joined his survey with that of his great predecessor. Bellingshausen followed this up with a survey of the South Shetlands. Then he pushed south into the ice. On January 18, 1820, the tough old *Mirnyi* bounced off a heavy ice floe, fortunately with little damage. She was constantly slowing up the voyage and the *Vostok* was always under shortened sail to allow her consort to keep up.

Bellingshausen continued his explorations along the ice in high latitudes until supplies began to get low and the winter season approached. Then, after conferring with Captain Lazarev in the shadow of a 400-foot-high iceberg, he decided to go to Port Jackson for fresh provisions and wood. The ships separated and the *Vostok* (cheered by the warm New South Wales weather and green shores) arrived off that port late in the afternoon of March 29. The next day, anchored in Sydney Cove, the weary sailors could begin to relax.

Bellingshausen lost no time paying his respects to Governor Lachlan Macquarie. Soon he also got his first sight of Australian aborigines. "About midday," he relates, "a family of natives arrived on board, in a dirty European boat from the north shore. They spoke a little broken English bowed very low to the Europeans, and made grimaces to express their delight. One of them wore the worn-out trousers of a Brit-

* Golovnin had made an earlier circumnavigation in 1807–1809, which yielded little in the way of scientific results. In 1811 he did surveying in the Bering Sea area on both the Asia and American coasts and drew a more accurate map of the Kurile Islands than had been done previously.

ish sailor, decorated with red clay and mud, on his neck he wore a copper plate, in the shape of a crescent moon, with the inscription:

BOONGAREE
CHIEF OF THE
BROKEN — BAY — TRIBE
1815

This plate was attached to a strong copper chain. From this inscription we knew who our guest was, and he added that he had accompanied Captain Flinders and Lieutenant King in their voyages off the coast of New Holland. Boongaree presented his wife Matora to us. She was partially attired in a dress of English frieze, and had adorned her head with kangaroo teeth. A daughter was almost half white, handsome in face and figure, which gave evidence of European blood, the son, like his father, was dark; all were naked. Boongaree, pointing to his companions, said, 'These are my people.' Then pointing to the whole north shore, 'This is my Land.' I ordered that they should be given a glass of grog each and of sugar and butter as much as they wished. Seeing this liberality they begged for tobacco, old clothes and ropes, and whatever they happened to notice. I ordered him to be given some Brazilian tobacco twist, and told him that they would receive clothes and ropes if they brought fish, live birds, a kangaroo and other animals. His reply to all this was 'Oh yes, yes.' They left the ship half drunk, shouting horribly. Matora, who called herself 'Queen,' behaved with even greater vulgarity than the other guests."

In early April, the lumbering *Mirnyi* finally beat up the bay to join *Vostok*, and on May 8, 1820, the two ships weighed anchor, bound for New Zealand.

At Queen Charlotte Sound, on May twenty-seventh, twenty-three of the inhabitants came out to the ships in two canoes. Bellingshausen bought their fish and "specimens of their handiwork," and invited the chief to dine. In return, the Maoris sang songs for the sailors and performed a war dance. Bellingshausen, Lazarev, the artist Paul Mikhailov, and the astronomer Ivan Simanov then visited a local village. They all admired the chief's house, with its heavy posts carved into grotesque, red-painted human figures, its fine mats, and weapons hanging from the walls. As the party returned to their landing, sailors bartered nails for beautifully made and highly polished weapons of hard wood, whalebone, and greenstone. Among the curios eagerly traded and acquired, one stood out. "When we were saying good-bye," Bellingshausen says, "the old man detained me. By his orders, his men brought a mace 8 feet in length, the top being halbert-shaped, carved and inlaid with shells like eyes, the lower end being shaped like a narrow paddle. I thought that he was making me a present of the mace, but on my accepting it and being about to place it in the cutter, the old man seized it with both hands and I then understood that he was not giving it to me but wished to exchange it. To gratify him I gave him two arsheens [1½ yards] of red cloth; he was very pleased with his profitable deal and told all his fellow natives about it at the top of his voice." Bellingshausen's descriptions of the dress, ornaments, and canoes of the New Zealanders, it should be added, were thorough, and he is constantly comparing his own observations with those of his predecessor and hero, the immortal Cook.

The expedition sailed from Cook Strait on June 9, 1820, and twenty days later sighted Rapa, which Vancouver had discovered in 1791. Immediately, fifteen canoe loads of Polynesians, offering little to trade except shellfish, taro, and poi, surrounded the ships, and a chief cautiously ventured on board the *Vostok*. The canoes were back the next morning, their occupants still consumed with wonder. As Bellingshausen described it, "the islanders were astonished at the size of the ship and all the things, which were quite new to them. One measured the length of the ship on the upper deck with the span of his arms, by lying down on the deck each time to stretch out his arms to their full extent. He also measured the width of the quarter-deck. Our guests did not leave the ship by the companion ladder but dived straight into the water and then climbed into their canoes."

Bellingshausen spent the month of July sailing through the Tuamotus, where he surveyed numerous islands and made several new discoveries. The first of his discoveries in the Tuamotus was on July 10, when he came upon Angatau and named it Count Arakscheev Island. Two days later he came upon two islands originally discovered by Queirós in 1606 — Takume and Raroia (where the raft *Kon-Tiki* came ashore on Heyerdahl's famous voyage from Peru). These he named for two Russian princes. The coral reef and violent surf prevented a landing, but one enterprising native managed to board the ship and was immediately dressed up in the red uniform of a Russian Imperial Guardsman and had a medal hung around his neck. When he rubbed noses with the officers, the treatment so delighted him that he returned later with "a young woman, some dried cuttle-fish and some shelled mussels, dried and strung on to bark fibre. It is probable that this food which he brought from the island represents the object of their trading and their roamings over the inhabited islands. We invited the woman into the cabin, I made her a present of a mirror, ear-rings, a ring and a piece of red cloth, which she wrapped round her body from the waist to the knee; her own fine matting plaited skilfully of grass she left with us, and it is now kept in the Museum of the Imperial Admiralty Department among the rarities."

On the fourteenth Bellingshausen discovered Nihiru and Taenga. (He called the latter Lieutenant-General Yermolov Island, with that ear for euphony so acute among Russian explorers.) The following day he sighted Makemo Island, originally discovered by Captain John Buyers in the *Margaret* in 1803, and that same afternoon the well-wooded northern shore of Tepoto came into view. This was another new discovery and Bellingshausen named it General Raevski Island; it is southernmost of three islands still known as the Raevski group. Then, during the next twenty-four hours, he sighted in quick succession Tahanea and Faaite, and gave them Russian names (although they had been seen by earlier navigators). Fakarava was an important new discovery. He correctly identified Toau and Kaukura as two of Cook's Pallisers. He discovered tiny Niau, calling it Greig Island after the vice-admiral under whom he had served in the Black Sea; he sailed along a whole chain of the Tuamotus and called them "The Russian Islands" — but the name never stuck.

Bellingshausen now decided to go to Tahiti in order to get fresh provisions and especially to check his chronometers at Point Venus, a place whose longitude was well established. This would enable him to ascertain the accuracy of the longitudes that he had established for the various islands just visited and discovered. Stopping at Makatéa with its high pockmarked cliffs and unfathomable water, he picked up four Polynesian castaways from Anaa, two hundred miles to the southeast. These unfortunates had originally been ten in number but the others were killed by castaways from another island with whom they had been at war.

Like all sailors after a long voyage, Bellingshausen appreciated the amenities of Tahiti, which he sighted on July twenty-first, and Matavai Bay, whither he was led by one of King Pomare's pilots. "My pen," Bellingshausen said, "is wholly unequal to the task of expressing a sailor's pleasure on finding himself at anchor after a long weary voyage, in a spot which needs only to be seen to fire the imagination. We were almost surrounded by land. The level green plain of Matavai, with the clumps of cocoa-palms, orange and lemon-trees, extending to the very shore; the tall breadfruit trees towering above the cocoa-nut palms; behind them to the right the high mountains and deep valleys of Otahiti Island covered with woods; along the sandy beach some little houses — all this together formed an enchanting view."

Henry Nott, an English bricklayer turned missionary, who had been left in Tahiti by the *Duff* in 1797, came on board at this point and informed Bellingshausen that he would be visited by the king. And, indeed, His Majesty's large canoe shortly came into view, bearing Pomare, his queen, a ten-year-old daughter, and other women. "We were, all of us, anxious to see him," Bellingshausen writes, "and all crowded to the gangway, with exclamations of 'Here he comes.' The double canoe, in which the King was seated, was approaching slowly; on the horizontal, projecting fore part of the canoe a seat resembling a drake's bill was errected on which the King was seated. Over a white calico shirt he wore a piece of white cloth with an opening in it large enough to pass it over the head, with the points hanging down before and behind. The lower part of the body was draped in another piece of white calico, from his belt down to his very feet. His hair was cropped close in front, but from the crown of his head down to the nape he wore it twisted in a drooping tress. His face was dark, with deep-set black eyes under thick black eyebrows; he had thick lips, and a black moustache, and his enormous stature gave him a really royal appearance."

The Russian commander entertained the royal family in the cabin, with Nott acting as interpreter. Then, as the party ascended to the deck, an ear-shattering salute was fired in the king's honor. Pomare reciprocated with a gift of four hogs and a canoe load of vegetables. Bellingshausen later returned the king's visit, and while ashore met Nott's English wife. (The Notts had become completely acclimated to Tahiti — where they are now buried — and neither had any desire to return to England.) During this visit, the king secretly took Bellingshausen into his bedroom and closed the door, so that the missionary could not see what was going on. "From the box," Bellingshausen records, "he took an inkstand, a pen and a few scraps of paper, which he gave to me, asking me to write in Russian that the bearer of the note should be given a bottle of rum. I wrote to the effect that he should be given three bottles of rum and six bottles of Teneriffe wine."

Until July 27, when the Russians sailed, the king and chiefs spent much time on the ships, drinking rum and admiring the skyrockets set off for their amusement. Before leaving, Bellingshausen distributed silver medals with the head of Czar Alexander I to the chiefs and similar bronze ones to the commoners. His notes on Tahiti are extensive, and summarizing his reasons for stopping there, he writes: "Although our stay at Otahiti had been short, it had been a great help to us in many ways. My chief reason for touching at this island had been the large number of coral islands which we had discovered and whose longitudes had to be verified by reference to Venus Point so as to establish for certain the geographical position of this archipelago, so full of dangers to the navigator."

Sailing north from Tahiti, Bellingshausen discovered Matahiva. (He named it Lazareff Island.) On August 1 he discovered and surveyed uninhabited Vostok Island. Turning westerly, he arrived off Rakahanga and named it Grand Duke Alexander Island, while the islanders, armed with spears and clubs, lined the shore.

On August 11 Bellingshausen set his course for Port Jackson and the next day sighted Byron's Danger Island (or Pukapuka, as it is now known). He observed the high northern shore of Vavau on the sixteenth and three days later discovered Tuvana-i-Tholo and Tuvana-i-

Ra at the southern extremity of the Lau group of the Fijis, naming them Mikhailov and Simoniv islands. His last discovery of a tropical Pacific island came in the night of August 20, when he nearly ran on the reef at Ono-i-Lau (which may have been seen by the *Bounty* mutineers).

Bellingshausen's Pacific islands exploration was substantially completed when, after anchoring in Sydney Cove September ninth, he sailed for a second swing to the Antarctic on October 30, 1820, and sighted the beautifully green Macquarie Island, its shore covered with sea elephants, penguins, and European sealers. By November 29, he was in heavy ice. On January 11, 1821 he discovered and named Peter I Island. Surveying along the shores of the South Shetlands on January 25, he saw eight British and American sealing vessels and had a memorable meeting with Captain Nathaniel B. Palmer, working for Edmund Fanning.

After collecting a stuffed young penguin for the Admiralty Museum in St. Petersburg, Bellingshausen headed for Rio and home. He had circumnavigated the world eastward and now corrected his date by having two consecutive February thirds. Anchoring at Rio on March 27, he visited the U.S. Frigate *Congress* (which had buried seventy men at sea in a ninety-day voyage from Canton). After a month's stay he left Rio and transported the Russian ambassador to Lisbon. He arrived at Kronshtadt on July 25, after a voyage of 751 days, covering — as he precisely states — 57,073½ miles.

In March 1823, Alexander I appointed Otto von Kotzebue to command another scientific voyage to the Pacific and ordered a new ship, the *Predpriatie* (Enterprise), especially built for the purpose. (A medium-sized frigate, armed with twenty-four six-pounders, *Predpriatie* was larger than the *Rurik* and was the first vessel ever built indoors in Russia.) As originally planned, the voyage was to be purely scientific. But then it was decided to have the *Predpriatie* carry a cargo to Kamchatka and proceed to northwest America and take station for several months to protect the Russian-American Company against foreign encroachment.

Professor Escholtz, who had sailed with Kotzebue on his first circumnavigation, and Dr. Lenz were the naturalists. Other scientific personnel included Preux (an astronomer), Hoffman (a mineralogist), and Siegwald (a physician). In all, 145 persons were to embark on *Predpriatie*. In June the ship arrived at Kronshtadt and by July 14 (old style, as are all dates for this voyage) she was fully equipped and ready to sail. The Czar came on board that day and wished the company a happy voyage.

Kotzebue took leave of his wife and sailed on July 28, 1823, with a fresh wind. (Before things were snugged down, they were hit by a sudden storm, and a well-fed pig fell through a cabin skylight into the midst of twenty young officers and seasick scientists.) *Predpriatie* made a two-day stop at Copenhagen and reached Portsmouth on August 25, so that Kotzebue could go up to London again for charts, chronometers, and astronomical instruments. Kotzebue attempted to sail on September 6, but was driven back by head winds and brought into Portsmouth again by a drunken pilot. *Predpriatie* finally sailed on September 15 for Teneriffe and from Rio on November 28.

Between the Falklands and Patagonia Kotzebue spoke an American whaler. "The dirty ship," he recorded, "and the crew smeared with blubber, had indeed a disgusting appearance; but if we consider to what toils and dangers these poor men are exposed during their voyages, which commonly last several years, in the most tempestuous seas, sometimes sailing about for months without seeing a fish, and suffering in the meanwhile from the want of wholesome food, yet pursuing their object with invincable perseverance, it is impossible to deny them compassion and even commendation. The North Americans display an industry and perseverance in their commercial undertakings, which is not exceeded even by the English, they are to be met with upon every sea, and in the most unfrequented regions, disdaining nothing, however trivial, from which they can derive profit."

Predpriatie doubled Cape Horn on Christmas Day, 1823, and came to anchor in Concepción Bay, Chile (now in revolt against Spain) in mid-January of 1824. Kotzebue next headed for the Tuamotus, to confirm the location of the islands he had seen and discovered on his first voyage: in three weeks he sailed four thousand miles. Late in the afternoon of March 2 he discovered Fangahina, which he sailed completely around without finding a landing. (He named it Predpriatie Island for his ship.) Proceeding a little to the west, he found Bellingshausen's Arakscheev Island (Angatau) exactly where that explorer had located it, but saw none of the inhabitants his compatriot had reported. He next saw Bellingshausen's Wolchonsky Islands (Takurea) and on March 8 made Romanzov Island, which he had discovered on his first voyage. He discovered Aratika on March 9. Islands were all around him now, including two that he could not identify, as well as Carlshof (discovered by Roggeveen in 1722), the Pallisers, Greig Island, and, finally, Tahiti, where he anchored in Matavai Bay on March 14. The pilot who took him in was a Russian-speaking Englishman named Williams, who had served with the Russian-American Company and was settled in Tahiti with a native wife and family.

Kotzebue had an interesting time with the English missionaries, but he did not have a high opinion of their accomplishments. Nott, the head of the mission, was now an old man, and Wilson had also been there twenty years. Bennet and Tyrman were the only young toilers in the vineyard. Tahitian culture had greatly changed, also. The Tahitians now dressed in cast-off European clothing of all kinds. There were no more great canoes. Few mats were made. Playing the flute, dancing, and mock battles were not allowed.

Kotzebue took a house on shore, where he was visited by the queen and the adolescent king. The queen arrived at the head of a long procession bringing three hogs, sweet and white potatoes, yams, and fruit as presents. Kotzebue returned the compliment with calico, silk handkerchiefs, and beads. Meanwhile, aboard the ship, the crew were selling all their old clothes to the Tahitians at exorbitant prices.

Kotzebue left Tahiti on March 24, 1824, and decided to go to the Navigators' Island (Samoa). He sighted the easternmost of the group on April 2 and in the course of the next five days did the most complete chart of the group up to his time.

The Samoan island of Upolu was the most productive for provisions that Kotzebue had found. There he obtained sixty large pigs and an abundance of fowls, fruits, and vegetables in exchange for some old iron, beads, and a few nails. The Samoans also brought tame pigeons and sparrow-sized parrots, lively red and green birds with red tails four times the length of their bodies. These lovely pets sat on their masters' hands and took food from their mouths. The Russians bought them in numbers.

Kotzebue sailed from Samoa on April 7, 1824, bound northwest towards his favorite islands, the Radak chain of the Marshalls. Calms delayed the passage, but *Predpriatie* was at Kotzebue's old anchorage at Otdia by the end of the month. After their eight years' absence Kotzebue and Escholtz were recognized and joyfully welcomed by their Micronesian friends. Kadu, the Caroline Islander who had gone with Kotzebue to the Bering Sea, had moved to Aur and taken with him all of the domesticated animals left on Otdia on the first voyage (excepting the cats who had gone feral). Kotzebue added to his previous surveying of the Radak chain, but he spent only about a week on this visit.

A month later, on June 8, the *Predpriatie* was anchored in the harbor of Petropavlovsk. During the summer Kotzebue sailed along the southern coasts of the Aleutians to Sitka and the Russian-American Company post there. He arrived on August 9. Finding that his presence to relieve the frigate on station there was not required until March 1, 1825, he sailed down the Northwest Coast, spent a couple of months at San Francisco, and then headed for the Hawaiian Islands. When he arrived in mid-December, he discovered that Honolulu had become a European harbor. A regular pilot now took vessels in and out, and there were many whalers and other ships there. In Hawaiian homes Chinese porcelains had replaced gourds and coconuts for both domestic use and display.

Kotzebue returned home via the Radaks (discovering Bikini, which he named Escholtz Island after his friend the scientist), Guam, Manila, the Cape of Good Hope, and St. Helena. He arrived on June 3 at Portsmouth, where he spent a few days, and dropped anchor at Kronshtadt on July 10, 1826.

Thus, in addition to his valuable surveys and observations of islanders, Kotzebue discovered three new islands — Fangahina, Aratika, and Bikini — on his second voyage.

The final Russian voyage in this series, which deserves a paragraph, was that of Captain Fedor P. Lütke from 1826 to 1829 in the sloop *Senyavin* with the *Moller* as consort. No full account of this voyage has been published in English. Lütke's expedition left Kronshtadt on August 16, 1826, entered the Pacific via Cape Horn, stopped at Valparaiso, and in June 1827 reached Sitka, where Baron Wrangel was governor. Like his countrymen before him, Lütke combined exploration in the Bering Sea area and among the tropical islands. Lütke's great contribution to Pacific exploration was his survey of the Caroline Islands from November 1827 throughout 1828. In the course of this charting he discovered Eauripik. His chart of the Carolines was the best yet made. Besides his surveying, Lütke, who had two naturalists and an ornithologist with him, made numerous meteorological and hydrographical observations.

Indeed, Lütke's expedition, along with Bellingshausen's and Kotzebue's, was among the most successful sent out by any country. Unmarred by tragedy, these expeditions were commanded by able, humane officers who made significant contributions to the geographical, ethnological, and other scientific knowledge of the Pacific.

15

Return of the French

AFTER Baudin's voyage no French expeditions were sent into the Pacific for over a decade: France's resources, both human and monetary, had been spent by the Napoleonic Wars. Following the Restoration, however, with peace established once more and Louis XVIII returned to his ancestral throne, France hoped to recover through scientific achievement some of the pride that she had lost through military defeat. Thus new outbursts of French activity took place almost simultaneously with the Russian voyages.

From 1816 until 1840 there were few years when at least one French navigator was not encircling the globe. Most of these voyages were sponsored by the French government. Some, in fact, were not scientific at all, but rather French naval cruises for showing the flag or for other political reasons. Since the time of La Pérouse and Baudin, the emphasis and purposes of expeditions had changed. Although there were immense amounts of charting remaining to be done, much of the glamour of discovery had gone and unknown coasts were few and insignificant. Expeditions now went forth seeking information to assist the whale fishery and were prepared to put in long months of intensive and dreary investigation in physics, magnetism, hydrography, and meteorology, as well as in the more immediately stimulating disciplines of biology and ethnology.

The first voyage (and not a government one) in this second round of French activity was that of Camille de Roquefeuil, a merchant captain, who sailed from Bordeaux, on October 11, 1816, on a fur-trading voyage to the Northwest Coast. Rounding the Horn in the *Bordelais*, Roquefeuil made the usual calls at Valparaiso and at Callao, where he met the Russian-American Company ships *Kutusov* and *Suwarov*. (The two Russian vessels had been separated in a great storm at Cape Horn and had just been reunited.) Continuing north, he stopped at San Francisco in August and then proceeded with his not very successful fur trading around Nootka Sound. At the end of the season he returned to San Francisco, leaving there on November 20, 1817, for the Marquesas for sandalwood to help fill out his cargo. Then he returned to California and the Northwest Coast for another season's fur trading at Nootka, Sitka, and around the Queen Charlotte Islands. The voyage terminated when the *Bordelais*, after a three-year absence, entered the Gironde on November 21, 1819.

Roquefeuil made no geographical discoveries, but he added details to the charts of the West Coast and gave excellent reports on the Polynesians of the Marquesas and Hawaiian islands.

While Roquefeuil was bartering for furs with the Indians in the early autumn of 1817, the first of the great French government expeditions was fitting out at the naval base at Toulon. Nicholas Baudin had died on his voyage; his work on the Australian coast was uncompleted. But beyond completing the Australian survey, it was not expected that the new voyage would have significant geographical results. The ebullient Jacques Etienne Arago, artist of the expedition, summed it up when he wrote: "There is scarcely a midshipman in our navy who could not now, if required, steer a vessel to Kamtschatka to Otaheite, or to New Zealand. The Pacific Ocean has been so frequently explored, that it is almost better known, and certainly less dangerous, than the Mediterranean, which bathes our shores." No, studies in terrestrial magnetism, physics, meteorology, ethnography, and languages were to be concentrated on this time, and collections were to be made for the French museums. It was no coincidence that the program for the new expedition was largely planned by Humboldt, Cuvier, and other leading French scientists.

Two of the ablest officers on the Baudin expedition had been Lieutenant Louis Claude de Saulces de Freycinet, the cartographer, and his younger brother Henry, who afterwards became an admiral. At the time of the Baudin voyage, Louis, who was born at Montélimar, Dauphiné on August 7, 1779, was twenty-one years old. He had entered the navy at fourteen, fought in several engagements against the English, and was on his way up the ladder. Ever since his return to Paris in 1805 he had been employed at the Ministry of Marine, editing the reports and preparing the maps and plans of the Baudin expedition.

Now thirty-eight years old, de Freycinet was selected to command the corvette *Uranie* on the scientific voyage *autour du monde*. He, in turn, carefully selected each officer and supernumerary, and secured the best of equipment and provisions then available. (Among his officers was Louis Isidor Duperrey, who in a few years would be commanding his own expedition.) De Freycinet was at pains to select as many sailors as possible who were also skilled as carpenters, sailworkers, blacksmiths, or in other useful trades. Romantic interest on the voyage was assured when, the afternoon before sailing, de Freycinet, perhaps taking the clue from Matthew Flinders, smuggled his pretty wife aboard dressed as a youth. Rose de Freycinet remained in disguise (not a very successful disguise) on her visit to the lieutenant governor at Gibraltar and until the *Uranie* had left The Rock. Then, like Madame Baré on Bougainville's expedition, she continued the circumnavigation of the globe. She was probably the second woman in history to do so.

The *Uranie*, amply provisioned for two years and equipped with the most up-to-date machines for distilling salt water and remedies for scurvy, sailed from Toulon on September 17, 1817. From Gibraltar and Teneriffe, she sailed to Rio de Janeiro, arriving on December 6. Here de Freycinet stayed for nearly two months making pendulum observations, while the naturalists collected specimens and curiosities. From early March to April 5, 1818, *Uranie* conducted similar observations in Table Bay at the Cape of Good Hope. (At Table Bay the young Rose lived onshore in a private home. It was at Table Bay, also, that de Freycinet exchanged visits with Otto von Kotzebue, homeward bound in the *Rurick* on his first voyage. Rose wrote: "You can imagine the satisfaction the two commandants took in their meetings with each other.") The expedition continued its scientific work at

Mauritius, where *Uranie* was careened and her copper repaired, and where the officers and Rose enjoyed the dinners, balls, horse races, and gay social life for which Port Louis was famous.

Uranie crossed the Indian Ocean in mid-summer and arrived at Shark Bay on the western coast of Australia on September 12, to resume in earnest the unfinished survey begun on the Baudin voyage. Among the scientific collections that *Uranie* carried away from Shark Bay when the survey was completed September twenty-sixth was a unique historical relic, which de Freycinet had hankered for ever since seeing it with Baudin seventeen years before. On the northern tip of Dirk Hartogs Island, which he named Cap de l'Inscription, Dirk Hartog, captain of the Dutch ship *De Eendracht* had, in 1616, nailed an inscribed pewter plate to a post on the cliff. In 1697 Hartog's countryman William Vlamingh found this original plate* and carried it away, substituting another, onto which he copied Hartog's inscription and added the record of his own visit. The Vlamingh plate had been found in the sand by members of Baudin's expedition, and de Freycinet had wanted to take it away, but was overruled. Instead, the plate had been set up once more, nailed to a new post. Now, however, Louis Claude de Saulces de Freycinet was in command. The Vlamingh plate was his.†

Uranie spent a little over a fortnight at Koepang in Dutch Timor. Her departure was prolonged: coasting along Timor's northern shore, she was becalmed in scorching heat for twenty-four days. With food short and men sick, de Freycinet took advantage of the first breeze to get into Dili, the capital of Portuguese Timor, where the colony's governor swiftly provided for their needs. On his departure the governor presented de Freycinet with four children from the interior of the island to take to Europe as curiosities. The captain endeavored to avoid this expression of kindness, but was finally compelled to accept one boy, who was subsequently baptized Joseph Antonio and died in Paris at the age of sixteen.

From Timor the leisurely expedition crossed the Banda Sea to the

---

* Now in the Rijks Museum.
† Today after incredible vicissitudes the plate is in the museum in Perth, Western Australia.

Moluccas, landing on Pisang, and, on December 16, anchoring at Rawak near Waigeo off New Guinea's northwestern tip. Magnetic studies continued all the while, along with astronomical observations and geographical research. The health of de Freycinet's people was, however, rapidly deteriorating due to dysentery and scurvy. He was compelled to push on for Guam, where relief would be available.

No sooner was the anchor down at Guam, March 18, 1819, than Don Medinilla y Pineda, the governor, came on board anxiously inquiring about their needs. It took over two months, until early June, for the sick — who were taken ashore — to recover. But the generous governor would accept no payment for the supplies he had provided, even apologizing for their skimpiness. Meanwhile, for the healthy, there were endless rounds of banquets and luxurious dinner parties, where the amount of rich food consumed was limited only by the capacities of the Frenchmen's stomachs. For entertainment there were cock fights — sham combats — gorgeously costumed dancers. There seemed to be no limit to Guam's hospitality.

Despite the social distractions, however, and the slow recovery of ill crew members, Duperrey made a successful survey of the island, and the scientific work of the expedition continued more or less unimpeded. *Uranie* ultimately weighed anchor on June fifth, cruised north of the Marianas to get in a higher latitude, and then sailed east for Hawaii. Mauna Kea was sighted on August 6, 1819.

At Kealakekua Bay, *Uranie's* impulsive artist Jacques Arago immediately paid a visit of piety to the site of Cook's death. But he was not impressed with the Hawaiian court. "A miserable hut," he wrote, "built of straw, from twenty-five to thirty feet long, and from twelve to fifteen feet broad, the entrance to which is by a low and narrow door; some mats, on which several half-naked giants are reposing, and who bear the titles of ministers and generals; two chairs, on which are seated, on days of ceremony, a large fat, dirty, heavy, proud man, and a stout half-naked woman, who allows herself to coquet [*sic*] with every stranger, without betraying her fidelity to her large-jowled husband, who is eat up with I know not how many horrible diseases . . . such is the palace of the monarch of the Sandwich Isles; and such are the King and Queen of Owhyhee, and such is their dignified court!"

In due course, de Freycinet received an invitation from King Liho Liho, who met him on the beach. The king was dressed in the best regal fashion in the full uniform of an English captain, and surrounded by chiefs in red and golden feather helmets. Even more splendiferous must have been the dress of de Freycinet's party. For when King Liho Liho's minister Kraimokou (Kalanimoku) saw *Uranie*'s chaplain in clerical garb, he immediately asked to be baptized — and King Liho Liho requested that he be allowed to attend the ceremony with his suite. At the two-hour reception that followed the ceremony, enough rum, brandy, and wine were consumed to constitute a three-month's supply for ten men of normal thirst. And when the party was over, the king requested an additional two bottles of brandy from de Freycinet, so that he might successfully drink to the commander's health and to the success of the voyage.

Uranie moved over to Maui on the fifteenth of August and spent ten days there before proceeding to Oahu. The reception by the European residents of Honolulu made de Freycinet regret he had not come there in the first place. Then Boki, the governor of Oahu, learned that his brother, Kalanimoku, had been baptized and also requested the sacrament. It was a pleasant month spent about the Hawaiian Islands.

De Freycinet had hoped to make Tahiti his next port of call. Like Byron, however, he could not get his ship to windward and was forced reluctantly — to the bitter disappointment of his young officers — to bear away for Australia and Port Jackson. On this run, he made the only new geographical discovery of the voyage: passing a tiny coral island east of Samoa, he gallantly named it Ile Rose. (Arago, who throughout his book makes no direct reference to Madame de Freycinet's presence on board, comes closest to it on describing this occasion. He writes, with a touch of asperity: "Let us see; what shall we call it? Let it be a flowery name. Shall it be Green Island, Red Island, or . . . No, I suppose it will be Rose Island.")

De Freycinet and his officers were entertained at Sydney by Governor Lachlan Macquarie, while the ship was refitted. Six weeks later,

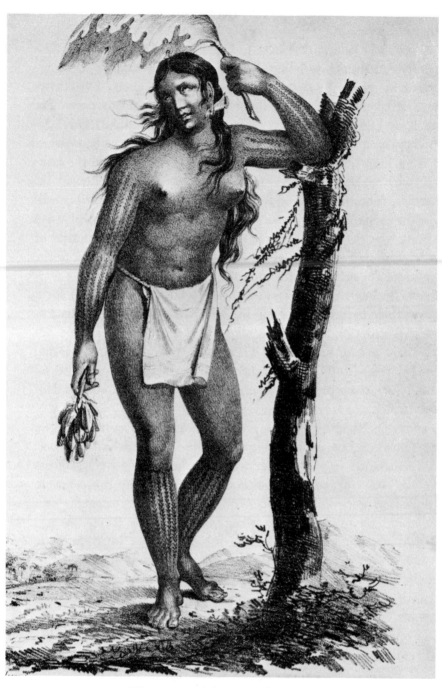

Woman of Tinian, Caroline Islands
(after Arago, in Freycinet's Voyage)

on Christmas Day, 1819, the *Uranie* passed out through Sydney Heads and began the long run through the South Pacific for Cape Horn.

Now de Freycinet's luck began to turn against him. A few days out, ten convict stowaways were discovered on board; and on February 14, 1820, while entering Berkeley Sound, East Island, in the Falklands, the *Uranie* hit a rock and was holed so badly that she had to be beached. Journals and papers relating to scientific observations were saved, but many of the ethnological and natural history collections stored in the bottom of the hold were lost. Arago lost ten portfolios of sketches and finished drawings.*

Because rescue was highly unlikely, de Freycinet set up an encampment on shore and immediately began altering the longboat so that Lieutenant Duperrey could make the thousand-mile voyage to Montevideo for assistance. During the arduous two and a half months that *Uranie*'s crew were marooned, supplies ran short and the crew had to hunt seals, penguins, and wild horses for subsistence.

Just as Duperrey was about to leave for South America, however, two other vessels appeared. The first ship, *General Knox*, commanded by Captain Orne of Salem, was sealing in the Falklands with a schooner and sloop as tenders. While de Freycinet was negotiating with Orne, another American ship, the *Mercury*, with Captain John Galvin, arrived under Spanish rebel colors. Bargaining with the two American captains was a tight affair, since each intended to get as much money from the French government as possible. Eventually, de Freycinet made arrangements with Galvin to take his party to Rio in the *Mercury*, and he finally purchased the vessel at Montevideo. Ironically, an English whaler and the English Antarctic explorer Captain James Weddell arrived at the Falklands only a few days after de Freycinet made his contract with Galvin. Both Englishmen would have gladly helped the unfortunate castaways out of their perilous circumstances.

The French commander renamed Galvin's *Mercury* the *Physicienne*. After repairs at Rio de Janeiro she took the expedition home,

---

* The two New Zealand tattooed heads he saved (he probably picked them up in Australia) were later stolen from him at Rio.

arriving at Le Havre on November 13, 1820. De Freycinet was acquitted honorably at a pro forma court martial for losing his ship and given a promotion. Nor was anything more said about his disobedience in taking his wife along.

It must be said that the actual results of de Freycinet's expedition, while substantial (numerous new species of fishes, reptiles, and invertebrates, for example, were discovered), were not commensurate with the preparations for the voyage or with its length. It must also be observed that, with so many young officers on board, Rose's presence created a disciplinary problem and that, because of Rose, the voyage became a social tour at all of the European-governed ports. To be sure, de Freycinet was conscientious about his various observations, but soon even these would be obsolete. Perhaps the most solid long range results of the voyage were the fine natural history and ethnographical collections and the voluminous notes and drawings relating to the various countries and islands visited.

Following his return de Freycinet spent much of his life supervising the publication of the results of the voyage. It took twenty years — from 1824 to 1844 — for the eight quarto volumes and several folio atlases to appear, and the work was never completed. De Freycinet was elected to the Academy of Sciences in 1825 and was one of the founders of the Paris Geographical Society.* He died on August 18, 1842.

Like the English and Russians, the French were building a dynasty of naval officer–explorers. De Freycinet, after cutting his teeth on the Baudin expedition, had led the first of the new series of voyages after peace had settled on his troubled land. One of his lieutenants on the circumnavigation in *Uranie* was Louis Isidor Duperrey, a young man of ability and experience.

Duperrey was born in Paris in 1786 and entered the navy in 1803. In 1809 and 1810 he took part in military operations at Brest and Rochefort. Before sailing with de Freycinet, he gained hydrographical experience in a survey of the coast of Tuscany. In 1821 Duperrey,

---

* Along with Duperrey and D'Urville. It is the oldest and one of the most distinguished organizations of its kind.

with his friend and fellow officer Dumont d'Urville, presented a plan for another naval voyage of exploration to the Marquis de Clermont Tonnerre, Minister of Marine, in which special attention was to be given to magnetism, meteorology, and the configuration of the globe. "In the geographical department," said Duperrey, "we would propose to verify or to rectify, either by direct, or by chronometrical observations, the position of a great number of points in different parts of the globe, especially among the numerous island groups of the Pacific Ocean, notorious for shipwrecks, and so remarkable for the character and the form of the shoals, sandbanks, and reefs, of which they in part consist; also to trace new routes through the Dangerous Archipelago and the Society Islands, side by side with those taken by Quiros, Wallis, Bougainville, and Cook; to carry on hydrographical surveys in continuation of those made in the voyages of d'Entrecasteaux and of Freycinet in Polynesia, New Holland, and the Molucca Islands; and particularly to visit the Caroline Islands, discovered by Magellan, about which, with the exception of the eastern side, examined in our own time by Captain Kotzebue, we have only very vague information, communicated by the missionaries, and by them learnt from stories told by savages who had lost their way and were driven in their canoes upon the Marianne Islands.

"The languages, character, and customs of these islanders must also receive special and careful attention."

In addition to the proposed scientific plans, one of the primary purposes of the voyage would be to locate harbors and to help in any other way possible the economically important French whaling industry in the Pacific.

It was a tall order.

The Academy of Sciences nevertheless endorsed the plan and supplied information on various points where accurate scientific information was badly needed. Duperrey was chosen to lead the expedition and Dumont d'Urville was selected as his second-in-command.

The corvette *Coquille*, then lying at Toulon, was selected and refitted for the voyage. Duperrey left Toulon in her on August 11, 1822, less than two years after he had arrived at Le Havre in *Physicienne*. Following a survey of the lonely mid-Atlantic island of Ascension, he intended to sail to the Falkland Islands, but damage to the *Coquille* forced a stop at St. Catharine Island, Brazil. The voyage continued on October 30, and when Duperrey arrived at Berkeley Sound in the Falkland Islands, he revisited the campsite where he had lived for three months and where the remains of the poor old *Uranie* were now embedded in the sand. The melancholy sight remained in his mind's eye for many a day.

Duperrey's published narrative of the voyage is unfinished: it ends with his departure from Chile. However, we know that he sailed north to Callao and visited Lima and Paita, Peru, before setting sail for Tahiti in March 1823. We also know that he was nearly wrecked on the low coral atoll of Réao in the Tuamotu Archipelago during the night of April 22. (He named the atoll, which he thought to be a new discovery, Clermont-Tonnerre for the Minister of Marine.) *Coquille* arrived at Tahiti on May 3, for a brief visit.

From the leeward Society Islands to Bora Bora, from Niue and Tonga to the Fijis, from Santa Cruz in Melanesia to the coasts of Bougainville and Buka in the Solomons, from Port Praslin in New Ireland to the Schouten Island and northern New Guinea — *Coquille* cut a wide swathe through the Pacific. Duperrey spent two weeks in early September investigating the anchorages and people at the island of Waigeo, and in the process discovered the southern bay that nearly cuts that island in two. The voyage then continued to Amboina and Timor and on to western and southern Australia. *Coquille* arrived in Sydney on January 17 for revictualing and repairs. She departed Sydney on March 20, 1824.

From the Bay of Islands, New Zealand, Duperrey sailed almost due north to Rotuma, where he found four beachcombers, who had deserted from the whale ship *Rochester*, tattooed and smeared with yellow powder, happily raising native families. The *Coquille* continued her northerly course through the Gilberts, while Duperrey made an especially close examination of Nonouti, and discovered Matthews Island. (Actually, Matthews Island — it is now called Marakei Atoll — may have been seen before, but Duperrey nailed its position down firmly for the first time.) *Coquille* then sailed in a northwesterly direction past Ebon (which Duperrey called Les Iles Boston) and called

Men of New Ireland (from Duperrey, Voyage Autour du Monde)

at Jaluit, where one of the islets was named in her honor La Coquille. A general chart was made of the Mulgraves at this time.

In the Carolines, at Kusaie or Strong's Island (which he called Ile Oualan), Duperrey commented on the beauty of the women. Since the island, though discovered in 1804, was uncharted, Duperrey decided to make an exact survey of it. He spent ten days at this pleasant task, enjoying the island's friendly people and ample fresh food. A few days later, on June 18, 1824, he discovered the island of Mokil (which possibly had been seen by the Spaniard, Alvaro de Saavedra) and named it Ile Duperrey. He subsequently discovered the twin atolls of Losap and Nama (also possibly seen by Saavedra), on June twenty-third, as well as accomplishing a great amount of charting. At the end of June he left the Carolines, bound home. Duperrey arrived at Marseille in the spring of 1825, after an absence of two and one half years.

The voyage of *Coquille* was a successful one, during which not a single man was lost. Its results were published in six quarto volumes and four superb atlases (although the narrative and ethnological sections of the text were never completed). Duperrey's hydrographical surveys, especially in the Tuamotus, Societies, and Carolines, were outstanding, and generated fifty-one carefully drawn charts and plans, as well as enormous collections of astronomical, magnetic, and meteorological data. *Coquille*'s crew acquired much new information concerning Pacific currents. Duperrey's numerous pendulum observations served to determine the magnetic equator and to prove the equality of the flattening of the two hemispheres. In addition, important geological, zoological, and ethnological collections were accumulated, and the surgeon and zoologist René Primevère Lesson — the first naturalist to observe birds of paradise in their native environment — later published extensively on that aspect of the results of the voyage.

Duperrey, who devoted most of the rest of his life to the investigation of terrestrial magnetism, was recognized for his work by admission to the Academy of Sciences in 1842. He died in August 1865.

Duperrey's second-in-command aboard *Coquille* had been Jules Sebastien Cesar Dumont d'Urville, four years Duperrey's junior. Born in Normandy in 1790, Dumont d'Urville went to sea as an apprentice seaman in the navy in 1807. During his first twelve years of naval service, he advanced slowly. But he had a great talent for languages, and studied botany and entomology in addition to the standard subjects that an officer must master. In 1820, his erudition began to serve him in good stead. During a survey voyage in the eastern Mediterranean, the French consul on the island of Milos took him to see a statue that had recently been unearthed. D'Urville immediately recognized it as a figure of extraordinary beauty and quality, and his rapturous report to the French Ambassador at Constantinople was influential in obtaining the famous Venus de Milo for the Louvre.

When d'Urville returned to Paris in 1821, he joined his friend Duperrey in planning the scientific circumnavigation of the *Coquille*. But he was not especially satisfied with some of the scientific results of the voyage of the *Coquille*, believing that certain fields had been neglected. Upon his return in 1825 he quickly began laying plans for another expedition, to visit New Zealand, the Fiji Islands, the Loyalty Islands, New Britain, and New Guinea. These plans, too, were ap-

Captain J. S. C. Dumont D'Urville, the greatest Pacific explorer after Cook
(*D'Urville*, Voyage of the Astrolabe *1826–29*)

proved, and he was given further orders, based on a rumor that an American captain had found a Cross of St. Louis and some medals in the hands of natives on an island between New Caledonia and the Louisiades, to make another search for La Pérouse. The *Coquille*, refitted for another arduous voyage, was, at d'Urville's request, renamed *Astrolabe*, in memory of La Pérouse's flagship. Lesson, who obviously enjoyed voyaging, was once more the surgeon, and Messrs. Quoy and Joseph-Paul Gaimard, who had been with de Freycinet on the *Uranie*, were engaged as scientists.

D'Urville sailed from Toulon on April 25, 1826, thirteen months after his return with Duperrey, to explore the western Pacific in a continuation of Duperrey's work. His passage, which ran well south of the cape and past St. Paul and Amsterdam islands, was a rough one, but October 7, 1826, found the *Astrolabe* safely anchored in King George Sound on the southern Australian coast. Fresh water and a suitable site for an observatory were soon found. And while sailors pitched the tents, several officers made a tour of the bay (They found the local aborigines peaceful and shy, although one courageous fellow spent two days on board the ship standing by the galley fire and eating anything that came his way.) The officers also worked at their hydrographical and astronomical observations and mapped the entire area, while the naturalists accumulated extensive botanical and zoological collections.

From King George Sound, *Astrolabe* sailed to Jervis Bay and Sydney, and one entire volume of d'Urville's narrative is devoted to New South Wales. *Astrolabe* subsequently crossed the Tasman Sea, arriving at Tasman Bay, New Zealand on January 14, 1827. As a result of this survey of its shores — the first — d'Urville Island was found to be separated from the main South Island by the geographical feature that d'Urville named French Pass. He had good reason to know, too, for here he nearly wrecked his ship. *Astrolabe* now sailed through Cook Strait, doubled Cape Palliser, and worked her way up the east coast of the North Island, making numerous refinements of the positions of geographical features as she went. During the cruise, d'Urville kept close contacts with the Maoris, who supplied him with pigs and potatoes as well as information. He examined the Bay of Plenty and Mercury Bay and finally arrived at the Bay of Islands. On his return run south, he made an extensive exploration of Hauraki Gulf and predicted that the present site of Auckland would be a good location for a city.

D'Urville left New Zealand, to which he devotes another entire volume of his narrative, on March 18, 1827, bound for Tongatabu. By the sixteenth of April he was off Nomuka, and two days later at Eua. A severe storm nearly proved fatal to the *Astrolabe*, before d'Urville managed to bring her safely to Tongatabu.

At this period, a number of Europeans, including the Wesleyan missionaries, were living at Tongatabu. Quantities of fruits and vegetables, fowls and pigs were available at phenomenally low prices, along with large collections of carved clubs and other arms, household articles, ornaments, and native manufactures of all kinds. Although d'Urville had no reason to mistrust the Tonga people, on May 9 he discovered a native plot to take the ship. He decided to leave as soon as possible and prepared to set sail on the fourteenth, but on that day several of his sailors were kidnapped. It took ten days of bombardment and negotiation before the sailors were returned unharmed. The *Astrolabe* finally took her departure on the twenty-fourth. As it turned out, d'Urville left just in time, for his boatswain found out that over half of his sailors, beguiled by the easy Polynesian life, were ready to jump ship and take up the beachcomber's indolent calling.

Astrolabe spent twenty days among the Fiji Islands, which she entered through the passage between Ongea and Vatoa into the deep but reef-strewn Koro Sea. Cautiously she turned back from these dangerous waters and shaped a southerly course, piloted by some Fijians whom d'Urville had on board. On this leg, d'Urville discovered Totoya and Matuku, two of the three Moala group in the Laus.

Among the acquaintances d'Urville made in the Fijis were a well-traveled Tongan and a man from Guam, both of whom gave d'Urville the names of many islands in the Fiji group. As he pursued his exploration of these islands, d'Urville nearly wrecked the *Astrolabe* on June 5, 1827, on the thirty-mile reef which he named for his ship. Its existence had already been recorded by Captain Bligh, but the reef is still known as the Great Astrolabe Reef. It forms a loop and terminates in a ring of reefs called North Astrolabe.

One of d'Urville's most important accomplishments on the voyage was the accurate charting of the Loyalty Islands. This work was followed by a survey of tiny Huon Island and the chain of reefs running from it to the northern tip of New Caledonia. From here d'Urville sailed in six days to the Louisiade Archipelago. When foul weather forced him to abandon his plan to pass through Torres Strait, he navigated the treacherous waters of the Louisiades and proceeded to survey over a thousand miles of New Guinea's largely unexplored northern coast. His attempted survey of New Britain was, however, frustrated by incredible rains.

D'Urville arrived at Amboina on September 24 to replenish supplies before making the long circuit around Australia for Hobart, Tasmania. No French ship had been in Hobart since Baudin's visit twenty-five years before. But no sooner had he entered the Derwent River, than d'Urville heard of Captain Peter Dillon's discovery of La Pérouse relics on Tikopia and Vanikoro.* He therefore abandoned plans to return to New Zealand, deciding instead, to follow up the news of La Pérouse, as he had been instructed. After stowing his provisions, buying new anchors, and repairing the ship and her dilapidated rigging, d'Urville put to sea again on Janury 5, 1828, heading north. At Tikopia, on February 9, and at Vanikoro, he confirmed Dillon's discovery of the fate of La Pérouse, and collected an 1800-pound anchor and other relics overlooked by Dillon, as well as erecting a monument to his countryman's memory.

D'Urville had intended to go to the Solomons to look for La Pérouse survivors, but a large number of his men were now sick. As Duperrey had done before him, he turned northwest; he sailed through the Caroline Islands and arrived at Guam on May 2. It was nearly a mouth before his ailing crew had recuperated sufficiently to proceed. The *Astrolabe* arrived at Marseilles on March 25, 1829. In August of 1829, d'Urville was promoted to post captain.

The results of this expedition were immense. Forty-five new charts

* Chapter 16 contains a full account of the Dillon discovery.

Fijian sailing canoe (D'Urville, Voyage Au Pole Sud)

were drawn, and the natural history collections were so enormous that every inch of the facilities at the Jardin du Roi was filled. (Lesson, for example, had collected some sixteen hundred pressed plants.) The data on magnetism, water temperatures, meteorology, philology, and anthropology were no less voluminous. Yet, while the voyage resulted in one of the largest and handsomest publications on the South Seas, d'Urville himself was severely criticized, especially for neglecting to survey Torres Strait.

French whaling interests and commerce in the Pacific increased steadily during the second quarter of the nineteenth century, and one of the duties of the series of government expeditions during this period was to find and survey new harbors and anchorages where whalers could find shelter and refreshment. This was, in fact, the primary object of the voyage of the frigate *Venus*, commanded by Captain Abel Aubert Du Petit-Thouars.

Du Petit-Thouars was forty-three years old when he sailed from Brest on December 29, 1836, for his voyage round the world. Proceeding to the Hawaiian Islands, the captain promptly became involved in a dispute over the attempted expulsion of two priests — French Catholic missionaries — from the islands. Fortunately Du Petit-Thouars and Captain Edward Belcher, who arrived about the same time in H.M.S. *Sulphur*, were able to persuade the king that the priests could remain in Honolulu temporarily, although both captains gave pledges that the two fathers would leave at the first opportunity. In order to insure the rights of French citizens to come and go freely in the Hawaiian Islands, Du Petit-Thouars exceeded his authority by making a treaty with Kamehameha III, signed July 24, 1837. In this treaty, the same protection was guaranteed Hawaiians traveling in France.

After that heady interlude in international politics, the *Venus* went about her business of exploring for the benefit of whalers. She arrived at Petropavlovsk, Kamchatka on August 31, 1837, and left a fortnight later to sail along the Aleutian chain and to coast the continent to Monterey, California, exploring safe anchorages for the wide-ranging whalers. The winter, she spent exploring the Mexican coast, devoting particular attention to the harbors of Mazatlán, San Blas, and Acapulco. Because of contrary winds, Du Petit-Thouars was unable to make his next desired destination in the Galápagos. He did, though, sight Easter Island, where he surveyed its northern coast for the first time. Returning to Valparaiso, he finally reached the Galápagos and charted that group before going on to explore the northwestern Marquesas.

After leaving the Marquesas, Du Petit-Thouars sailed to Tahiti, where he became involved again in politics. Queen Pomare, like her royal colleague in the Hawaiian Islands, had expelled two French Catholic priests. For this Du Petit-Thouars exacted an indemnity of $2,000, along with an apology and a salute to the French flag. He also made another treaty without authority. This was preliminary to his return four years later as an admiral, when he established a French protectorate over the Society Islands.

After this display of power politics, Du Petit-Thouars visited New Zealand and then returned home by way of Réunion and the Cape of Good Hope, arriving in France in June 1839. While some charting and surveying was accomplished, especially along the western American continental seaboard, this voyage was more famous for its political overtones than for its contributions to knowledge.

So, too, were two other French naval voyages that occurred during the same years. Captain A. N. Vaillant took the corvette *Bonite* around the world in 1836 and 1837, but on his Pacific crossing stopped only to show the flag and obtain provisions at the Hawaiian Islands. In the years 1837 to 1840, Captain John B. T. Cécile made a voyage in the southern hemisphere comparable to that of Du Petit-Thouars in the northern, primarily for the benefit of the whale fishery. In addition to charting bays and harbors he surveyed Chatham Island and the Ilots de Bass (Morotiri).

Captain Cyrille Pierre Théodore Laplace, who was born in 1793 (the same year as Du Petit-Thouars), had made a circumnavigation of the world in 1830 to 1832, in the frigate *Favorite*. During this voyage he made a minute examination of the Bay of Islands, New Zealand, to the complete bafflement of Maori and English settlers alike. He made another voyage in the frigate *Artémise* in 1837 to 1840, primarily for political purposes, and in July 1839 delivered a manifesto to the king of the Hawaiian Islands regarding his treatment of catholics. Fine publications resulted from both voyages.

One of the most interesting sources of information on the central Pacific is the work of Jacques A. Moerenhout, a Fleming who made three voyages in the Pacific between the years 1828 and 1834. He later settled down in Tahiti, where he became the French Consul for that island and United States Consul for Polynesia. On a voyage from Chile to Tahiti in the *Volador* he discovered Maria Atoll in the Tuamotus on March 1, 1829. This was his only discovery, but he made valuable ethnological contributions on the peoples of Pitcairn, the Tuamotus, Easter Island, Rapa, the Austral Islands, Mangareva, and the Society group.

Of all the French navigators of the nineteenth century, d'Urville towers above the others as much as Cook outshines his eighteenth-century English compatriots. After d'Urville returned from his voyage in the *Astrolabe*, he began writing up the massive results of that voyage. This work was interrupted when he was called upon to escort King Charles X to England and exile. D'Urville was a bluff, untactful seaman and he was strongly criticized for the manner in which he carried out this assignment. He retired to sulk in Toulon, where he developed plans for an expedition to study the native peoples of the Pacific. At heart, Dumont d'Urville was a frustrated anthropologist, but he had no luck in selling his plan to the government until Admiral Claude de Rosamel became Minister of Marine. In approaching the admiral with his scheme he said: "I have the vanity to believe that few men today know the Pacific Ocean as I do," and he was right. King Louis Phillipe approved the plan but added to its complexity by stipulating that penetration should be made into the Antarctic. D'Urville, a warm-water boy, was not enthusiastic about frozen seas, but had no other choice than to accept the Citizen King's desire.

D'Urville at this time was not a well man, but he was a determined one. He took command of his old *Astrolabe*, the corvette like himself a veteran of two Pacific voyages, and as a consort chose the corvette *Zelée*. Captain Charles-Hector Jacquinot was given command of her.

Easter Islanders dancing on the deck of the Venus (Du Petit-Thouars, Voyage Autour du Monde)

Clément-Adrien Vincendon Dumoulin was the hydrographer and Louis Le Breton the official artist.*

D'Urville sailed from Toulon on September 7, 1837. Early in the new year he made his attempt to sail closer to the South Pole than Weddell had done. The French were entirely inexperienced in ice navigation and their ships were not equipped for it. Only some flimsy and entirely inadequate metal sheathing had been added to the bows of the vessels. The ships were stopped by the ice pack (which d'Urville wisely decided not to attempt to penetrate) in 63° 39′ south latitude on January 22, 1838, far short of Weddell's farthest point. After spending two months among the icebergs, the ships headed for the Pacific on March 5.

In the central Pacific, d'Urville stopped at Mangareva, the Marquesas Islands, and Tahiti, and spent three months surveying in Samoa and the Fiji Islands (continuing the work of his previous voyage). One of his duties in the Fiji Islands was to avenge the capture of the French bêche-de-mer trading brig *Amiable Josephine* by Mbau and Viwa chiefs, on July 19, 1834. The captain and most of the crew of *Amiable Josephine* had been massacred, and, because of the Fijians' lack of sailing skill, the vessel was wrecked on a reef. D'Urville arrived with his corvettes in October 1838, and the chiefs guessed why he came. A native pilot took his ships safely through the reefs between Ovalau and Mbau. At Mbau the blame was placed on the Viwa people, who all had time to escape. On the sixteenth, d'Urville sent eighty men to destroy the deserted Viwa village anyway. It was rebuilt the next year; Wesleyan missionaries established a headquarters nearby.

D'Urville surveyed definitively along the Solomons before turning northwesterly through the Carolines to Guam. Freshly supplied, he went south once more through the Palau Islands and the Moluccas to Batavia and thence around western and southern Australia to Hobart, Tasmania, where he arrived in late 1839.

By now he had heard of the two great British and American expeditions, commanded by James Clark Ross and Charles Wilkes, for high southern exploration. He did not need to make another attempt to

* The Academy of Sciences was lukewarm about this expedition but encouraging letters were received from foreign scholars, including Humboldt and Krusenstern.

The French entertained at Nuku Hiva, Marquesas Islands (D'Urville, Voyage Au Pole Sud)

penetrate the Antarctic, but national pride drove him on to participate in what had become an international competition. He had also become interested in terrestrial magnetism and hoped to find the south magnetic pole somewhere between 120° and 160° east, south of Tasmania. He did not realize that the sealer Captain John Balleny had already anticipated him on that section of coast. Sailing through enormous ice islands, d'Urville managed to reach the sixty-sixth parallel on January 20, 1840, and was prepared to cross the Antarctic Circle when he came upon an unbroken high coast stretching as far as the eye could reach in either direction. After landing on some rocky islets, d'Urville named the whole coast Adélie Land for his wife.

The ships continued eastward along the land for two days, until the good clear weather, with which they had been blessed, turned stormy and the ships were briefly separated in a gale. The bad weather continued, and on January 29, 1840, a strange brig came out of the fog flying American colors. She was the *Porpoise* under Lieutenant Ringgold of the Wilkes expedition. Before they could speak to each other they were again lost in the fog. D'Urville regretted this episode very much, as he had wanted to compare notes with the Americans, although later the ill-tempered Wilkes accused him of deliberately running away to avoid speaking. On February 1, d'Urville turned north to Hobart Town.

The final Pacific cruise of his voyage took d'Urville to the Auckland Islands and again to New Zealand, a land of which he was especially fond. He spent some time at the Bay of Islands. Then, sailing to the Loyalty Islands, he filled in some gaps left from his previous voyage and followed this with a geographical survey of the Louisiade Archipelago. To correct one of the major lapses of his previous voyage, he now surveyed treacherous Torres Strait with the greatest care. (In the course of this work both of his ships ran aground and were gotten off only with difficulty.) D'Urville refreshed at Timor, touched at Réunion in his crossing of the Indian Ocean, and at St. Helena in the Atlantic. He arrived back in Toulon on November 6, 1840.

After his return Dumont d'Urville was rewarded again by a promotion to rear admiral. In 1841 he became president of the Paris

Geographical Society and was awarded the society's gold medal. It was while working on the monumental account of his voyage that he went on a holiday to Versailles with his wife and son. On the way home, on May 8, 1842, all three perished in a train accident near Meudon.

Book Four

16

British Ships on Other Errands

ALTHOUGH captains on commercial voyages by the second decade of the nineteenth century seldom made discoveries of any great consequence, and although systematic exploration was being carried out exclusively by official expeditions, four English voyages not primarily organized for Pacific exploration made significant geographic contributions.

On December 30, 1813, H.M. Frigate *Briton*, thirty-eight guns and 300 men, under the command of Sir Thomas Staines, sailed from Spithead with an East Indies and South American fleet. Shortly after she sailed, a storm disabled the Indiaman *Fort William*, and Sir Thomas was forced to stand by in *Briton* until *Fort William* could be gotten into Funchal. As the two ships were now separated from the fleet, the *Briton* escorted the Indiaman to Rio, whence the *Briton* planned to sail with the *Fort William* round the Cape of Good Hope. However, orders were received for her to proceed to the Pacific around Cape Horn and to seek out the U.S. Frigate *Essex*, said to be refitting at Valparaiso, and put a stop to David Porter's depredations on English whalers. Sir Thomas arrived at Valparaiso on May 21, 1814, only to find that the *Essex* had already been captured by H.M.S. *Phoebe* and *Cherub* a few weeks before. H.M. Frigate *Tagus* was also at anchor at Valparaiso. Ten days later the *Phoebe* sailed for England with her prize, while the *Briton* and *Tagus* sailed for Callao.

After visiting several small ports along the Peruvian coast the two frigates went to the Galápagos Islands, where they took in over a hundred tortoises. (Several of these monsters weighed upwards of 370 pounds and one, on the *Briton*, so greatly exceeded all the others in size that it was named Lord Chatham by the sailors.) Well supplied with fresh tortoise meat, the *Briton*, still in company with the *Tagus*, sailed on August 4. She made the 3,000-mile run to Nuku Hiva in the Marquesas in fourteen days and dropped the hook at Port Anna Maria (Taiohae) — the same anchorage where Porter had laid in the *Essex*. One of the first people to greet *Briton* was an English sailor named Wilson, who had been living at Port Anna Maria for ten years and was now performing the duties of self-appointed harbor pilot. Almost immediately the friendly local chief asked Sir Thomas how many pigs, breadfruit, coconuts, and ladies he would require for the two ships.

During the fortnight spent at the Marquesas, Sir Thomas paid a visit to the king. Lieutenant John Shillabeer, who wrote the published account of *Briton*'s voyage, described the palace as "an open hut, situated near the sea-side, [that] has nothing, except its size, to distinguish it from any of the others. One of the rooms was curiously decorated with the skeleton heads of pigs, exceedingly clean, and well preserved. These animals, to a great number, had been sacrificed at the death of the king's mother, and whose heads were fixed round this apartment, by way of keeping her alive in his memory; but however dear she might have been to him, he did not hesitate to barter a couple of the best for an old razor." Lt. Shillabeer and two companions subsequently walked over the mountains to visit the Typees, whom the English found to be a kindly people, although American officers in Valparaiso had said they were especially hostile. With considerable justification Shillabeer condemns Porter's unreasonably harsh treatment of the Marquesans.

The ships moved over to Tahuata Island and then sailed from the Marquesas on September 2, bound back to Valparaiso. It was reckoned that the course laid out should carry the ship nearly three degrees of longitude to the eastward of Pitcairn's Island. Staines and his officers were astonished, therefore, when that lofty, lonely island made its unexpected appearance during the second watch. At daylight they could easily see huts, people, and signs of cultivation, and boats putting out through the surf. The officers of the *Briton* and *Tagus* prepared to practice their Polynesian.

What then was their surprise to be hailed in perfect English! Until that moment, thoughts of Bligh and the *Bounty* had not entered their heads. They were but dimly aware that descendants of the mutineers and their Tahitian wives lived on Pitcairn. Before the *Briton* had sailed from Spithead, the British Admiralty had received in 1813 a letter from Captain Mayhew Folger of Nantucket, reporting that, while he was in command of the Boston ship *Topaz* on a sealing voyage in 1808, he had stopped at Pitcairn and found the mutineers' descendants and one surviving member of the *Bounty* crew — Alexander Smith (who later preferred to be known as John Adams). Folger's report had been looked on with some scepticism in England. Now the proof was before the officers' eyes. According to Shillabeer, after an exchange of pleasantries the first man aboard asked, "Do you know one William Bligh, in England?" Shortly Fletcher Christian's son, Friday Fletcher October Christian, was also on board. It soon emerged that, although four ships had been sighted since Folger's visit, the *Briton* and *Tagus* were the first to stop.

The young Pitcairner Mackey (McCoy), who had been first on deck, received the fright of his life when a small black terrier suddenly appeared. Running behind one of the officers, he pointed at the creature and said, "I know what that is, it is a dog, I never saw a dog before — will it bite?" Then, turning to young Christian, he remarked in admiration, "It is a pretty thing too to look at, is it not?" Some of the officers, but not Shillabeer to his regret, went ashore and interviewed Alexander Smith (John Adams), the last mutineer. He gave them several of Captain Bligh's books, later owned by Fletcher Christian, with marginal notes by Bligh. The Pitcairn Islanders and English officers alike were fascinated and excited by the accidental visit of the two frigates.

Leaving Pitcairn, the *Briton* and the *Tagus* made the run to Valparaiso in thirty days, left shortly thereafter for home, and arrived at Plymouth on July 7, 1815, where for the first time they heard the news of Napoleon's return from Elba and the Battle of Waterloo.*

* In cruising about the west coast of South America, the two frigates called at Juan

When King Kamehameha II (Liho Liho) of the Hawaiian Islands decided to visit his royal colleagues in England, he embarked with his queen and retinue on the English whaler *Aigle*, commanded by Captain Starbuck, an American. The party arrived at Portsmouth on May 21 or 22, 1824, and went directly to London.

The English were, understandably, taken by surprise at this royal visit, but they rallied round and the Hawaiians were entertained in a manner becoming their rank. Indeed, an audience with George IV was in the planning stage, when both Kamehameha II and Queen Kamamalu contracted measles, then epidemic in London. Both sovereigns were dead before the middle of July.

Everything possible was done by the British government to atone for this misfortune, and H.M.S. *Blonde*, commanded by George Anson Lord Byron (grandson of "Foul Weather" Jack the circum navigator, and cousin of the poet, whom he succeeded to the title), was selected to return the bodies. The royal remains were taken on board at Woolwich. Then the ship went around to Spithead, where Boki, the governor of Oahu, and other survivors of the Hawaiian party embarked. She sailed the next day, September 29, 1824, for the Pacific.

This was not, of course, a voyage of discovery. Yet Whitehall obviously intended that the opportunity be taken to add to natural knowledge, especially of the Sandwich Islands. Robert Dampier, an excellent artist, boarded H.M.S. *Blonde* at Rio de Janeiro; James Macrae, a Scottish botanist and horticulturalist, was sent out by the Horticultural Society of London (predecessor of the Royal Horticultural Society) to carry plants to the islands as well as to make botanical collections; and Andrew Bloxam (whose older brother, Reverend Rowland R. Bloxam, was chaplain of the ship) sailed as naturalist.

The *Blonde* touched at Madeira and Rio and sailed from St. Catharine's, Brazil, on New Year's Day, 1825. By February 4, 1826, she was

---

Fernández for wood and water. Here again they reenacted some of Captain Folger's experiences. A tent that they set up on shore was plundered by Spaniards living on the island. A few years before, Folger in the *Topaz*, after making his discovery of the *Bounty* people's descendants at Pitcairn, had a number of things stolen from him at the same place, among them Captain Bligh's chronometer, which John Adams had given to Folger to return to Bligh.

Interior of Pitcairn Island (Beechey, Voyage to the Pacific)

at Valparaiso, where several other English naval vessels, including the *Briton*, then lay. Here the *Blonde* overtook Captain Richard Charlton, first English Consul to the Society and Sandwich islands, who (according to Andrew Bloxam) sailed two days later for the Hawaiian Islands with a "most extraordinary cargo on board, consisting of donkeys and Jew's harps — harmony combined." Unhappily, it was here, too, that Kapihe, the likable and intelligent Hawaiian chief who had charge of all the king's vessels, died. Because Kapihe was a heretic the Chileans would not allow his burial on land, and so he was taken out and buried at sea. Following this tragedy, an outbreak of smallpox on board ship delayed the sailing further. In the midst of all this travail, several Welsh seamen provided a St. David's Day interlude by getting exuberantly drunk.

H.M.S. *Blonde* finally sighted Hilo on May 3, 1825. Two days later Lord Byron, Bloxam, and others landed at Lahaina on Maui. The entire party of Hawaiians brought from England came ashore dressed in their European clothing. The following day the *Blonde* was taken over to Oahu, where, because of her size, she was forced to anchor outside the shallow, intricate channel into Honolulu Harbor.

Byron lost no time in giving a public reception for the young King Kauikeaouli (soon to be known as Kamehameha III), the Queen Mother Kahumanu, other members of the royal family, and the leading chiefs. Richard Charlton and the principal white residents, including the American missionaries Bingham and Stewart, were also present. Lord Byron made a gracious speech on behalf of His Britannic Majesty and distributed gifts to the assembled Hawaiian dignitaries. Hiram Bingham, the self-appointed leading missionary, delivered a dull, long-winded prayer. Then came the refreshments.

James Macrae, always a diligent collector of plants and other natural history specimens, made an unsuccessful attempt to escape this boring ceremony. "Being tired of waiting any longer at this mock formality," he recalled, "I slipped away unperceived, to look for plants, but being missed by Lord Byron, I was sent for to return, and was presented to the Regent as the person who had brought them plants from the Horticultural Society of London. He was informed that I wanted permission to collect the wild plants of the country for the Society.

View of Honolulu, 1826 (Original watercolor by R. Beechey. In the collection of the Peabody Museum of Salem)

Mr. Pitt, Regent, kindly granted me full liberty to collect what plants I wished. Lord Byron, however, requested me not to begin collecting until the funeral was over."

The royal bodies were brought ashore on May 6, and the funeral held shortly thereafter. With the solemn mission accomplished, Macrae and Andrew Bloxam made a two-day botanizing excursion up the Nuuanu Valley collecting plants and land snails. (Among the valley's residents, they met a Tahitian who had served in the British Navy and suffered wounds at Algiers.) Macrae and Bloxam descended the Pali and spent the night in the hut of a Bengalese tailor who had been in an Indiaman wrecked on Oahu, and had married a Hawaiian woman and settled down and raised a family. The Hawaiian melting pot was already simmering well.

Macrae has left an interesting description of the Hawaiians living in the valley at this time. "Both sexes," he writes, "are generally tatooed irregularly, with figures of goats, muskets and even letters of the alphabet. Name and birthplace with date of the year are often seen tatooed along the arm. Many of the men shave their heads, and cut their hair in the form of a helmet, the crest of which is often stained with lime, so as to be of a light whitish colour. The women esteem it cut short, with a rim over the forehead bleached white and standing up in front like bristles. Sometimes a long curl is preserved in the middle of the forehead, which is combed backwards. Some suffer their hair to grow and tie it up behind in a bunch. Many of the females, different from any of the other sex, have a tatooed line about two inches broad inside the thigh down as low as the ankle, where it terminates in the form of a ring generally on the right foot. Most of them had a looking glass and a wooden tabacco pipe tied round the neck in a handkerchief or piece of tapa cloth. They are very fond of smoking, and are seldom seen without a pipe. . . ."

Dampier, meanwhile, the expedition's artist, was kept busy painting his distinguished portraits of the royal family. And important ethnological specimens (today in various institutions) were collected. "Our coming to reside on shore," Lord Byron wrote, "has been the signal for all the petty traffickers in curiosities to gather round us. Feather tippets and cloaks, war-helmets, weapons, mother-of-pearl fish-hooks, and even gods are brought to market; and as the latter article has been in much demand, the handicraftsmen have set to work and manufactured a few new ones, just as good as the old, but that they have never been worshipped — and do not the antiquemakers in Rome do the same?" On May 21, Bloxam remarked, "I procured today for a dollar two very old and curious carved idols, or native gods, one of which I presented to Lord Byron, the other is now in the Oxford Museum."

In a last stroll through Honolulu, Macrae "noticed a young woman walking along the street, and at the same time suckling several puppies that were wrapped up in a piece of tapa cloth hanging round her shoulders and breasts. The custom of suckling dogs and pigs is common to the natives of the Sandwich Islands. These animals are held by them in great estimation, little inferior to their own offspring, and my journeys to the woods in search of plants often afforded me an opportunity of being an eye witness to this habit. I often saw them feeding the young pigs and dogs with the poi made from the taro root, in the same way as a mother would her child."

After a month's stay at Honolulu, where the *Blonde* was victualed entirely from the estate of Boki, the governor of Oahu, Lord Byron sailed on June 7 to Hilo, taking Queen Kahumanu, John Young, and a party of chiefs with him. Here His Lordship intended to refit, and Queen Kahumanu provided a commodious and convenient house for his use. Byron moved on shore with half a dozen of his officers and took up residence, while Kahumanu and her party lived nearby in five temporary hastily constructed huts. During the refitting of the ship, various shore parties explored the island. Macrae climbed Mauna Kea and made a memorable descent into the active crater of Kilauea on the flank of Mauna Loa. Although Alexander Menzies, the surgeon with Vancouver, had probably been the first human being to reach the summit of Mauna Loa, Macrae was the first botanist to notice and collect the rare Silver Sword plant, which he described as being "in growth much like a Yucca, with sharp pointed silver coloured leaves and green upright spike of three or four feet producing pendulous branches with brown flowers, truly superb, and almost worth the journey of coming here to see it on purpose." He also visited the beautiful Waianuenue (Rainbow) Falls.

Macrae reported to Byron that "each island, and each division on Hawaii, has some peculiar article, in the manufacture of which its inhabitants excel. The mats of Onehow and those of Taui are incomparably softer and finer than those of the other islands. The women in the neighbourhood of Woraray are said to be more dexterous than others in preparing the bark of the broussonettia [paper mulberry tree] for cloth, and stamping on their tapas the ingenious figures which adorn them. The occupations of the chiefs were making the fishing-tackle, arms, war-cloaks, and helmets; but the wars of Tamehameha, which introduced gunpowder, the progress of civilization, which has made them acquainted with money, commerce, and the arts of reading and writing, have produced a change of occupation among the chiefs; and it is probable that the ornamented pahoe [wooden dagger], the pearl fishhook, and the splendid war-cloak, will soon be more easily found in the cabinets of Europe than among the islands of the Pacific."

The *Blonde*, her refitting completed, now prepared to sail back to Oahu. She took an enormous amount of Hawaiian luggage on board, including 2,000 pieces of tapa that belonged to Queen Kahumanu. (Rents at this time were partially collected in tapas, and quantities of the now priceless barkcloth were sold by the government to the Robinson and Lawrence ship repair yard, where it was used as felting under copper sheathing.) On July 12 Byron left Honolulu and returned to Kealakekua Bay to pick up a surveyor who had reamined on Hawaii to map the coast.

Byron's description of his visit to the no longer sacred royal morai near Honaunau, the City of Refuge,* suggests his fascinated interest in Hawaiian culture. "After rowing along the coast to the southward for a short time," Byron recounts, "we came to a pretty creek called Honaunau, where the morai, overshadowed with cocoa-nut trees, stood. The exterior appearance of the building itself does not differ from that of the grass houses of the native chiefs. It is surrounded by a palisade formed of the trunks of palm-trees, and the court within the palisade is filled with rude wooden images of all shapes and dimen-

* It has recently been restored by the National Park Service.

sions, whose grotesque forms and horrible countenances present a most extra-ordinary spectacle. Most of these idols are placed in the same attitude; one, however, was distinguished by a greater degree of skill in the carving; it had a child in its arms. There were also a number of poles with carved heads in various parts of the court, and, immediately in front of the morai, and outside of the palisades, there was a kind of sentinel deity of a very grotesque shape. On entering the morai we saw on one hand a line of deities made of wicker-work, clothed in fine tapa, now nearly destroyed by time, and adorned with feathered helmets and masks, made more hideous by rows of sharks' teeth, and tufts of human hair; each differing a little from the other, but all preserving a strong family likeness. Under these the bones of the ancient kings of the Island are said to be deposited; and near them the favourite weapons of deceased chiefs and heroes, their ornaments, and whatever else might have been pleasing to them while alive."

Chief Kalaimoku readily gave permission to Byron and his officers to remove whatever they desired. In short order a fortune (in today's market) in primitive art was turfed on board the *Blonde*.

Bloxam, who drew a sketch of this last remaining morai in nearly perfect condition, also has left a description of it. And Macrae, who visited the same place the day after his commander, rather glumly remarks: "The party with Lord Byron that had visited here the day before, had taken away any memorials of the morai that could be taken, so we asked the old priest to be allowed to take some of the ancient weather-beaten carved figures outside." Later, Macrae continues, "On board we found the old priest awaiting us for some presents in return for the old images he had allowed us to take from outside the morai. We gave him several articles of clothing with which he was more pleased than if we had given him money."

During four busy days at Kealakekua, Lord Byron erected an inscribed cross as a memorial to Captain Cook at the spot where his distinguished predecessor was killed. He then weighed anchor and departed on July 18.

For ten days Byron tried unsuccessfully to work to windward and make Tahiti. When on July 29 he saw low land in the distance, he took it to be Starbuck Island. But repeated observations revealed it to be a new discovery. Byron promptly named it Malden Island for his surveyor.

This remnant of coral had not always been uninhabited. "There are traces of human occupation," Byron later reported, "if not of habitation. Large square areas raised to the height of three feet above the ordinary surface are here and there to be seen, supported by blocks of wrought coral, and each having in the centre what we may call an altar or table-tomb."

On the first of August Byron sighted the real Starbuck Island, an uninviting scrap of soil on which a landing was impossible. A week later *Blonde* was off Mauke in the Cook Islands. As the ship lay about three miles offshore, several canoes approached. "The first that reached us was a single man," Byron wrote, "whose costume soon convinced us that we were not the first visitors of this solitary place. He wore a straw hat, shaped like a common English hat; and besides his maro or waist-cloth, he wore a cloak of tapa, of the same form with the South American poncho. The language of this man seemed to bear some affinity to the Hawaiian, but not sufficient for any of our people to comprehend him fully; however, we made out that the Island was called Mauti. While we were questioning our visitor, another canoe, of very singular construction, came alongside of us." Byron's supposition that he was not the first foreign visitor was confirmed when two native Tahitian missionaries of the London Missionary Society stepped from the second canoe. It quickly emerged that the Reverend John Williams, while at Atiu in the chartered vessel *Endeavour* two years before, had heard of both Mauke and Mitiaro and visited them in July 1823 — the same year that he also discovered Rarotonga.

Landing, the Polynesians carried the officers through shoal water. People pressed forward to shake hands, and they guided the English towards the village, about two miles distant. "Our path" Byron wrote, "lay through a thick shady wood, on the skirts of which, in a small open space on the left, two handsome canoes were building. They were each eighty feet long; the lower part, as usual, of a single tree, hollowed out with great skill." Bloxam was equally impressed with them but judged them about ten feet shorter.

On August 10 Byron gave up all hope of reaching Tahiti and bore up for Valparaiso, which *Blonde* reached in twenty-one days.* She arrived at Spithead on March 15, 1826.

Two months and five days after Lord Byron brought the *Blonde* back to England, another smart British frigate, H.M.S. *Blossom*, sailed for the Pacific. Hers was not a mission of sadness; it was primarily another endeavor to pass along the frozen Arctic coast of North America. It was related to another voyage planned to approach the Arctic coast from the Atlantic.

In 1824 William E. Parry began his third attempt to penetrate the Northwest Passage — this time by way of Prince Regent's Inlet. At the same time Captain John Franklin, back from his brilliant discoveries at the mouth of the Coppermine River, headed an expedition to descend the Mackenzie River. His associate, Dr. John Richardson, was to explore the coast eastward while Franklin was to follow the shore line westward as far as possible. It was realized that, if either Parry or Franklin were successful in reaching the open sea at Bering Strait, provisions would be nearly exhausted. The government, therefore, decided to send a well-supplied ship — the *Blossom* — to Bering Strait to await the arrival of the two expeditions. And as the *Blossom* would reach the Pacific a good many weeks before her presence was required in the north (the summer of 1826 and, if necessary, that of 1827, was specified), her skipper, Beechey, was instructed to survey and explore "such parts of the Pacific as were within reach, and were of the most consequence to navigation."

Entrusted with this errand, Captain Frederick William Beechey, a son of the painter Sir William Beechey and a veteran of ice navigation, was given command of H.M.S. *Blossom*, a small frigate of twenty-six guns. (Ten of her guns were removed to lighten her for exploration purposes.) Among *Blossom's* officers were Lieutenant Edward Bel-

---

* On March 7, midway across the Atlantic, the *Blonde* rescued four men and two women from the lumber-laden wreck of the ship *Frances Mary* of New Brunswick, bound for Liverpool. The wretched people, after a thirty-two days' ordeal, were the only survivors of a group of seventeen. They had resorted to cannibalism to live. Later the *Frances Mary* was salvaged by H.M.S. *Diamond* and brought into the Azores.

cher, just returned from the Pacific in the *Blonde*, and midshipman Richard B. Beechey — the captain's nephew and an artist of no small talent. George Tradescant Lay was appointed naturalist. The ship was strengthened and a large schooner-rigged boat was stowed on deck as a tender. Articles of trade, antiscorbutics, spirits for both internal consumption and the preservation of specimens, and all other necessary supplies were provided in abundance.

Beechey was instructed to visit Easter Island, search for Sala-y-Gomez Island, determine whether or not Ducie and Elizabeth islands were one and the same, visit Pitcairn, and survey through the Tuamotus all the way to Tahiti. If he had time he was to go to Samoa, establish the true position of Suvorov Island, and leave dispatches at Hawaii, where food and water could be replenished before he went north. The date for his rendezvous with Franklin at Bering Strait had been fixed for not later than July 10, 1826, but if Franklin failed to appear, Beechey was to remain there until the end of October or as late as the season allowed. If neither Parry nor Franklin arrived at all, Beechey was to return to the rendezvous in 1827. Specimens were to be collected in the islands of the Pacific. After obtaining at least two specimens of each kind for the public museums, officers were allowed to collect for themselves. Journals were to be kept and charts and drawings made.

The *Blossom* sailed from Spithead on May 20, 1825, and on July 11 anchored in the middle of a British squadron at Rio de Janeiro. She sailed from Rio a month later, rounded the Horn, and after a two-day layover at Valparaiso headed, on October 29, across the Pacific.

Off Sala-y-Gomez, Beechey noted that Kotzebue's latitude for those lonely rocks was, as published, nine miles in error. (He generously suggested that it may have been a typographical mistake.) When Easter Island was sighted on the afternoon of November 16, Beechey ordered two boats launched under the command of the ship's first lieutenant, George Peard. The boats finally landed, after encountering severe difficulties from numbers of natives in the water who impeded their progress. "All those in the water were naked," Beechey wrote, "and only here and there, on the shore, a thin cloak of the native cloth was to be seen. Some had their faces painted black, some red; others black and white, or red and white, in the ludicrous manner practised by our clowns; and two demonlike monsters were painted entirely black."

As other navigators had noted, the Easter Islanders were not the friendliest Pacific islanders. The British were crowded by the motley throng and shortly Beechey noted that "one of the natives, probably a chief, with a cloak and head-dress of feathers, was observed from the ship hastening from the huts to the landing-place, attended by several persons with short clubs. This hostile appearance, followed by the blowing of the conch-shell, a sound which Cook observes he never knew to portend good, kept our glasses for a while riveted to the spot." As the boats pulled from the shore under a shower of stones, Beechey decided to leave Easter, reflecting that there would be little loss to knowledge, as the place had been well described by others.

Blossom picked up a trade wind and soon was in sight of Ducie Island — a clear lagoon surrounded by an oval of coral rising a bare twelve feet, at most, above the sea's surface. Only the birds and trees bending in the trades gave Ducie Island life. But the water surrounding it (so clear that the bottom could be distinctly seen where no sounding could be obtained with a thirty fathom line) teemed with fish and sharks.

Beechey next sailed to Elizabeth (more properly called Henderson) Island, with which Ducie could not possibly be confused. For Henderson, one of those rare islands thrown up by some great convulsion of the earth, is composed entirely of dead honeycombed coral. From its flat surface, nearly eighty feet above the sea, perpendicular cliffs drop to the ocean on all sides but the north. Landing here is hazardous; the summit is difficult to attain.*

Following his instructions to the letter, Beechey went on to Pitcairn, which he sighted on December 4, 1825. Old John Adams, rowed by ten husky young men of the island, visited *Blossom* in a whaleboat. The islanders had apparently forgotten the visit of the *Briton* and *Tagus* eleven years before, for they allowed that they had

---

* Henderson Island was actually discovered by some of the survivors from the American whaler *Essex*, sunk by a sperm whale, who lived here for several months until rescued by an English whaler.

never seen a ship "so rich" as the *Blossom*. The vessels that occasionally called at Pitcairn were mostly grubby whalers or small traders. Adams's oarsmen skillfully landed the officers of *Blossom*, two at a time through the surf, at the foot of cliffs that tower above rock-strewn Bounty Bay.

Beechey stayed at the island until December 21 and wrote the most extensive account of Pitcairn, its people, their customs, and life that had yet appeared. He reported that tapa was still being manufactured — a craft learned from the islanders' Tahitian ancestors — and that the island swarmed with houseflies, a nuisance imported by H.M.S. *Briton*. He reported that the population of Pitcairn Island at this time was sixty-six.

As the officers of *Blossom* walked the island paths, they discovered that one trail led to a steep cliff called "the Rope," overlooking a small sandy bay at the eastern end of the island, and at its foot they found stone adzes. "The hatchets," Beechey wrote, "of which we obtained several specimens, were made of a compact basaltic lava, not unlike clinkstone, very hard, and capable of a fine polish. In shape they resembled those used at Otaheite, and by all the islanders of these seas that I have seen." On the peak of "the Rope," Beechey and his men found further evidence of earlier Polynesian occupation: "four images, about six feet in height, placed upon a platform; and, according to Adams's description, not unlike the morais at Easter Island, excepting that they were upon a much smaller scale. One of these images, which had been preserved, was a rude representation of the human figure to the hips, and was hewn out of a piece of red lava."

Blossom covered the ninety miles from Pitcairn to Oeno in two days. But when Beechey sent a crew to Oeno in a landing attempt, one sailor was lost and Lieutenant Edward Belcher nearly drowned as the boat was smashed on the reef. The remainder of the boat's crew was rescued through the heroism of Lieutenant John Wainwright, who risked his own life to take a line to the stranded men on the reef and get them off with a raft.

On December 29 Beechey sighted Mangareva Island (which had been discovered by Captain James Wilson in the *Duff*) and ordered boats lowered to investigate the lagoon and find a passage for the ship.

Mangarevan raft (*Beechey,* Voyage to the Pacific)

At this point, Beechey writes, "several small vessels under sail were observed bearing down to us. When they approached we found they were large katamarans or rafts, carrying from sixteen to twenty men each. . . . We were much pleased with the manner of lowering their matting sail, diverging on different courses, and working their paddles, in the use of which they had great power, and were well skilled, plying them together, or to use a nautical phrase, keeping stroke. They had no other weapons but long poles; and were quite naked with the exception of a banana leaf cut into strips, and tied about their loins, and one or two persons who wore white turbans." When Beechey offered presents to the islanders, they in turn gave him bundles of poi tied up in leaves of such an overpowering odor that Beechey dropped his instantly. Then, as frequently happened with South Sea Islanders, the Mangarevans tried to make off with everything that was not nailed down (and, in the case of the boat's rudder, succeeded). The boat party spent the night on a bar. At daylight, Beechey guided the ship through a pass and into a bay to a safe anchorage.

Because fresh water had become a necessity, the ship was shortly moved across the lagoon, where two bountiful streams flowed down the side of Mount Duff. Beechey and Belcher landed here with two boatloads of sailors, and while Beechey was rubbing noses with a chief in the standard Polynesian gesture of friendship, his fowling piece was stolen. Later, while sailors filled the water casks, Beechey strolled about the village near the foot of Mount Duff and noticed several places where bodies, apparently mummified, had been laid out on racks. He encouraged his surgeon to investigate the methods employed for their preservation. Meanwhile, Lieutenant Belcher, who got about the islands more than anyone else, found an interesting morai. It was, as he described it for Beechey, "a hut, about twenty feet in length by ten wide, and seven high, with a thatched roof, of which the eaves were three feet from the ground, contained the deity. . . . Along the whole length of the interior of the hut was a trough elevated about three feet from the ground; in the centre of which was an idol three feet high, neatly carved and polished; the eyebrows were sculptured, but not the eyes; and from the manner in which the muscles were defined it was evident that these people were not regardless of the anatomy of the figure. . . . In the trough beneath the image were several paddles, mats, coils of line, and cloth, offerings which had been made to the deity; and at his feet was placed a calabash, which the natives said contained water 'avy.' [Kava]" Because of the serious attitude of the people Belcher abstained from trespassing on the sacred ground. However, he "endeavoured to purchase this idol; but valuable as his offer must have been to these poor people, the temptation did not prove sufficient."

Visiting the village near Mount Duff on January 8, 1826, Beechey passed two more mummified bodies, wrapped in many sheets of tapa and raised about three feet off the ground on carved posts. Beechey also met "a venerable looking person about sixty years of age, with a long beard entirely grey; he had well proportioned features, and a commanding aspect; his figure was rather tall, but lassitude and corpulency greatly diminished his natural stature; he was entirely naked except a maro, and a crown made from the feathers of the frigate-bird, or black tern; his body was extensively tattooed, and from the loins to the ankles he was covered with small lines, which at a distance had the appearance of pantaloons. Long nails, and rolls of skin overhanging his hips, pointed out his exemption from labour, and an indulgence in luxuries which in all probability attached to him in virtue of his birth-right. He was introduced to us as an areghe or chief; he did not rise from his seat, but gave the nasal salutation in his squatting posture, which in the Friendly Islands is considered a mark of respect."

While Beechey visited with the chief, Belcher, a man of continuing intellectual curiosity, "discovered three drums, very similar to those at Otaheite, as described by Captain Cook. The largest was about five feet six inches high, and fourteen inches in diameter. . . . It was brought to me," writes Beechey, "and I offered the areghe some knives in exchange, which he refused until the number was increased. When the bargain was concluded, the young chief showed the manner of playing upon the instrument, and convinced us that his skill must have been the result of long practice."

Unfortunately Beechey's purchase was never concluded: "On re-moving the drum which had been sold by the areghe, two of the na-tives laid violent hands upon it, and demanded something more than had been given. To avoid disturbance I complied with their request by doubling the original sum; but this, so far from securing the drum, rendered the probability of our obtaining it without force more re-mote. I brought the old chief back to explain the matter to him, but he would not interfere; and foreseeing the consequence of persisting, I left our purchase in their hands, disgusted with their dishonesty and cunning."

During the stay at Mangareva, Beechey and his men made a good chart of the Gambier group, named the individual islands, and took many soundings in the lagoon. Beechey described the physical and geological features of the island in detail, noted the plants, fruits, and vegetables; rats, lizards, and birds. He observed that the natives re-sembled other Polynesians, "that they were fairer and handsomer than Hawaiians, less effeminate than Tahitians."

Of the tattooing, which was elaborate and universal among the men, Beechey wrote, "the effect is becoming, and in a great measure destroys the appearance of nakedness. The patterns which most im-prove the shape, and which appear to me peculiar to this groupe [*sic*], are those which extend from the armpits to the hips, and are drawn forward with a curve which seems to contract the waist, and at a short distance give the figure an elegance and outline not unlike that of the figures seen on the walls of the Egyptian tombs. . . . Imitations of blue pantaloons and breeches are also very common, the sleeves which divide at the wrist, and extend along the convexity of the metatarsal bones to the tips of the fingers and thumbs, leaving a space between the thumb and forefinger, on which the mark V is punctured. The chief had this mark, the crosses, the slender waist, and pantaloons. The women are very little subjected to this torture."

It will be recalled that when Beechey arrived at Mangareva he was approached by a fleet of rafts. His extended stay confirmed the unusual fact that canoes were lacking here. "Rafts or katamarans are used instead," he says. "They are from forty to fifty feet in length, and will contain upwards of twenty persons. They consist of the trunks of trees fastened together by rope and crossbeams: upon this a triangular sail is hoisted, supported by two poles from each end; but it is only used when the wind is very favourable; at which time, if two or three katamarans happen to be going the same way, they fasten on and perform their voyage together."

The *Blossom* weighed anchor on January 13, 1826, and Beechey began an island-hopping survey through the Tuamotus that took him all the way to Tahiti. *Blossom*'s boats circled Lord Hood's Island (Marutea) and sighted a stone hut on a platform on one of the points, indicating that the place had once been inhabited. (However, wrote Beechey, "the only living thing seen upon the shore was a grey heron gorging itself with black star-fish.") On January 18 *Blossom* raised Réao.* The heavily breaking seas made a landing impossible here, although nervous natives put out in several canoes. Nor was it possible to land on Serle Island (Pukaruha) on the twenty-first. Beechey had better luck at Whitsunday Island (Pinaki), and landed there briefly, albeit with difficulty. He observed several houses and other evidences of occupation but no inhabitants. "But what most attracted our atten-

---

* Named Clermont-Tonnerre by Captain Duperrey on his voyage in the *Coquille*. He considered it a new discovery, not knowing that the *Minerva* had beaten him to it.

Blossom's officers attacked by the Mangarevans (Beechey, Voyage to the Pacific)

tion was a heap of fish bones, six feet by five, neatly cleaned, and piled up very carefully with planks placed upon them to prevent their being scattered by the wind."

Next on Beechey's course was Queen Charlotte's Island (Nukuta-vake), where huts were seen, but again no people. Then, two hours' sailing from Queen Charlotte, Beechey came to Cook's Lagoon Island (Vahitahi) and sent two boats towards shore. "The natives seeing them approach came down to the beach armed with poles from twenty to twenty-five feet in length, with bone heads, and short clubs shaped like a bill-hook; but before they reached the surf they laid down their weapons." He goes on to describe them: "The men were a fine athletic race, with frizzled hair, which they wore very thick. In complexion, they were much lighter than the islanders of Clermont Tonnere: one man, in particular, and the only one who had whiskers, was so fair, and so like an European, that the boat's crew claimed him as a countryman. . . . The women had a mat wrapped about their loins as their only covering: some wore the hair tied in a bunch upon one side of the head, others had a plaited band tied round it. They were inferior to the men in personal appearance and mostly bow-legged; but they exerted an authority not very common among uncivilized people, by taking from the men whatever articles they received in exchange for their fruit, as soon as they returned to the shore."

On January 27, 1826, Beechey made his first discovery: he sighted Vanavana, which he named Barrow's Island for the secretary of the admiralty. Here a tiny oval of land enclosed a shallow lagoon, and large trees provided welcome shade from the scorching sun. Although black and white terns, tropic and frigate birds, and soldier crabs were Vanavana's only inhabitants, this had not always been the case. "Under these trees were three large pits containing several tons of fresh water and not far from them some low huts similar to those described at the other islands, and a tomb-stone shaped like that at Whitsunday Island. We judged that the huts had been long deserted, from the circumstance of the tern and other aquatic birds occupying some calabashes which were left in them. Among several things found in this deserted village were part of a scraper used by merchant-ships, and a large fish-hook, which we preserved, without suspecting that they would at a future day clear up the doubt that these articles were calculated to throw upon the merit of discovering this island, to which we otherwise felt an indisputable claim."

Before Beechey reached Carysfort Island (Tureia) he came upon two coral islands. Sailing around the larger, he saw two anchors lying high up on the reef and the remains of a wreck, which he speculated was the whaler *Matilda*, lost in this vicinity in 1792. This fourteen-mile-long island with its excellent lagoon harbor was Mururoa. Some twenty miles southeast of it lay Fangataufa, which became, on January 29, 1826, Beechey's second discovery. Two days later Beechey discovered Ahunui, which he named Byam Martin Island for the comptroller of the navy, Sir Thomas Byam Martin. He was astonished to be met at Ahunui by forty shipwrecked Tahitians — a party of native Christian missionaries, complete with testaments and hymn-books printed in Tahitian. Their double canoe, in which they had made this remarkable voyage 600 miles to windward of Tahiti, had been repaired (in anticipation of a return voyage) and placed under a shed. Since there was not space on the *Blossom* to take all forty of the shipwrecked party back to Tahiti, the best Beechey could do was to ship one man with his wife and family, who would carry the word to friends and relatives.

Leaving Byam Martin Island, Beechey passed so close to the windward of Gloucester that the coral nearly scraped the barnacles off the bottom. Later the same day he arrived at Bow Island (Hao), first seen by Bougainville in 1768. Here Tuwarri, the Tahitian passenger, met his brother, whom he had left at Chain Island (Anaa) three years before.

Beechey, with his ship safe in the lagoon, made a careful examination of Bow Island. He left it on February 20 and continued his survey through the Tuamotus, correcting errors of longitude made by Bellingshausen, Duperrey, and others. He remarked that Turnbull's observed positions were impossibly inaccurate. (In all he visited thirty-two islands in succession, of which twelve, including Pitcairn, were inhabited.) Finally, on March 15, 1826, he sighted Mehetia, Tahiti's near neighbor to the eastward, and soon afterward the Tahitian mountains came into view.

From Tahiti *Blossom* sailed on to Honolulu, where the naturalist of the expedition, Mr. Lay, who had not been well, was left to recover his health. Beechey arrived at Petropavlovsk in late June to find dispatches telling him of the return of Captain Parry's expedition to England (and thereby enabling him to cancel that part of his instructions relating to Parry). *Blossom* next sailed northward through Bering Strait as far as Icy Cape and then sent a party eastwards in the tender, commanded by Mr. Elson, the mate, to endeavor to meet Franklin. (Elson got as far as Point Barrow, but although he and Franklin reached within 160 miles of each other, they did not meet.) Then San Francisco, then the Sandwich Islands again, then Macao, then the Ryukyu Islands, then Kotzebue Sound. *Blossom* returned home at last to Spithead via the west coast of South America, Cape Horn, and Rio de Janeiro. The ship was paid off at Woolwich on October 12, 1828.

Beechey's contribution to our geographical knowledge, especially of the Tuamotus, was considerable; his surveys were notable; his reports on the Pitcairn Islanders and various Polynesian groups were significant. Beechey died on November 29, 1856 at the age of sixty.

Almost forty years had passed since La Pérouse sailed from Botany Bay into oblivion. Official searches had long since been given up. Time, and the vast Pacific, had swallowed the great French expedition. Yet now, through a series of fortuitous circumstances, combined with his own quick analytical powers of observation, Captain Peter Dillon, an obscure trader, solved the long-standing mystery.

It all began when Dillon made a sandalwood voyage from Calcutta to Fiji in 1812 and 1813 as an officer of the ship *Hunter*. Captain Robson, the vessel's commander, became involved in one of the incessant tribal wars going on in the Fijis at this time. He was on the losing side, and Dillon, after a skirmish, found himself one of only three members of a boat's crew to escape massacre. Robson, after such disastrous losses, decided to sail for China. As an act of humanity he took with him several people who had fought on his side and who would have been eaten had they remained in Fiji. He told Dillon, however, that he would land these people on the first island they came to. This island turned out to be Tikopia, a Polynesian outlier in the Santa Cruz group. Among those he landed was a white man named Martin Bus-hart and his Fijian wife. The *Hunter* went on to China, and Dillon, in command of the ship's cutter, sailed to Port Jackson.

Thirteen years went by and on May 13, 1826, Peter Dillon, now in command of the ship *St. Patrick*, once more came within sight of Ti-kopia. He decided to stop and see how Bushart and the others had fared. Before he could land, Bushart and a Lascar sailor (who had also been one of the group) came on board. The Lascar gave Dillon a silver sword guard, and from Bushart Dillon learned of other Euro-pean relics that had been brought in canoes from Vanikoro (or, as he called it, Malicolo), where — the Tikopians said — two large ships had been wrecked at a time when those on the island who were now old men had been boys. Dillon correctly concluded that, since no other two ships had been lost in this general area of the Pacific during

Martin Bouchert, whom Dillon left at Tikopia
(*D'Urville,* Voyage of the Astrolabe *1826–29*)

the period described, these must be the ships of La Pérouse. He made an immediate attempt to go to Vanikoro, but within sight of the island he was becalmed for several days. A leaky ship and shortage of provisions forced him, as soon as he got a wind, to sail for Bengal, where he arrived in September.

Announcing his discovery to the Bengal government, Dillon offered his ship (provided the government would repair it at their expense) to go to Vanikoro and attempt to rescue any possible survivors of the French expedition. After considerable negotiations his ship was turned down, but he was given command of the Honorable East India Company's ship *Research*. Early in the new year he worked downriver and on January 23, 1827, discharged the pilot. Sailing south, he coasted western Australia and arrived at Derwent River, Tasmania, on April 5 and then went on to Port Jackson.* From Port Jackson he sailed to New Zealand, Tonga, and Rotuma before he sighted Tikopia again on September 5.

But once on the scene, Dillon energetically pursued his search. He obtained some chain plates, iron bolts, and a crowbar from a man who had been to Vanikoro. More important, he heard the story from the natives of how the two vessels had been wrecked in the night. One vessel, a total and immediate loss, had hit the reef at a spot called Whannow; the other drove over the reef at a place called Paiow, and her men were apparently able to salvage some stores and useful articles. Establishing themselves within a palisade, the French built a small two-masted vessel from parts of the stranded ship and from trees cut nearby. In this craft all but two men had sailed away never to be seen again.

Dillon's trading officer purchased thirty-one more relics, including fourteen native tools made of beaten iron, an old sword blade, a rasp, a razor, a china plate, one half a brass globe, several bells, and a silver sword handle, which was immediately recognized as belonging to the same sword as the sword guard that had been obtained the previous year.

* Dillon was not really hurrying to get to the Santa Cruz Islands. He had a constant running battle, including a lawsuit in Port Jackson, with a Dr. Robert Tytler, whom he had taken along in an ill-advised moment and who turned out to be a madman.

Having apparently exhausted the possibility of getting information at Tikopia, Dillon took along a couple of natives as pilots, and sailed over to Vanikoro, where he arrived late in the afternoon of September 7. Here he immediately began interrogating Vanikoroans and offering to buy anything from the wrecked ships. He heard again the story of the wrecks in a dreadful storm and the building of the escape vessel. There were many discrepancies concerning the number of men lost and whether or not any or many from the first vessel had been massacred. But it did emerge that, of the two Frenchmen who had remained on the island, one had died and the other had fled with a local chief to another island. Dillon purchased quantities of iron, copper, and brass, including the iron tiller of a large ship, iron knees, tools, and utensils. Among the brass and copper objects was a large ship's bell, twelve and a half inches in diameter, decorated on the front with a cross, the Virgin Mary, and a holy man, and on the back with three figures in an ellipse with the sun shining over them. It was inscribed *Bazin m'a fait* [Bazin made me].

Dillon obtained a remarkable statement relating to the wreck of the second ship from a man named Owallie. "A long time ago," Owallie began, "the people of this island, upon coming out one morning, saw part of a ship on the reef opposite to Paiow, where it held together till the middle of the day, when it was broken by the sea, fell to pieces, and large parts of it floated on shore along the coast. The ship got on the reef in the night, when it blew a tremendous hurricane, which broke down a considerable number of our fruit-trees. We had not seen the ship the day before. Four men were saved from her, and were on the beach at this place, who we were about to kill, supposing them spirits, when they made a present to our chief of something, and he saved their lives. They lived with us a short time, and then joined their people at Paiow, who built a small ship there and went away in it. None of those four men were chiefs: they were only subordinate men. Those things which we sell you now have been procured from the ship wrecked on the reef, on which, at low water, our people were in the habit of diving and bringing up what they could find. Several pieces of the wreck floated on shore, from which we procured some things; but nothing has been got from it for some time back, as it has become rotten and been drifted away by the sea. We killed none of the ship's people at this place, but several dead bodies were cast on shore, with the legs and other members mutilated by the sharks. The same night another ship struck on a reef near Whannow and went down. There were several men saved from her, who built a little ship, and went away five moons after the big one was lost. While building it, they had a great fence of trees round them to keep out the islanders; who being equally afraid of them, they consequently kept up but little intercourse. The white men used often to look at the sun through something, but we have none of those things. Two white men remained behind after the rest went away; the one was a chief, and the other a common man, who used to attend on the white chief, who died about three years ago. The chief with whom the white man resided was obliged, about two years and a half ago, to fly from his country, and was accompanied by the white man. The name of the district which they abandoned was Pawcorrie; but we do not know what has become of this tribe. The only white people or foreigners the inhabitants of this island have ever seen were, first, the people of the wrecked ships, and secondly, those before me now."

Dillon made an excursion to the spot where the escape vessel was built, hoping that some inscription or message might be found, but except for a clearing and some stumps of trees all evidence had vanished in thirty-nine years. Dillon did, however, discover a plank over four feet long and thirteen inches wide, decorated with a fleur-de-lis and other ornamental carving, built into a house, as well as a small millstone for grinding grain and a copper boiler of fifteen to twenty gallons' capacity. And he found a piece of blue glass tube, the proud possession of a man who had it transversely fixed like a yardarm through the cartilage of his nose.

After exhausting all of the information and material obtainable at Vanikoro, Dillon sailed on October 8, 1827, to Ndeni, the largest of the Santa Cruz group, in the hopes of finding the lone Frenchman who had fled in that direction. He was unsuccessful and retraced his steps to the Bay of Islands, New Zealand, which he left December 27 for Port Jackson. By April 5, 1828, he was taking a pilot off the

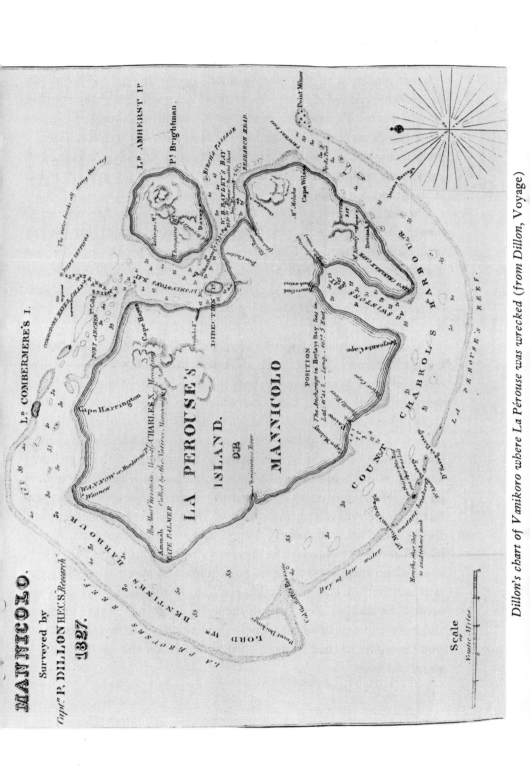

Dillon's chart of Vanikoro where La Pérouse was wrecked (from Dillon, Voyage)

mouth of the Hooghly River and shortly thereafter arrived at Calcutta.

After reporting to the Marine Board of the Bengal Government, Peter Dillon packed up his precious relics and took passage on the ship *Mary Ann* for Europe. He landed at Plymouth on October 25, and immediately went to London to see the French ambassador. After a preliminary trip to Paris to arrange publication rights, he returned to Paris again with the relics on February 6, 1829: at last what was left of the gallant La Pérouse expedition returned to France.

Charles X rewarded Dillon liberally for his efforts. He was reimbursed for all of his expenses, given a 4,000-franc annuity for the rest of his life, and made a Chevalier of the Legion of Honor. He was granted an interview with the king and met, on several occasions, the Viscount de Lesseps — the only person of the La Pérouse expedition still alive — who had made the phenomenal overland journey from Kamchatka.

De Lesseps examined all of the relics carefully, and Dillon has recorded his remarks. "The piece of board with the *fleur de lis* on it, [he observed] had most probably once formed a part of the ornamental work of the *Boussole*'s stern, on which the national arms of France were represented, as she was the only one of the ships bearing such an ornament. The silver sword-handle and silver spoon he also examined, and said that such swords were worn by the officers of the expedition, and that it was not unlikely the guard and spoon belonged to him, as he had left such articles on board the expedition, considering them burthensome on his long journey over snows, deserts, mountains, and through the wilds of Siberia. With regard to the brass guns, having looked at them attentively, he observed that the four largest were such as stood on the quarterdeck of both ships, and that the smallest gun was such as they had mounted in the long-boats when going on shore among the savages. On noticing the small millstone, he turned round suddenly and expressed his surprise, observing, 'This is the best thing you have got: we had some of them mounted on the quarter-deck to grind our grain.'"

17

Darwin and the *Beagle*

WHILE the French expeditions were crisscrossing the Pacific in the second quarter of the nineteenth century, amassing collections and publishing monumental tomes, the English were quietly slogging out the details of coastal delineation. Tenacious, dedicated, professional navy hydrographers in small ships worked some of the most intricate waters in desperately bad climates in order that accurate charts could be made to guide the world's commerce. Theirs was the bedrock of exploration.

The voyage of H.M.S. *Beagle* in 1832–1836 is one of the most outstanding of these expeditions. *Beagle*'s Pacific crossing was hasty (although not originally intended so), and there were no island discoveries. But the accurate and detailed survey work and charting, the meridial observations, and, above all, the fact that a young naturalist named Charles Darwin was on board, contributed results in new areas of knowledge that make this voyage a classic.

The origin of the voyage goes back to an earlier one in which the *Beagle* was involved. With the rapid expansion of the whale fishery and the ever wider search for furs, sandalwood, pearl shell, and other products suitable especially for the China trade, the number of ships entering the Pacific had risen rapidly in the first thirty years of the nineteenth century. It was estimated that by 1830 there were five hundred British and American vessels in the Pacific. Nor were French, Russian, Spanish, and other ships uncommon. The only two ways for a ship to sail to the Pacific and to Asia were via Cape Horn or the Cape of Good Hope. (By this time, it was realized that even if a Northwest Passage were discovered it would be commercially useless.) Since neither the southern African nor South American shores had been properly surveyed, the British Hydrographic Office, under a series of energetic hydrographers, was pushing coastal surveys as rapidly as funds and personnel allowed. After years of work, the African survey was completed by Captain William FitzWilliam Owen in 1826. The same year the much more difficult southern South American survey began.

In 1825 the Lords Commissioners of the Admiralty had ordered two ships equipped for the South American survey. By May 1826 the ship *Adventure*, 330 tons, and the bark *Beagle*, 235 tons, were ready in Plymouth Sound. Philip Parker King, son of the former governor of New South Wales, Philip Gidley King, was appointed commander of the *Adventure* and of the expedition. (Captain King had already become expert while completing Matthew Flinder's Australian surveys. As a boy he had seen that great hydrographer when Flinders came to call on his father after the disaster at Wreck Reef.) Captain Pringle Stokes was given command of the *Beagle*.

Instructions were specific. Supplying a total of twelve chronometers for the two ships, the commissioners demanded that longitude be determined with the greatest accuracy. They ordered the expedition to make several stops on the Atlantic crossing to Rio de Janeiro, and then to survey the coast from the River Plate, around Tierra del Fuego, to Chiloé Island on the west coast of South America, as the state of the seasons or other circumstances determined. Furthermore, this service was to be continued until the work was completed.

The ships sailed from Plymouth on May 22, 1826, and arrived on August 10 at Rio, where they remained until October 2. By the thirteenth they were anchored in Maldonado Bay, where they stayed for a month while the north side of the River Plate was surveyed. Leaving Montevideo on November 19, King decided to survey the southern coasts of Patagonia, Tierra del Fuego, and the Strait of Magellan first, in order to take advantage of the season.

For the next two years, the men of *Adventure* and *Beagle* pursued their work in one of the world's most atrocious climates, charting the Strait of Magellan and the maze of intricate channels from its western

The Beagle laid ashore in the Santa Cruz River (Darwin, Voyages of the Adventure and Beagle, Vol. II)

end to the southern coast of Tierra del Fuego.* Gales were frequent. Thick weather often hampered the work. Ships became worn. Men became exhausted. Sometimes the vessels were in company and at other times worked their separate projects. After an extended separation in the summer of 1828, the *Beagle* rejoined the *Adventure*, and Captain Stokes, physically and mentally worn out, committed suicide by shooting himself; he died on August 12 and was succeeded by Lieutenant W. G. Skyring.

King took his battered expedition back to Rio de Janeiro, where the vessels were repaired and Admiral Sir Robert Otway appointed Robert Fitzroy to the command of the *Beagle*. Then the little fleet returned to Port Famine, the base in the Strait of Magellan, and the monotonous work continued.

While charting was the principal object, continual observations were also made on the natural history of this little-known part of the world; and the Fuegian Indians came in for more attention than they had hitherto received, partly because they were constantly pilfering anything they could lay their hands on. In the course of retrieving a stolen boat, Fitzroy ended up with a nine-year-old girl whom he named "Fuegian Basket" and two young men called "York Minster" and "Boat Memory." Later he was given another boy about fourteen years old, from a different tribe, in exchange for a few beads and buttons. (Indeed, the boy was christened "Jimmy Button.") Finding it impossible to return these young people to their proper tribes, Fitzroy decided to take them to England and trust that they could be returned home on another voyage. It was this circumstance that set the scene for the *Beagle*'s second voyage and gave the young Darwin his opportunity.

Beagle and *Adventure* met at Rio de Janeiro and arrived in company at Plymouth Sound on October 14, 1830. During the voyage home Robert Fitzroy, considering the situation of his Fuegian guests, wrote a letter to his commander, Captain King, explaining that these Indians were being maintained at his own expense, and that, unless His

---

* The survey was interrupted only once, when the expedition returned to Montevideo in April 1827, for the crew to recuperate. At Montevideo the schooner *Adelaide* was purchased and added to the expedition.

Majesty's government directed otherwise, he would find homes for them, educate them as much as possible, and, in three or four years, either take or send them home with such useful articles as he could collect to improve their lives. King forwarded Fitzroy's letter to the Admiralty, and five days after his arrival in Plymouth had a letter from John Barrow for the Lords Commissioners, granting Fitzroy's request and an assurance that the Fuegians would be given passage home.

Fitzroy lost no time in having the Fuegians taken to the Royal Naval Hospital in Plymouth and innoculated for smallpox. "Boat Memory" died as the result of his vaccination. The other three were boarded with the Reverend William Wilson in Walthamstow, where they were taught English and simple and useful crafts. Fitzroy completed his duties relating to the survey in March 1831. In the summer of that year he took the three Fuegians, at the wish of William IV, to St. James's palace, where they had a royal audience with the king and with Queen Adelaide, who gave the little girl one of her own bonnets, a ring, and money for a new outfit of clothes.

As the year wore on, Fitzroy was appalled to learn that the Lords of the Admiralty had decided to discontinue the South American survey. He had even made arrangements to charter a merchantman to return his charges to Tierra del Fuego at his own expense, when, through the intervention of an influential relative, the lords reversed their decision. The *Beagle* was fitted out at Devonport, and Fitzroy was appointed to command her again. Besides returning the Fuegians, the Admiralty agreed, at the request of the Reverend William Wilson, that two volunteers could be taken along to live among the Fuegians and attempt to establish a civilized Christian community. (As it turned out only one, Richard Matthews, was willing to take the chance.) The kindhearted people of Walthamstow collected chests of articles for the Fuegians to take back with them, including such useless things as chamberpots, much to the sailors' amusement.

It was the desire of Sir Francis Beaufort, hydrographer of the Admiralty, that Fitzroy complete the South American survey and then cross the Pacific and carry a chain of meridian distances around the world. The *Beagle* was commissioned on July 4, 1831, and immediately taken into dry dock, where she was sheathed and coppered. Her comfort and seaworthiness were improved by raising the deck, which increased her burden to 242 tons. Her new rigging, spars, and sails were of the best, and she carried many improved devices, as well as six new superior boats for the survey crews, and no less than twenty-two chronometers in the captain's cabin.

Two of Fitzroy's lieutenants, John C. Wickham and Bartholomew J. Sulivan, who had served on the first voyage, were again appointed. But the great fame of the voyage rests on the selection of one of the supernumeraries. Fitzroy felt strongly that a naturalist should be appointed, and made the proposal to Beaufort. Beaufort agreed and, through a friend at Cambridge, sent Fitzroy twenty-three-year-old Charles Darwin, only three years the captain's junior. The two young men liked each other, and Darwin was invited to be Fitzroy's guest for the voyage. Although Darwin's father opposed the plan, Darwin succeeded, through the help of his uncle Josiah Wedgwood, in overcoming his father's objections. Augustus Earle was engaged as an artist and George James Stebbing was employed to keep the chronometers and other instruments in order. In all there were seventy-four persons on board when the *Beagle* sailed from England.

Beaufort gave very detailed plans for the voyage. First, the longitude of Rio de Janeiro should be settled once and for all. Fitzroy was not to waste time duplicating the work of a French expedition "now engaged in the examination of the coast between St. Catherine's and the Rio de la Plata," but to continue south from the river, filling in the gaps left by the previous expedition. Following the completion of the east coast, Fitzroy was to move to Concepción or Valparaiso for provisions and to fill in the intervals remaining between the western end of the Strait of Magellan and Valparaiso. Accuracy was to be stressed — Beaufort's memorandum reminds the captain that "the only general knowledge we have [of the coast south of Valparaiso] is from the Spanish charts, which seem, with the exception of certain ports, to have been merely the result of a running view of the shore. Of this kind of half-knowledge we have had too much: the present state of science, which affords such ample means, seems to demand that whatever is now done should be finally done; and that coasts, which are constantly visited by English vessels, should no longer have the motley appearance of alternate error and accuracy."

After leaving the South American coast Fitzroy was to survey the Galápagos Islands and, if time permitted, search for some coral islands supposed to be five or six degrees south of Pitcairn and for several other doubtful islands that had crept into the charts. "But whatever route [across the Pacific] may be adopted," Beaufort admonished, "it should conduct her to Tahiti, in order to verify the chronometers at Point Venus, a point which may be considered as indisputably fixed by Captain Cook's and by many concurrent observations. Except in this case, she ought to avoid as much as possible the ground examined by Captain Beechey."

From Tahiti Fitzroy was to proceed to Port Jackson, touching at as many intervening islands as possible to divide the run into judicious chronometer stages. At Port Jackson the longitude of the observatory at Paramatta had been absolutely determined. Thus Fitzroy from Point Venus to Paramatta would be running between two longitudinally fixed points. Depending on the season, alternate routes from Port Jackson were suggested for completing the voyage. There were general instructions on the making of charts, plans, and sketches. And Beaufort further cautioned: "Trifling as it may appear, the love of giving a multiplicity of new and unmeaning names tends to confuse our geographical knowledge. The name stamped upon a place by the first discoverer should be held sacred by the common consent of all nations; and in new discoveries it would be far more beneficial to make the name convey some idea of the nature of the place; or if it be inhabited, to adopt the native appellation, than to exhaust the catalogue of public characters or private friends at home. The officers and crews, indeed, have some claim on such distinction, which, slight as it is, helps to excite an interest in the voyage."

Tides, winds, currents, and astronomical and meteorological observations were all to be given attention. And Darwin was almost certainly inspired to do one of his most important pieces of research by Beaufort's comment that "the circularly-formed Coral Islands in the Pacific occasionally afford excellent land-locked harbours, with a sufficient entrance, and would be well adapted to any nice astronomical observations which might require to be carried on in undisturbed tranquillity. While these are quietly proceeding, and the chronometers rating, a very interesting inquiry might be instituted respecting the formation of these coral reefs."

Finally, reports were to be sent home to the Hydrographic Office at every opportunity as insurance against the loss of the ship, and the Beaufort scale was to be used for denoting the force of the wind.

The *Beagle* was ready for sea in November, but gales delayed her sailing for over a month. She finally got under way on December 27, 1831. Fitzroy was pleased with his ship. "Never, I believe, did a vessel leave England better provided, or fitted for the service she was destined to perform, and for the health and comfort of her crew, than the *Beagle*," he wrote. Even when a strong gale drove the heavily laden bark south across the Bay of Biscay with her scuppers under, "though so deep in the water, our little vessel's movements were uncommonly easy, and all our best timekeepers being hung in particularly good jimbals [*sic*], I had no fear of their rates being altered, except by the effect of a change of temperature."

After anchoring at Santa Cruz, Fitzroy was told that he would have to remain in quarantine for twelve days. He decided that the delay was not worth it and sailed on, much to the disappointment of Darwin, who had hoped to visit the peak of Teneriffe. *Beagle* next sailed to Porto Praia on the island of São Tiago and here, on January 16, Darwin began his narrative.

Once begun, Darwin for the remainder of the voyage commented on everything that met his inquiring eye: the habits of the octopus and vampire bats; the discoloration of seas; birds, spiders, plants, and all living things. He was deeply interested in the Indians and South Sea Islanders and their customs. He studied the geology. His intellectual curiosity was truly all-consuming.

The *Beagle* anchored briefly at Fernando de Noronha on February 19, 1832. After making stops at Bahia (Salvador) and Rio de Janeiro, she entered the River Plate on July 22. Fitzroy began his surveys at once and pursued them energetically on the Atlantic side and around Tierra del Fuego for the next year and a half. The returning Fuegians got their first elated glimpse of their homeland when the *Beagle* anchored off Santa Inés, Tierra del Fuego. After weathering a gale off the Diego Ramírez Islands, Fitzroy landed his three Fuegians and Richard Matthews in late January 1833. His great concern for the safety of Matthews warranted his picking up the young man again on February 6. Matthews's missionary efforts fell on stormy ground. He was in constant danger of his life. He agreed with Fitzroy that if he had been left longer he would probably have been killed.

At the Falkland Islands (which he surveyed) on March 1, Fitzroy anchored near the beach at the south side of Berkeley Sound, where de Freycinet had run the *Uranie* ashore in 1820. Here he bought from a sealer the fine schooner *Unicorn* and renamed her the *Adventure*, out of sentiment for the last voyage, to use as a tender. Fitzroy went north to Montevideo for wintering and refitting and sailed south from there December 6, revisiting his pet Fuegians in March 1834.

Once his work on the Atlantic side was completed, Fitzroy stood out into the Pacific through Cockburn Channel and sailed directly to Valparaiso, where he learned from dispatches that his funds were cut. This cut would, he thought, curtail his work on the Chilean coast and the intended examination of islands in the Pacific. But although he was forced to sell the *Adventure*, he continued his work: he completed the important survey of Chiloé Island on February 5, 1835, and then, by great skill and tenacity, completed the survey of the coast of southern Chile, which he had earlier despaired of doing.

Fitzroy's work was interrupted when H.M.S. *Challenger* was wrecked near Concepción on May 19, 1835. (Fitzroy played an important part in rescuing her survivors.) Soon, however, the *Beagle* was on her way up the South American coast. She sailed from Callao on September 7 for the Galápagos and sighted Chatham Island (San Cristóbal) on the fifteenth. At Albemarle Island (Isabela) the *Beagle* was anchored in the same cove where Lord Byron had moored the *Blonde* ten years before.

During the five weeks' survey of the Galápagos — the best yet done of this desolate group — Darwin made the most detailed remarks on the geology and natural history of these fascinating islands up to his time and for a long time thereafter. "The natural history of this archipelago is very remarkable," he began, "it seems to be a little world within itself; the greater number of its inhabitants, both vegetable and animal, being found nowhere else."

On Chatham Island Darwin visited small glowing hot craters. Curious sights met his eye at every turn. "In my walk I met two large tortoises, each of which must have weighed at least two hundred pounds. One was eating a piece of cactus, and when I approached, it looked at me, and then quietly walked away: the other gave a deep hiss and drew in its head. These huge reptiles, surrounded by the black lava, the leafless shrubs, and large cacti, appeared to my fancy like some antediluvian animals." On Albemarle Island, "the rocks on the coast abounded with great black lizards, between three and four feet long; and on the hills, another species was equally common. We saw several of the latter, some clumsily running out of our way, and others shuffling into their burrows." These were Darwin's first sights of two of the remarkable animals of the Galápagos.

Darwin not only described everything he saw, but collected in every branch of natural history as completely as time permitted. He found that the two or three hundred people then living in those islands believed the giant tortoises to be deaf. "Certainly they do not overhear a person walking close behind them," he writes. "I was always amused, when overtaking one of these great monsters as it was quietly pacing along, to see how suddenly, the instant I passed, it would draw in its head and legs, and uttering a deep hiss fall to the ground with a heavy sound, as if struck dead. I frequently got on their backs, and then, upon giving a few raps on the hinder part of the shell, they would rise up and walk away; — but I found it very difficult to keep my balance." He notes that there are both aquatic and terrestrial species of the large lizards and describes them and their habits. Commenting on tortoises and lizards, he observes that the Galápagos are not remarkable for the number of species of reptiles found there, but "there is no other quarter of the world, where this order replaces herbivorous mammalia in so extraordinary a manner."

By October 20 the survey of the Galápagos was completed and the *Beagle*'s bow turned towards Tahiti, 3200 miles away. So far, in spite of the cutback, Fitzroy had managed to complete everything that his instructions called for. It had been his intent to take meridian readings

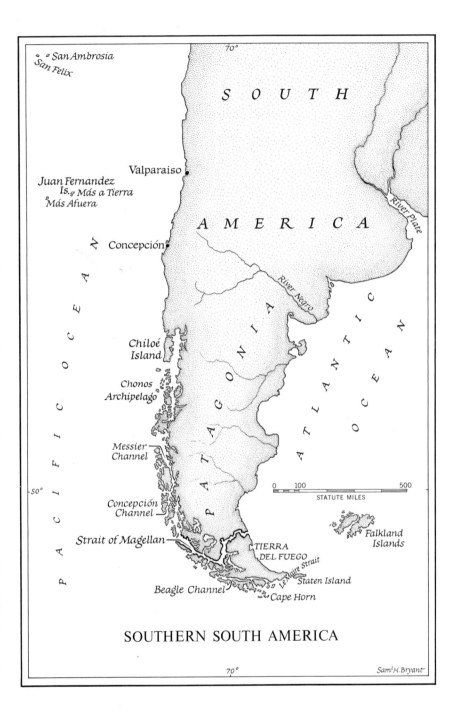

SOUTHERN SOUTH AMERICA

at several of the Tuamotu Islands and to give Darwin an opportunity to examine their coral structure. The elderly Krusenstern had sent Fitzroy a copy of his atlas containing a chart of the Tuamotus. But now it was necessary to push on, and Fitzroy hastened through the archipelago without stopping.

The first of the Tuamotus was sighted on November 9, 1835, and as others were passed, Darwin became intrigued by the long brilliant white beaches, capped by green palm trees. From the masthead he looked down on smooth lagoons within their rings of coral. He wondered that such small and fragile-looking bits of land were not over-whelmed by the ocean. At daylight on November 15, Darwin re-marked, "Tahiti, an island which must for ever remain as classical to the voyager in the South Sea," came in view, and he was immediately impressed with the bountiful luxuriance of the land. "The low land which comes down to the beach of coral sand, is covered by the most beautiful productions of the intertropical regions. In the midst of ba-nanas, orange, cocoa-nut, and breadfruit trees, spots are cleared where yams, sweet potatoes, sugar-cane, and pineapples, are cultivated. Even the brushwood is a fruit-tree, namely, the guava, which from its abun-dance is as noxious as a weed."

Darwin liked the Tahitians and found their color pleasing: "To see a white man bathing by the side of a Tahitian, was like comparing a plant bleached by the gardener's art, with one growing on the open fields." He found their tattooing graceful and "thought the body of a man thus ornamented, was like the trunk of a noble tree embraced by a delicate creeper." Fitzroy agreed as far as the men were concerned, but he thought the reputation of the women for beauty greatly over-rated. "Perhaps my eyes were prejudiced in favour of features and complexion," Fitzroy comments, "for the shambling gait and flat noses of the native women had no charms for me. I saw no beauty among them; and either they are not as handsome as they were said to be, or my ideas are fastidious. The men, on the other hand, exceed every idea formed from the old descriptions."

Fitzroy lost no time making the necessary observations at Point Venus. As he had been sailing west a day had been lost, and the six-teenth by ship calendar was changed to the seventeenth to agree with the Tahiti date. The site of Cook's observatory was a famous one, from which most of the geographical positions of islands were reckoned. Its position had been precisely determined by such notable astronomers as Wales, Green, and Bayley. An Englishman named John Middleton, living in Tahiti, produced a chart of the Tuamotus showing the islands with their native names, and Fitzroy added this information to Krusenstern's chart. He added to the chart still more data from Mr. Hall, the son of the missionary.

While Fitzroy was pursuing his various observations, Darwin with some companions made a three-day excursion into the mountainous interior. Following up a stream, Darwin discovered that "the valley soon began to narrow, and the sides to grow lofty and more precipitous. After having walked between three and four hours, we found the width of the ravine scarcely exceeded that of the bed of the stream. On each hand the walls were nearly vertical; yet from the soft nature of the volcanic strata, trees and a rank vegetation sprung from every projecting ledge. These precipices must have been some thousand feet high: and the whole formed a mountain gorge, far more magnificent than any thing which I had ever before beheld."

It was a hazardous climb, as anyone who has seen those precipitous mountains knows, "for it was necessary to pass the face of a naked rock, by the aid of ropes, which we brought with us. How any person discovered that this formidable spot was the only point where the side of the mountain was practicable, I cannot imagine. We then cautiously walked along one of the ledges, till we came to the stream already alluded to. This ledge formed a flat spot, above which a beautiful cascade, of some hundred feet, poured down its waters, and beneath it another high one emptied itself into the main stream. From this cool and shady recess, we made a circuit to avoid the overhanging cascade. As before, we followed little projecting ledges, the apparent danger being partly hidden by the thickness of the vegetation. In passing from one of the ledges to another, there was a vertical wall of rock. One of the Tahitians, a fine active man, placed the trunk of a tree against this, climbed up it, and then by the aid of crevices reached the summit. He fixed the ropes to a projecting point, and lowered them for us, then hauled up a dog which accompanied us, and lastly our luggage. Beneath the ledge on which the dead tree was placed the precipice must have been five or six hundred feet deep; and if the abyss had not been partly concealed by the overhanging ferns and lilies, my head would have turned giddy, and nothing should have induced me to have attempted it."

The *Beagle* departed Tahiti on November 26, 1835, and sighted New Zealand on December 19. "We may now consider ourselves as having nearly crossed the Pacific ocean," Darwin reflected. "It is necessary to sail over this great sea to understand its immensity. Moving quickly onwards for weeks together we meet with nothing, but the same blue, profoundly deep, ocean. Even within the Archipelagoes, the islands are mere specks, and far distant one from the other. Accustomed to look at maps, drawn on a small scale, where dots, shading, and names are crowded together, we do not judge rightly how infinitely small the proportion of dry land is to the water of this great sea." Two days later, on December 21, *Beagle* entered the Bay of Islands, where between two and three hundred Englishmen then lived. The place was a distinct comedown after Tahiti. And like their landscape, the Maori suffered by comparison with the Tahitian. Both Fitzroy and Darwin made extensive comments on the life and habits of the Maori and upon the mostly worthless English who had settled there.

The observation instruments were set up on a little island called Paiha — "a pretty spot." And again Darwin set off on one of his inland jaunts. "The introduction of the potato," he noted as he explored the countryside, "has been the most essential benefit to the island; it is now much more used, than any native vegetable. New Zealand is favoured by one great natural advantage; namely, that the inhabitants can never perish from famine. The whole country abounds with fern; and the roots of this plant, if not very palatable, yet contain much nutriment. A native can always subsist on these, and on the shells which are abundant on all parts of the sea-coast."

Guided by a Maori chief, who talked his ear off, Darwin visited the missionary headquarters at Waimate. Here in five years the missionaries had accomplished wonders. They lived in substantial English farmhouses, and their rich acres were cultivated with every variety of

European grain, fruits, and vegetables, as well as some tropical species. Nearby Darwin was shown a forest of the famous kauri pine. "I measured one of these noble trees," he wrote, "in a part which was not enlarged near the roots, and found it to be thirty-one feet in circumference. There was another close by, which I did not see, thirty-three; and I heard of one, no less than forty feet. The trunks are also very remarkable from their smoothness, cylindrical figure, absence of branches, and having very nearly the same girth through a length from sixty to even ninety feet. The crown of this tree, where it is irregularly branched, is small, and out of proportion to the trunk; and the foliage is likewise diminutive as compared with the branches. . . ." On the outskirts of the wood he saw growing in abundance the native flax, from which the Maori wove their clothing.

Darwin returned to the Bay of Islands on horseback on December 24, and the next day he and Fitzroy celebrated Christmas by attending a long, dull church service, conducted simultaneously in English and Maori. They had been absent from England two days short of four years.

On the last day of the year the *Beagle* sailed past North Cape bound for Port Jackson. She anchored in Sydney Cove on January 12, 1836. The capital of New South Wales was now a thriving city and here Fitzroy stayed until the thirtieth. The *Beagle* then sailed for Tasmania and spent ten days off Hobart Town, while Darwin made several pleasant little excursions into the country to examine the geology. On March 6, anchor was dropped in King George Sound near the southwest corner of Australia.

From Australia, *Beagle* crossed the Indian Ocean to the Cocos Islands. While Fitzroy charted the Cocos, Darwin began the examination and collection of coral, which he had originally planned to do in the similarly formed Tuamotus. "I am glad we have visited these islands," Darwin wrote on April 12, "such formations surely rank high amongst the wonderful objects of this world. It is not a wonder, which at first strikes the eye of the body, but rather, after reflection, the eye of reason."

The voyage home was by way of Mauritius, Simons Bay, St. Helena, Ascension, Brazil, the Cape Verdes, and Azores. The *Beagle* completed her circumnavigation at Falmouth, where Darwin left her, on October 2, 1836, after an absence of four years and nine months. Fitzroy took his last meridian traverse at Greenwich. The ship was paid off at Woolwich on November 17.

Just as Fitzroy had completed an arduous task magnificently, so Darwin's mind was magnificently opened by his five years in diverse ecological regions. The Galápagos, with their different species confined to particular islands, sowed the seeds of the theory of evolution in Darwin's mind. His delightful stay in the Cocos Islands started him on his theories of coral reef formation.

Yet, while Darwin and Fitzroy had remained surprisingly good friends through nearly five years of sharing a small cabin, they did not maintain close contact thereafter. Indeed, Fitzroy, a firm believer in creation, attacked *The Origin of Species* when it was published. Fitzroy later returned to New Zealand for five years as governor. After ten years as superintendent of the Meteorological Office, he committed suicide by slitting his throat with a razor — another victim of long, hard years of grueling work, severe climates, and oppressive responsibility.

18

The Wilkes Expedition

B Y the late 1830's there were probably more American vessels trading and whaling in the Pacific than those of any other nationality.
Numerous reefs and islands had been discovered and reported by
these merchant captains, the most extensive being the northern Marquesas, or Washington Islands, by Captain Ingraham in the *Hope*. But
whalers and traders were not equipped for exploration and their longitudes were notoriously inaccurate. They were out to make money;
geography, unless it yielded a marketable product, was incidental to
them. And, although the British, Russian, and French governments
had been sending out their several exploring and scientific expeditions,
the government of the United States had so far done nothing.

This apathy was at the federal level. For years Americans who in-
vested in whaling, sealing, or trading, especially from the New England ports, had been petitioning the government to send naval vessels
to the Pacific. There was charting to be done and they wanted the flag
shown at the various islands where American ships habitually called
for supplies and refreshment and where there were difficulties with
obdurate chiefs. Before the War of 1812, Captain Edmund Fanning
had proposed an expedition of discovery to President Madison, but
then the war prevented it. President John Quincy Adams, a New
Englander in all respects, understood the importance of an American
expedition and proposed such a venture to Congress in 1825. Three
years later the House voted to send a small naval vessel on a surveying
voyage to the Pacific. To be sure, the House neglected to appropriate

any funds for the purpose. Nevertheless, Samuel L. Southard, secretary of the navy, made the sloop of war *Peacock* available for such a voyage. Secretary Southard sent Jeremiah N. Reynolds — who had been lecturing throughout the country and urging that a government scientific expedition be sent to the South Seas — on a tour of New England ports to interview captains and ascertain what sort of information a government expedition should collect. He also sent Lieutenant Charles Wilkes, superintendant of the Depot of Charts and Instruments (as the Hydrographic Office was called then), to England and the Continent to buy chronometers and other scientific instruments. Both men did their work well, but unfortunately the money was not forthcoming and the idea was abandoned.

In 1829 and 1830 Captain Fanning, becoming impatient, sent two brigs, the *Annawan* and *Seraph*, under Captains Nathaniel B. Palmer and Benjamin Pendleton, with Reynolds, Dr. James Wights, a naturalist from Albany, and others, to seek new sealing grounds in high southern latitudes. It was a combination sealing and scientific voyage, with the one paying for the other. Yet, although the name Palmer Land was added to the Antarctic continent and there was a meeting with Bellingshausen's Russian expedition, little was accomplished, and Reynolds left the voyage in Chile to join the frigate *Potomac* as private secretary to Commodore John Downes. The collections made on the *Annawan* and *Seraph* were sent to the Museum of Natural History in New York, the Philadelphia Academy of Sciences, the Boston Society of Natural History, and the Albany Institute.

When the U.S. frigate *Potomac* returned from her Pacific cruise, Reynolds, who had been on the tail end of it, and Francis Warriner, who had made the entire cruise, both published books on the voyage. Meanwhile, the sloop of war *Vincennes* had also just returned from a Pacific cruise, and her sailing master, Matthew Fontaine Maury, reported that charts were very poor for the west coast and that the area around the mouth of the Columbia River was particularly ill delineated. Both Maury and Reynolds bombarded Congress with petitions. Eventually there was a Treasury surplus and Congress appropriated funds through the Navy Department for a voyage of exploration.

On June 29, 1836, Captain Thomas ap Catesby Jones, the veteran

Cape Codder who had made a notable cruise to the Pacific in 1826 and 1827, during which he apprehended the mutineers of the whale ship *Globe* and interfered with the rules on prostitution and shipping in Honolulu, was offered — and he accepted — command of the proposed expedition.* Jones had exaggerated ideas regarding the organization of a venture of this sort. Most of the famous European expeditions had consisted of one or two vessels. It had been demonstrated time and again that frigates were too large for exploratory work. Small vessels were better suited for the close inshore navigation demanded. Nevertheless, Jones requested the frigate *Macedonian*, two brigs, and two schooners. Jones continued in a running fight with Secretary of the Navy Mahlon Dickerson over everything connected with the expedition. He insisted on constructing small brigs and schooners especially for the voyage and they turned out to be unsuitable. His firm feelings concerning personnel led to further unfortunate differences of opinion. The situation reached an impasse, and when, in December 1837, Jones requested that he be relieved of the command, Dickerson was only too ready to comply.

It was no easy matter to find another commander for the United States Exploring Expedition — as the enterprise was officially called. Senior officers refused the offer, men deserted, and the public, once so enthusiastic, became critical and then apathetic. After interminable wrangling, command was offered to Lieutenant Charles Wilkes, a competent hydrographical surveyor, who had made the trip to Europe to purchase instruments for the expedition that had first been voted nearly ten years before. Wilkes received his orders to command on March 20, 1838.

Enthusiasm, advice, and support for the expedition came from the East India Marine Society of Salem, Massachusetts, the town that had sent more traders to the Pacific than any other. On December 16, 1834, there was submitted to the Twenty-third Congress a "Memorial of the East India Marine Society of Salem, Massachusetts, praying that an expedition be fitted out by the government to make a voyage of discovery and survey to the South Seas," endorsing a recommenda-

---

* Reynolds, at the suggestion of President Jackson, was offered the job of secretary to the commander, but turned it down.

Commodore Charles Wilkes, Commander of the U.S. Exploring Expedition
(*from* Narrative of the U.S. Exploring Expedition)

tion to the same effect made by the Rhode Island Legislature the previous month. Some sense of the urgency (and righteous indignation) of the Salem merchants is suggested by their rhetorical question: "Without attempting to designate the groups or islands most important to be examined, your memoralists would simply call the attention of your honorable body to one point, which may serve as an index to the rest. The Feejee or Beetee Islands, what is known of them? They were named but not visited by Captain Cook, and consist of sixty or more in number. Where shall we find a chart of this group, pointing out its harbors and dangers? There are none to be found, for none exist! And yet have we no trade there? We speak not for others, but for ourselves." Support also came from the whaling interests in New Bedford and Nantucket, and from the Naval Lyceum in New York. The Philadelphia Academy of Natural Sciences and the American Philosophical Society were generous with their advice on collecting, and in recommending scientists.

Wilkes was opposed to using a frigate, and the brigs and schooners that Jones had had built were unsatisfactory. The vessels finally selected were two sloops of war — *Vincennes*, 780 tons, and *Peacock*, 650 tons — the survey brig *Porpoise*, and the storeship *Relief*. Two New York pilot schooners, the *New Jersey*, of 110 tons, and the *Independence*, of 96 tons, were purchased for shoal water work and renamed *Sea Gull* and *Flying Fish*. Wilkes chose his friend Lieutenant William L. Hudson as his second-in-command and as captain of the *Peacock*, and Lieutenant Cadwalader Ringgold as third officer of the expedition and captain of the *Porpoise*. Both were competent officers, but inexperienced in surveying.

Wilkes, who was far from satisfied with the expedition's equipment, left Washington for Norfolk on August 10, 1838, and joined the fleet at Hampton Roads. The first sentence of his instructions, dated August 11, succinctly states the purpose of the voyage. "The Congress of the United States," they begin, "having in view the important interests of our commerce embarked in the whale-fisheries, and other adventures in the great Southern Ocean, by an act of the 18th of May, 1836, authorized an Expedition to be fitted out for the purpose of exploring and surveying that sea, as well to determine the existence of all doubtful islands and shoals, as to discover and accurately fix the position of those which lie in or near the track of our vessels in that quarter, and may have escaped the observation of scientific navigators."

Like the British explorer Fitzroy two years before, Wilkes, according to his instructions, was to establish the longitude at Rio de Janeiro when he called there for supplies. He was then to make a particular examination of the Rio Negro and proceed to Tierra del Fuego, leaving the two larger ships with the scientists to examine that area and sending the *Porpoise* and the two tenders to explore the Antarctic. *Porpoise* and her tenders were to reach as high a southern latitude as possible and to follow Weddell's 1823 track. Meanwhile, those left at Tierra del Fuego were to make surveys extending or verifying those of King and Fitzroy — and, particularly, to investigate such coves, inlets, harbors, and soundings as might be serviceable to American whaleships making their passages between the Atlantic and Pacific oceans. After reassembling, the squadron was to stretch westward and southward as far as Cook's *ne plus ultra* at 105° west, and then turn north to Valparaiso, where a storeship would be waiting for them in March 1839.

The Pacific surveys were to be primarily in the Samoan and Fiji groups, noting the best harbors for shelter and supplies, and the Society Islands were to be visited if possible. The next supply depot was to be Sydney, whence another swing into the Antarctic south of Tasmania and as far west as 45° east of Enderby Land was to be made. Rendezvous was to be no later than the end of March 1840 at Kerguelen Island, whence they were to sail to the Sandwich Islands to meet another storeship in April.

The next project was to make a survey of the northwestern United States coast, especially of the Columbia River and San Francisco Bay and the coast in between. This completed, Wilkes should cross the Pacific to the coast of Japan, taking in as many islands as possible on the way. If desirable, he could enter the Sea of Japan. He was to take care to arrive at Mindoro or in the Sulu Sea at the proper season to make a thorough examination of this sea, to ascertain if there might be a safe route through it that would shorten the passage of American vessels going to China. Following this survey, he was to proceed to Sunda Strait, then turn back and examine the Straits of Billiton, meet a storeship at Singapore in April 1841, and return to the United States via the Cape of Good Hope.

No trade was to be carried on except for necessities or curiosities. The rights of natives were to be carefully protected and, above all, lives were not to be risked unnecessarily.

"Although the primary object of the Expedition," went Wilkes's instructions, "is the promotion of the great interests of commerce and navigation, yet you will take occasions, not incompatible with the great purposes of your undertaking, to extend the bounds of science, and promote the acquisition of knowledge." And further: "The hydrography and geography of the various seas and countries you may visit in the route pointed out to you in the preceding instructions, will occupy your special attention; and all the researches connected with them, as well as with astronomy, terrestrial magnetism, and meteorology, are confided exclusively to the officers of the navy, on whose zeal and talents the Department confidently relies for such results as will enable future navigators to pass over the track traversed by your vessels, without fear and without danger."

Particular attention was to be paid to the comprehensive reports of the committees of the Salem East India Marine Society and the American Philosophical Society. These, together with a communication from the Naval Lyceum of New York, were to be regarded as part of the intructions. All journals, memoranda, sketches, and notes of any kind regarding the expedition were to be collected before the ships returned to United States waters.

Nine scientists and artists were engaged for the voyage. Joseph Draton and Alfred T. Agate were the draftsmen. Dr. Charles Pickering and Titian R. Peale (son of Charles Wilson Peale and himself a talented artist) were the general naturalists. James D. Dana was mineralogist; Horatio Hale, philologist; John P. Couthony, conchologist; William Rich, botanist; and William D. Brackenridge, horticulturist. A taxidermist and an expert to care for the scientific instruments

M

completed the roster of supernumeraries. Some who had originally expected to go on the voyage withdrew either because of the interminable delays or from professional jealousies.*

The distinguished Russian navigator, Vice-Admiral Krusenstern, was as helpful to the United States expedition as he had been in the voyage of the *Beagle*. Again he provided the most up-to-date charts of his atlas, gave valuable advice, and took a deep interest in the enterprise.

The fleet got under way at three o'clock in the afternoon of August 18, 1838, and sailed out of Hampton Roads bound for Madeira. (Because of the prevailing winds and currents, the only easy way to make a voyage to Rio de Janeiro from the United States in the days of sail was to cross the Atlantic twice.) *Peacock* proved to be the fastest sailer and *Relief* by far the slowest. Madeira was reached in less than a month; a brief call was made at Porto Praia in the Cape Verdes (where the *Relief* should have arrived but hadn't), and Rio de Janeiro was reached in late November. The fleet remained here until January 6, 1839, and by the thirtieth they were in Orange Harbor, Tierra del Fuego.

The forty-year-old Wilkes was energetic, decisive, and competent. He was also a martinet. His personality became so impressed on the voyage that it has ever since been known as the Wilkes Expedition, rather than by its official name.

On February 25 Wilkes, now in the *Porpoise* accompanied by the *Sea Gull*, sailed to the southeast for Palmer's Land and Weddell's track. The same day the *Peacock* and *Flying Fish* sailed to the southwest in an attempt to penetrate beyond Captain Cook's farthest south. The *Vincennes* and *Relief* remained at Orange Harbor. Both Antarctic groups encountered fearful weather and ice conditions. The *Porpoise*, *Sea Gull*, and *Flying Fish* returned to Orange Harbor from this first penetration of the Antarctic, while the *Peacock* sailed directly to Valparaiso. There too went *Relief* after nearly foundering in a gale off Cockburn Channel. The other ships trickled in to port by May 19,

---

* Among these were Lieutenant Matthew F. Maury, Jeremiah N. Reynolds, the naturalist James Eights, and the botanist Asa Gray.

except for the *Sea Gull*. Neither she nor her fifteen men were seen again after April 28.

At Valparaiso it was found that the *Relief* and the storeship *Mariposa* had gone to Callao, and in about a week's time the other ships of the squadron followed. Stores from the *Mariposa* were taken in all the vessels and the remainder loaded on *Relief*, which was detached from the expedition and ordered to land part of her stores at the Sandwich Islands and the rest at Sydney, and then to proceed home around Cape Horn.

Now well supplied for his Pacific crossing, Wilkes decided to follow the recommendations of Krusenstern regarding charting in the Tuamotus. He arrived on August 13, 1839, at Clermont-Tonnerre, to begin his surveys and to allow the naturalists to begin their various researches.* With four vessels at his command Wilkes was able to accomplish an enormous amount of surveying. He devised a method of charting islands that used his fleet to advantage. Wilkes conducted his running survey through the Tuamotus for a month, endeavoring to locate as many coral atolls as possible and charting sixteen different islands. He was unable to find three of his discoveries on any chart. These he named King (Taiaro), Vincennes (Kawehe), and Peacock (Ahii).

Landing on Hennake, or Honden, Island on August 19 — it had been visited by Schouten and Le Maire nearly two and a quarter centuries before — Wilkes was disillusioned after the first beautiful and romantic appearance of a coral island: "That verdure which seemed from a distant view to carpet the whole island, was in reality but a few patches of wiry grass, obstructing the walking, and offering neither fruit nor flowers to view; it grew among the rugged coral debris, with a little sand and vegetable earth." On August 24, as he was surveying Byron's Disappointment Islands, natives approached in twelve- to fifteen-foot canoes made of strips of coconut palm wood sewn together. Their wiry beards and mustaches set them apart from the peo-

---

* The geographical positions that Duperrey and Beechey had laid down for Clermont-Tonnerre did not agree, but Wilkes was able to prove that the French navigator was correct.

ple of any other island. They had nothing to trade except some old matting, for they ridiculed the idea of parting with their well-made, backward-bending paddles. The survey of the Disappointment Islands was successfully completed.

When Wilkes discovered King Island (he named it for the sailor who had spotted it from the masthead) no inhabitants were found, but there was evidence that pearl fishermen had been there. The naturalists took advantage of the landing by adding a substantial number of plants to their collections. At Raraka, twenty miles to the southwest, Wilkes was welcomed by flag-waving Tahitians. The Tahitians had arrived in two thirty-five-foot double canoes on a shelling voyage. Nearby was another tiny island not laid down on the chart, where Wilkes was befriended by an old tattooed chief, one of whose hands had been bitten off by a shark while he was pearl diving.

The local practice of catching fish enabled the naturalists to add more specimens here than they had elsewhere. "The way of catching fish practised here is quite amusing," Wilkes wrote, "and to it we owe the many specimens in that department of natural history which we obtained. The natives enjoy the sport amazingly, and both old and young are all in some way participators in it. Near the mouth of the lagoon are laid some coral stones, forming a rude and shallow pen, with a channel leading to it; several natives proceed about one-third of a mile up the beach of the lagoon, where they enter the water, ranging themselves in a row, the tallest in the deepest water. They then move along down towards the pen, quite noiselessly at first, driving the fish before them. As they approach, they begin to splash and make a noise; the clamour gradually increases, until it becomes one continued shout. They then contract themselves towards the pen, and the fish are seen jumping and dashing in all directions, as if very much alarmed, until they are forced to enter the pen, which is then closed with a few stones; afterwards the natives begin to spear them with great dexterity, and many were obtained." Wilkes named the sixteen-mile-long coral strip near Raraka, Vincennes Island.

Now he sent his ships off among many islands on various surveying errands, in order to accomplish as much work as possible. (At Aratika, or Carlshoff, Island, he met a native who "was tatooed only on one side, from the pubis to the sternum, bounded by broad blue bands, which divided and terminated under each ear.") Wilkes endeavored to examine as many coral islands as possible in the Tuamotus. In due course the *Vincennes* arrived at Tahiti, and found the *Porpoise* already there. The *Peacock* and *Flying Fish* soon followed. All vessels anchored in Matavai Bay by September 14, 1839.

The next day being Sunday, as many of the officers and men as could be spared attended divine service in the mission church. But at the same time, work overhauling the vessels began, the sick were sent on shore, and an observatory was established on Point Venus. Wilkes visited the Reverend Mr. Wilson, the senior missionary, and in turn received S. R. Blackler, the Reverend Pritchard, and J. A. Moerenhout, the voyager who settled in Tahiti, consuls for the United States, British, and French governments, respectively.

Something of Wilkes's character comes out in his opinion of Tahitian women. "I hesitate to speak of the females of this island," he says (as Fitzroy said before him), "for I differ from all who have gone before me in relation to their vaunted beauty. I did not see among them a single woman whom I could call handsome. They have, indeed, a soft sleepiness about the eyes, which may be fascinating to some, but I should rather ascribe the celebrity their charms have obtained among navigators, to their cheerfulness and gaiety. Their figures are bad, and the greater part of them are parrot-toed. They are exceedingly prone to prattling, or may rather be said to have a tattling disposition, for they cannot keep even their own secrets."

The *Porpoise* was dispatched to work in the western Tuamotus with orders to rendezvous with the *Vincennes* at de Freycinet's Rose Island. Meanwhile Wilkes surveyed the harbors of Tahiti and spent a few days at Moorea. He made the uninhabited Bellingshausen Island on September 29, where he conducted magnetic experiments and collected many fish. On October 7 the *Vincennes* and *Porpoise* met off Rose Island. Ringgold in *Porpoise* had connected the survey of Rangiroa (or Dean's) Island with Krusenstern (Tikahau) and Lazareff (Matahiva) islands. The *Peacock* and *Flying Fish* (with which Wilkes wanted to sail in company) could not leave Tahiti until after October 10, when repairs to the pilot boat were completed.

At this point Wilkes began his important running survey of Samoa. "As it was my intention to make a thorough examination of this group," he explained, "I resolved, in order to accomplish it in the least possible time, to divide the squadron, so as to put all the remaining islands under examination at the same time. The island of Tutuila being the most central, and, from the information I had obtained, the best position for my astronomical observations, I selected it for the *Vincennes*. That of Upolu was reserved for the *Peacock* and *Flying Fish* when they should arrive; and in case of their being detained longer then I anticipated, I should be ready to take up the survey of the latter, or assist in completing it. The *Porpoise* was ordered to examine the island of Savaii; and one of the naturalists, Dr. Pickering, was directed to join her, for the purpose of exploring the interior of the island during her operations in its vicinity. Lieutenant-Commandant Ringgold was therefore directed to land him for the purpose, and take him on board when the survey should be concluded." The surveys of Tutuila were, in fact, completed on November 23. And as the expedition departed, Wilkes wrote feelingly of sailing "along the southern shore of the island, admiring its diversified surface, its luxuriant groves, and the smiling villages that crown its bays."

The thirty-six miles to the rich and fruitful island of Upolu were quickly passed and soon they saw the *Peacock* lying in Apia Harbor. While "Messrs. Dana and Couthouy visited a lake called Lauto, which lies . . . in the center of an extinct crater," Peale, one of the naturalists, and a party traveled the Stone Road from Vivimanga to Sanga, a region of lava caves. The largest of these caves, at Sanga, "was dedicated to the god 'Moso,' who was supposed to reside in it. The entrance was found to be closed by an artificial wall built across it, about three feet thick." It had been reported, the narrative adds, "that this cave was frequented by a peculiar kind of swallow, which never ventured into the light of day. Mr. Peale . . . found swallows in abundance, which made a bat-like noise, or rather one having a resemblance to the rattling of pebbles. So far, however, from their being a peculiar species, as they had been represented, they were the common species of the islands. . . ."

Carrying out his duties, Wilkes often sat in judgment over disputes between South Sea Islanders and whites. He also tried natives who had killed Americans, and discussed with Samoan chiefs regulations for the activities of whale ships on their periodic visits. For Wilkes, and for his entire crew, the stay at Apia was a busy, but rewarding one.

The entire squadron assembled in the harbor of Apia on November 10, 1839, having completed surveys of all the harbors and all the different islands of the Samoan group (with the exception of the south coast of Upolu, which was completed the following year). Besides the surveys, parties had crossed the islands in various directions, conducted magnetic experiments, and made extensive natural history collections and ethnological investigations. Astronomical observations were also made and a full record kept of the tides. Small wonder that, when the squadron weighed anchor and sailed westward, Wilkes was well satisfied with the work that had been accomplished. The *Vincennes* and the *Peacock* anchored at Sydney Cove at 10:00 P.M. on November 26, and the *Porpoise* and *Flying Fish* joined them twenty-four hours later. Following a Christmas spent with new-found friends, the squadron sailed from Sydney on December 26 — the very date called for by the master plan, as originally prepared so many months before leaving the United States.

The next two and a half months Wilkes and his men spent in their second period of Antarctic exploration. Almost immediately the *Flying Fish* was separated from the three larger vessels in a dense fog. (She was not seen again until they reached New Zealand, where she had already arrived at the Bay of Islands.) The *Peacock*, badly damaged by ice, narrowly escaped destruction and was forced to return to Sydney. The *Porpoise* followed the *Flying Fish* to the Bay of Islands. Wilkes turned the *Vincennes* north on February 21, 1840, and arrived back in Sydney on March 11, relieved to find the *Peacock* safely there. Wilkes did not linger for repairs to his consort, but left on the nineteenth for New Zealand, giving orders to Hudson to follow as soon as possible and meet him at Tongatabu.

On March 30 he groped his way into the Bay of Islands after dark, to find the *Porpoise* and *Flying Fish* snugly anchored. The scientific

[343]

men had not gone on the Antarctic cruise but had taken passage direct from Sydney to the Bay of Islands on the British brig *Victoria*. Here they were occupied with their collecting and studies of the Maori.

"The trade in native curiosities is not quite so great as it used to be," Wilkes reported, "particularly in tattooed heads. So great at one time was the traffic in the latter article, between New Zealand and Sydney, that, in 1831, it was prohibited by law. In Governor Darling's administration of the colony, the chief Shougi is supposed to have made large sums by it, and there are some persons who, in part, impute his wars to his desire of gain; for, having been in England, he became acquainted with the value set upon them, and the demand for them. It is generally thought that many of the heads thus sold have been prepared by the white runaway convicts, who have learnt the mode of doing this from the natives. They are still to be obtained, though great precaution is used in disposing of them.

"A missionary brig, lying at the Bay of Islands, had many curiosities on board, in the possession of the steward; and after the buying of mats &c., had been finished, he invited our officers to step down to his little store-room, under the forecastle, where he had a curiosity which could not be brought out. After this mysterious enunciation, they followed him to the bottom of the ladder; he then told them he was about to put his fate into their hands, believing that they were too much men of honour to betray him. He then proceeded to inform them that he had two preserved heads of New Zealand chiefs, which he would sell for ten pounds. He could not venture, he said, to produce them on board the brig, but if they would appoint a place, he would bring them. The penalty for selling them was fifty guineas, and he conjured them to the most perfect secrecy. These proved to be beautiful specimens, and now form a part of our collections. So effectually has the fine prevented this traffic, that it is an extremely difficult matter to obtain a head; they are as rare now as they have been common heretofore; and the last place in which it could have been expected to find them, would have been on board a missionary vessel."

Vincennes, Porpoise, and *Flying Fish* sailed from the Bay of Islands for Tongatabu on April 6, 1840, bound for the Fijis. The crews had no regrets at leaving New Zealand. They had found it a dull place.

Wilkes's flagship, the U.S.S. Vincennes, in the ice (Original oil painting. In the collection of the Peabody Museum of Salem)

The Fijis were as beautiful in the 1840's as they are today, but the people were savage then and the coral-strewn Fiji waters virtually uncharted. Although Wilkes had an enormous task laid out before him, he tackled it with his usual thoroughness and energy. He began his main survey by landing at Levuka, Ovalau, where he was fortunate in meeting David Whippey, a New Englander from a whaler who had lived in these islands for eighteen years. Whippey was extremely useful to Wilkes, especially in dealing with the Fijians. Benjamin Vanderford, the Salem captain who had made several bêche-de-mer voyages to the Fijis and was now a pilot with Wilkes, was no less useful during the Fiji survey.

When Wilkes had landed his instruments, he climbed Mt. Andulong with the help of Fijians. From the top he had a wide view of the beautiful valleys of Ovalau: coconut and breadfruit groves, towns, and cultivated areas lay spread out before him. It was the ideal place to take a series of angles between all the many points, peaks, and islands that could be seen. Setting up a base camp on a point of Ovalau, Wilkes now began laying out plans and distributing the work for a complete survey of this intricate group. Rigid instructions were given to the survey crews to avoid conflicts or entanglements of any kind with the Fijians. Wilkes drove his men unmercifully to accomplish the Fiji work.

On May 12, while Wilkes was absorbed in his observations, he received a distinguished visitor. The great canoe of Tanoa, king of Mbau, was seen rounding the southern point of the island. "It had a magnificent appearance," Wilkes wrote, "with its immense sail of white mats; the pennants streaming from its yard, denoted it at once as belonging to some great chief. It was a fit accompaniment to the magnificent scenery around, and advanced rapidly and gracefully along; it was a single canoe, one hundred feet in length, with an outrigger of large size, ornamented with a great number (two thousand five hundred) of the Cypraea ovula shells; its velocity was almost inconceivable, and every one was struck with the adroitness with which it was managed and landed on the beach."

Vanderford and Tanoa, who were old friends from bêche-de-mer trading days, greeted each other warmly. (Vanderford had once been

Tanoa, King of Mbau, Fiji
(*from* Narrative of the U.S. Exploring Expedition)

wrecked in the Fijis and resided at Mbau, where the royal rascal had stolen everything from him but his skin, while protecting him from others who might have turned the destitute captain into long pig in the stone ovens.) Tanoa's visit was followed in a few days by one from his son and successor Seru (or Thakombau, as he was later called), an able but ruthless young cannibal, who was to become the principal ruler of Fiji and to negotiate the eventual acceptance of the islands as a British crown colony.

One of the most useful chiefs to the expedition was Thokanauto. This keen fellow, who called himself the white man's friend, was a reformed cannibal generally known as Mr. Phillips: a name he adopted from Stephen C. Phillips of Salem, a merchant whose ships were active in the Fiji trade. Another of the leading chiefs was Vendovi, who a few years previously had taken a leading part in the massacre of part of the crew of the Salem trader *Charles Doggett* and whom Wilkes was to capture and bring to New York. Between his duties Wilkes managed to find time to exchange numerous hospitalities with Fijian chiefs and to dine with the Wesleyan missionaries and their wives, who had been active in Fiji for about a year.

The Fijian hospitality was impressive. One of the more unusual entertainments was an exhibition of native dances, which included a performance by a Fijian clown. "His body was entirely covered with green and dried leaves," Wilkes remembered, "and vines bound round in every way; on his head he wore a mask somewhat resembling a bear's head, painted black on one side, and orange on the other; in one hand he carried a large club, and in the other, one of the short ones, to which our men had given the name of 'Handy Billy;' his movements were very much like those of our clowns, and drew down immense applause from the spectators."

John Sac, the New Zealand Maori sailor on the expedition, reciprocated by performing one of his violent war dances, to the utter astonishment of the Fijians. Despite the Fijians' reputation for cannibalism, no proof of it was seen by any member of the expedition until July 2, when the *Peacock* anchored in Naloa Bay off the village of Fokasinga. Then the proof came with a vengeance. "One human body had already been brought over and just feasted upon. Shortly afterwards a canoe came alongside, bringing the skull yet warm from the fire, much scorched, and marked with the teeth of those who had eaten of it. The brain had been roasted and taken out, as well as the eyes and teeth. Another canoe came alongside with some roasted flesh in it. While Mr. Spieden and others were agreeing with the natives for the purchase of the skull for a fathom of cloth, a native stood near him holding something in his right hand, which he soon applied to his mouth, and began to eat. To their utter astonishment they discovered it to be the eye of the dead man, which the native had plucked from the skull a few moments before."

Wilkes and his men celebrated Independence Day, 1840, with a turtle feast (perhaps to blur the memory of the cannibal feast) and a double allowance of grog. Then the *Peacock* and *Vincennes* met in Mbau Bay, and Wilkes reviewed the work of the expedition to date. So much remained to be done that it was obvious that the Fiji survey must remain unfinished, unless more time were devoted to it than had originally been planned. Wilkes rightly concluded that the survey of the Fiji Islands was the most important project of the entire voyage. He therefore resolved to complete it. At the same time, because of the protracted stay, he ordered the men's provision allowance reduced by one-third.

Throughout their work, the members of the Wilkes Expedition had maintained friendly relations with the Fijians. But on July 10, Wilkes ordered a village burnt to the ground, in revenge for the theft of a launch, even though the boat was subsequently returned. Then Lieutenant Joseph A. Underwood and Wilkes's nephew, Midshipman Wilkes Henry, both popular young men who were trading at the island of Malolo for food, were attacked and massacred. (The bodies were recovered and buried in a common grave on a little island.) Once again Wilkes took swift and awful revenge: all canoes on the island were destroyed; the two villages of Sualib and Arro were burned flat; all of the islands' best warriors — some fifty-seven — were killed, and the surviving men of Malolo were forced to crawl to meet their conquerors on their hands and knees. This incident is the prime example of Wilkes at his worst. Proud, querulous, and impatient, his grossly vindictive actions on these occasions may not be excused even by the most chauvinist American.*

For all the blood he had so senselessly spilled, Wilkes was satisfied with his survey of the Fijis. "It gives me great pleasure," he summarized his work, "to be able, with but few exceptions, to bear witness to the untiring zeal of those who were attached to the Expedition, and to the accuracy with which the work was performed; and in the cases where error or careless work was suspected, the doubtful parts were resurveyed, correcting any mistake which might have been committed in the first instance, and verifying the survey where it was accurate."

On August 10, 1840, the squadron sailed from the Fiji Islands, taking Chief Vendovi with them.† Wilkes had separated his ships for the voyage to Honolulu. *Porpoise* was dispatched to finish surveying details and to search for the crew of a wrecked ship. *Flying Fish* was to chart a reef before shaping her course northward, and the two sloops of war were put on separate courses, the better to search for doubtful islands and obtain more information on winds and currents.

Vincennes anchored off Honolulu on September 24. She was joined by the *Peacock* six days later. On October 8 the *Porpoise* arrived. The season was by now too far advanced for a cruise to the Northwest Coast. As soon as he heard of the exploring fleets' arrival, however, King Kamehameha III invited Wilkes, with his officers and scientists, to an audience. At his request, the harbor of Waialae was surveyed.

After refitting his vessels Wilkes sent the *Peacock* and *Flying Fish* to Upolu to complete the Samoan survey and the *Porpoise* to finish the work in the Tuamotus and to survey Penrhyn and Flint islands. Wilkes himself proceeded in the *Vincennes* to Hilo, accompanied by Dr. Garrett P. Judd and Mr. Brinsmade, the United States consul.

---

* Following this brutal episode, the officers of the *Vincennes* and *Peacock* wore badges of mourning for thirty days. They took up a collection among themselves, with which a memorial to the two officers and to Midshipmen Reid and Bacon, lost with the *Sea Gull*, was later erected in Mt. Auburn Cemetery, Cambridge, Massachusetts.

† He died of pneumonia three days after the *Vincennes* returned to New York.

Vendovi, Chief of Rewa, Fiji
(Watercolor. In the collection of the Peabody Museum of Salem)

During his extended stay at Hawaii, Wilkes ascended Mauna Loa with a party of two hundred Hawaiians and a fantastic amount of equipment and established a camp at Pendulum Peak. During the month of December (including Christmas, spent on the mountain) he made extensive pendulum observations on the summit.

"It was not with out some nervous excitement," Wilkes wrote, "that I placed my instrument on the highest point of Mauna Loa, within a few feet of its crater, and turned it upon Mauna Kea, to measure the difference in the Height of these twin giants of the Pacific.*

"The very idea of standing on the summit of one of the highest peaks on the midst of this vast ocean, in close proximity to a precipice of profound depth, overhanging an immense crater 'outrageous as a sea,' with molten rock, would have been exciting even to a strong man; but the sensation was overpowering to one already exhausted by breathing the rarefied air, and toiling over the lava which this huge cauldron must have vomited forth in quantities sufficient to form a dome sixty miles in diameter, and nearly three miles in height."

Before beginning his descent on January 13, Wilkes had the words "Pendulum Peak, January 1841, U.S. Ex[ploring] Ex[pedition]" cut in lava by the campsite. The party returned by way of Kilauea and arrived back at Hilo on January 23, after an absence of forty-two days.

While Wilkes was working at Hawaii and Maui, Hudson and Ringgold had been carrying out their respective assignments. The *Porpoise*, which had left Honolulu on November 15, returned on March 24, at which point Ringgold reported on the completion of work at several of the islands in the Tuamotus and on the difficult coral-boring experiments made by Lieutenant Robert E. Johnson on Aratika (Carlshoff) Island. (It was a laborious process — and the greatest depth reached was twenty-one feet.) Ringgoid's account of his experience at Penrhyn Island (which was found to be thirty miles farther west than its location on Arrowsmith's Chart) was especially dramatic. "The vessel stood off and on [Penrhyn Island] all night, and on the 16th, at sunrise, canoes were discovered approaching the brig, in great numbers, many of them large. At seven o'clock two came alongside, and

---

* Mauna Kea proved to be the winner.

others soon followed them. As the numbers of the visitors increased, they became more bold, and clambered up the sides, uttering loud and savage yells. They were the wildest and most savage-looking beings that had been met with, vociferating in a frightful manner, and accompanying their exclamations with the most violent contortions and gesticulations; they seemed frantic with excitement." The natives were armed with eight-foot coconut wood spears and wore ornaments of braided human hair decorated with fingernails half an inch long.

The *Porpoise* had to be recoppered at Honolulu before she left with the *Vincennes* for the Northwest Coast on April 5, 1841. And since the *Peacock* and *Flying Fish* had not returned, Wilkes left orders for Hudson to join him off the mouth of the Columbia River.

Meanwhile, Hudson with his two vessels had located and surveyed Washington and Jarvis islands, and had returned via the Phoenix group (Enderbury, Birnie, and Hull). Hudson also surveyed Duke of York (Atafu) Island and nearby Duke of Clarence (Nukunono) and discovered Fakaofo, which he named Bowditch Island for the great Salem navigator. About this time, Hudson heard of the existence of another island from a whaling captain. He located it at 11° 05′ south, 170° 55′ 15″ west, and named it Swains for his informer.

The *Peacock* and *Flying Fish* went to Upolu and completed a survey there, then sailed to Funafuti in the Ellice Islands, arriving on March 14, 1841. Nukufetau was the next island Hudson surveyed. (It had been called Depeyster's Island for the captain of that name, who discovered both it and Funafuti in 1819.) Then came the small island of Nanomanga, which Hudson named after himself.

Hudson's first landfall in the Gilberts was Tabiteuea, the island that Captain Bishop had named Drummond in 1799. Hudson found the Gilbertese good-looking, thievish, and lightly tattooed. The Gilbert warriors were armed with long spears and swords edged with sharks' teeth, and their arms and legs exhibited irregular scars from the gashing effects of these formidable weapons. Their physical features, ornaments, canoes, customs, and artifacts were described by Hudson in great detail, and he added that the women were some of the prettiest that had yet been seen in the South Seas.

As Hudson conducted his survey, Peale and the botanist William

Rich crossed the island collecting plants, birds, and shells. They took care to be well armed, for the natives were not of the friendliest. Indeed, after a skirmish, John Anderson, an able seaman, was reported missing, and although tobacco was offered as ransom, Anderson could not be found. Presumably he had been killed. Hudson burned the village of Utiroa in revenge, much to the delight of the inhabitants of a neighboring village, who proceeded to loot it.

Hudson continued north to the middle of the Gilberts, where he surveyed in quick succession Nonouti, Kuria, Abemama, and Maiana. At Kuria he picked up a young Irish beachcomber, John Kirby, who had deserted from the English whaler *Admiral Cockburn* three years before. He had settled down to family life with the chief's daughter, but now requested to be taken back to civilization. His request was granted and his heartbroken wife was given alimony in the form of an old jacknife.

By the time *Peacock* and *Flying Fish* sailed through these islands, various navigators had already contributed much to the accumulating knowledge about them. In charting coral islands, however, it had often been the custom of the earlier explorers to give a separate name to each islet — or *motu*, as it is called in Polynesia — around an atoll and to refer to the whole as a group under another name. When this information was transferred by engravers to published charts, it created great confusion. "The published charts [for the Gilberts] were found so inaccurate," according to Wilkes's surveyors, "as to be a cause of danger rather than of safety; for in them the islands are multiplied, and every hummock or detached islet on the same reef is represented as separate, and a name assigned it. Thus a confusion exists, that it is almost impossible to unravel. How so many errors could be committed, can only be accounted for by the fact that those who had the publication of the charts formerly were generally ignorant, and did not take that care to sift and examine the information that was essential to accuracy."

From Kuria, Hudson sailed to Tarawa, and Abaiang. He finished his Gilbert Islands survey with an examination of Marakei (or Matthews) Island, Makin (which he calls Taritari), and Little Makin (which he calls Makin). At Little Makin, some twenty canoes appeared and in one was another beachcomber — a Scot named Robert Wood, who had jumped ship from the English whaler *Janie* and had not seen another white man for seven years. His English had become unintelligible, but with practice soon straightened out. Like the Irish beachcomber, he requested and was given passage back to civilization.

In their brief encounter, the crew of the *Peacock* noticed a great difference between the natives of Little Makin and the other Gilbert Islands — in respect to their appearance, as well as in character. The features of the Makinese "were regular, and by some thought handsome; they had fine teeth, with glossy black hair, flowing in ringlets about their heads; they were also of a lighter colour than the rest of the natives with whom they are grouped; their figures were, for the most part, rotund, and they seem to have an abundance of food to become fat upon. In walking, they appeared like a moving mass of jelly; every laugh set not only their sides in motion, but their whole frame and flesh."

There was no begging or stealing at Makin. The canoes were larger and better built than in the other Gilberts. The women were not offered for prostitution. Polygamy was the custom among the upper classes, the principal chief having over fifty wives. (One chief had his wives sewed up in mats when he went away on a canoe trip.) To be sure, the shortage of women created a difficult situation. Poorer men could not afford any, and one lonely chief attempted to leave the island by hanging on to a man rope trailing from the *Peacock*. He was discovered and sent back to his sexless island existence.

The Gilbert survey had taken so long that upon its completion Hudson was forced to place his crews on reduced allowances of food and water, as he sailed north between the Ralik and Radak chains of the Marshalls to the northernmost of that group, then known as the Pescadores (now Rongerik). He surveyed Kotzebue's Kossakoff Island (now Rongelap) and from there steered easterly for Honolulu, where the *Peacock* and *Flying Fish* arrived in mid-June within three days of each other.

On June 21 the two vessels sailed for the Columbia River to rejoin the squadron. They reached soundings off the river on July 17, and the next day the *Peacock* piled up on the bar across the river mouth and became a total loss. Although no lives were lost, and the charts, documents, and nautical instruments were saved, some of the collections were destroyed.

To strengthen his weakened fleet, Wilkes bought the brig *Oregon*. Doggedly he continued surveys of the Columbia River, San Francisco Bay, and the coast between. By November 17, 1841, the fleet was back in Honolulu, where they spent a scant ten days before sailing for Manila. The *Porpoise* and *Oregon* were detached to explore the reefs and shoals extending for over a thousand miles northwest of the Hawaiian Islands. *Vincennes* and *Flying Fish* proceeded to Manila and a rather cursory survey of the Sulu Sea.

One suspects that by this time everyone was weary, homesick, and ill-tempered. When the fleet reassembled at Singapore, the *Flying Fish*, now in poor condition, was sold and the other three vessels sailed for home around the Cape of Good Hope. *Vincennes* anchored off Sandy Hook on June 10, 1842, and the *Porpoise* and *Oregon* arrived about three weeks later.

The many important results of the United States Exploring Expedition were overshadowed by controversy. Charges and countercharges flew thick and fast between Wilkes and his officers. Wilkes, along with several of his officers, was courtmartialed after his return. The court began on July 25 on board the U.S.S. *North Carolina* at Brooklyn Navy Yard. There were thirty-five charges against Wilkes, of which nine were stricken, but the charges were for trivia — wearing an unauthorized uniform, "god-damning" his officers, severe punishment of men beyond regulations, etc. There was little mention of loss of ships and none of the fifty-seven slaughtered Fijians. He was sentenced to be publicly reprimanded by the secretary of the navy.

When all is said and done, Wilkes carried out his assignment most effectively. He was a temperamental, severe, and proud man who drove himself harder than he drove his men. The charts resulting from the expedition were many and excellent, and some have been superceded only in recent years. His five-volume *Narrative*, written in a remarkably short time, is a treasure house of geographical, ethnological, and historical information. First published at the end of 1844, by

1858 it had gone through fifteen editions. The twenty-two ponderous volumes of the scientific series, produced by the various scientists, are a monument to their diligence and a great contribution to knowledge. The fact that they were published in absurdly small editions has limited their usefulness.

Yet perhaps too much time and ink in the past has been devoted to stressing the acrimonious aspects of the arguments between personalities involved before, during, and after the expedition returned, and not enough to its solid accomplishments. One cannot help sympathizing with Wilkes's bitter disappointment over the indifference of the public and the accusations of some of his officers after the completion of a notable achievement.

19

The English Finish Up

THE major scientific voyages of the 1830's and 1840's substantially brought to a close the geographical exploration of the Pacific. They had also made known much of the flora and fauna and had enlightened the world on various island dwellers. In general, one could say that with each expedition there was a diminishing return of new geographical knowledge, but a greater return of biological and ethnographical data.

While the major expeditions were in progress and their results were being published in massive reports, there were other voyages, mostly English, that were clearing up geographical details in obscure corners of the Pacific. Individually, these voyages did not amount to much. Their total contribution, however, ranging from the 1830's to the 1870's, is impressive.

Eleven years after he first sailed for the Pacific in H.M.S. *Blossom* to meet Sir John Franklin beyond Bering Strait, Frederick William Beechey was again dispatched on a surveying voyage to fill in blanks in the charts along America's Pacific seaboard — this time aboard *Sulphur*.

After establishing certain precise meridian distances in the Atlantic, his instructions called for Beechey to round the Horn and complete the detailed survey of the western coast of South America, beginning where Captain Fitzroy's survey in the *Beagle* terminated. Unfortunately Fitzroy had not returned to England by the time the *Sulphur* sailed, but it was supposed that his termination point would be known in Valparaiso. (It was also thought, however, that there would be no duplication if Beechey began his survey at Coquimbo, pending the return of the *Beagle* or the arrival of her dispatches.) Except for the ports of Guayaquil and Callao, there existed no detailed knowledge of the entire long coasts of Chile, Peru, Ecuador beyond two Spanish charts based on running surveys. And as to those, Beechey's instructions declared: "The half-knowledge to be obtained by this kind of survey, has always acted as a check on the advance of geographical and nautical information, and is in itself useless; for the native coaster wants nothing beyond his local experience; the regular foreign trade employs a pilot; and the occasional visitor sees that all the details are so unlike the truth, that he does not even attempt to correct."

Next in importance to laying down the coastline with accuracy, Beechey's instructions stated, was the need for precise soundings and recordings of bottom quality. If possible, Beechey should determine the position of the tiny St. Felix Island, nearly six hundred miles off the South American coast, and the dangerous London Bank, reported by the brig *Cannon* in 1827 at 27° 6' south and 92° 16' west. He was also to determine the length of Cocos Island, long in doubt, and at all times he was to keep records on the direction, strength, and depth of ocean currents; on the comparative temperatures of the atmosphere and the sea; on the rise and fall of tides; and on wind forces, including the periods and limits of trade winds, monsoons, and rainy seasons.

Beechey was to make observations on magnetic variation and the dip of the needle at certain geographical points; he was to take barometric readings regularly, and meteorological observations. He should keep written nautical descriptions and directions for ports within the survey, paying particular attention to places of refuge where water, wood, and other supplies could be obtained. Among the atolls, he was to make borings in coral formations in order to find out if they rested on old volcanoes; and while it was not the object of this expedition to make large geological or natural history collections, Beechey was to keep his eyes open to obvious opportunities.*

---

* A botanical collector, taken along to gather plants and seeds for His Majesty's Garden at Kew, was to be given all reasonable assistance as long as it did not interfere with the surveying.

Captain Beechey in the *Sulphur*, accompanied by the schooner *Starling* commanded by Lieutenant Henry Kellett, sailed from Portsmouth on December 24, 1835, and touched at Madeira, Teneriffe, Rio de Janeiro, and Montevideo on the voyage out. The two vessels arrived at Valparaiso within the limits of their primary survey on June 9, but here Captain Beechey, a veteran of many arduous cruises, became too ill to continue and was invalided home in H.M.S. *North Star*. Lieutenant Kellett assumed command of the expedition and went on with the work. As soon as the Lords of the Admiralty received notice of Captain Beechey's return, they appointed Captain Edward Belcher, Beechey's old shipmate and assistant surveyor on the *Blossom* voyage, to succeed him. Belcher received his appointment to H.M.S. *Sulphur* in November 1836. He proceeded by steamer to Panama and crossed the isthmus, where he was met by the *Sulphur* and took over command.

Belcher completed *Sulphur*'s hydrographical work on the South American coast and then sailed for the Hawaiian Islands. Almost from the moment he arrived, on July 7, 1837, he was involved in the case of the French Catholic missionaries and the government's attempt to force a British flag vessel to transport them from the islands. Belcher, a volatile man at best, nearly had apoplexy during his confrontation with the Reverend Hiram Bingham of the American Mission, under whose insistence the orders were being carried out; but at this critical moment, Captain du Petit-Thouars in the frigate *Venus* arrived in Hawaii on his circumnavigation. The English and French captains joined forces and obtained a temporary restraining order on the expulsion of the Catholic fathers.

From Kauai the *Sulphur* sailed to Port Etches in King William Sound, Alaska, where Belcher fixed the position of lofty Mount Saint Elias. *Sulphur* then proceeded down the coast to Nootka Sound and San Francisco. The entire year of 1838 Belcher spent on the survey, working along the Central American coast to Cocos Island. By May 29, 1839, the *Sulphur* was once more off Honolulu. Belcher sailed again from the islands to the northwest on June 16.

After finishing his work along the western American littoral,

Belcher was instructed to cross the Pacific and return home around the Cape of Good Hope. He began his homeward voyage from San Blas on December 25, 1839, thence to the islands of Socorro and Clarión, downhill to the Marquesas. On January 20, *Sulphur* raised Nuku Hiva. Entering beautiful Anna Maria Bay, Belcher erected an observatory on the precise spot where both Porter in 1814 and d'Urville on his second voyage had placed theirs.

The voyage continued to Hao (or Bow) Island in the middle of the Tuamotu Archipelago. Belcher had been at Hao before in the *Blossom*; now he spent nearly two months there, principally to conduct experiments in coral boring. While the arduous borings were going on, he made tidal, magnetic, and astronomical observations and accumulated a good fish collection. Belcher has left an excellent account of the Bow Islanders and speaks of the physical changes in the island — one islet, for example, that had disappeared — since his visit fourteen years previous.

On April 4 *Sulphur* dropped anchor in Matavai Bay, Tahiti. She moved over to Papeete the next day (assisted, when the wind dropped, by the boats of thirteen American whale ships moored in the harbor). Belcher spent a scant four days in this now comparatively civilized port before sailing to Huahiné and then on to the Cook Islands. *Sulphur* made a scheduled stop at Vavau in the Tonga group to determine the meridian. She departed Vavau on May 23, and in three days raised the easternmost of the Fiji group, where she grounded and sheared her rudder pintles. About this time Belcher heard that Wilkes was still surveying in the Fijis and sent Kellett in the *Starling* to find the Wilkes ships. Kellett was successful: Wilkes immediately sent three pintles from the *Peacock*. Wilkes then followed up with a visit to Belcher on June 15, when the two commanders spent nearly eighteen hours together comparing notes, exchanging information, and talking over matters of mutual interest.

By June, the Belcher expedition had reached the New Hebrides — Port Resolution, Tana. The vessels left on the twenty-fourth; Belcher examined the inner side of Guadalcanal and then went to Port Carteret, which he surveyed along with other harbors of New Ireland. When tedious, thick weather and a long sick list rendered a complete investigation of New Ireland impossible, Belcher pushed on past the Admiralties to the mainland of New Guinea.

The costume of the nervous, but good-humored, natives there "was entirely new to us," Belcher recorded, "resembling nothing we have seen. The hair, which is permitted to grow to a great length, is confined behind by a conical case, having the crown as its base, and generally tapering at eighteen inches length to three at the point, the hair curling over. Into this preposterous appendage they stick their feather ornaments, either birds of paradise or canes with gaudy feathers of parrots or other birds neatly worked on, which add about eighteen inches to the length. They are generally in a state of nature, but in many cases, particularly the older people, have a dirty tapa about their loins. In stature they seldom reach the height of five feet four inches, and average about five feet."

As Belcher moved along the northern coast, he was "visited by many natives, from whom we purchased weapons, and other trifles." The island population seemed to increase as he moved westward. Well-built short canoes, each manned by a crew of two or three men, came laden with bows, arrows, coconuts, and plantains offered in exchange for hoop iron and beads. (Large china blue beads were the favorites.) One plate of tortoiseshell was honestly traded for six inches of rusty hoop iron. But the islanders' tarnished bird of paradise plumes, worn as ornaments, were not for sale.

Belcher had a sharp eye for the differences among the various tribes he encountered during this part of his voyage. He noticed especially the changes in canoe styles. "These were of two kinds," he writes of one group of canoes: "one intended for extensive fishing, and with trifling ornament; the other entirely state, and gorgeously ornamented in sculpture at the stern, which was further decorated by plumes of birds of paradise. This latter had a kind of frame work, which could be immediately converted into a house, by mats there in readiness, and I am inclined to believe they generally sleep in them in preference to landing."

From New Guinea Belcher entered the Moluccas, visited Buru, and rejoined Kellett (who had gone on ahead in the *Starling*) at Amboina

Ornamental bow carving of a New Guinea canoe
(*Belcher*, Voyage Around the World, *Vol. II*)

on September 3, 1840. From here he proceeded to Singapore, where orders were awaiting him to go to Canton. He took an active part in operations against the Chinese and was finally able to sail for England late in 1841. He anchored at Spithead on June 19, 1842.

The cruise of the *Sulphur* was long, and mostly unexciting. But it filled in much of the detail for the eastern Pacific continental shores and produced accurate charts of many island harbors, especially in the western Pacific.

As the population of Australia (largely in Sydney and environs) grew, more ships began using the tortuous and dangerous passes through the northern end of the Great Barrier Reef into Torres Strait, and there was a growing and pressing need to have all passes precisely charted and marked by beacons or buoys. To begin this work, the Admiralty dispatched the survey vessel *Fly* under Captain F. P. Blackwood, accompanied by the cutter *Bramble*, commanded by Lieutenant C. B. Yule, as tender.

[363]

Hitherto most of the charting of the Great Barrier Reef had been on the lagoon — or western — side. Now Blackwood was instructed to survey its exterior — or eastern — edge from Breaksea Spit to the New Guinea shore. He was to examine all channels through the barrier chain and make detailed plans of all those offering a safe passage. Next he was to devise a method for marking the best passes with wood, stone, or iron beacons and discuss with the governor at Sydney his suggested method. He was also to determine the positions and dimensions of reefs and shoals to the southward of the Great Barrier Reef and others westward of New Caledonia. In Torres Strait itself he was to collate the previous surveys of Flinders, Bligh, and King and make a complete survey of Endeavour Strait.

These were the primary purposes of the expedition. If time remained and it seemed feasible, however, Blackwood was free to explore and chart the southern shore of New Guinea, the southwestern Louisiades, and the western side of New Caledonia. Blackwood's instructions concluded with the admonition: "Whatever you do is to be done effectually."

The most modern, approved, and costly instruments were provided for Blackwood for research in magnetism, and certain of the officers were specially trained for performing these observations. Two naturalists, J. Beete Jukes (who wrote the narrative of the voyage) and John MacGillivray, were employed for the expedition. H. S. Melville was appointed artist. Brief accounts of the progress of the work were to be sent John Barrow, secretary of the Admiralty, at every opportunity.

The vessels sailed in company from Falmouth on April 11, 1842, and arrived at Simon's Bay, Cape of Good Hope, on June 19. They left Simon's Bay a little over three weeks later, bound for Hobart, Tasmania. By the fifteenth of October they were at Sydney, and here they remained until November 24, when Blackwood left to begin his herculean survey at Breaksea Spit. For the remainder of 1843 Blackwood was employed in the Great Barrier Reef survey.

As the *Fly* approached Murray Island in the entrance of Torres Strait in early August 1843, the crew saw many natives on the beach and a line of large dome-shaped huts, surrounded by fences of tall

poles ornamented with large shells. The Murray Islanders had a reputation for ferocity and treachery. Blackwood was therefore cautious
as he approached land. Soon he was surrounded by about a hundred
shouting, yammering people, offering plates of tortoiseshell, coconuts,
and bows and arrows in barter for iron and knives (which they called
"knipa").

From Murray the survey transferred to barren and uninteresting
York Island. On his second cruise out of Sydney in 1844, Blackwood
went to Cape York and spent some time at Darnley (Erub) Island.
Fifty or sixty people greeted his landing and, like the Murray Islanders, offered coconuts, tortoiseshell, and axes for trade. They were a
brown people of middle height with handsome fine — indeed, rather
semitic — features. Their hair was dressed in long pipelike ringlets
smeared with red ochre, while some wore wigs.

The islanders of Torres Strait were famous for their tortoiseshell
masks, and *Fly*'s naturalist Jukes was elated when he "purchased for a
knife a curious tortoise-shell mask, or face, made to fit over the head,
which was used they told me, in their dances. It was fairly put together, with hair, beard and whiskers fastened on, projecting ears, and
pieces of mother-of-pearl, with a black patch in the centre for the
eyes." A little later one of the officers was fortunate to obtain for an
axe a tortoiseshell figure of a boy, three feet high. The mask, along
with Jukes's other ethnological collections, ended up in the British
Museum, and the tortoiseshell boy in the Museum of the United Service Institution in London.

After a second circumnavigation of Australia, Blackwood arrived
on September 25 at Sydney, where he found orders to return home
with the *Fly* but to leave Lieutenant C. B. Yule in the *Bramble* to
continue the survey. Blackwood purchased a small schooner called the
Castlereagh, fitted her out as *Bramble*'s consort, and left for home on
December 19. The *Fly* arrived at Spithead on June 19, 1846, after an
absence of four years and eleven weeks.

The results of this voyage were considerable. Five hundred miles of
the outer line of the Great Barrier Reef, from latitude 16° 40′ to its
northern extremity, were surveyed, as well as one hundred and ten
miles of the main coastline of Australia, from West Hill to the north-

ern part of Whitsunday Passage. The Capricorn Islands and Swain Reefs, Port Bowen, and Rockingham Bay were charted. A beacon was erected on Raine Islet. Endeavour Strait and all of the eastern portion of Torres Strait from Cape York to the coast of New Guinea (an area of some 7,000 square miles, crowded with reefs and islands) were surveyed, in addition to 140 miles of the New Guinea coast. Between four and five thousand zoological specimens were collected. The geological and ethnological collections were also large, and a great deal of linguistic and ethnological data was accumulated.

But the job was not finished.

The *Fly* arrived home in June 1846, and on September 24 of the same year Captain Owen Stanley commissioned the twenty-eight-gun ship *Rattlesnake* at Portsmouth. Stanley's orders were to continue the work of Blackwood. Although the specific objects of the *Fly* voyage had been completed with the survey for the erection of a durable beacon marking Raine Island Passage, much remained to be done to make those seas secure, and it was desirable to locate another entrance to Torres Strait farther to the northward for vessels overshooting the latitude of Raine Islet. As with the previous voyage, surveying was to be Stanley's primary object, but he was not to overlook the natural sciences. John MacGillivray, who had been naturalist on the *Fly*, was employed in the same capacity for the *Rattlesnake* and wrote the official account of the expedition. The second naturalist and assistant surgeon was a young man who would become as famous as Darwin: Thomas Henry Huxley was only twenty-two when he embarked on this adventure, which gave him experience similar to that of his older contemporary.

Again, every reasonable facility was to be given the naturalists in making and preserving collections, but they were not to interfere with surveying. Brief accounts were to be sent home to the secretary of the Admiralty at every opportunity and a constant correspondence kept up with the hydrographer, Sir Francis Beaufort. When the surveys (and sailing directions) were completed, both *Rattlesnake* and *Bramble* were to return to Spithead, unless *Bramble* was unfit to make the voyage. Further instructions from Beaufort cautioned Stanley to

Murray Islanders eager to barter (Voyage of the H.M.S. Fly, *Vol. 1*)

lose no opportunity to verify the positions and improve the details on the Australian coast laid down by Captain P. P. King. He was also to examine those parts of the Coral Sea traversed by ships heading for Torres Strait and carefully explore the northernmost (or Bligh) channel (apparently the safest entrance from the Pacific). And he was to connect the islands and Warrior Reefs with a survey of the New Guinea coast. Like Blackwood, Stanley was given complete freedom to execute his instructions in any order he desired.

H.M.S. *Rattlesnake* left Spithead on December 3, 1846, and took the same passage as the *Fly*. She anchored in Simon's Bay on March 8, 1847. Stanley made good use of his time here by constructing a chart of the bay and its neighborhood, which was later incorporated with an earlier survey made by Sir Edward Belcher in H.M.S. *Samarang*. By May 4 the *Rattlesnake* was beating up to Port Louis, Mauritius, to leave £15,000 for the colony's use.

Port Louis was a cosmopolitan seaport. "The first thing to engage attention," the naturalist MacGillivray wrote, "is the strange mixture of nations, — representatives, he [the visitor] might at first be inclined to imagine, of half the countries of the earth. He stares at a Coolie from Madras with a breach cloth and soldier's jacket, or a stately, bearded Moor, striking a bargain with a Parsee merchant; a Chinaman, with two bundles slung on a bamboo, hurries past, jostling a group of young Creole exquisites smoking their cheroots at a corner, and talking of last night's Norma, or the programme of the evening's performance at the Hippodrome in the Champ de Mars; his eye next catches a couple of sailors reeling out of a grogshop, to the amusement of a group of laughing negresses in white muslin dresses of the latest Parisian fashion, contrasting strongly with a modestly attired Cingalese woman, and an Indian ayah with her young charge. Amidst all this the French language prevails; everything more or less pertains of the French character, and an Englishman can scarcely believe that he is in one of the colonies of his own country."

Rattlesnake spent twelve days at Mauritius, then Stanley was requested to take more specie to Hobart, Tasmania. He therefore abandoned plans for stopping at King George Sound and sailed to Hobart, where he arrived June 24. He reached Sydney the fifteenth of the following month. Soon after he sold *Castlereagh* and recommissioned the *Bramble* as a tender for *Rattlesnake*.

In a series of cruises to the northward Captain Stanley systematically carried out and fulfilled his instructions. On one cruise he concentrated on the Cape York area. Blackwood had surveyed 140 miles of the southeast New Guinea coast, and Lieutenant Yule had surveyed two degrees more of longitude of that coast to the westward of and connecting with Blackwood's survey. Stanley charted a large part of the Louisiade Archipelago, beginning at Rossel Island (named after one of d'Entrecasteaux's officers), the easternmost island of the group. He continued making his traverses, returning intermittently to Sydney, until the work was completed.

There were many contacts with the inhabitants, for this whole region was well populated. At Redscar Bay, in the eastern side of the Gulf of Papua, Huxley and the talented marine artist Oswald W. Brierly received a scare when they were surrounded by a group of painted Papuans laden with material to trade. Suddenly the visitors produced ten-foot-long spears that had been concealed in the grass. Their behavior became rude and insolent, and a cautious retreat by Huxley and Brierly narrowly prevented open hostility. Since the entire region is one where a wide variety of personal ornaments are worn, Huxley collected an abundance of necklaces of shells, black seeds, and dogs' canine teeth; nose sticks (called yardarms by the sailors), pendants, tortoiseshell combs, and lime spatulas. At Brierly (Daddahai) Island, named for the artist, Huxley and MacGillivray wandered about unmolested, making notes and sketching, while one of the officers traded for yams. One islander, upon acquiring an axe he particularly fancied, "became quite wild with joy, laughing and screaming, and flourishing the axe over his head." In all, 368 pounds of yams were obtained for seventeen axes and a few knives.

Huxley and MacGillivray made particularly close observations of the material culture of the Brumer Islands, including excellent descriptions of the various kinds of canoes seen along the coast. At every stop the two naturalists were avidly building up superb ethnological and natural history collections. They also discovered eight or nine new species of birds.

In due course Stanley left Cape York and sailed through Torres Strait, along the southeast New Guinea coast, to the Louisiades and thence to Sydney, reversing his previous course. He made numerous stops along the way. At Mount Ernest, writes MacGillivray, "not far from the village, under the shade of an aged mimusops tree on the outskirts of the wood, we observed a cleared oval space where ten human skulls — of former members of the tribe, as we were informed — were arranged upon a plank raised on stones a foot or so from the ground. The skulls were mostly old and weather-worn, and some of them had pandanus seeds stuck in the orbits by way of eyes. In front was a large smooth stone painted red and black, and partially imbedded in the earth, and beside it were some painted human leg and arm bones, shells and other ornaments."

Rattlesnake made a call at Darnley Island, whose people were so well described on the *Fly* voyage, where Lieutenant Yule was sent to connect the surveys of the *Fly* and *Rattlesnake* and thus complete the coastline of the whole of the southeast part of New Guinea. Yule and MacGillivray left *Bramble* behind for a few weeks at the Duchateau Islands to obtain a meridian distance and to fill up blanks. "Although rather a better sample of the Papuan race than that which we had lately seen at Redscar Bay," MacGillivray commented on the Duchateau Islanders, "there was no marked physical distinction between these inhabitants of the Louisiade and the New Guinea men. The canoes, however, are as different as the language; here, as throughout the Archipelago, the canoes have the semblance of a narrow coffin-like box, resting upon a hollowed out log, the bow having the two characteristic ornaments of the tabúra, or head-board, and the crest-like carved wood work running out along the beak."

But while the ethnographical exploration was extensive and yielded rich results, MacGillivray was well aware of its complication in this region. "The ethnology of New Guinea," he wrote, "is involved in so much confusion and obscurity for want of sufficient *data*. . . ." Until very recently it remained so.

When the Torres Strait survey was at last completed, it emerged that "the most important practical result of Capt. Stanley's survey of the Louisiade Archipelago and the south coast of New Guinea, was ascertaining the existence of a clear channel of at least 30 miles in width along the southern shores of these islands, stretching east and west between Cape Deliverance and the north-east entrance to Torres Strait — a distance of about 600 miles. This space was so traversed by the two vessels of the expedition without any detached reefs being discovered, that it does not seem probable that any such exist there, with the exception of the Eastern Fields of Flinders."

Soon after the *Rattlesnake* arrived at Sydney, Captain Owen Stanley died suddenly, on March 13, 1850, at the early age of thirty-nine. All further plans for the *Rattlesnake* to go to Singapore were canceled. Lieutenant Yule was appointed to command, with orders to proceed direct to England. He left Sydney on May 3. After stopping at the Falklands and Fayal, the *Rattlesnake* arrived home and was paid off at Chatham on November 9, 1850.

Blackwood's and Stanley's expeditions are perpetuated in many names in southern and eastern New Guinea: the Fly River, the great Owen Stanley Range, Rattlesnake Mountain on Tagula Island in the Louisiades, for example. Now treacherous, tricky Torres Strait and its approaches were at last charted and reasonably safe for all shipping — especially for the widening commerce from Sydney.

In 1849 Captain John Elphinstone Erskine, R.N., made a cruise through the islands of the western Pacific in H.M.S. *Havannah*, a razeed frigate originally of 960 tons. Erskine was sent out by Governor Sir George Grey of New Zealand to make an inspection of all of the islands of consequence within the limits of his command. There were no scientific objects of this cruise beyond examining and hastily surveying previously unknown anchorages. Its principal purposes were to show the flag, to encourage and regulate British trade among these islands, and to furnish an eyewitness account of their state.

Erskine sailed from the Bay of Islands on June 25, 1849, and the prevailing winds determined the order in which he visited the islands. Niue was his first stop, followed by Samoa, Vavau in the Tonga group, the Fijis, the New Hebrides, the Loyalty group, New Caledonia, and the Isle of Pines. Erskine arrived at Sydney on October 7. Part of the way Erskine escorted the bishop of New Zealand on his tour of the missions. Erskine's book contains a wealth of historical and ethnological information on these islands, but his only contribution of any consequence to exploration was in the Loyalty Islands. Erskine had obtained a tracing of Dumont d'Urville's chart of the Loyalties showing d'Urville's survey of the northern and eastern sides of the islands. Erskine helped to fill in the picture by making a very hasty and sketchy outline of their southwestern sides. The following year he cruised back through the islands, visiting New Caledonia, the Solomons, and the New Hebrides before returning to New Zealand.

The great island of New Guinea is shaped like a buzzard. Perched on the tip of the Cape York Peninsula of Australia, its head — now called Vogelkop — faces west; its tail ends in a forked tip formed by Milne Bay. Captain Owen Stanley had never rounded the eastern tip, for he commenced his survey three miles southwest of Heath Island and ran westward. Thus when Captain John Moresby sailed for the Australian station, the eastern tip of New Guinea had still not been established; between Heath Island and Huon Gulf there were over 350 miles of unknown coast, where but two positions had been laid down by d'Entrecasteaux.

Moresby steamed out of Sydney in H.M.S. *Basilisk*, a ship of 1031 tons, on January 15, 1871, bound for Cape York. He carried horses and stores for the settlement at Somerset. Due to the admirable surveys of Blackwood and Owen Stanley, the waters of the Great Barrier Reef were now safe for navigation, and after three months the *Basilisk* was back in Sydney Harbor. In May 1872 she was dispatched on a cruise (to check the illegal kidnapping of natives) that took her to Norfolk, Wallis, Fotuna, and Rotuma. By July 30 she was at the two southernmost of the Ellice Islands, from where Moresby went to the Santa Cruz Islands. Here Moresby surveyed, for the first time, Utupua (or Edgecombe) Island; he was rather proud of discovering a channel leading into the fine anchorage, which he named Basilisk Harbor. He then called at the New Hebrides and arrived at Nouméa, New Caledonia, on September 12, 1872, after visiting fifty-three islands. He dropped anchor at Sydney on the twenty-fourth, where orders were awaiting him to proceed once more to Torres Strait for four (afterwards changed to six) months.

Moresby left Sydney on December 8, 1872. He stopped at Brisbane to pick up Navigating Lieutenant Connor, a good surveyor, and then went to Cape York, where Connor was detached to make detailed surveys among the Torres Strait islands. Moresby went to Darnley Island and then stood across the Gulf of Papua for Redscar Bay to visit the mission station, where he found the missionaries starving and took them on board. After exploring up a river he continued a close examination of the coast for fifty miles east, discovering in the process the spacious, magnificent sheltered harbor of Port Moresby, the best port on the southwest coast of New Guinea. Another fifty miles of coast was examined and then *Basilisk* returned to Redscar Bay. Connor and Midshipman Pitt, who had been surveying the northern shore of Torres Strait, returned to *Basilisk* with their nine men and two boats at this time.

Moresby was hankering to fill in the last blank on the New Guinea coast, but his orders confined him to west of longitude 148° east, only a little beyond Port Moresby. He had other orders, however, to search for the famous Russian traveler Miklucho Maclay, who had disappeared into the wilds of New Guinea some months before. So, after detaching Connor again to continue his work along the Torres Strait shore of New Guinea, Moresby went to Cape York and then examined Hammond Island in the entrance of the strait.

The three-mile-long Hammond Island was blessed with a lovely little river emptying into the bay. "We followed the stream up through a deep rocky gorge," Moresby wrote, "amongst scenes as picturesque as can be imagined. Sometimes it was lost to sight in a gloomy depth, overhung by tropic growth, then it rose again, racing and foaming over huge boulders, forming here waterfalls ten or fifteen feet deep, and there deep stilly pools, from which it slipped softly down. On reaching the summit we found that the hills spread themselves out into a large concave plain, forming a great natural reservoir, from which many streams descended. . . ."

Moresby next sailed to Yule Island and charted the waters of Rob-

ert Hall Sound behind it — another good anchorage. He ascended the
Ethel River for ten miles and then on April 6 stood for eastern New
Guinea.

Now Moresby learned that Bougainville, d'Entrecasteaux, d'Urville, and Owen Stanley, all of whom thought that they had seen the
eastern tip of New Guinea, had actually seen only islands: from East
Cape along the northern shore for 190 miles as the crow flies was coast
unseen by a white man. Although d'Entrecasteaux had sighted land
indistinctly and named it Cape Sud Est, his position fell twelve miles
inland. There was another forty-mile blank to d'Entrecasteaux's
Richie Island — in reality, a point. A further unknown gap of sixty
miles carried the coast to Huon Gulf, from which point the coast had
been traced with tolerable accuracy.

Moresby's survey of Heath (Rogeia) Island joined with Captain
Stanley's. Since the waters off eastern New Guinea are reef-strewn
and dangerous, Moresby hoped that by moving out to Teste (Wari)
Island, twenty-two miles south of the then supposed tip of New
Guinea, he would be able to get around the barrier reef. Yet from
Teste, Moresby soon discovered that the so-called southeast extremity
of New Guinea was only a point on one of a lofty group of small
islands. As the *Basilisk* anchored near the end of what was supposed to
be the mainland, a score of canoes approached manned by nervous
armed natives, ready to take instant flight. When one, bolder than the
rest, climbed the ladder, and, standing on the quarterdeck, squeezed
his nose spasmodically with one forefinger and thumb and his navel
with the other, the delighted officers responded to this navel salute in
kind; immediately the most harmonious relations prevailed.

It did not take long for Moresby to discover that Fortescue Strait
cut off fourteen miles of what had hitherto been thought of as New
Guinea and to name it Moresby (Basilaki) Island. In quick succession,
boat surveys discovered China Strait and Hayter (Sariba) and Basilisk
(Sideia) islands.

After conning the *Basilisk* through China Strait, Moresby, in the
name of Her Majesty Queen Victoria, took formal possession of the
newly discovered islands at an anchorage at Hayter Island that he
called Possession Bay. When Moresby rounded the great bluff end of

New Guinea, he considered that he was now fairly to the north of the island, and stood west, supposing that the land seen to the northwest belonged to the d'Entrecasteaux group of islands. What was his surprise, after some sailing, to find himself embayed. Thus was discovered noble Milne Bay, named for the first lord of the Admiralty.

Completing his survey of Milne Bay, Moresby finally found the true East Cape of New Guinea, with the d'Entrecasteaux Islands afar off in the ocean and distinctly separate. It turned out that the eastern end of the island was fork-shaped; the upper tyne terminating in East Cape, and the lower prong in Moresby Island.

Moresby was now running out of coal and reluctantly decided to give up seeking a good way through the maze of reefs around East Cape. Before leaving, however, he rounded the cape in boats and "steered to the west for several miles along a shore more luxuriant and beautiful than words can describe. . . ." He sketched the d'Entrecasteaux Islands from this position for the first time. Then, turning the other way, he observed: "The great Owen Stanley range may be said to terminate at the head of Milne Bay, but one of its spurs, named by me Sterling Range, runs at a diminished elevation through this new neck of land or narrow peninsula which terminates in East Cape. The double-topped hill which marks this henceforth important promontory on the map of the world, was crowned to the summits, when first we saw it, with tropical forest, but the noble trees afterwards fell to our axes, as we made it a theodolite station."

Basilisk left East Cape on May 3, her skipper well satisfied with the results of the cruise. Besides the new discoveries and surveys, "the ship was," according to Moresby, "full of strange pets and curiosities. The most remarkable of the pets was a cassowary from Cornwallis Island; there were some New Guinea pigs, some varieties of cuscus, and any amount of birds. We had stone and wood weapons and instruments of all kinds; amongst which the large greenstone axes used by the natives in making canoes were the most conspicuous — the blades very sharp, and the stone resembling the prized greenstone of New Zealand. We had canoe paddles made of a fine dark wood. . . . There were gourds of all sizes and shapes . . . cocoa-nuts, used to carry water, and carved all over; bowls of red firebaked clay . . . baskets . . .

netted bags, fish-hooks . . . plumes of the cassowary and red bird of paradise; fillets for the head, and breastplates made of fibre, and beautifully embroidered with shells and berries."

A ten-day passage took *Basilisk* to Somerset at Cape York, where she was rejoined by Lieutenant Connor and Mr. Grant, who had completed a survey of forty-six miles of the great Warrior Reef and 148 miles of the south coast of New Guinea and islands along Torres Strait. By July 2 the *Basilisk* was again at Sydney after an eventful six months' cruise to be refitted. She subsequently proceeded to New Zealand, where Moresby was met by Lieutenant Dawson, the Admiralty surveyor, who gave him permission by mail to return home around northern New Guinea and to complete the work along the unknown coast. Moresby was allowed six weeks for additional surveys, and Dawson had come provided with a supply of the best surveying instruments for the purpose. Moresby reached Sydney yet again on January 6, 1874. H. M. Schooner *Sandfly* was ordered to accompany the *Basilisk* as a tender and Moresby borrowed a steam pinnace from the New South Wales government.

Moresby sailed from Sydney the last day of January. On reaching Teste Island, he rated his chronometers and made a trigonometrical survey between that island and East Cape. The pinnace was a great success. On one occasion it took fourteen canoes in tow, while the owners shouted with admiration and pleasure, till the officer caused extreme consternation by blowing the steam whistle.

On March 4 Moresby visited the D'Entrecasteaux group, on which no white man had ever before set foot. He discovered the strait separating the two southernmost large islands and named them Normandy and Fergusson. The people of these islands, he said, were similar to those of New Guinea, and "our seamen made themselves popular with their dusky friends by getting them on board and painting them with quaint devices in tar and red paint; and those thus ornamented became objects of an envy on shore that produced only too many candidates for the paint-brush." Another strait was found, separating Fergusson from the northernmost large island, which was named Goodenough for Commodore James Graham Goodenough, commander of the Australian Station. All of this hitherto unseen side of these islands was

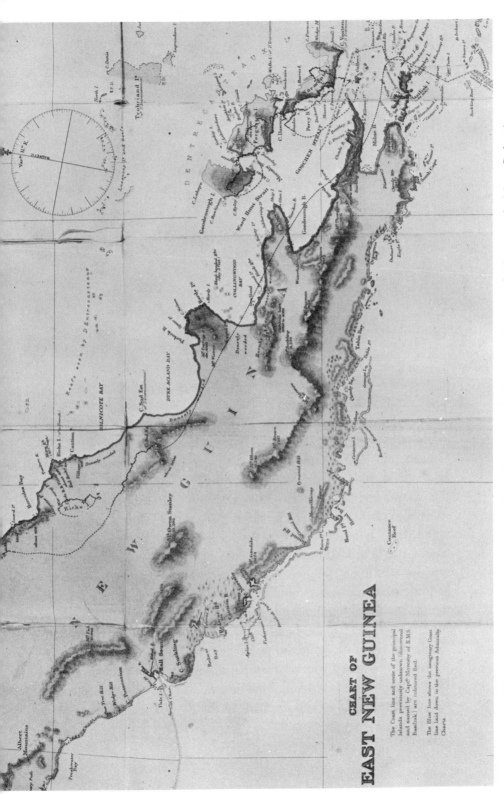

Moresby's survey of northeastern New Guinea coast (Moresby: Voyage of Discovery in New Guinea)

Men of New Guinea (from Duperrey, Voyage Autour du Monde)

mapped. Moresby felt that the *Basilisk* had opened a new and accurately surveyed highway for commerce between Australia, New Guinea, and China. On April 27 he began his running survey of the north coast, made easier by the fact that no barrier reef exists along this shore. He distributed names liberally and most of them have stuck. Goschen Strait, Goodenough Bay, Ward Hunt Strait, Collingwood Bay, Dyke Ackland Bay for his friend Sir Thomas Dyke Ackland, Cape Ward Hunt, and Hercules Bay after Sir Hercules Robinson, are all still on the map. When Moresby arrived at Huon Gulf he had explored the last extensive unknown coastline in the habitable world, thereby completing a work begun by Dampier in 1696 and continued by d'Entrecasteaux, d'Urville, and others. Overlapping somewhat with d'Urville, he terminated his survey at Astrolabe Bay.

Moresby reached the western extremity of New Guinea on May 27. About a week's sail from Amboina, he found a convenient anchorage in Threshold Bay and cleaned up the *Basilisk* in order not to disgrace his service when meeting a Dutch man-of-war. The old ship was rusty from long sea work, and her decks were dyed a dark mahogany color from the stacks of wood that had been collected for fuel after her coal gave out. With painting and smartening-up completed, *Basilisk* bade farewell to New Guinea and arrived at Amboina on June 2. The homeward voyage continued with a stop at Singapore, where Dawson and the pinnace were left to go back to Australia. Moresby hauled down his pennant at Sheerness on December 15, 1874, after an absence thirty-nine days short of four years.

No part of the coastline of New Guinea between Heath Island and Huon Gulf had been laid down before the voyage of the *Basilisk*. The cruise had also added to the chart 140 islands (twenty-five of them inhabited) and many excellent harbors and anchorages. Moresby's name is perpetuated in the spacious harbor and the island off New Guinea's eastern tip — and by the fact that his was the last voyage to make major geographical discoveries in the Pacific.

20

Last of the Old, First of the New

As the 1870's drew near, the surface of the Pacific was known in considerable detail. Its floor, however, was still a mystery, as were the deeps of all the oceans. Faced with such oceanographic obscurity, the Royal Society in 1868 succeeded in persuading the Admiralty to place H.M.S. *Lightning* at its disposal for six weeks of work along the British coast. In that short time *Lightning* did enough sounding and dredging at 650 fathoms (the greatest depth yet attempted) to whet the British appetite for more extended work of this kind. The following year the society secured H.M.S. *Porcupine* for deep-sea exploration. Working off the Irish coasts, *Porcupine* had successful results, first from 1,500 fathoms and then from 2,400 fathoms. So the *Porcupine* was again sent out, in 1870, to the southwest and the coast of Portugal. The results showed that life existed at unsuspected depths, that there were peculiar variations in deep-sea temperatures, and that there were strange movements of currents and circulation of water at different depths.

Following the success of these test cruises, the Council of the Royal Society proposed that a ship be outfitted for a three- or four-years' cruise around the world. The purposes of the expedition were to sound the ocean depths, dredge the ocean floors, examine the chemical and physical properties of seawater at different depths, collect and study all oceanic creatures from surface dwellers to those that lived on the ocean floor, measure currents below the surface, take daily magnetic and meteorological observations, and, finally, examine the plants, animals, and geology of all oceanic islands visited. In this ambitious program the Admiralty concurred, adding surveying instructions so dear to the hearts of naval officers and so important to maritime commerce. The navy was to man the vessel and the society to provide the civilian scientific staff.

H.M.S. *Challenger*, a steam corvette of 2,300 tons, was selected and altered for the unwarlike mission. Most of her guns were removed and her spars were shortened. Below decks, her quarters were modified for the scientific staff; and laboratories and tons of dredging equipment were installed, as well as storage for the thousands of feet of hemp line to be used for dredging and sounding. Captain George Strong Nares, an experienced surveying officer, was appointed to command the expedition. The civilian staff, chosen by the Royal Society, was directed by Professor C. Wyville Thomson and included three naturalists, H. W. Moseley, John Murray, and R. von Suhm (who died on the voyage). There was also a chemist, J. Y. Buchanan. J. J. Wild was secretary and artist.

The latest scientific equipment of all kinds was provided, including the newly invented Baillie sounding machine. If by modern standards this equipment was bulky and clumsy, nevertheless no expedition had ever been prepared to do so much scientific work in such variety on a circumnavigation. Although this was an entirely new kind of expedition, equipped "to carry on whatever researches might throw light on the physical, chemical, and biological conditions of the deep sea," the older traditions of exploration also lingered on. While the scientists were conducting their researches, the naval officers, whenever opportunity offered, were to make surveys of harbors and islands to collect plants, and to make ethnological observations whenever practicable.

The *Challenger* sailed from Portsmouth on the shortest day of the year, December 21, 1872, on a voyage that lasted three and a half years. It is a well-known voyage. The scientific results were published in some fifty ponderous volumes between 1880 and 1895; several popular books on it were written by various members of the expedition. Other accounts have been published in recent years. For our purposes, however, the portion of the cruise pertaining to the Pacific deserves a brief retelling. It is really the end of our story.

After leaving England and crossing the Bay of Biscay, where *Challenger* sighted a ship floating bottom up, a routine shipboard procedure of scientific investigation was established that was followed from the time the vessel left Teneriffe till the very end of the voyage. *Challenger* spent almost a year in the Atlantic, proceeding to St. Thomas in the West Indies, Bermuda, Halifax, Bermuda again, thence to the Azores, Madeira, and the Cape Verdes, Bahia, Brazil, and Tristan da Cunha (in mid-October). On the twenty-eighth of October, Nares finally dropped anchor at the Cape of Good Hope.

On December 2 *Challenger* left the cape and proceeded to the Marion and Crozet islands (which had been discovered within ten days of each other by Marion Du Fresne in January 1772, one hundred and two years before) and then continued on to Christmas Harbor at the Kerguelen Islands. Nares and his party examined the Kerguelens carefully, for one of their objects was to ascertain the most suitable site for the observations of the transits of Venus that were to occur in 1874 and 1882 — the same errand that had taken Captain Cook to Tahiti on his first voyage over a century before.*

After she left mountainous Kerguelen, *Challenger* sighted McDonald and Heard islands, and then continued through a dirty green sea until, on February 16, she met an ice barrier that formed an immense wall rising from one to two hundred feet in height and stretching in either direction as far as the eye could reach. Now Nares turned north for Australia, sighting Port Phillip on St. Patrick's Day, 1874. He remained at Melbourne until April 1, and arrived on the sixth at Sydney, where the collections made on the Arctic cruise were packed, catalogued, and sent to England in sixty-five large boxes and ten casks.

After an extended stay, *Challenger* left New South Wales on June 12 and made a rough passage of the Tasman Sea. (She spent four days bucking a head wind in Cook Strait, where a leadsman was washed overboard and drowned. During the crossing Nares had ordered a line of soundings taken, to facilitate laying a cable between New Zealand and Australia.) But Nares finally dropped anchor in Wellington Harbor, New Zealand, at four in the afternoon on June 28.

---

* The 1874 transit was observed at the Kerguelens from October 9, 1874, to February 27, 1875, by the *Volage* expedition, sent out for the purpose.

Nares next proceeded to Tongatabu, anchoring off Nukualofa, exactly one hundred years after Cook. At Nukualofa he found three whaling vessels — whalers came here each year for the humpback whale season, which around the Tonga Islands lasted from mid-June to the end of October — and from them he learned that an American family who had settled on Raoul (or Sunday) Island in the Kermadecs had abandoned their lonely home when a volcano suddenly erupted there and a shoal rose and sank again in the island's west bay. When the *Challenger* passed by that island, however, all was quiet and there was not the slightest sign of smoke or volcanic activity.

Once in Tonga the sailors were quick to notice that the large, handsome women had fine figures, but the missionaries now insisted that breasts be covered. When Lieutenant Herbert Swire, an officer with unusual artistic talent, went ashore at Nukualofa on the Sunday after arrival, the Tongans were all going to the missionary church. Most of the men were dressed in coats, boots, and trousers, but no hats; the women wore bright dresses and bonnets, but no shoes. The Polynesian spirit, however, had changed little. "The girls were all very larky," Swire wrote, "and it was great fun to see them dressing as they walked to church; some would come out of their houses with nothing on but the tapa, or native cloth, petticoat, carrying dress and bonnet over the arm, which would be adjusted whilst smiling and giggling round us newcomers." Nor did legal measures have any effect. "The King, advised by the missionaries, is trying, by means of heavy fines, to instill Wesleyan morality into his subjects, but even the wisdom of Solomon would not suffice to create so radical a change in the character of the Polynesian race."

The Tongan ironwood trees reminded the Englishmen of Australia. Small herons waded about the coral reefs catching fish, kingfishers sat on dead twigs alert to dart at their prey, lonely little swifts swooped among the coconut trees, and a beautiful small fruit pigeon, green with a purple patch on its head, cooed in the thick masses of foliage. As dusk approached large fruit bats ate the bright red flowers of a tree.

Amid this tropical scene lizards, insects, plants, and corals were energetically collected during the short stay, which ended on July 22.

"This was," Wild later wrote, "one of the pleasantest episodes of our cruise round the world, and we were loath to part from an island which seemed to realise the dream of the idyllic poet. The sun of a primitive civilisation is fast sinking below the western horizon of the Pacific. We were fortunate enough to gather some of its last rays."

Challenger spent a day at the island of Matuku, in the Fijis, about seventy miles east of Kandavu, where an observatory was set up on the edge of the ancient crater forming the harbor, and a party ascended the island's highest peak — some twelve hundred feet. While they dredged off Matuku, *Challenger*'s crew brought to the surface the only living specimen of the pearly nautilus collected on the expedition.

At Ngaloa Harbor on Kandavu (which had been made a port of call for the Sydney and San Francisco mail steamers), *Challenger* conducted another survey. This was now a fair-sized town for the South Seas, with lovely paths leading away through peaceful valleys among dense groves of breadfruit and coconut trees. Meanwhile, a party of officers and naturalists made a trip in the barge to Mbau and Rewa. At Mbau they viewed with some apprehension the stone against which the heads of human victims intended for the great ovens were bashed. (This stone is now the baptismal font in the Methodist Church at Mbau.) The party paid a visit to King Thakombau, the reformed old cannibal, who received his visitors lying on his stomach reading his Bible. They also ascended the Rewa River and purchased quantities of clubs, spears, kava bowls, and other implements at the villages along its banks. The naturalist Moseley has left a fine account of this trip and of the Fijians, and Lieutenant Swire also has written at some length on their customs. But these were, by now, long-familiar subjects, and already Fijian children were writing class papers in the Fijian language. The *Challenger* left Ngaloa Harbor, Fiji, on August 10, taking on board several New Hebrides laborers who had completed their contracts and wished to return home.

The *Challenger* reached the New Hebrides on August 17, 1874, and landed her passengers at Api Island. She went on her way to Raine Islet, marked by the beacon tower erected by the *Fly* expedition, where the naturalists were allowed time to go ashore. At Somerset,

A Tongan in ceremonial dress
(*from* Exploring Voyage of the H.M.S. Challenger, *Vol. 1*)

Cape York, the wonderful twelve-foot-high anthills and the deplorable condition of the aborigines were equally impressive.

It is interesting to note how ethnological material could by now be collected out of context. Cape York was, according to Thomson's account, "a sort of emporium of savage weapons and ornaments. Pearl-shell gathering vessels ('pearl-shellers' as they are called) come to Somerset with crews which they have picked up at all the islands in the neighborhood, from New Guinea, and from all over the Pacific, and they bring weapons and ornaments from all these places with them. Moreover, the Murray Islanders visit the port in their canoes, and bring bows and arrows, drums and such things for barter. The water police stationed at Somerset deal in these curiosities, buying them up and selling them to passengers in the passing steamers, or to other visitors. Hence all kinds of savage weapons have found their way into English collections, with the label 'Cape York,' and the northern Australians have got credit for having learnt the use of the bow and arrow. Apparently, however, no Australian natives use the bow at all. Weapons from very remote places find their way to Cape York, and thus no doubt the first specimens of Admiralty Island javelins reached the English museums. Accurate determination of locality is of course essential to the interest of savage weapons. Surgeon Maclean of the *Challenger* had a large New Guinea drum of the crocodile form thrust upon his acceptance as a fee for visiting a patient on board one of the 'pearl-shellers.' "

Leaving Somerset on September 8, 1874, the *Challenger* sailed westward out of Torres Strait to the Aroe Islands, where both the islanders and their natural history received considerable attention. The vessel then proceeded on her leisurely way, surveying and dredging around the Kai and Banda islands to Amboina, whose green hills were seen at daylight on October 4. After a six-day stay there she made a two-day run to Ternate in the Moluccas.

From Ternate a rather hazardous trade was carried on by the Malays with New Guinea. A wrecked Malay proa was fair game for the Papuans, but desire for the valuable bird of paradise plumes lured the Malays on. According to the official *Narrative:* "The Malay collectors who are sent every year with the traders to New Guinea from Ternate, to collect Birds of Paradise and other birds, are some of them extremely expert in preparing and preserving bird-skins. They mount them with a small stick stuck into the tow stuffing, and protruding at the tail; the skin is handled by the stick, and thus the bird's feathers are prevented from being injured. There are several Mohammedan dealers in bird-skins in the town of Ternate. A Papuan Bird of Paradise (*Paradisea papuana*), well-skinned, costs about eight shillings, and a well-skinned Red Bird of Paradise (*Paradisea rubra*) fourteen shillings."

A ball in honor of the "Challengers" was held in Government House at Ternate, attended by all the rank and beauty of the town, including Arabs, Chinese, Malays, Dutchmen, and the lone English resident. On the seventeenth the *Challenger* left Ternate for Zamboanga, and then continued through the intricate interisland waterways of the Philippines, arriving at Manila on November 4. After a week at the Philippine capital the cruise continued to Hong Kong. Here all of the specimens collected since leaving Sydney were packed in 129 cases and several casks and placed on board the H.M.S. *Adventure* for shipment to England. It was at Hong Kong that Captain Nares found orders for him to return home to take command of an Arctic expedition being planned. Captain Frank Turle Thomson, then serving on the China station, was appointed to the *Challenger*, and took command of the expedition on January 2, 1875. Four days later the ship sailed from Hong Kong to Manila, then once more made her way through the Philippine Islands, and turned westward to Humboldt Bay, named by Dumont d'Urville, on the north coast of New Guinea. The *Challenger* was again in Pacific waters.

As the ship entered Humboldt Bay on the evening of February 23, signal fires glimmered and flashed from one side of the bay to the other, bright lights moved among the pile-built villages, and warning shouts of many voices came over the water. Men clad in white cockatoo feathers or wreaths of bright scarlet flowers, in exploratory canoes, asked for "sigor," and cigars were passed to them on their fish spears. (Later it was learned that the word meant iron, which was really what was wanted.) At daybreak the number of canoes surrounding the ship continued to increase until there were sixty-seven of them. The air was filled with shouts and the booming of conch shell trumpets.

This golden opportunity to collect ethnological specimens was not neglected. "To see them depriving themselves of their weapons and ornaments," Wild wrote, "the result of much toil and inventive skill, and handing them over to us in return for a few inches of rusty hoop iron, was a singular sight, and could not fail to impress us with the immense value which this metal must have in the eyes of a man hitherto compelled to spend month after month in chipping out his canoe from the trunk of a tree with a stone hatchet or the sharp edge of a shell. . . .

"Laden with the 'spoil of the Egyptians,' whose store of bows and arrows, three-pronged fish-spears, carved paddles, stone hatchets, bone daggers, earrings, nose ornaments, necklaces, breast-shields, bracelets, and wigs we had no doubt considerably reduced — I fear the next gathering of the warriors of the tribe must have fallen short of its usual splendour — we steamed, before sunset, out of Humboldt Bay."

Swire, who made wonderful notes and superb watercolors of the people, was an avid collector. "During all this time," he wrote, "no end of trade had been going on between us on board the ship and the occupants of the canoes. They would on no account be persuaded to come on board, but traded alongside in a most confident manner. In exchange for butcher's knives, axes, hoop iron, beads, they would give their bows and arrows, armlets, earrings, belts, or wigs, or, in fact, anything they possessed. The wig, which I certainly ought to have mentioned before, is worn on the front part of the head, being tied under the hair; it is made of black cassowary's feathers, clipped to even lengths, and certainly is very becoming. They do not all wear them, those who do being, I suppose, the dandies. Red Handkerchiefs they would take, but they evidently did not care much about them; cigars were not much valued, and tobacco was despised. Iron, especially in the shape of axes and knives was the great demand; 'segaw, segaw, oh segaw,' being the constant cry all day."

After leaving the New Guinea coast, the expedition reached the

Admiralty Islands on March 3, where they named a long crescent-shaped coral reef after d'Entrecasteaux, who had discovered it in 1792. The Admiralties were not well known, and the official account of the people (who were more friendly than those of Humboldt Bay) is one of the most important ethnographical accounts of the expedition. After the *Challenger*'s visit, the Russian explorer of Melanesia, Baron N. de Miklucho Maclay, whom Captain Erskine of the *Basilisk* had searched for on the New Guinea coast, made several visits to the Admiralties.

Challenger acquired large collections of weapons, tools, ornaments, and utensils in exchange for hoop iron. Most of the ornaments were made of shells or tusks. "It must be remembered," the writer of the *Narrative* observes, "that the native ornaments of the Pacific Islands are all made to show on a dark skin. White shell or tusk ornaments look exceedingly well against the dark skins of natives, although when removed and handled by whites they show to little advantage. The young girls at the Admiralty Islands sometimes wear a necklace or two, but they are never decorated to the same extent as are the men, who seem averse to part with any of their finery to the women."

The excellent, beautifully illustrated account of the material culture of the Admiralty Islands is a classic. Amusingly enough, there is an impressive pair of carved human male and female figures illustrated and described in the *Narrative*. The prudish Wild, illustrating the same figures, deletes all genitalia and piously writes: "I have reproduced them with a few immaterial alterations."

Nothing was admired more by *Challenger*'s people than the spectacular large wooden food bowls. As Moseley describes them: "These resemble somewhat those of the Solomon islanders, being, like them, blackened, but in the present case they are most remarkable for their graceful forms and delicately carved handles. The bowls are worked with wonderful precision, considering the tools available, to the circular form, appearing as true as if turned. They are widely open, and are provided with a pair of curved handles, which rise above the level of the tops of the bowls, and are sometimes ring-like, sometimes cut in a delicate spiral. They are always ornamented with perforated carving, and often bear a pair of Crocodiles, or roughly executed human figures on their outer margins. The bowls stand always on four short legs, like the Fijian kaava bowls."

Challenger sailed from the Admiralties on March 10, and, after making thirteen soundings on the way to Japan, arrived at Yokohama a month later, where she was docked for overhaul. "The tedious voyage from the Admiralty Islands to Japan occupied us thirty-two days," the young Swire wrote, "and I think I was never so glad to get in to harbour as on the occasion of our arrival at Yokohama."

From Japan *Challenger* crossed the open Pacific to the Hawaiian Islands, taking a course between the two courses of the U.S.S. *Tuscarora*, which had made a deep-sea sounding cruise the previous year (1874) from San Francisco to Japan via the Hawaiian Islands and returned in a great circle to the north, skirting the Aleutians. Honolulu, where the expedition arrived in late July, was now a thoroughly American town with an Oriental flavor. A large shop dispensed Chinese and Japanese curiosities; photographers sold souvenirs; passengers on the mail steamers that stopped there could buy corals imported from the Marquesas and fake native implements at high prices. Already the seeds of modern Honolulu had been planted. King Kalakaua visited the *Challenger* and took keen interest in the work of the expedition. After a fortnight at Honolulu, during which a series of ancient Hawaiian skulls was collected, the ship was moved over to Hilo for a week's stay. She sailed for Tahiti on August 19 and arrived there a month later.

During the stay at Papeete, *Challenger*'s party made a careful examination of the coral reef and Lieutenant Swire conducted the first survey of the seaward slope of the barrier reef. (The excursion into the mountains, following Darwin's footsteps, was now almost a tradition with all of the later nineteenth-century expeditions at Tahiti.) On October 3 the *Challenger* steamed out of Papeete Harbor with her band playing the lively Tahitian anthem. When she arrived at Valparaiso in November, after stopping at Juan Fernández, she was greeted by the band on a French man-of-war playing the same tune. On December 11 the *Challenger* swung ship in Valparaiso Harbor to ascertain compass errors. Twenty days later she entered the Gulf of Peñas and from there proceeded down the inland passages to the Strait of Magellan. She was now on the final leg of her voyage home. In May 1876 she passed the Needles and sailed up the Solent towards Spithead, with a cold northeaster whipping down the channel. She arrived home on the twenty-fourth.

Challenger's voyage covered 68,890 nautical miles and involved observations at 362 established stations. She lost fifty-seven miles of dredging line in her travels.

"Writing now after the Commission has come to a close," the director of the scientific party, Sir C. Wyville Thomson, began, "I think I am justified in saying that the objects of the Expedition have been fully and faithfully carried out. The instructions of the Lords Commissioners of the Admiralty, founded upon the recommendations of a committee of the Royal Society, were followed so far as circumstances would permit. We always kept in view that to explore the conditions of the deep sea was the primary object of our mission, and throughout the voyage we took every possible opportunity of making a deep-sea observation. We dredged from time to time in shallow water in the most remote regions, and we have in this way acquired many undescribed animal forms; and collections of land animals and plants were likewise made on every available occasion; but I rather discouraged such work, which in our case could only be done imperfectly, if it seemed likely to divert our attention from our special object."

The systematic collections, including examples of animal life at all depths, made at the different stations were sent to the University of Edinburgh, where they would be convenient for Wyville Thomson, who was to oversee the publication of the scientific results of the expedition. The botanical collections were sent directly to Kew Gardens, and the incidental zoological and ethnological collections went to the British Museum. John Murray, lecturing in the Hulme Town Hall at Manchester on December 18, 1877, observed: "The Challenger has not robbed the ocean of all her secrets, but she has made captures for almost every branch of science. She has drawn a line of observations around the world, and through the deep sea, from which all future investigations must take their start."

The results of the expedition were published in some fifty massive volumes, first under Thomson, then, on his death in March 1882, by his assistant John Murray, who had been one of the scientists on the entire cruise. In addition to the official *Narrative* and scientific volumes, various members of the expedition wrote popular accounts of their experience — often their edited journals, or letters that they had sent home. The expedition was an outstanding success; the Admiralty sent letters of commendation to both Captain Thomson and Wyville Thomson for their successful leadership and the carrying out of their assignments.

All modern oceanographic research in the Pacific starts with the *Challenger* expedition. While her equipment may have been clumsy and inadequate by today's standards, she managed to procure an enormous amount of information. Only with the moon landings of the Apollos has a new body of data of such dimensions been made as was brought back by the *Challenger* expedition. At the same time, she was the last expedition in the tradition that had become standard since Captain Cook. Surveying, botanical and zoological collecting on islands, and observations of native peoples were all still expected. Other expeditions followed — indeed, are still going on — but their purposes are limited and their research specialized and defined. Thus the *Challenger* closed one era and began a new. She brings to a fitting close the century of Pacific exploration after Captain Cook.

There were no more islands to discover. The flora, fauna, and people of the Pacific basin and its surrounding shores were reasonably well known. Vancouver, Broughton, Flinders, Fitzroy, Erskine, and others had filled in the long stretches of coast bordering its shores. The numerous other voyages, naval and merchant, professional and amateur, that we have followed had crisscrossed the broad waters from Valparaiso to Singapore and from Bering Strait to the Antarctic Continent.

Yet the new era begun by the *Challenger* continues, for the Pacific Ocean will provide fields for investigation so long as the world exists.

Carved wooden bowl from the Admiralty Islands
(*from* Exploring Voyage of the H.M.S. Challenger, *Vol. 1*)

Bibliography

BOOKS FOR THE GENERAL READER

Bassett, Marnie. *Realms and Islands: The World Voyage of Rose de Freycinet in the Corvette* Uranie *1817–1820*. New York: Oxford University Press, 1962.

Beaglehole, J. C. *The Exploration of the Pacific*. Palo Alto: Stanford University Press, 1966.

Dunmore, John. *French Explorers in the Pacific*. Vol. I: *The Eighteenth Century*. Vol. II: *The Nineteenth Century*. Oxford: The University Press, 1965, 1969.

Friis, Herman R., ed. *The Pacific Basin: A History of Its Geographical Exploration*. New York: American Geographical Society, 1967.

Ritchie, G. S. *Forward*, Challenger. London: Hollis & Carter Ltd., 1957.

———. *The Admiralty Chart: British Naval Hydrography in the Nineteenth Century*. New York, 1967.

Sharp, Andrew. *The Discovery of the Pacific Islands*. Oxford: The University Press, 1960.

Tyler, David B. *The Wilkes Expedition*. Philadelphia: American Philosophical Society, 1968.

Woodward, Ralph Lee. *Robinson Crusoe's Island: A History of the Juan Fernández Islands*. Chapel Hill: University of North Carolina Press, 1969.

CHAPTER 1

There is a vast literature on this period of Pacific exploration. For general summary works I have relied on J. C. Beaglehole, *The Exploration of the Pacific* (Stanford University Press, 1966); Peter H. Buck, *An Introduction to Polynesian Anthropology* (Honolulu: Bishop Museum Press, 1945); *Pacific Islands*, Vol. I: *General Survey*. (Naval Intelligence Division [British], 1945); and A. Sharp, *The Discovery of the Pacific Islands* (Oxford, 1960). Beaglehole's new edition of *The Journals of Captain James Cook on his Voyages of Discovery* for the Hakluyt Society (Vol. I and Portfolio, Cambridge, 1955; Vol. II, 1961; Vol. III, 1967), covering Cook's three voyages, are indispensable to anyone interested in this subject. For data on specific voyages I have referred to J. A. Robertson, *Magellan's Voyage Around the World By Antonio Pigafetta* (Cleveland, 1906); R. E. Gallagher, *Byron's Journal of his Circumnavigation 1764–1766* (Cambridge: Hakluyt, 1964); H. Carrington, *The Discovery of Tahiti. A Journal . . . by . . . George Robertson* (London: Hakluyt, 1948); Hellen Wallis, *Carteret's Voyage Round the World 1766–1769* (Cambridge: Hakluyt,

1965); L. A. de Bougainville, *A Voyage Round the World* (London, 1772). There are several good reference works on the islands of the Pacific. I have found the most useful, although the oldest, to be *An Index to the Islands of the Pacific Ocean* by William T. Brigham (Honolulu: Bishop Museum Press, 1900). I have also referred to the *Times Atlas*, to National Geographic Society maps, and to Hydrographic Office charts.

CHAPTER 2

For de Surville's voyage I have relied on *French Explorers in the Pacific*, by John Dunmore (Oxford, Vol. I, 1965; Vol. II, 1969) and B. G. Corney, *The Voyage of Captain Don Felipe Gonzalez* (Cambridge, 1908). The latter was used also for Gonzalez himself. Dunmore has also been useful for Marion du Fresne's voyage, but I have preferred for this H. Ling Roth, *Crozet's Voyage to Tasmania, New Zealand, the Ladrone Islands, and the Philippines in the Years 1771-1772* (London, 1891). For Boenechea the three volumes of B. G. Corney, *The Quest and Occupation of Tahiti by Emissaries of Spain During the Years 1772-1776* (London: Hakluyt, 1913, 1915, 1919), are indispensable. The only account of Maurelle's voyage was sent back from the Pacific by La Pérouse and is printed in L. A. Milet-Mureau, cited for the next chapter.

CHAPTER 3

For most of this chapter I have relied on L. A. Milet-Mureau, *A Voyage Round the World, Performed In the Years 1785, 1786, 1787, and 1788, By the* Boussole *and* Astrolabe, *Under the Command of J. F. G. de La Pérouse*, 2 volumes (London, 1799). Included are La Pérouse's journals, some of his letters, various odds and ends and a short dissertation on the Easter Islanders and the Hawaiians of Maui by M. Rollin, the surgeon of *Boussole*, and his speculation upon the introduction of venereal disease among the latter. He did not believe that it was introduced by Cook's sailors because it was so widespread and advanced. La Pérouse also contributed astute observations on the sea otter trade. Two other works providing important supplementary information are *Travels in Kamtschatka, During the Years 1787 and 1788. Translated From the French of M. de Lesseps, Consul of France, and Interpreter to the Count de la Pérouse, now Engaged in a Voyage Round the World, by Command of His Most Christian Majesty*, 2 vols. (London, 1790), and John Hunter, *An Historical Journal of the Transactions at Port Jackson and Norfolk Island, with the Discoveries which have been made in New South Wales and in the Southern Ocean, since the publication of Phillip's Voyage, compiled from the Official Papers; Including the Journals of Governors Phillip and King and of Lieut. Ball; and the Voyages From the first Sailing of the Sirius in 1787, to the Return of that Ship's Company to England in 1792*.

CHAPTER 4

The principal sources for this chapter are Nathaniel Portlock, *A Voyage Round the World; but more particularly to the North-West Coast of America: Performed in 1785, 1786, 1787, and 1788 in the* King George *and* Queen Charlotte, *Captains Portlock and Dixon* (London, 1789); George Dixon, volume of identical title and date; *The Dixon-Meares Controversy*, edited by F. W. Howay (Toronto, 1929); and *The Life and Adventures of John Nicol, Mariner* (London, 1822). The latter is a rare book, which has been reprinted twice—first, in a badly bowdlerized account entitled "The Adventures of John Nicol, Mariner, during Thirty Years at Sea" in *The Sea, The Ship and the Sailor: Tales of Adventure From Log Books and Original Narratives* (Salem, 1925), pp. 105-167; and second, in an excellent accurate edition with the original title and an interesting Foreword and Afterword by Alexander Laing (New York: Farrar & Rinehart, 1936).

CHAPTER 5

The principal references for this chapter are *Voyages Made in the Years 1788 and 1789, from China to the North West Coast of America* by John Meares (London, 1790); *The Journal of Captain James Colnett Aboard the* Argonaut *from April 26, 1789 to Nov. 3, 1791,* edited with introduction and notes by F. W. Howay (Toronto, 1940); *Voyages of the "Columbia" to the Northwest Coast 1787–1790 and 1790–1793,* edited by F. W. Howay (Boston, 1941); and *A Voyage to the South Atlantic and Round Cape Horn into the Pacific Ocean, for the Purpose of Extending the Spermaceti Whale Fisheries . . . ,* by Captain James Colnett (London, 1798).

CHAPTER 6

For this chapter I have relied largely on the following sources. Lieutenant George Mortimer's now rare book on the voyage of the *Mercury* was published in London, 1791, entitled *Observations and Remarks made during a Voyage to the Islands of Teneriffe, Amsterdam, Maria's Islands near Van Diemen's Land; Otaheite, Sandwich Islands; Owhyhee, the Fox Islands on the North West Coast of America, Tinian, and from thence to Canton, in the Brig* Mercury, *Commanded by John Henry Cox,* Esq. For Captain Bligh's first voyage I have used his own book, *A Voyage to the South Sea, undertaken by Command of His Majesty, for the purpose of Conveying the Breadfruit Tree to the West Indies, in His Majesty's Ship the* Bounty (London, 1792); and *The Log of the Bounty* with Introduction and Notes by Owen Rutter (London, The Golden Cockerel Press, 1937). Basil Thompson's edition of the narratives of Captain Edward Edwards and George Hamilton, *Voyage of the H.M.S. 'Pandora' dispatched to Arrest the Mutineers of the 'Bounty' in the South Seas, 1790–91,* with its excellent Introduction and additional material, has been used rather than the Berwick, 1793, edition. I have also found *Pandora's Last Voyage,* by Geoffrey Rawson (London, 1963), very useful. The principal published reference for Bligh's second voyage is Ida Lee's *Captain Bligh's Second Voyage to the South Sea* (London, 1920). For ascertaining various facts I have found *The Life of Vice-Admiral William Bligh,* by George Mackaness (New York, n.d.), excellent.

CHAPTER 7

Several rare and important books have been relied on for this chapter. George Keate's book, *An Account of the Pelew Islands, situated in the Western Part of the Pacific Ocean Composed from the Journals and Communications of Captain Henry Wilson and some of his officers, who, in August 1783, were there Shipwrecked, in The* Antelope, *a Packet belonging to the Honourable East India Company* (London, 1789, third edition), is a classic. One of the most important works for any study relating to Pacific history is *The Voyage of Governor Phillip to Botany Bay* (London, 1789), which includes the journals of Lieutenant Shortland, Watts (who was with Sever), Ball, and Captain Marshall. Captain Thomas Gilbert published his own journal, entitled *Voyage from New South Wales to Canton, in the Year 1788, with Views of the Islands Discovered* (London, 1789). Seventeen eighty-nine was a big publishing year for voyages. The most detailed account, "Historical Notes on the Gilbert and Marshall Islands," *The American Neptune,* Vol. IV (1944), pp. 87–118, of the discovery of these was written during World War II by Samuel Eliot Morison. (This essay was reprinted in Morison's *By Land and By Sea,* New York, Knopf, 1953, pp. 124–157.) Recently the Hakluyt Society (Series II, No. CXXXI) has published *The Journal and Letters of Captain Charles Bishop on the North-West*

Coast of America, in the Pacific and in New South Wales 1794–1799, edited by Michael Roe (Cambridge, 1967).

CHAPTER 8

The principal source for Marchand's voyage is the very good book written by C. P. Claret Fleurieu, which is based on a journal kept by Captain Chanal and supplemented by that of the surgeon, Claude Roblet. The book is entitled *A Voyage Round the World, Performed During the Years 1790, 1791, and 1792, by Etienne Marchand, Preceded by a Historical Introduction, and Illustrated by Charts, etc.*, 2 vols. (London, 1801). The two main sources for d'Entrecasteaux's expedition are *Voyage in Search of La Pérouse, Performed by Order of the Constituent Assembly during the Years 1791, 1792, 1793, and 1794, and Drawn up By M. Labillardiere* (London, 1800), and *Voyage de Dentrecasteaux, Envoyé a la Recherche de la Pérouse*, by M. de Rossel, 2 vols. (Paris, 1808). For both voyages, Dunmore's *French Explorers in the Pacific*, Vol. 1 (Oxford, 1965), has been most helpful.

CHAPTER 9

The primary source for this chapter is the magnificent three-volume work *A Voyage of Discovery to the North Pacific Ocean, and Round the World; in which the coast of North-West America has been carefully examined and accurately surveyed. Undertaken by His Majesty's Command, Principally with a view to ascertain the existence of any navigable communication between the North Pacific and North Atlantic Oceans; and performed in the Years 1790, 1791, 1792, 1793, 1794, and 1795, in the* Discovery *Sloop of War, and Armed Tender* Chatham, *under the command of Captain George Vancouver* (London, 1798).

Also helpful have been *Vancouver A Life, 1757–1798* by George Goodwin (London, 1930), and *Surveyor of the Sea: The Life and Voyages of Captain George Vancouver*, by Bern Anderson (Seattle, 1960).

CHAPTER 10

The three principal books relied on for this chapter are William Robert Broughton's *A Voyage of Discovery to the North Pacific Ocean . . . Performed in His Majesty's Sloop* Providence, *and her Tender, in the Years 1795, 1796, 1797, 1798* (London, 1804); James Wilson's *A Missionary Voyage to the Southern Pacific Ocean, performed in the Years 1796, 1797, 1798, in the Ship* Duff (London, 1799); and John Turnbull's *A Voyage Round the World in the Years 1800, 1801, 1802, 1803, and 1804* (London, 1813, second edition).

CHAPTER 11

The basic reference is Matthew Flinders's great work *A Voyage to Terra Australis; undertaken for the purpose of completing the Discovery of that vast Country . . . in . . . 1801, 1802, and 1803 in His Majesty's Ship the Investigator . . .*, 2 vols. and atlas (London, 1814). Also important are *Matthew Flinders' Narrative of his Voyage in the Schooner Francis in 1798 . . .*, by Geoffrey Rawson (The Golden Cockerel Press, 1946), and *Drawings by William Westall: Landscape Artist on board H.M.S. Investigator during the circumnavigation of Australia by Captain Matthew Flinders R.N. in 1801–1803*, edited by T. M. Perry and Donald H. Simpson (London, 1962).

The account of Baudin's voyage was written by François Péron, *Voyage de Découvertes aux Terres Australis, Exécuté par Ordre de La Majesté l'Empereur et Roi . . . Pendant les Années 1800, 1801, 1802, 1803, et 1804 . . .* (Paris, Vol. I, 1807; Vol. II, 1816); and Louis de Freycinet, *Voyage de Découvertes aux Terres Australis, Naviga-*

tion et Géographie (Paris, 1815). An English translation of Vol. I of Péron, *A Voyage of Discovery to the Southern Hemisphere* . . . appeared in London in 1809. A short account of Baudin's voyage appeared as an appendix in John Trumbull's *A Voyage Round the World* . . . (London, 1813, second edition), pp. 474-490.

There are a multitude of secondary sources. Some of the most useful have been James D. Mack, *Matthew Flinders, 1774-1814* (Nelson, 1966); Andrew Sharp, *The Discovery of Australia* (Oxford, 1963); and Herman R. Friis, ed., *The Pacific Basin* (New York, 1967).

CHAPTER 12

Most of the information for this chapter is contained in the following books on the voyage. I have used the English editions. *Voyage Round the World, in the Years 1803, 1804, 1805, & 1806* . . ., by Captain A. J. von Krusenstern, 2 vol. (London, 1813); *A Voyage Round the World in the Years 1803, 4, 5, & 6* . . . , by Urey Lisiansky (London, 1814); and *Voyages and Travels in Various Parts of the World, during the Years 1803, 1804, 1805, 1806 and 1807*, by G. H. von Langsdorff (London, 1813). Also *Atlas de l'océan Pacifique dressé par m. de Krusenstern*. Publié par ordre de Sa Majesté impériale (St. Petersburg, 1827). *The Memoirs of the Celebrated Admiral Adam John de Krusenstern The First Russian Circumnavigator, translated from the German by his daughter Madam Charlotte Bernhardi and Edited by Rear-Admiral Sir John Ross, C.B.* (London, 1856), contains numerous details of Krusenstern's life.

CHAPTER 13

Six books constitute the major sources of information for this chapter. The first is "An Account of a recent discovery of seven Islands in the South Pacific Ocean, by Joseph Ingraham, Citizen of Boston, and Commander of the brigantine *Hope*, of seventy tons burthen: of, and from this Port, bound to the N. W. Coast of America," contributed by Jeremy Belknap, in *Collection of the Massachusetts Historical Society, For the Year 1793*, Vol. II (Boston, 1810), pp. 20-24. Amasa Delano's *Narrative of Voyages and Travels, in the Northern and Southern Hemispheres: Comprising Three Voyages Round the World; together with a Voyage of Survey and Discovery in the Pacific Ocean and Oriental Islands* (Boston, 1817) is a classic. So, too, is Edmund Fanning's *Voyages Round the World; with Selected Sketches of Voyages to the South Seas, North and South Pacific Oceans, China, etc*. . . . *between the Years 1792 and 1832* (New York, 1833). Fanning followed up this best seller with a second book, *Voyages to the South Seas, Indian and Pacific Oceans, China Sea, North-west Coast, Feejee Islands, South Shetlands, etc., etc.* , . . . *Between the Years 1830-1837* (New York, 1838), in which he makes a strong plea for an American Exploring Expedition to go to the South Seas. In 1924 the Marine Research Society published a badly bowdlerized edition of Fanning's first book, entitled *Voyages and Discoveries in the South Seas 1792-1832*. After the War of 1812 was over, David Porter published his experiences in the Pacific in *Journal of a Cruise Made to the Pacific Ocean, by Captain David Porter in the United States Frigate Essex, in the Years 1812, 1813, and 1814* (New York, 1822, second edition), 2 vols. Finally, the last and least reliable of the American sealing accounts came from the pen of Captain Benjamin Morrell, Jr., with the pretentious title *A Narrative of Four Voyages, to the South Sea, North and South Pacific Ocean, Chinese Sea, Ethiopic and Southern Atlantic Ocean, Indian and Antarctic Ocean. From the Year 1822 to 1831* . . . [the title goes on for much longer] (New York, 1832). On the last of his four published voyages, Morrell was accompanied by his second wife, Abby Jane Morrell, who wrote a little book on her travels entitled *Narrative of a Voyage to the Ethiopic and South Atlantic Ocean, Indian Ocean, Chinese Sea, North and South Pacific Ocean in the Years 1829, 1830, 1831* (New York, 1833).

CHAPTER 14

Three valuable books were published by members of Kotzebue's first voyage. Kotzebue's own *A Voyage of Discovery into the South Seas and Beering's Straits for the Purpose of Exploring a North-East Passage, Undertaken in the Years 1815–1818* was the first to appear—in German, at Weimar in 1821, and in English, in three volumes at London the same year. Louis Choris's *Voyage Pittoresque Autour du Monde* was published in Paris in 1822. *Reise um die Welt*, by Adelbert von Chamisso, appeared in 1836; he had already written a section on scientific observations for Kotzebue's book.

No account of Bellingshausen's voyage was published in English until the Hakluyt Society (Series II, Vols. XCI and XCII) translation, *The Voyage of Captain Bellingshausen to the Antarctic Seas 1819–1821*, by Frank Debenham, appeared in 1945. The primary authority for the third voyage discussed in this chapter is *A New Voyage Round the World, in the Years 1823, 24, 25, and 26* by Otto von Kotzebue, two vols. (London, 1830). The book that he wrote about his second circumnavigation, however, cannot compare with his earlier work on the first voyage. Much of the second book is based on the writings of Cook and other earlier explorers. In his second book Kotzebue seems to be trying too hard to write a best seller, and he had not the advantage of having the talented Chamisso and Choris with him.

CHAPTER 15

The multivolumed official accounts of the nineteenth-century French voyages are the most voluminous of any for a group of related expeditions. For the most part they have never been translated into English. The plates of the atlases are magnificent. These works are now all of great rarity and very costly when they appear on the market, which is seldom. The principal works relating to the major voyages are: *Journal d'un Voyage Autour du Monde, Pendant les Années 1816, 1817, 1818 et 1819*, by Camille de Roquefeuil (Paris, 1823), 2 vols.; *Voyage Autour du Monde, Entrepris par ordre du Roi . . . Exécuté sur les Corvettes de S.M. l'Uranie, et la Physicienne, pendant les Années 1817, 1818, 1819 et 1820 . . .*, by Louis C. D. de Freycinet (Paris, 1824–1844), 7 vols. and atlas. Jacques Arago's account of the same voyage has been published in both French and English. I have used the English translation *Narrative of a Voyage Round the World, in the* Uranie *and* Physicienne *Corvettes, Commanded by Captain Freycinet, during the Years 1817, 1818, 1819, and 1820* (London, 1823). The woman's point of view has been published in *Campagne de l'Uranie* (1817–1820); *Journal de Madame Rose de Saulces de Freycinet . . .*, edited by Charles Duplomb (Paris, 1927), and *Realms and Islands, The World Voyage of Rose de Freycinet in the Corvette* Uranie *1817–1820*, by Marnie Bassett (London, 1962). Sources for the other principal voyages are *Voyage Autour du Monde, Exécuté par Ordre du Roi, Sur la Corvette de La Majesté, La Coquille, Pendant les Années 1822, 1823, 1824 et 1825 . . .*, by L. I. Duperrey (Paris, 1828), 6 vols. and 4 atlases; *Voyage de la Corvette L'Astrolabe Exécuté par Ordre du Roi, Pendant les Années 1826, 1827, 1828, 1829, sous le Commandant de M.J. Dumont D'Urville . . .* (Paris, 1830–1835), 22 vols. and 7 atlases; *Voyage Autour du Monde sur la Frégate La* Venus, *Pendant les Années 1836–1839 . . .*, by Abel du Petit-Thouars (Paris, 1840–1855), 10 vols. and 4 atlases; *Voyage Autour du Monde Exécuté Pendant les Années 1836 et 1837 sur la Corvette La* Bonite *. . .*, by Captain A. N. Vaillant (Paris, 1840–1866), 17 vols. and 3 atlases; *Voyage au Pole Sud et dans l'Oceanie sur les Corvettes L'Astrolabe et la Zélée, Exécuté par Ordre de Roi Pendant les Années 1837, 1838, 1839, 1840, Sous le Commandement de M.J. Dumont D'Urville . . .* (Paris, 1841–1854), 23 vols., 4 atlases; *Voyage Autour du Monde par les mers de l'Inde et. de Chine, Exécuté sur la Corvette de l'état La* Favorite *Pendant les Années 1830, 1831, et 1832*, by C. P. T. Laplace (Paris, 1833–1839), 5 vols. and atlas; *Campagne de Circum-*

navigation de la Frégate L'Artémise Pendant les Années 1837, 1838, 1839 et 1840 . . . , by C. P. Laplace (Paris, 1844–1848), 6 vols.

CHAPTER 16

The visit of the *Briton* and *Tagus* to the Marquesas and Pitcairn is recorded by a lieutenant of the Royal Marines, John Shillibeer, on board the *Briton* in his *A Narrative of the* Briton's *Voyage, to Pitcairn's Island . . .* (London, 1817). For Byron's return of the bodies of the Hawaiian monarchs, the principal sources are the handsome but inadequate compilation edited by Mrs. Maria Graham, *Voyage of H.M.S. Blonde to the Sandwich Islands, in the Years 1824–1825* (London, 1826), compiled from various journals; the *Diary of Andrew Bloxam Naturalist of the "Blonde,"* published as Special Publication 10 of the Bishop Museum (Honolulu, 1925); and extracts from the diary of the Scottish botanist James Macrae, entitled *With Lord Byron at the Sandwich Islands in 1825* (Honolulu, 1822).

The authorized Admiralty account of the Beechey voyage is *Narrative of a Voyage to the Pacific and Beering's Strait, to Co-operate with the Polar Expeditions: Performed in His Majesty's Ship* Blossom *Under the Command of Captain F. W. Beechey, R.N. in the Years 1825, 26, 27, 28* (London, 1831), 2 vols. There are also other editions of this voyage. Captain Peter Dillon's book was published in French in Paris, 1830 and an English edition, *Narrative and Successful Result of a Voyage in the South Seas, . . . to Ascertain the Actual Fate of La Pérouse's Expedition . . . ,* was published in London in 1829.

CHAPTER 17

The most important source for this chapter is the three-volume *Narrative of the Surveying Voyages of His Majesty's Ships* Adventure *and* Beagle, *Between the Years 1826 and 1836 Describing Their Examination of the Southern Shores of South America and the* Beagle's *Circumnavigation of the Globe* (London, 1830). The first two volumes, by Robert Fitzroy, are devoted to the two voyages. The third volume is Darwin's classic narrative. A second edition of his work, somewhat modified, was published in 1845; with an Introduction by Gavin de Beer and engravings by Robert Gibbings, it was reprinted in 1957 by the Heritage Press in New York. Darwin's journal was not published until 1933, when it appeared as *Diary of the Voyage of H.M.S. Beagle,* edited by Nora Barlow (Cambridge).

CHAPTER 18

There is an enormous amount of both published and unpublished material available on the Wilkes Expedition, but the most important single source is still the five volumes of the *Narrative of the United States Exploring Expedition During the Years 1838, 1839, 1840, 1841, 1842,* by Charles Wilkes (Philadelphia, 1845). In 1942 the New York Public Library published Daniel C. Haskell's bibliography of the expedition, with an Introduction by Harry M. Lydenberg, entitled *The United States Exploring Expedition, 1838–1842, and its Publication 1844–1874.* This is an indispensable piece of scholarly work for anyone interested in the expedition. The most thorough history of the voyage is *The Wilkes Expedition,* by David B. Tyler, published by the American Philosophical Society in 1968. Tyler's book contains an invaluable bibliography on both the unpublished and published sources relating to the expedition. The American Philosophical Society devoted its *Proceedings,* Vol. LXXXII (1940), pp. 519–600, to a series of papers on various aspects of the expedition. This society, which provided advice when the expedition was being planned, has always shown more interest in the recognition of the expedition's work than any other organization. Besides the publications already mentioned, it published in 1961 *Titian Ramsay Peale, 1799–1885, And His Journals of The Wilkes Expedition.*

o

CHAPTER 19

Good books were published on all of the voyages covered in this chapter. Frederick Debell Bennett's account of his circumnavigation is an excellent two-volume work entitled *Narrative of a Whaling Voyage Round the Globe, from the Year 1833 to 1836* . . . (London, 1840). Sir Edward Belcher, who wrote books on all three of his important voyages, published the cruise of H.M.S. *Sulphur* in two volumes in London, 1843, as *Narrative of a Voyage Round the World, Performed in Her Majesty's Ship* Sulphur, *During the Years 1836–1842, Including Details of the Naval Operations in China, From Dec. 1840, to Nov. 1841.* The books on the voyages of the *Fly* and the *Rattlesnake* were written by two of the naturalists. The earlier, by J. Beete Jukes, was *Narrative of the Surveying Voyage of H.M.S. Fly, commanded by Captain F. P. Blackwood, R.N. in Torres Strait, New Guinea, and other Islands of the Eastern Archipelago, During the Years 1842–1846* . . . (London, 1847), 2 vols. The surveying sequel by John MacGillivray is the *Narrative of the Voyage of H.M.S. Rattlesnake, Commanded by the late Captain Owen Stanley, R.N., F.R.S. etc. During the Years 1846–1850. Including Discoveries and Surveys in New Guinea, the Louisiade Archipelago* . . . , another two-volume work (London, 1852). The story of the cruise of H.M.S. *Havannah* was written by her captain, John Elphinstone Erskine, as *Journal of a Cruise Among the Islands of the Western Pacific, Including the Feejees and Others Inhabited by the Polynesian Negro Races, in Her Majesty's Ship* Havannah (London, 1853). Again it was a naturalist, Dr. Karl Scherzer, who recorded the Austrian voyage in *Narrative of the Circumnavigation of the Globe by the Austrian Frigate* Novarra . . . *in the Years 1857, 1858, & 1859* (London, 1863), 3 vols. T. H. Hood wrote *Notes of a Cruise in H.M.S. "Fawn" in the Western Pacific in the Year 1862* (Edinburgh, 1863). Captain John Moresby, R.N., published his own important work — *Discoveries & Surveys in New Guinea and the D'Entrecasteaux Islands: A Cruise in Polynesia and visits to the Pearl-Shelling Stations in Torres Straits of H.M.S.* Basilisk (London, 1876).

CHAPTER 20

The results of the *Challenger* expedition were published in fifty large volumes between 1880 and 1885, under the editorship of Sir C. Wyville Thomson and John Murray, and were entitled *Report on the Scientific Results of the Voyage of H.M.S. Challenger During the Years 1873–76 Under the Command of Captain George S. Nares, R.N., F.R.S. and the Late Captain Frank Tourle Thomson, R.N.* The most important single source for this voyage is Vol. I, Parts 1 and 2 of this work, entitled *Narrative.*

Other sources on the voyage which I have found useful include the following: John Murray, *The Cruise of the* Challenger. *Two lectures delivered at Hulme Town Hall, Manchester, December 11 and 18, 1877*; John James Wild, *At Anchor: A Narrative of Experience Afloat and Ashore During the Voyage of H.M.S. "Challenger" From 1872 to 1876* (London, 1878); W. J. J. Spry, *The Cruise of Her Majesty's Ship* Challenger (New York, 1877); Lord George G. Campbell, *Log-Letters From "The Challenger"* (London and New York, 1877); C. Wyville Thomson, *The Voyage of the "Challenger": The Atlantic* (London, 1877), 2 vols.; H. N. Moseley, *Notes by a Naturalist on the "Challenger"* (London, 1879); and Herbert Swire, *The Voyage of the* Challenger: *A Personal Narrative of the Historic Circumnavigation of the Globe in the Years 1872–1876* (The Golden Cockerel Press, 1938), 2 vols. The story of the voyage has been written numerous times in recent years—see, for example, G. S. Ritchie, Challenger: *The Life of a Survey Ship* (London, 1957).

Pacific Voyages of Exploration, 1767–1876

Commander	Nationality	Ships	Sailed	Returned
Jean de Surville	French	St. Jean Baptiste	Brittany, June 1767	Port-Louis, Brittany, August 1773 (de Surville drowned at Callao)
Felipe Gonzáles Antonio Domonte	Spanish	San Lorenzo Santa Rosalia	Callao, Peru, 10 October 1770	Chiloé Island, 15 December 1770
Marion Du Fresne Julien Crozet	French	Castries Mascarin	Mauritius, 18 October 1771	Guam, 20 September 1772 (left Guam 19 November)
Domingo Boenechea	Spanish	Santa María Magadalena [Aquila]	Callao, 26 September 1772	Valparaiso, 8 March 1773
Yves J. de Kerguelen-Tremarec	French	Fortune	Mauritius, 16 January 1772	
Yves J. de Kerguelen-Tremarec	French	Gros Ventre	Mauritius, 18 October 1773	
Domingo Boenechea José de Andiá y Varela	Spanish	Aquila Jupiter	Callao, 20 September 1774	Callao, 8 April 1775
Juan de Langara	Spanish	Aquila	Callao, 27 September 1775	Callao, 17 February 1776
Francisco Antonio Maurelle	Spanish	La Princessa	Sisiron, Philippine Ids., 21 November 1780	San Blas, Panama, 27 September 1781
Henry Wilson	British	Antelope	Macao, 21 July 1783	Wrecked, Palau Islands, 10 August 1783
J. F. G. de La Pérouse Paul Antoine de Langle	French	Boussole Astrolabe	Brest, 1 August 1785	Last seen when they sailed from Botany Bay, 11 March 1788
Nathaniel Portlock George Dixon	British	King George Queen Charlotte	Spithead, 16 September 1785	Margate, 24 August 1788 Dover, 17 September 1788
John Meares	British	Nootka	Bengal, March 1786	
James Colnett Charles Duncan	British	Prince of Wales Princess Royal	England, September 1786	Macao, 12 November 1788
William Bligh	British	H.M.S. Bounty	Spithead, 23 December 1787	Captured by mutineers, 28 April 1789 Bligh arrived Plymouth, 14 March

William Douglas	(under Portuguese colors)	*Iphigenia Nubiana*		Macao, 5 October 1789
Henry L. Ball	British	*Supply*	Port Jackson, 14 February 1788	Port Jackson, 1788
Capt. Sever	British	*Lady Penrhyn*	Port Jackson, 5 May 1788	Macao, 19 October 1788
William Marshall, Thomas Gilbert	British	*Scarborough, Charlotte*	Port Jackson, 6 May 1788	Macao, 9 September 1788
John Shortland	British	*Alexander*	Port Jackson, 14 July 1788	Batavia, 18 November 1788; England, 29 May 1789
Robert Gray, John Kendrick	American	*Columbia, Lady Washington*	Boston, 30 September 1788	Boston, 1790
James Colnett	British	*Argonaut*	China, 1789	Macao, 30 May 1791
John Henry Cox	British	*Mercury*	Downs, 28 February 1789	Macao, 27 December 1789
Joseph Ingraham	American	*Hope*	Boston, 1790	1793
Robert Gray	American	*Columbia*	Boston, 2 October 1790	Boston, 29 July 1793
Edward Edwards	British	*H.M.S. Pandora*	Jack-in-the-Basket, 7 November 1790	Wrecked 28 August 1791, Edwards arrived Portsmouth, 19 June 1792
Etienne Marchand	French	*Solide*	Marseilles, 14 December 1790	Toulon, 14 August 1792
George Vancouver, William Robert Broughton	British	*H.M.S. Discovery, H.M.S. Chatham*	Falmouth, 1 April 1791	In the Thames, 20 October 1795; 17 October 1795
John McClure, Amasa Delano	British, American	*Panther, Endeavour*	Macao, 27 April 1791	Macao, March 1793
William Bligh, Nathaniel Portlock	British	*H.M.S. Providence, H.M.S. Assistant*	England, 3 August 1791	Dungeness, 2 August 1793
Antoine Raymond Joseph Bruni d'Entrecasteaux, Huon de Kermadec	French	*Recherche, Espérance*	Brest, 28 September 1791	France, 12 March 1796

Commander	Nationality	Ships	Sailed	Returned
James Colnett	British	H.M.S. *Rattler*	England, 7 January 1793	Cowes, 2 November 1794
William Robert Broughton	British	H.M.S. *Providence*	Spithead, 15 February 1795	Wrecked, Ryukyu Islands, 17 May 1797, continued survey in schooner, arrived England, February 1799
James Wilson	British	*Duff*	Spithead, 24 October 1796	The Thames, 11 July 1798
Edmund Fanning	American	*Betsey*	1797	New York, 26 April 1799
Amasa Delano	American	*Perseverance*	Boston, 10 November 1799	Boston, 1 November 1802
Edmund Fanning	American	*Aspasia*	New York, May 1800	New York, March 1802
John Buyers John Turnbull	British	*Margaret*	England, 2 July 1800	Wrecked, Tuamotus, 1803, arrived England, August 1804
Nicholas Baudin Emmanuel Hamelin	French	*Géographie* *Naturaliste*	Le Havre, 19 October 1800	France, *Géographie* returned 1804
Matthew Flinders	British	H.M.S. *Investigator*	Spithead, 18 July 1801	Port Jackson, 9 June 1803
A. J. von Krusenstern Urey Lisiansky	Russian	*Nadeshda* *Neva*	Kronshtadt, 7 August 1803	Kronshtadt, 19 August 1806
Amasa Delano Samuel Delano	American	*Perseverance* *Pilgrim*	Boston, 25 September 1803	Boston, 26 July 1807
Isaac Pendleton	American	*Union*	1804	Fiji, wrecked 1804
Reuben Brumley	American	*Hope*	New York, August 1806	New York, May 1808
V. M. Golovnin	Russian	*Diana*	Kronshtadt, 25 July 1807	Kronshtadt, 25 September 1809
Edmund Fanning	American	*Tonquin*	New York, 26 May 1807	New York, 6 March 1808
Reuben Brumley	American	*Tonquin*	New York, 15 June 1808	Sold on Northwest Coast?
David Porter	American	U.S.S. *Essex*	The Delaware, 28 October 1812	Captured, Valparaiso, 28 March 1814
Sir Thomas Staines	British	H.M.S. *Briton* H.M.S. *Tagus*	Spithead, 30 December,	Plymouth, 7 July 1815

Camille de Roquefeuil	French	*Bordelais*	Bordeaux, 11 October 1816	The Gironde, 21 November 1819
V. M. Golovnin	Russian	*Kamchatka*	Kronshtadt, 26 August 1817	1819
Louis C. de S. de Freycinet	French	*Uranie Physicienne*	Toulon, 17 September 1817	Le Havre, 13 November 1820
Thaddeus Bellingshausen Mikhail Lazarev	Russian	*Vostok Mirnyi*	Kronshtadt, 4 July 1819	Kronshtadt, 25 July 1821
Louis Isidor Duperrey	French	*Coquille*	Toulon, 11 August 1822	Marseille, spring of 1825
Otto von Kotzebue	Russian	*Predpriatie*	Kronshtadt, 28 July 1823	Kronshtadt, 10 July 1826
Benjamin Morrell, Jr.	American	*Tartar*	New York, July 1824	New York, 8 May 1826
George Anson Lord Byron	British	*H.M.S. Blonde*	Spithead, 29 September 1824	Spithead, 15 March 1826
Frederick William Beechey	British	*H.M.S. Blossom*	Spithead, 20 May 1825	Spithead, October 1828
J. S. C. Dumont d'Urville	French	*Astrolabe*	Toulon, 25 April 1826	Marseille, 25 March 1829
Fedor P. Lütke	Russian	*Senyavin Moller*	Kronshtadt, 16 August 1826	1829
Peter Dillon	British	*Research*	Bengal, 23 January 1827	Hooghly River, 5 April 1828
Jacques A. Moerenhout	Dutch–French	*Volador*	Three voyages from 1828	to 1834
Benjamin Morrell, Jr.	American	*Antarctic*	New York, 2 September 1829	New York, 27 August 1831
Cyrille P. T. Laplace	French	*Favorite*	1830	1832
Robert Fitzroy	British	*H.M.S. Beagle*	Barn-pool Mt. Edgecumbe, 27 December 1831	Falmouth, 2 October 1836
Edward Belcher (Succeeding F. W. Beechey) Henry Kellett	British	*H.M.S. Sulphur* *H.M.S. Starling*	Portsmouth, 24 December 1835	Spithead, 19 June 1842

Commander	Nationality	Ships	Sailed	Returned
A. A. Du Petit-Thouars	French	*Venus*	Brest, 29 December 1836	France, June 1839
A. N. Vaillant	French	*Bonite*	Toulon, 6 February 1836	Brest, 6 November 1837
J. B. T. Cécile	French	*Heroïne*	1837	1840
Cyrille P. T. Laplace	French	*Artémise*	1837	1840
J. S. C. Dumont d'Urville / Charles H. Jacquinot	French	*Astrolabe* *Zelée*	Toulon, 7 September 1837	Toulon, 6 November 1840
Charles Wilkes / William L. Hudson / Cadwalader Ringgold	American	U.S.S. *Vincennes* / U.S.S. *Peacock* / U.S.S. *Porpoise* / U.S.S. *Sea Gull* / U.S.S. *Flying Fish* / U.S.S. *Relief*	Hampton Roads, 18 August 1838	New York, 10 June 1842 (*Vincennes* only)
Francis P. Blackwood / C. B. Yule	British	H.M.S. *Fly* / Cutter *Bramble*	Falmouth, 11 April 1842	Spithead, 19 June 1846 (*Fly* only)
Owen Stanley	British	H.M.S. *Rattlesnake*	Spithead, 3 December 1846	Chatham, 9 November 1850
John Elphinstone Erskine	British	H.M.S. *Havannah*	Bay of Islands, N.Z., 25 June 1849	Sydney, 7 October 1849
Karl Scherzer (scientist on voyage)	Austrian	*Novarra*	Trieste, 30 April 1857	Trieste, 26 August 1859
T. H. Hood (author)	British	H.M.S. *Fawn*	Sydney, 7 May 1862	Sydney, September 1862
John Moresby (2 cruises)	British	H.M.S. *Basilisk*	Sydney, 15 January 1871	Sheerness, 15 December 1874
George S. Nares / Frank T. Thomson	British	H.M.S. *Challenger*	Portsmouth, 21 December 1872	Spithead, 24 May 1876

Index

[409]

*o

Index

Essex, U.S.S., 227, 285, 286, 299*n*, 406
Etches, John, 54, 68, 70, 72
Etches, Richard Cadman, 44, 70, 135
Etea, Queen, 98
Ethel River, 374
Etoile, 13
Eua, Tonga, 127, 271

FAAITE, 248
Fair American, 142, 148
Fakaofo, 87, 353
Fakarava, 248
Falkland Islands, 45–46, 220, 227, 228, 229, 252, 263, 266, 323, 371
Fangahina, 253, 254
Fangataufa, 307
Fanning, Edmund, 251; voyages of, 220–227, 332, 406; promotes exploring expedition, 331
Fanning Island, 224–225
Fatu Hiva, 14, 115, 200
Favorite, 275, 407
Fawn, H.M.S., 408
Fayal, 371
Fearn, John, 112
Federal Island, 213. See also Nuku Hiva
Feenou (chief), 128, 129
Felice Adventurer, 61–69 *passim*, 405
Fenis and St. Joseph, 144
Fergusson Island, 376
Fernando de Noronha, 322
Fiji Islands, 10, 88, 230, 251, 266, 268, 335, 336, 371; Bligh at, 92–93, 94; and Tonga, 129–130; d'Urville at, 271, 278; Dillon at, 308–309; Wilkes Expedition at, 346–350, 361; *Challenger* at, 384
First Fleet, 40, 106, 113
First Squadron, 243
Fitz Hugh Sound, 150
Fitzroy, Robert, 318–330, 336, 341, 358–359, 392, 407
Fleurieu, C. B. Claret, 119–120
Flinders, Ann Chappell, 181*n*
Flinders, Matthew, 157, 195, 246, 258, 316, 364, 371, 392; with Bligh, 89, 92; with Bass, 178, 180; survey of Australia, 180–192, 406
Flinders, Samuel W., 181, 192
Flinders Passage, 186
Flint Island, 350
Flora, 243
Fly, H.M.S., 363–366, 368, 370, 384, 408
Fly River, 371
Flying Fish, 335, 338, 341–344, 350, 353, 354, 356, 408
Fokasinga, 348

Folger, Mayhew, 287, 288*n*
Formosa, 17, 32, 37, 159, 160, 209
Fortescue Strait, 374
Fortuna Island, 9
Fortune, 21*n*, 404
Fort William, 285
Fotuna Island, 372
Fowler, Robert, 183
France, eighteenth-century explorations, 12–13, 16–24; and Spanish expeditions, 29; La Pérouse's voyage, 30–42; war with England, 30–31, 94, 133, 192; Marchand's voyage, 114–120; search for La Pérouse, 120–134; Baudin's voyage, 184, 185, 190, 192–194; and Flinders, 192, 194; *1817* expedition, 256–264; *1822* expedition, 265–268; *1826* expedition, 268–274; treaty with Kamehameha III, 274; political voyages, 274–276; d'Urville's voyage, 276–281; return of La Pérouse relics, 314
Frances Mary, 297*n*
Francis, 180, 192
Franklin, Sir John, 30, 178, 181, 297, 298, 308, 358
Franklin, 216. See also *Antelope*
Franklin Island (Motuiti), 213
Frederik Hendrik Island, 22
French East India Company, 16
French Frigates Shoal, 36
French Pass, 270
French Revolution, 120, 133
Friendly Cove, 65, 66, 68, 158
Friendly Islands. See Tonga
Friendship, 107, 108
"Fuegian Basket" (Fuegian), 318, 319
Funafuti, 113, 353
Funter, Capt., 69
Furneaux, Tobias, 14, 20, 80, 177, 178
Furneaux Islands, 178, 180

GAIMARD, JOSEPH-PAUL, 270
Galápagos Islands, 219, 229, 275, 286, 321; Colnett at, 74, 75; Darwin at, 323–324, 330
Galvin, John, 263
Gambier Islands, 167, 303. See also Mangareva
Gamboa, Pedro Sarmiento de, 7
Gayangos, Tomas, 28
General Knox, 263
General Raevski Island (Tepoto), 248
Geographe Bay, 193*n*
Géographie, 184, 185, 190, 192, 193, 194, 406
George IV, King of England, 288

[415]

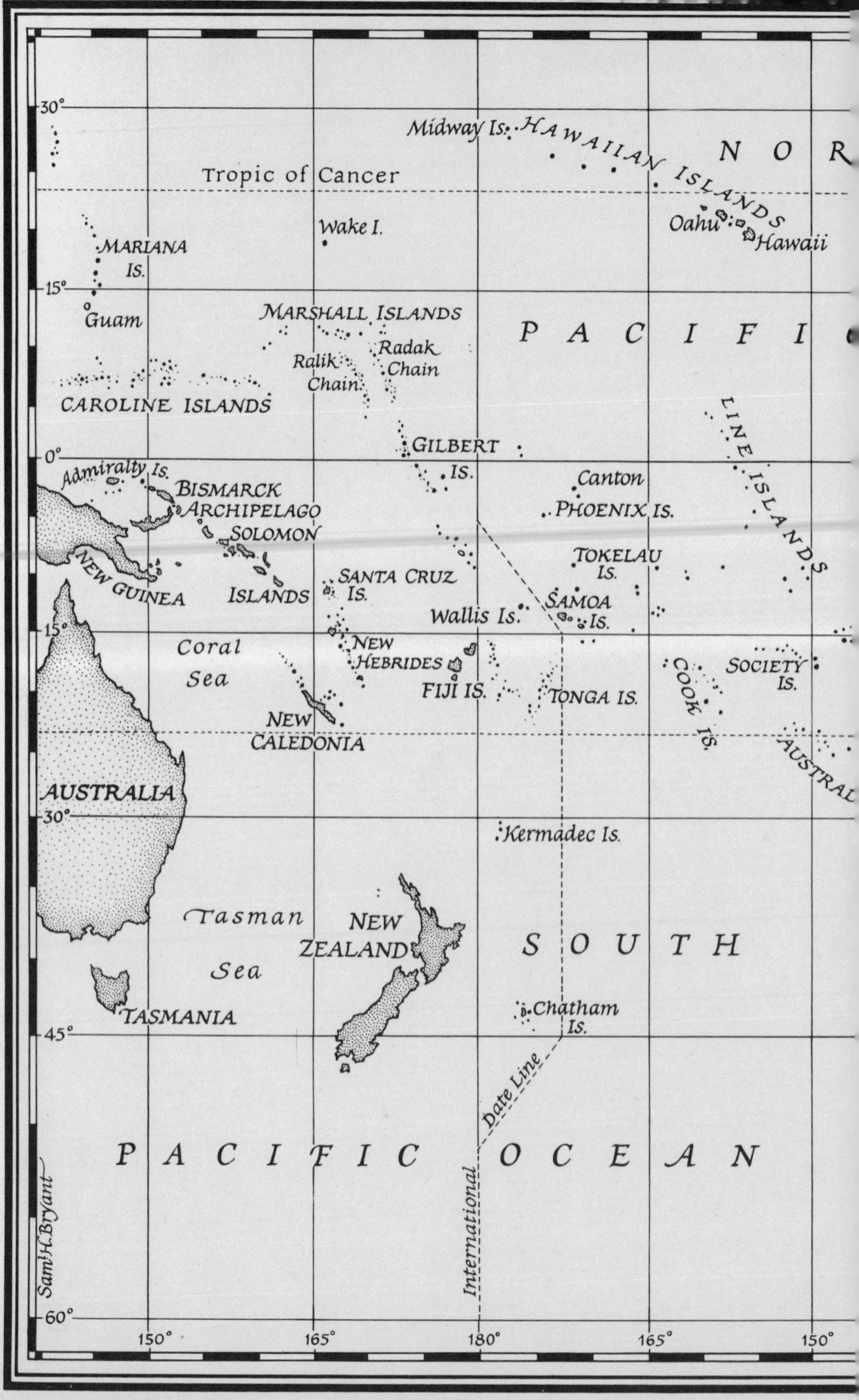

Midway Is.
HAWAIIAN ISLANDS
NOR
Tropic of Cancer
Oahu
Hawaii
Wake I.
MARIANA IS.
Guam
MARSHALL ISLANDS
Ralik Chain
Radak Chain
PACIFI
CAROLINE ISLANDS
LINE ISLANDS
GILBERT IS.
Admiralty Is.
BISMARCK ARCHIPELAGO
Canton
PHOENIX IS.
SOLOMON ISLANDS
NEW GUINEA
TOKELAU IS.
SANTA CRUZ IS.
SAMOA IS.
Wallis Is.
Coral Sea
NEW HEBRIDES
FIJI IS.
TONGA IS.
COOK IS.
SOCIETY IS.
NEW CALEDONIA
AUSTRAL
AUSTRALIA
Kermadec Is.
Tasman Sea
NEW ZEALAND
SOUTH
TASMANIA
Chatham Is.
International Date Line
PACIFIC OCEAN
Saml H. Bryant
30°
15°
0°
15°
30°
45°
60°
150°
165°
180°
165°
150°